Foster Care
Therapist
Handbook

Relational Approaches
to the Children and Their Families

Edited by
Robert E. Lee and Jason B. Whiting

CWLA
PRESS

CWLA Press is an imprint of the Child Welfare League of America. The Child Welfare League of America is the nation's oldest and largest membership-based child welfare organization. We are committed to engaging people everywhere in promoting the well-being of children, youth, and their families, and protecting every child from harm. All proceeds from the sale of this book support CWLA's programs in behalf of children and families.

CHILD WELFARE LEAGUE OF AMERICA, INC.
HEADQUARTERS
2345 Crystal Drive, Suite 250, Arlington, VA 22202-4815
E-mail: books@cwla.org

CURRENT PRINTING (last digit)
10 9 8 7 6 5 4 3 2 1

Cover and text design by Marlene Saulsbury
Edited by Kathleen Ruby

Printed in the United States of America

ISBN-10: 1-58760-046-3
ISBN-13: 978-1-58760-046-3

Library of Congress Cataloging-in-Publication Data

Foster care therapist handbook: relational approaches to the children
and their families / Robert E. Lee and Jason B. Whiting, editors.
        p. cm.
    Includes index.
    ISBN 978-1-58760-046-3 (pbk.)
    1. Foster home care—United States—Handbooks, manuals, etc.
    2. Foster parents—United States. 3. Foster children—United States.
    I. Lee, Robert E., 1943- II. Whiting, Jason B. III. Title.

    HV881.F646 2007
    362.73'3—dc22

2007026001

Contents

Part 3. Important "Other" Issues

Preface

This book is far more passionate than the average textbook. Like you, we have worked for a long time in the trenches of the foster care system. Like you, we understand very well why there is such a high turnover rate among the therapists, caseworkers, and administrative staff who serve foster care agencies. We know what it means to care about beneficial outcomes for our clients in the face of sometimes-overwhelming complexity, frustration, and criticism. We recognize that, even when a case is going very well, it is difficult to keep everything coordinated. We speak collectively in a strong voice throughout this book because we have learned some very important lessons about working with these child clients and their birth and foster families. No one can guarantee positive outcomes all of the time. *But there are things we all can do to maximize the probability of desirable things happening.* This book is about that. Children in foster care primarily benefit from a family-centered, relational therapy approach. Even play therapy for traumatized children must include a family therapy component if it is to be truly effective.

Our goal for this book is to provide a readable and helpful set of chapters for agency therapists and caseworkers. We believe that busy professionals prefer usability to dense, theoretical treatises. *"What works with my case, right here, right now? What will help me help them?"*—these are the questions that need answering. We have asked agency therapists and children in care what topics are most important. We then picked contributors with meaningful child welfare agency experience and an investment in these topics. As a result of these efforts, we are offering you a comprehensive, practical, reader-friendly, relatively thin, and affordable handbook.

We begin with an all-encompassing conceptual framework. Next, we offer advice about issues with various children, birth families, and foster families. Finally, we address specific areas about which foster care therapists and staff have requested direction. Case examples bring each chapter to life and show you clearly how the work has been done effectively. If the voices and ideas in this book inspire you to think and act in new ways, then we all can take satisfaction in working together as we serve families and children.

This book was born in the decade from 1987 to 1997. One author, a faculty member at Michigan State University, had been working with Detroit-area foster care agencies. In time he confided his disillusionment to the other author, a doctoral student in family and child ecology, and to Majorie Kostelnik, their gifted department chairperson. Dr. Kostelnik listened empathically and observed that little good would result from focusing on the negative side of foster care. *This advice was influential.* She recommended setting out to discover what works in various foster care and child welfare settings and then employing these techniques in our own agencies. She suggested finding approaches that increased the probability of desirable outcomes and testing them out. This is known as "best practices" service research.

This was a wonderful idea! A cynic once suggested that "insanity" could be defined as doing the same thing over and over, but hoping for a different outcome. That's what the authors had been doing for ten years. Upon shifting to a "best practices" orientation, positive thinking replaced negativism and cynicism. Curiosity and active searching replaced "doing more of the same old stuff." Hope replaced pessimism. And, wonderfully enough, entire agencies got caught up in this spirit. Employee attrition went down and morale went up.

This is very powerful stuff. It involves: 1) understanding what will elicit and maintain desirable and undesirable results in birth families, agency staff, and foster parents, and 2) emphasizing the former and inhibiting the latter. In this regard, we apply what we

have learned about family therapy and cultivating beneficial relationships between parents and children. We drew from sources in
family science, infant mental health, and social psychology to find
out about attitudes, interpersonal relationships, families, and other
social systems. We discovered that listening to the stories of foster
children while they were in care was a valuable tool in evaluating
the system that was designed to help them. Interviews with foster
parents also illuminated our viewpoint. Many other individuals,
especially the contributors to this book, enabled us to learn, and
this handbook is the product. This handbook is a heartfelt cele-
bration of what we have been doing for so long and is part of our
attempts to "make a difference."

About the Authors

Editors

Robert E. Lee, PhD, ABPP, is Professor of Marriage and Family Therapy at Florida State University, College of Human Sciences, Department of Family and Child Sciences. He has been intimately involved with the foster care system since 1987. At first, he alternated supportive consultations with agency staff and traditional psychological evaluations of children and parents. But over the years, he became dissatisfied with the nature of his work and what he was bringing to the child welfare agencies. The problems in day-to-day foster care seemed insurmountable. Investigating what successful people in other settings were doing when they faced similar problems enabled him to develop a "best practices" approach in foster care, informed by contemporary family therapy outcomes research, the infant mental health movement, child development, and family science.

Jason B. Whiting, PhD, is Assistant Professor of Marriage and Family Therapy at the University of Kentucky, Department of Family Studies. As a therapist and a father, he has great interest in the welfare of children. His clinical experience includes work in agency, school, and private practice settings with at-risk children and their families, including those involved in the foster care system. As a researcher, Jason has studied the experiences of foster children and foster parents. Other areas of interest include couple conflict and violence, parenting, and moral issues in therapy.

Contributors

Larry Barlow, PhD, is Coordinator of the Center for Marriage and Family Therapy at Florida State University. He serves as Executive Director of the Florida Association for Marriage and Family Therapy, and is co-founder of the DADS Family Project. He lives in Tallahassee where he has a private practice for individuals, couples, and families.

Sandra M. Barlow, PhD, is the Clinical Supervisor for the therapeutic visitation program at the Center for Marriage and Family Therapy at Florida State University. She maintains a private practice in Tallahassee treating children, adolescents, and adults. She also is a registered play therapist and a graduate of the FSU Harris Institute for Infant Mental Health.

Robert Brammer, PhD, is Associate Professor of Counseling at West Texas A&M University. He is the father of two adopted children and has worked in the foster care system for nearly a decade. His book, *Diversity in Counseling: Exploring Gender and Ethnic Issues,* was published by Brooks/Cole in 2004.

Rachel Brown, MD, MBBS, MPhil, is Professor in the Department of Psychiatry and Behavioral Science at Mercer University School of Medicine, Macon, Georgia, and is board certified as a psychiatrist and child and adolescent psychiatrist in the United Kingdom and the United States. She is interim department chair, teaches and supervises medical students and marriage and family therapy students, and provides clinical services through Mercer Health Systems. She is a foster and adoptive parent.

Debra D. Castaldo, PhD, has specialized in the field of foster care and adoption for 27 years. She was previously the Director of Clinical Services for Children's Aid and Adoption Society of New Jersey, and Manager of Pediatric Social Work at the Babies and

Children's Hospital of New York–Presbyterian Hospital. She is an adjunct faculty member at Columbia University School of Social Work and previously was adjunct faculty at Ramapo College of New Jersey and Rutgers University School of Social Work, Continuing Education. She maintains a private practice in Englewood, New Jersey.

Patricia McKinsey Crittenden, PhD, directs the Family Relations Institute in Miami, Florida. She has a multidisciplinary background tied to the needs of at-risk families, and has worked as a lecturer, researcher, administrator, program manager, psychotherapist, service provider, and teacher. Her specific fields of expertise include attachment theory, family systems, and child maltreatment.

Douglas Davies, MSW, PhD, is Clinical/Practice Associate Professor at the School of Social Work, University of Michigan, Ann Arbor. He is an infant mental health specialist and has published several articles on intervention with young children and families. His 2004 book, *Child Development: A Practitioner's Guide* (2nd edition, published by Guilford Press), describes how to apply child development theory to clinical practice.

Patricia D. Donovan, MS, is a doctoral student in marriage and family therapy at Florida State University. Her research interests are related to adult survivors of child sexual abuse and couple functioning. She is a supervisor in training and student member of the American Association for Marriage and Family Therapy and the National Council on Family Relations.

Mary Dozier, PhD, received her doctorate in clinical psychology from Duke University in 1983 and subsequently completed an internship and postdoctoral fellowship at St. Elizabeths Hospital in Washington, DC. For the last 10 years, Dr. Dozier has studied challenges faced by children in the foster care system, and has developed an intervention designed to enhance relationships between children and their caregivers. Dr. Dozier was promoted to Professor at the University of Delaware in 2003 and was named to the Amy E. Dupont Chair of Child Development in 2004.

Steve Farnfield, PhD, is at the School of Health and Social Care, University of Reading, in the United Kingdom. A former psychiatric social worker and play therapist, he currently offers consultation and staff training with regard to assessing attachment in children and adults, child and family observation, family placement, interviewing children, and object relations theory.

Tomi Gomory, PhD, is Associate Professor, the Florida State University College of Social Work. His research domain is mental health with a focus on the evaluation of mental health interventions and policy. Before becoming an academician he worked as a therapist and administrator in agencies providing mental health and homeless services.

Terry D. Hargrave, PhD, is Professor of Counseling at West Texas A&M University in Canyon, Texas. He has written numerous articles and four books on the contextual family therapy approach, including *The New Contextual Therapy: Guiding the Power of Give and Take* (Brunner-Routledge, 2003).

Paul T. Huber, MA, is currently working towards a PhD in family studies at the University of Kentucky. He has been a foster parent for over 12 years and is a licensed minister, serving a Lexington-area church as the pastor to children and families.

Kathleen Burns Jager, PhD, is Assistant Professor in the marriage and family therapy specialization at Michigan State University. She also is the acting director of the University's Family and Child Clinic. A licensed marriage and family therapist and a certified family life educator, Dr. Jager has several years' experience in a family-based services in-home therapy program.

Michelle Knights, MS, received her master of science degree in human development and family studies from the University of Delaware in 2002, and she has been a parent trainer with Dr. Mary Dozier's Infant Caregiver Project since October 2002. Her interests include developing and implementing programs that support optimal development for children. She is particularly interested in factors that promote secure attachment in young children.

Erin Lewis, BA, received her degree in psychology from the Pennsylvania State University in May 2004, and is a doctoral student in clinical psychology at the University of Delaware. She also works as a research assistant on Dr. Mary Dozier's Infant Caregiver Project. Her research interests include children in foster care, environmental influences on developmental psychopathology, and intervention for at-risk child populations.

Mallory Maier, MS, received a dual master's degree in social service and law and social policy from the Bryn Mawr College Graduate School of Social Work and Social Research in 2001. She works as a parent trainer with Dr. Mary Dozier's Infant Caregiver Project, and her interests include clinical interventions with children who have experienced problematic early care, as well as child and adolescent psychotherapy.

Laura McDuff, PhD, is Assistant Professor in Counselor Education at West Texas A&M University. She teaches play therapy and other types of child counseling, and has written and reviewed various articles and chapters related to this field.

Lenore M. McWey, PhD, is Assistant Professor of Marriage and Family Therapy at Florida State University. Her professional interests are in the areas of foster care and marital and family therapy research. She is an approved supervisor and clinical member of the American Association for Marriage and Family Therapy. She is also a member of the National Council on Family Relations.

John K. Mooradian, PhD, ACSW, is a Clinical Assistant Professor in the School of Social Work at Michigan State University, where he coordinates the Certificate Program in Clinical Social Work with Families. Dr. Mooradian also maintains a private practice in which he treats adolescents, adults, couples, and families using relational and ecological approaches. He has accumulated over twenty years of clinical experience with families that face multiple challenges, including substance abuse.

Alice Nadelman, PhD, has worked with children and families for over 35 years, specializing in early childhood trauma and impaired attachment. She maintains a private practice in Teaneck, New Jersey, and has served as a consultant and trainer for the State of New Jersey Division of Youth and Family Services, Hackensack University Medical Center, and Children's Aid and Adoption Society of New Jersey. She is a faculty member at Rutgers University School of Social Work, Continuing Education.

J. Matthew Orr, PhD, is an Assistant Professor in the Marriage and Family Therapy Program, Department of Psychiatry and Behavioral Sciences, Mercer University School of Medicine, Macon, Georgia. He teaches and supervises family therapy students and medical students and is a family therapist with Mercer Health Systems where he specializes in working with children, adolescents, and their families.

Scott Ryan, PhD, is an Associate Professor at the Florida State University College of Social Work. Prior to that, he worked in the child welfare system for approximately 10 years. He has written extensively on child welfare issues, with a specific focus on adoptive families.

John Seita, PhD, is a former youth at risk who had lived in 15 different foster care homes as a child. Today he is on the faculty of the School of Social Work at Michigan State University. He also has appointments with MSU Extension and the Michigan Agricultural Experiment Station. His most recent book is *Kids Who Outwit Adults,* published in 2005 by the National Educational Service.

Ann M. Stacks, PhD, is an Assistant Professor in the Psychology Department at Wayne State University. She is the director of the Infant Mental Health Graduate Certificate Program. Her research is in the area of social-emotional development of young children in high-risk environments. She has worked as an infant mental health specialist in a variety of social service settings.

Kim Sumner-Mayer, PhD, works for the Children of Alcoholics Foundation (COAF), where she manages the Kinship Care program and Building Bridges. She is a licensed marriage and family therapist and has also worked at Children's Aid and Family Services, Inc., in northern New Jersey, where she specialized in therapy with traumatized children and families in foster care, family reunification, and adoption. She is an adjunct faculty member of the Syracuse University Family Therapy Summer Institute and she publishes and trains nationally in the areas of kinship care, substance abuse recovery and family reunification, cross-systems collaboration, and family therapy with the child welfare population.

Martell Teasley, PhD, is an Assistant Professor at the Florida State University College of Social Work. His primary area of research is on culturally competent practice with African American children and youth.

Edgar Tyson, PhD, is an Assistant Professor of Social Work at Florida State University. He has more than 10 years of practice experience with high-risk children and families, most of which have been involved in the child welfare system. His research interests are culturally sensitive assessment and intervention and youth culture as a treatment model.

Tracy Woodard-Meyers, PhD, is an Associate Professor in the Department of Sociology, Anthropology, and Criminal Justice at Valdosta State University. Prior to teaching, she worked with families while employed for seven years in a variety of child protective service positions. She is the author of several research articles and book chapters.

Part 1

The Culture and Environment of Foster Care

Introduction:
The Culture and Environment
of Foster Care

Robert E. Lee and Jason B. Whiting

We are working within a system that has heartbreaking challenges and shortfalls. These challenges underscore the importance of building positive relationships—families with their children, the foster care agency, and you. These problems also highlight the importance of a whole-family approach to foster care in general, and value of family therapy interventions as opposed to individual psychotherapy. It is also vital to look at birth families as small systems imbedded within larger systems, and to identify those relational factors that elicit and maintain desirable and undesirable custodial environments. Relational and contextual approaches address many of these needs.

Our temptation is to open with the usual statistics, for example, the number of foster children in the United States, their geographic and ethnic distribution, and so on. However, it occurs to us that, whatever the circumstances of this larger population, you are reading this book because of your concern about your own caseload of 10 to 60 children and, even more likely, the child in your office right now. You want to feel confident that you can heal this child and place him or her in an environment where—now and in the future—s/he can live a secure and fulfilling life. You want to feel good about what you do, both therapeutically and in your recommendations to the court.

In order to achieve this, you will need to work with that child in his and her context. This includes understanding the influences of the biological family, the agency, the current guardian, and his or her eventual placement. To have success and piece of mind, you need to create a healing context, rather than simply treat the individual child alone. As a family therapy guru said two decades ago, if fish are dying in a pond, you don't remove each fish and inject it with an antibiotic. *You work on the health of the pond* (Minuchin & Fishman, 1981). Therapists within the current foster care system are in the relationship-building business. Your task is to discover what inhibits people and their institutions (birth and foster families, agencies, courts, and schools, to name a few) from being the caretakers they optimally can be. We want to create circumstances that increase the probability of desirable things happening for our children and decrease the probability of undesirable things happening. For this to happen for the child in front of you, you need to focus on that child's context.

It's a tough time to be working in foster care. There is limited government money with which to address the needs of foster children and families at risk for foster care. The public has been jaded by media stories and sensational accounts of abuse and neglect. People are skeptical of the foster care system; at the same time, they have high expectations of it. Our society insists that family care is the best custodial environment for developing children, but it doesn't provide us enough foster care beds. Although we know that foster children should be matched by temperament and emotional and behavioral challenges with compatible foster homes, but, because of the desperate shortage of foster beds, children often go wherever beds are available. Frequently there are as many children in a household as they will accept. Although our overriding goal has been to rescue children from rugged backgrounds and put them into better lives, we discover instead that some of them are being reinjured—often in the very settings we had intended to help them.

We also know that extended foster care, especially for indefinite periods ("foster care drift"), is destructive for children, both while they are in care and beyond. And although we have the child in front of us, we may have no working alliance with their parents.

Moreover, despite the promises of foster care reform, there are many judges, referees, and magistrates who postpone decision-making for long periods of time—consequently, we find ourselves reduced to simply comforting children, as opposed to participating in the satisfactory rebuilding of their lives.

We recognize the importance of collaborative work between the birth family, agency, and foster family, the so-called foster care "triad." However, in many states foster parents are recruited from the ranks of those hoping to adopt. They are told that fostering is their best way to learn about the care of special needs children and that they will be the adoptive parents of choice should the birth parents' rights be terminated. This sets up competition between the birth and foster families, which sometimes is played out in the media, when foster parents attempt to prevent courts from sending the child back to the birth parents.

Similarly, kinship care was seen as a way of acquiring more foster beds while maintaining desirable family ties. However, relatives with foster placements claim that they get less financial support for the children in their care, and agency workers complain that these families sometimes collude with the birth parents in evading court-set limitations.

In short, despite changes in the laws and practice guidelines governing foster care, you know from your job, and from the child in front of you, that these things have not been resolved at the institutional level.

Who Are These Foster Children?

Child maltreatment may be said to exist when parents either are unaware of their children's needs or, although aware of these needs, are unable or unwilling to provide the appropriate response. When children are thought to be unsafe in their families, they are placed with surrogate parents until the unsafe circumstances can be fixed. The process of foster care begins when a court decides that the maltreatment is so extreme that it is too dangerous for children to continue to live in their homes. This may happen when family members inflict physical and emotional injury on children because of anger, cruelty, or bad judgment about discipline. Other problems might include sexual abuse, abandonment, or failure to provide adequate shelter, clothing, nutrition, supervision, health care, love, or attention. Children may also be exposed to extreme sexual or aggressive behavior between adults in the household. One parent may not protect the children from seeing and experiencing the abusive behavior of the other parent or adult in the home. Generally, more children are in foster care because of neglect than abuse, but many foster children have experienced both. As you have already discovered, many aspects of their maltreatment come to the surface well after the children are in foster care and in therapy.

There are about half a million such children and the number grows each year (U.S. Department of Health and Human Services, 2001). About 20% have been in foster care more than once. Native American, African American, and Hispanic children are disproportionately present in foster care. The majority of foster children are under six years of age. Half of them will spend less than a year in foster care. However, the other half may spend up to three years or more waiting for their cases to be resolved. This is especially likely when substance problems are involved. Ethnic minority children also typically have longer stays in foster care.

As we said, more children are in foster care because of neglect than abuse, but many have experienced both. How badly they are harmed by their maltreatment depends on:

- *their age when the maltreatment occurs.* Since the majority of them are under six years old, they probably do not have good coping resources. Furthermore, neglected children may have been born addicted to substances or suffered prenatal damage due to the mother's drug use or poor nutrition. Babies may fail to thrive physically, psychologically, and socially. All young maltreated children—infants, toddlers, and preschoolers— experience challenges with regard to physical skills, intelligence, language acquisition, the ability to regulate their emotions, and social skills.

- *how many destructive things happen and how extreme they are.* Many foster children have been maltreated in multiple ways. If the maltreatment were not extreme, the families would still be intact and receiving in-home services.

- *how long the maltreatment goes on.*

- *who is maltreating them.*

- *the behavior of the primary caretaking parent.* Because foster children generally have been disappointed by the primary caretakers in their lives, many are likely to be afraid of adults and feel unable to trust adults to protect them. Expect social problems such as hostility and deceit, and later delinquency and substance use.

In fact, you can expect the foster child in your office to demonstrate a variety of short- and long-term destructive effects of having been maltreated:

- inability to trust adults, peers, and the world;

- failure to develop physically, psychologically, and socially;

- falling behind in physical, cognitive, language, self-regulation, and social skills; and

- higher probability of later demonstrating learning and social problems in school, hostility, substance abuse, and delinquency.

Putting your client in foster placement was intended to help fix these deleterious consequences. Unhappily, the cure itself can be destructive in its own right.

- Your client probably has been removed from the only world he or she knows, and may have been put with strangers in a strange household.

- After a brief "honeymoon" period, your insecure client probably has misbehaved in the new home and elicited negative reactions from the adults and other children there.

- These reactions, in turn, may heighten your client's sense of insecurity and a negative spiral is likely. Your client's fears have been affirmed and so she or he demonstrates more emotional and behavioral upset. The new adults and siblings may react even more negatively to this misbehavior and your upset client may be moved to yet another foster home. This process may occur repeatedly, affirming each time your client's fears, and leading to more upset behavior.

- Another risk is that your client may abuse other children in the foster home, be abused by other children there, or even be abused by the foster parents. Since there are not enough foster families for the children who need them, agencies aren't always careful about whom they license. Moreover, even though it might be best for a child to be placed away from other children (because of a high likelihood of aggressive or sexual misbehavior toward them), this often does not happen. Unfortunately, your client also may have been split from siblings, and there may be no one to offer protection.

- If the case is not resolved quickly, and if the stay in foster care is of indeterminate length ("foster care drift"), your client may experience confusion, outrage, fear, inferiority, helplessness, and loyalty conflicts. As the child gets older, he or she may be at risk for multiple emotional, cognitive, social, and behavioral problems. Foster care drift is very harmful to your clients. They may be outraged that, in their minds, their parents don't love them enough to visit them frequently and to do what is necessary to bring them home (for example, quit drugs, get a job, or get rid of an abusive lover). And, due to this anger at the birth parents and distrusting replacement parents, your client may have been acting up in the foster home, which is how you got the referral. No doubt the other occupants of the foster home have been reacting in a manner that affirms your client's sense of not being lovable and of the world as not being a safe place. Furthermore, because his or her foster care is labeled as a temporary arrangement, your client is inhibited from making strong emotional investments. Finally, because your client has probably (before and after placement in foster care) been pre-occupied and upset during critical learning periods in his or her life, there is an increased probability that he or she will suffer intellectually, psychologically, emotionally, and socially. Your client may have been taking inventory of his or her merits and arrived at realistically low self-esteem and pessimism about his or her future.

Your Practice With "Special Needs Children"

From this population comes the majority of our "special needs children." Once these children become available for adoption, their long sojourn in foster care has made them more likely to have multiple bio/psycho/social problems. And they are older. Consequently, they often are less attractive to prospective adoptive parents and may remain in foster care as permanent wards of the state. Their lack of trust in the world and lack of self-esteem must seem well founded.

As you reach out to collaborate with the foster parents, you may discover unhappily that they are already alienated by a system that has not been totally honest with them. Despite changes in the law governing foster care, many foster parents still complain about agencies' lack of full disclosure about the history and nature of the children placed with them. The foster parents also may have discovered, as you have, that some agency personnel are overex-tended, poorly trained, unprofessional, of low morale, or not cul-turally literate with regard to their children and foster placements.

Given all of this complexity, and what you yourself know and have experienced in your attempts to be of service to these chil-dren, does it then surprise you that your own morale is often low—even lower than would be predicted by your high workload and low compensation? In fact, the agencies that employ therapists to help treat problematic child and family issues complain that they can't keep them. They have 50% staff turnover each year, which means that they lose 100% of their employees in a two-year period. What is to be done?

Relational Approaches to the Whole Family and the Larger System

In Chapter 2, we talk about how child maltreatment represents a failure of the entire system of which the child is a living part, and how foster care interventions need to be ecosystemic and have multiple impacts if they are to be effective. Leaving that argument aside for the moment, in this chapter we simply want to point out that your treatments in the service of your children should *primarily be family-centered* and relational. Your goal is the removal of those factors that make a household psychosocially inadequate for its children, while also addressing the emotional injuries done to the children by that household and their removal from it.

Often the first step is to work on the relationship that exists between parents and their children. However, if you are going to be able to do any transformative work with your families, you need for them to visit together in a regular, frequent, and constructive manner. This means that you probably need to work on creating a working alliance between the families and the agencies involved in their cases.

In foster care, the agency has the responsibility to oversee the removal of those factors that make the household unsafe for its children, and the agency must locate resources for this to happen. That responsibility is typically captured in some court-mandated agreement about what the family must do if its children are to return. (Notice the emphasis is often on what a family must *do*, and not what it must *become*.) For example, the birth parent(s) may be mandated to:

- demonstrate income and housing adequate to their custodial responsibilities,
- get rid of perpetrators (if any),
- demonstrate lack of illicit substance use,
- attend didactic parenting classes, or

- participate in individual counseling (often with nebulous treatment goals).

And, as you know from the children sitting in front of you, their children are often referred for psychotherapy.

The Problems of Traditional Individual Psychotherapeutic Approaches

Family emotional resources may not have been mobilized enough to get the parents moving on completing their parent-agency-court agreements. Often parents take a long time to "get it together" sufficiently to even begin working on the checklist given to them by the courts and overseen by the foster care agency. Indeed, as you already know in your experience with heartbroken and outraged children, many parents even take a long time to get involved in consistent supervised visitation with their children at the agency.

Aside from these motivational matters, our traditional interventions themselves may miss the mark of what is needed by the family. Think about a typical didactic parenting class: they happen away from the children, and are not tailored to a specific family. It may take another 10 months to a year after the class ends, before the parents can be reunited with the children. After all that time, do they remember what they learned in the parenting class? And can they apply it in their own situation? The classes do not help parents understand their own strengths and weaknesses, or help them apply what they are learning in their own family situations. What we need is an immediately relevant, useful, and credible experiential learning experience, instead of didactic classes which place parents in the *Catch-22* position of having to learn how to parent without actually doing it.

Similarly, individual psychotherapy is not the best approach for foster children and their birth and foster parents, because:

- it can't be used effectively with infants and toddlers, even if the child is of an age where s/he can do the acts of therapy. Unlike older clients, who carry us around in their heads, talk to us in there, and otherwise ponder what has occurred in a therapy session, young children can only deal with what is in front of them at the moment. The rest of us can expand our therapy experience and its lessons outside of the session. For infants and toddlers, therapeutic experiences are only one hour out of 168 in a week.

- individual therapy doesn't address relational context. If our concern is with problematic behaviors and emotions of children and their parents, we need to *contextualize* them, that is, identify what circumstances elicit and maintain undesirable and desirable states of being.

- moreover, if a major problem of parents and their children is that they are insecure or mistrustful of each other and ambivalently attached, you need to work on the relationship between parties involved.

- individual forms of psychotherapy are most indicated in cases of posttraumatic stress disorder. However, the parties involved need the corrective emotional experience of demonstrated parental capacity and willingness to keep them secure. In other words, children need to know that their futures will be different from the past—this assurance is only possible by actually witnessing improved parenting techniques being used by their parents (see Chapter 7, "Parent–Child Therapy for Traumatized Young Children in Foster Care").

There is one enormous additional problem with individual psychotherapeutic approaches: typically, therapists and other "helpers" are perceived by the birth family to be agents of the court (see Chapter 2, "An Ecosystemic Approach to Foster Care," and Chapter 20, "'But I Don't Trust You' Recognizing and Dealing with Parents' History of Trauma: The Story of Amy"). Many of our clients refer to all of us as "social workers" and defend themselves against us as if we were prosecuting attorneys. Sometimes this is a matter of subculture and lived experience. Sometimes it also comes from the adults' personal histories of current and past maltreatment by significant others.

So Why Do We Continue to Do Individual Therapy with Foster Children?

Given the contraindications, why are we all doing so much individual therapeutic work with foster children and their families? Perhaps we could find the answer in a "Top 10" survey.

FIGURE 1

The top 10 reasons why you may not do family therapy when children are referred for treatment:

Reason #10:　You are not trained/oriented to that.

Reason #9:　You like working with children!

Reason #8:　You can't just sit and watch parents mishandle their children in front of you.

Reason #7:　You don't like or you fear families.

Reason #6:　You lack faith in or feel animosity toward client parents ("perps").

Reason #5:　The child is the diagnosed "Identified Patient."

Reason #4:　Relational therapy is not convenient.

Reason #3:　The parents aren't sober or otherwise constructive and/or you can't get the parents to come in!

Reason #2:　A therapist can provide a Good Object for a child to internalize.

And the #1 reason for why folks don't do family therapy when children are referred is _____ (You complete the sentence.)

Success Requires Moving From the Little to the Bigger Picture

The above observations lead us to believe that we will be most successful as therapists to the foster care system to the extent that our interventions:

- take into account the whole family,
- are strengths-based,
- are respectful, and
- are collaborative and not adversarial.

In fact, for us to be maximally successful in our therapeutic endeavors with the clients assigned, the overseeing foster care agency needs to accept some important truths.

- First of all, interventions—including parent-agency-court agreements—need to be tailor-made. *One size doesn't fit all.* In the best of all possible worlds, assessment of family strengths and needs could be done collaboratively. Moreover, if assessment and planning were to be approached on a sensitive, case-by-case basis, individual assessments and intervention plans might be more respectful of sociocultural beliefs, values, and ways of doing things, and families would have less evidence that they were being stereotyped.

- Foster children are, first and foremost, children. And we know what all children need to thrive: loving and nurturing environments that are stable and predictable over time. Our job can be viewed as helping foster children have what all children need.

- The likelihood of children returning to their birth homes, and the speed at which this will happen, is directly related to the frequency of their parents' visitation with them while they are in foster care. Frequency of visitation, in turn, is directly related to the parents' relationships with their children and with the foster care agency. Our ultimate job as therapists is positive relationship building: between parents and their children and between parents and the agency.

To sum up thus far, as we go about working with these foster children and are involved with other individuals who work with these children, our superordinate benchmark is:

- we want everyone to take action to maximize the probability of desirable things happening,

- we want everyone to take action to minimize the probability of undesirable things happening, and

- we want everyone to address the court's and agency's doubts and fears.

Interventions that involve the whole family, and that are strengths-based and respectful, are most likely to meet these goals. The irony is that, unlike most innovations and "best practices in care," what we are suggesting here is more economical in terms of everyone's time and money than are the interventions they are to replace. When families are seen as units, only one session is required instead of one for each member. Moreover, some requirements not only can be met best, but also most economically, by multitasked family sessions. For example, supervised visitation may be an opportunity to do relational work, while also providing developmentally appropriate parenting lore (see Chapter 6, "The Case for Relational Therapy with Young Children in Foster Care"). The psychotherapy needs of the children and parents, and the parents' need for parenting classes are all met in one session. Therefore the child's per diem goes farther and the parents, probably already challenged logistically, do not have to find a way to attend several competing sessions a week.

Overview of This Book

Part 1 considers the culture and environment of foster care. Chapter 1 has begun this exploration and what it means for you as a therapist. In Chapter 2, we discuss the importance of considering the larger setting in which foster children and their families are situated, including discerning whose cooperation needs to be recruited and the sequencing of interventions and their goals. Chapter 3 takes a sensitive look at the sociocultural environments in which our children, their families, agency, court, and others are situated. Success requires culturally competent foster care and therapeutic interventions. What is therapeutic may be defined by the context, namely, *who* the clients and practitioners are, and the setting of each. Finally, in the last chapters (4 and 5) of Part 1, we learn how foster children make sense of their experiences and what they need.

In Part 2, we look at specific applications of relational therapy to clinical situations. Each chapter describes an approach and gives clinical illustrations of how to do it. Chapter 6 urges you to consider carefully why relational therapy is the treatment of choice when you are referred very young children. Chapter 7 describes the importance of family therapy even when traumatized children are referred. Since foster children have different needs and capacities at differing developmental stages (as do their parents and the families in which these individuals live), Chapter 8 considers what may be developmentally appropriate and how to use relational therapy to create a milieu that meets these needs. Since other chapters give clinical examples of families with younger children, here the illustration is focused on middle adolescents.

Chapter 9 reminds us that our therapeutic interventions must recognize the reality of two family groups, the birth family and the foster family, and tells us how to cultivate the resources of each. Next, in Chapter 10, placement of foster children with their relatives is considered and examples are given of how best to work with this unique situation.

Whether you are working with birth or foster families, it is important to appreciate the importance of family ties, which may be important to the individuals' sense of well-being and a major resource for their adjustment. Family ties also may be destructive if they take a negative turn. Therefore, Chapter 11 provides concrete guidelines for and ideas about experiential activities that can be used with families to establish, maintain, and strengthen interpersonal connections and also to identify important emotional issues. Then—lest we err on the side of too much emphasis on work with the birth family—Chapter 12 underscores the importance of secure and therapeutic foster care placements. It shows how to do family therapy within the foster home. Similarly, Chapter 13 details the support services that foster parents say that they need. Based on statewide surveys of foster families, this chapter explores the world of foster parents, including their stresses, strains, and satisfactions. The chapter describes how therapists can work most collaboratively with these parents.

The circumstances leading to foster placement may lead all parties to feel that they have been dealt with unjustly—by life and by society's institutions. And those maltreated as children often become maltreating parents. Chapter 14 gives an approach to family therapy that addresses the manifold perceptions of injustice on the part of family members and which is intended to reduce repetition across generations.

In Part 3, we show that we understand what it is you are facing in your day-to-day lives providing therapy to foster children. There are many complications and emergencies with which to deal, and our experienced experts offer practical help in managing them. Alleged sexual abuse imported into a foster home is one of the most explosive issues in child placement. Chapter 15 offers practical advice, involving an approach to the whole family, for effective management of these events. Just as with sexual abuse, foster children may bring aggressive behavior into their foster homes and school settings—Chapter 16 describes how to deal with these challenging situations.

Another difficult and common scenario is when substance dependence and abuse are prominent features in your case. Chapter 17 discusses how use of substances should be regarded and, when the adults are in recovery, how this may be supported and utilized.

Supervised visitation and extended visits—as opposed to didactic classes—provide an ideal time to provide child development and parenting skills. The goals of this psychoeducation are for the adults to have realistic expectations of their children and the capacity to recognize and respond to their cues in an appropriate and timely manner. Chapter 18 describes how to do this.

Chapter 19 talks about the end game, namely, what needs to be done with the birth family, the foster family, and the adoptive family during the transitional period when the children are to be returned to the birth home or placed for adoption.

Finally, we have been talking about an ecosystemic, collaborative approach. Yet many of our client families don't trust us at all.

Sometimes this is because the personal traumas experienced by the birth parents keep them from adequately using services meant to be supportive. Chapter 20 gives examples of this and describes approaches to removing these barriers.

There is one more important chapter: Chapter 21 has to do with taking care of yourself. We are impressed that foster care staff attrition is about 100% every two years. Sometimes agency staff members get better offers elsewhere; often, however, they complain of the disparity between idealistic expectations and reality. They also describe "compassion fatigue." Chapter 21 affirms such feelings and discusses ways to you can cope effectively and conserve your personal and professional self.

References

Minuchin, S., & Fishman, H. C. (1981). *Family therapy techniques.* Cambridge, MA: Harvard University Press.

U.S. Department of Health and Human Services, National Clearinghouse on Child Abuse and Neglect Information. (2001). *Child Maltreatment 1999: Reports from the States to the National Clearinghouse on Child Abuse and Neglect.* Washington, DC: United States Government Printing Office.

2

An Ecosystemic Approach to Foster Care

Robert E. Lee

Foster care remedial interventions into the needs of the triad *(child, birth parents, foster parents) must be performed in stages. They also must address the larger system of which all of the participants are a living part. Survival and case management needs must be addressed before early, mid-term, and final-stage goals. Foster care is a system with many influential members (court, state agency, community agencies, and foster family). The members must be identified and their overlapping areas of responsibility, conflicting goals, and alliances must be addressed.*

Preaching to the Choir

The wonderful thing about writing this book is that you, the readers, have had substantial experience in the child welfare trenches. Only you and your colleagues understand how complex your job is. You experience the fears and frustrations that come with the job, and you are probably reading this because you want to make things better. In short, you are bright, educated, and motivated—all the traits we've been told lead to positive intervention outcomes!

The best place to begin is for all of us to recognize that you already are an expert in foster care delivery systems and the human problems—staff, child, and family (birth and foster)—associated with foster care. You've lived it. By working within the system you've gone far beyond what you were taught in school. You have learned a lot by reflecting on your experience.

Let's celebrate and affirm all that you now know to be incontrovertibly true in your head—because of what you've read, been taught, and experienced.

I'd like to think of the following rules as—for you—nonnegotiable ground rules in your work with foster children and their families:

- Interventions need to be ecosystemic and have multiple impacts.

- Interventions need to be developmentally appropriate to all direct and indirect participants.

- Interventions also need to be done in stages.

Ecosystemic Thinking

I wanted to use a less exotic word than "ecosystemic," but there really isn't a substitute. It describes the complexity of what we do. Some people talk about children as if all children and their needs are the same. They talk about parents in the same way. But you recognize that every child and every parent is different. Each varies in intelligence, personality (temperament, adjustment style, values, attitudes, and expectations), health, and developmental level, to list just a few essential factors. And each child lives in a unique household, the context for diverse sibling, adult–child, and adult–adult relationships.

The household also is influenced by relationships with the court, educational, medical, and child welfare agency systems, and perhaps by the parents' occupational settings. The household, with its links to other systems, is also located within the larger environments of community, state, and nation. All of these different households may differ in resources (for example, family support services, jobs, public transportation) and values (for example, decisions about what to support, neglect, or even punish). There are also a myriad of other societal influences, including sexism, racism, and social class privilege, as well as current political administrations, legislative agendas, and the economy.

As a result, it is impossible to talk generally about "kids and their parents." We need to specify which child, in what family, in what setting, at what time in that child's, family's, and community's life. Assessing families means we must remain aware that there are many individual differences between children, between parents, and between parent–child and child–child relationships, from the child's birth onward. Each child and family member also has a social network that extends beyond the nuclear family, out into the community.

There also are differences between communities—each community lives in its own political, economic, and philosophical climate. These differences between communities have grave implications for foster care. For example, the average time spent in foster care in one county may be 8 months, in another 38 months. The first county may be suburban, with plentiful social welfare resources. In that county, the foster children often are from families that are temporarily down on their luck, and there are many families to both foster and adopt the children. The county where foster children linger may be a major urban area characterized by poverty and substance abuse. Many foster children may come from substance-using families with hard-core unemployment issues. Before these children can come home their parents must progress though substance recovery and discover marketable skills, adequate housing, reliable transportation, and affordable day care. As a result, the work and morale of caseworkers in each county's child welfare system may be quite different.

Ecosystemic thinking means that we recognize that all of these environments (the smaller embedded within the larger) transact to produce the unique total environment in which the child and his and her family are situated. Some people talk about this:

FIGURE 2

Children   Parents

More sophisticated folks talk in terms of this:

FIGURE 3

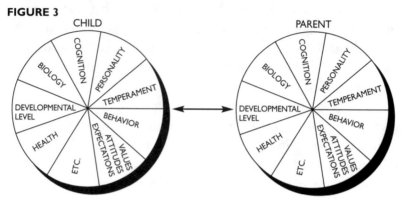

But we—who are intelligent, motivated, and courageous enough to look into things to the point where they become confusing—think in terms of this (Lerner, 1991):

FIGURE 4

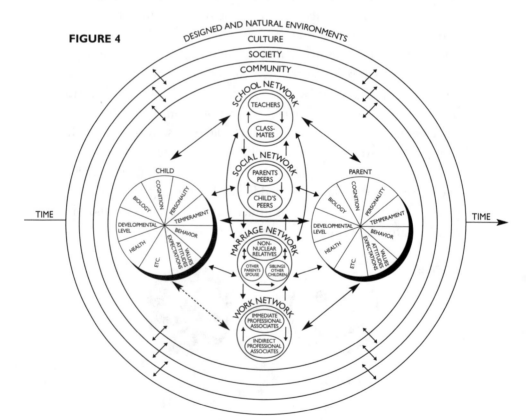

This level of insight may confuse us at times, or seem over-whelming, but it also empowers us because we know who all the players are for any single case. And our ecosystemic orientation tells us that sustained neglect and abuse of children always repre-sent the influence of the entire system of which the children are a living part. Indeed, child abuse and neglect often indicate the diminished capacity of (at least) the family subsystem. Another adult in the household or an older sibling was not able to step in and provide relief or summon aid. There were no concerned extended family members or neighbors to pitch in or to sound an alarm. Community resources, such as respite care, in-home family services, or available child protection workers, were either unavail-able or unused. There was inadequate financial aid for families in distress. Moreover, just as sustained neglect or abuse of a child is a product of many interacting things, so are positive foster care out-comes. Consider the following cases, and their outcomes, from an ecosystemic point of view.

Cases Lingering in Foster Care

The foster child was a baby girl, four months old. Her 20-year-old mother was mildly mentally impaired, and she neither knew who the baby's father was nor how a woman becomes pregnant. She demonstrated no apparent interest in her baby. For example, she would sit woodenly, gazing straight ahead, although her baby had been put in her lap and might even be crying. This woman's cog-nitive limitations were made worse by a passive adaptive style. She waited for others to attend to her needs and would not follow a vis-iting nurse's note card instructions in order to accomplish simple tasks. She had a certain "sleepy" quality, which she apparently used to tune out stress. The extended family wanted no involvement, either with the mother or the baby, and the mother was subse-quently placed in a group home. However, the community had no group home that would accommodate both a mentally impaired mother and her child. Given the child's developmental level (infancy), the mother's impoverished coping resources, the extended family's unwillingness to step in, and the community having little to offer beyond the fostering system, the outcome was inevitable.

A similar outcome befell a family of five children, ranging in age from four to 10 years old, who were found to be malnourished. The school-aged children were often truant from school and, upon investigation, their home was found to be unhygienic. Their mother had been diagnosed schizophrenic, schizoaffective type, and her husband was diagnosed with major depression. The mother had had many psychiatric hospitalizations but would not consistently take the medication that would keep her stable. The depressed husband deferred to his wife and generally was inactive within the home. They each had a small pension. While at the agency and in court, the mother was explosive and unable to advocate effectively for herself; her husband seemed to be at a loss, looking for external guidance. All five children had been placed in the temporary custody of their maternal grandmother, even though she did not report the neglect in the first place. She emphasized that she did not wish to be a permanent placement for the children. In this case, the family lacked personal and extended family resources, but there were abundant resources available to each parent and to the children in the community. However, even when aware of those resources, the parents were unable or unwilling to use them. The pensions provided the parents enough income to meet their own immediate needs for housing and sustenance, and enabled them to avoid those agencies they wished to avoid.

In another case, a 26-year-old single mother and cocktail waitress could not resist the men she met at work. She would go off with them for extended periods of time. In so doing, she left three children (aged five, four, and two) in the care of the eldest, a boy aged nine. The child welfare authorities became aware of this matter because the nine-year-old acquired too many absences from school while caring for his younger siblings. Upon visitation, it was clear that the mother loved her children. She was attentive, playful, and nurturing. She had appropriate expectations, set appropriate limits, and enforced them in developmentally appropriate ways.

She cried bitterly each time her visits would have to end. Unfortunately, the mother was continually unable to resist certain men and this was the third time in two years that she had abandoned her children in favor of extended recreation. Moreover, even while her children were in foster care, she missed supervised visitation sessions because she had eloped with yet another man. There were no resources for reunification in this case. The children were too young to take care of themselves. There were three fathers, but they were unavailable. One was in jail, another could not be located, and the third lived with another partner and children in a distant state. No members of the extended family wished to be involved, even as babysitters.

Families Who Were Reunited

Our first illustrative case, like the first one in the last section, also involves a mentally impaired, single mother of an infant. However, despite her intellectual deficiencies, this mother had a very active and alert adaptive style, could follow a list of instructions mechanically, recognized signs of distress in herself and her infant and, when she did, quickly called for help. And help was readily available. This individual had financial support and was linked by an attentive agency wraparound coordinator to a network of supportive services. The mother was able to recognize and to use community resources, and appropriate resources were available in her community setting.

In another successful case of reunification, the children were removed to foster care because their single mother, chronically abused by the men in her life, consistently failed to protect herself and the children from the men. Estranged from her family of origin, she wouldn't listen to her parents and siblings and would accept nothing from them. Nevertheless, the mother formed a bond with her caseworker and made good use of court-ordered psychotherapy, parenting classes, and other wraparound urban agency services, to secure a haven for herself and her children. Basically ambivalent about men, she decided to free herself and her children of her dependency on them. She acquired a job as a manager of an apartment complex; through this, she obtained housing and a modest income for her family and she could stay home and look after her children. In this family's case, personal and community resources made the positive difference.

In another family, the parents were both addicted to crack cocaine. However, the father had the good fortune to be a member of a large, urban, African-American family. The couple's three preschool children were put in kinship placement with the paternal grandparents. Their new home was the weekend gathering place for eight grown children, 22 grandchildren, and six great grand-children who lived in the immediate vicinity or nearby. This family did not like the idea of foster care. Their corporate belief was that "children should be raised to know their kinfolks." They subsequently demonstrated the collective ability of the entire family to take care of the previously neglected children.

What Influences Outcomes?

The aggregate contribution of personal, family, neighborhood, community, and national factors are what determine whether children remain neglected and abused, linger in foster care until they are adopted, or return home. As the above cases illustrate, different profiles of resources and help-seeking behavior characterize each case. Often, a deficit in one environment can be compensated by a larger amount in another. Parental personalities may or may not change, but their resources might. Children may grow to another, perhaps less needy developmental stage. Families of origin or adult partners may develop resources as support systems. Employment pictures may improve and neighborhoods change (and with them schools and support services). Federal programs may emerge that provide financial, housing, and job training resources.

In most cases, families involved in the neglect and abuse of children have multiple needs and their success as custodial families involves recognition and amelioration of them. The needs are not all of the same weight and it often isn't a matter of simple cause and effect. Deficient intellect for some, and/or specific sociocultural settings for others, may lead women to early pregnancies. This interferes with their education, which is associated with poverty and the absence of material and community resources (Hannan & Luster, 1991). Personality, in terms of values, talents, goals, and adaptive style, also plays a role (Bavolek, 1989; Crittenden, 1993). Personality manifests as a function of constitutional, developmental, family, and community influences (Davies, 2004). Families of origin, families of procreation, neighborhood, community, and even governmental policy have their influence in establishing climates supportive of problems or encouraging of change (Imber-Black, 1991). Ironically, as you surely recognize, our own service-providing agencies may play a helpful or maladaptive role (for example, see Dawson & Berry, 2002). Families and agencies may become stuck because of too much flexibility or rigidity, blurred boundaries, or unholy alliances between them (Colapinto, 1995). We will talk more about this in the final third of this chapter.

Multiple-Impact, Developmentally-Appropriate Interventions

As readers know from experience, foster care interventions have to address many concurrent problems relative to the safety of the children in their birth home and in the foster home. Whether or not reunification occurs and how long it takes—these potential events are known to be associated with the needs of the children, and the mental and physical health of the household (U.S. Department of Health & Human Services, National Center on Child Abuse & Neglect, 1996). These factors may include substance abuse, temperament, judgment, impulse control, and other mental health issues of the household. Also involved are matters related to income and financial decisionmaking, transportation, and knowledge about parenting (Family Resource Coalition, 1996). Finally, reunification is known to be associated with the frequency and quality of parental visitation (Littner, 1975; Marsh, 1986; Mech, 1985; Milner, 1987), the constructive attitude of agency staff

(Courtney, 1994; Laufer, 1994), and foster family attitude (Oyserman & Benbenishti, 1992).

If your healing interventions are to increase the probability of a positive outcome for the lives of your children, you need to influence the relationship between them and their parents, and between the parents and your agency. This involves the parents' capacity to perceive and respond appropriately to the children's needs—which, in turn, may involve education about their children, amelioration of baggage and competition (seductive people, addictions) from their own past and present lives, and the acquisition of parenting resources (personal, financial, and social resources that are needed for the support of a household).

As you will see in Chapter 8, "Providing Developmentally Appropriate Family Therapy," we recognize that where people are in their developmental trajectories determines what is important to them and what resources they have. So it is important to frequently make sure that what you are doing corresponds not only with the cognitive capacity but also the developmental stages of the child at hand, and that of all the significant others—family members and institutional personnel—who comprise that child's context. Everyone needs to be able to understand and buy into what you are intending.

To make this point, let's think about something basic—for example, the goal of returning the child to his or her birth parents. Is that something the child welfare agency workers want? What about the child's guardian ad litem? The judge? The parents' attorneys? Are the child's physical, emotional, and guidance needs compatible with the parents' current ability and motivation to recognize and meet them? Specifically, are the parents: 1) understanding what the child needs, 2) ready to focus primarily on that, and 3) sober or undistracted enough to be able to consistently do what is needed? If there are less than desirable qualities in the parents, we might also explore the extended custodial environment to see if there are grandparents or other family members with the motivation and means to supplement the household.

Your plans for the children in their families must also be stage-wise (see Bicknell-Hedges, 1995; Lee & Lynch, 1998). The family must be ready for your interventions psychologically and be able to use them to meet the needs that strike them as the most urgent at that point in time. When you offer treatments for which a family is not ready, they typically are rejected or otherwise fail (Rabin, 1995; Schatz & Bane, 1991). As Abraham Maslow (1962) pointed out long ago, survival needs will dominate an individual's consciousness until they are satisfied. Then, the person is ready to consider things less urgent, such as his or her treatment needs.

When you make plans for a birth family who have lost children to foster care, the sequence is obvious. Because the household has been considered unsafe for the children, those things that made it unsafe need to be fixed. In doing so, some things must occur first, and have predominance over others in the minds of all members of the foster care system. It is useful to think of five stages. Only as the tasks of each stage are resolved does it make sense to give full attention to those of the next stage. Because what happens to foster children over the short- and long-term is so influenced by the interdependent functioning of the entire foster care triad—birth family, foster family, child welfare agency—many innovative agencies involve all three parties to collaboratively plan each stage (see Lee & Lynch, 1998). All three parties could meet regularly to ascertain progress and decide what next might best serve family reunification. However, this mutual decisionmaking must focus on matters contained in the appropriate stage. Again, only as each step is successfully accomplished, is full attention given to the next stage.

Stage 1, the Immediate Survival Needs of the Birth Family

Prior to children being placed in your caseload, state authorities decided that keeping those children in their birth homes, even while making a multifaceted attempt to strengthen and support their families, was not warranted. Or perhaps such an attempt had been tried and had failed. Initially, your agency's most immediate action is to insure the safety of the children by finding them appropriate foster homes. If one or both of the parents also were at risk, those adults have to be found appropriate temporary havens as well.

The tasks of the first stage involve the immediate survival needs of the children, to be sure, but also of the birth family. You need to take immediate steps to assure the safety of all parties. As you know, this involves temporary foster care, but also may involve shelters, other short-term housing possibilities, and possibly medical settings for one or more adults. Concurrent with that, you will want to maintain connections for all of the family members (Littner, 1975). Especially be aware of the importance of the attachment between infants and their primary caretakers (see Davies, 2004), children's ambivalent emotions upon being removed to foster care (Whiting & Lee, 2003; see also Chapter 4, "The Perspective of the Consumer: Foster Children Tell Us What They Need"), the importance of sibling relationships to foster children's immediate adjustment (Lewis, 1995), and the practical importance of maintaining positive connections between members of the birth family (Littner, 1975; see also Chapter 8, "Providing Developmentally Appropriate Family Therapy"; Chapter 9, "An Integrative Approach Involving the Biological and Foster Family Systems"; and Chapter 10, "Kinship Placements: An Integrative Approach"), as well as positive ties between the birth and foster families (Minuchin, 1995; see also Chapter 9, "An Integrative Approach Involving the Biological and Foster Family Systems"; Chapter 12, "Intervening with Foster Infants' Foster Parents: Attachment and Biobehavioral Catch-Up"; and Chapter 13, "Supporting the Work of Foster Parents"). Obviously, there is a need to work out immediate, consistent, and meaningful visitation if at all possible (Browne & Maloney, 2002; Mapp, 2002).

However, as all experienced foster care workers and therapists recognize, although family linkages need to be maintained, children must be protected from predatory, blaming, and parentifying adults. Often this must be achieved by limiting visitation in one way or another, such as not letting certain adults attend the sessions, or by stopping visitation altogether. The problem with this approach is that the situation is not addressed within the family as it is happening, and thus is not fixed. Another unhappy result may be that the birth families (and perhaps the children as well) are alienated from the agency. When these relationships become everyone's focus, the birth family's self-interest may promote a more collaborative approach with the agency.

In the best of all circumstances, you are the therapist serving the birth family and are not expected to be your family's foster care worker as well. If so, you can play an important role in this beginning phase by facilitating initial meetings between case manager, birth family, and foster family. It is at this time that you develop a collaborative, strengths-focused approach and, as a result, cut back the birth family's defensiveness. There are strong beliefs and biases that both the birth family ("You know how social workers are …") and caseworkers ("Another crack mother with her crack baby") bring to their initial meetings. These feelings interfere with constructive collaboration. No matter where these toxic beliefs originate or how personal history, family, community, or subculture reinforces them, they must be neutralized for any cooperative birth family–agency effort to take place.

Stage 2, Initial Birth Family Stabilization

Now that the children are temporarily in a secure setting, the next step is to look at family stabilization. This often involves initiatives to the larger social system with regard to the family's basic needs: securing consistent and adequate food and shelter, getting the children in school, neutralizing negative parent–agency feelings, and helping parent surrogates address the children's immediate emotional needs. In this second stage, all potentially involved adults need to be identified, located, and recruited. As you are reading this, you are probably remembering times when a putative father suddenly showed up, did what he needed to do to establish paternity, and demanded to be involved in what was happening with a child. We are also thinking about the maternal and paternal extended families, members of which may wish to be considered for kinship foster placement. Various aspects of this are discussed in Chapter 10, "Kinship Placements: An Integrative Approach." For good or ill, kinship care is an ideal way to maintain family connections.

Moreover, early research has demonstrated the benefits of getting the birth family involved with the agency from the very beginning of foster placement. Having oriented the birth family, agency, and foster family toward each other in the first stage, and having suggested a collaborative approach, in this stage you try to make this happen in two primary ways:

- *First,* all parties need to learn to communicate effectively with one another, make their various needs, expectations, and fears known, advocate for themselves, and resolve conflicts.

- *Second,* as the therapist and an outsider to this foster care subsystem, you are in a position to point out overlapping areas of responsibility and inquire about role redundancies, goal conflicts, and unholy alliances so that everyone gets off to a good start.

In one example, as we will discuss later in this chapter, all three parties—the caseworker, the birth parents, and the foster family—may each validly believe that it is their role to "plan for the child." The birth family may automatically think that what is best for the child is for him or her to be returned home. A foster family may see its role as rescuing children to a better life. Now that many states allow foster families to adopt the children placed with them (if reunification attempts fail), many foster families may be opposed to birth family reunification from the outset. They may view fostering as the first step in an adoption process. In such a conflict between the birth family and the foster family, each of these parties may try to win over the caseworker, or even you, the family therapist. Then it's two against one, until the third party finds a strong ally.

Can you picture it? The foster family convinces the caseworker that parental rights should be terminated and the child adopted by the foster parents. Threatened by this, the birth parents try to convince you that they are the best recourse for their child. If they succeed, then it's two against two. In order to break this power struggle, one of the contesting parties probably will try to forge an alliance with a court official. And so on. Someone in a weak position recruits someone stronger, changing the balance of power, and then the other party does the same. As you know, this can go on and on. Your role as a systems-savvy outside consultant to the foster care system becomes crucial from the very moment foster children are placed.

It is also in this stage that you have the opportunity to assess and deal with destructive relationship issues within the family. These issues may be just the qualities that led well-meaning caseworkers to limit or terminate family visitation sessions. And this is the stage where you first address maladaptive use of substances in the family (see Chapter 17, "'We're in It Together' Family Therapy Where Substance Abuse Is a Problem"). In the beginning, that may mean that no one is to come to an agency, visitation, or therapy session intoxicated. And, as you have probably experienced, this may be an obstacle that cannot be overcome. If so, it makes no sense to move on to the third through fifth stages with the birth parents. The tasks at these advanced stages are irrelevant if the parents cannot be sober when they are with their children. Where adults have impulse control problems—anger, sexuality, substances, and so on—individual and relational therapy with the goal of behavioral control of these behaviors must take precedence over other goals.

Often the children, and also their parents, need crisis counseling to address any trauma elicited by the breakup of their homes or by matters leading up to that breakup. We can still hear the voice of the six-year-old girl who, weeks after removal from her home, cried and screamed about how her door was kicked in and she was forcibly taken away from her parents. As you know, many children also need immediate help with loyalty conflicts between their birth and foster families, and between the agency and their birth families. Birth parents may need to be encouraged to give their children permission to settle into their foster homes and to cooperate with the agency! The foster families and the agency personnel need to be sensitive to demands that typically pressure children into taking sides. Poignant examples of all of these circumstances are in Chapter 4, "The Perspective of the Consumer: Foster Children Tell Us What They Need."

It is in this stage that you, the therapist, need to hear and respect concerns of the foster parents about the children placed with them. Disrupted placements can be very destructive if they reinforce children's beliefs about rejection and the dangerous nature of the world and relationships. You have seen many examples where, after a brief honeymoon period, children engage in serious misbehavior. They may be anxious, grieving, or testing the good intentions of the foster parents. They also might be acting out relationships and events in which they were victimized. Unfortunately, if they frighten and frustrate the foster parents, the children may well be rejected from the household, which then increases their negative beliefs and emotions, which leads to more misbehavior, more rejection, and so on. Because of this, you may want to use the second stage to respond to concerns of the foster parents, even if your therapeutic agenda conflicts somewhat. In this stage, you may provide crisis counseling and problem solving for the foster parents and give them behavior modification methods to safely inhibit the children's behaviors that they find so difficult to endure. Giving foster parents insight into the world of those they are fostering is always helpful. However, such knowledge often is not enough, especially if the foster parents believe the foster children are a threat to the children already in the home (see Chapter 15, "'I Want This Child Out of Here Now!' How to Deal with Sexualized Acting Out in the Foster Environment: A 'SMART' Approach to Assessment and Treatment").

Stage 3, The Birth Family's Long-Term Survival Needs

If the tasks of the first two stages are accomplished effectively, then the family is in a safe place. It also has a relatively constructive relationship with the foster care system in which it has been embedded. The third stage builds on this foundation. If this is to be a viable household, the family needs to be able to accomplish the necessary activities of daily living—to acquire the resources to take care of all of its members in the long term. The first step is to acquire and maintain secure long-term shelter that is healthy for the children as well as other family members.

The parents need to find permanent solutions to their housing, food, medical, transportation, educational, and interpersonal challenges. They cannot fail to protect the children from abusive others and unhealthy events, be they matters of trauma, nutrition, hygiene, illness, education, or supervision. This means developing consistent adaptive skills that are "good enough" to meet day-to-day parental needs, and the absence of problematic substance use. Some of this requires a change in attitudes and motivation, which we will address in the next stage. But in the third stage, we are concerned that the family has acquired those tangible and social resources it needs in order to provide an adequate long-term home for its children. Social resources include identifying and nurturing social support systems, which often involves working out better relationships with both the maternal and paternal extended families. Once the family has the physical, financial, and interpersonal resources it needs, then the next step is to get the parents to use them consistently.

Many of your foster children will need extensive educational assessment and school interventions. Many more will need the social skills and behavioral controls necessary to establish and maintain gratifying social relationships outside the home, including peer and other school relationships. Many of these children have strong mixed feelings about relying on institutionalized authorities. These include not only the foster parents but also teachers, caseworkers, and you!

Finally, in this stage we expect the birth family, the foster family, and the agency to more fully develop a constructive working relationship with each other. This means that goals are shared and there exists a positive relationship to support work on those goals. This can grow into a generalized alliance and communication with the entire foster care system, so that future family problems can be identified and handled. In this stage, more than ever, the situation requires your ecosystemic understanding and your skill in recognizing dyadic and triadic methods of conflict resolution. You need to be alert to triangulations, blurred boundaries, coalitions, and other dysfunctional relationships taking place within the larger system in which all these parties transact (Colapinto, 1995).

Since traditional family therapy is not likely to work at a time when the family members are driven to deny evidence, transfer blame, and protect the group (DeMaio, 1995), your therapy probably will involve substantial individual and couples treatment for the adults, and individual treatment for the children. The goal of this individual work is to remove the obstacles to working together on relational issues—obstacles that might involve large doses of anger, fear, guilt, and baggage from earlier days (including the adults' own childhoods). When children and adults will not give each other explicit signs of what they need and, even when they do, the other parties cannot respond in adequate ways, then the inter- and intrapersonal obstacles to such sensitivity and constructive responsiveness need to be addressed and removed. This stage is described at length in Chapter 6, "The Case for Relational Therapy with Young Children in Foster Care," and Chapter 17, "'We're in It Together' Family Therapy Where Substance Abuse Is a Problem." The job of individual and couple therapy is to get family members ready for profitable family therapy in the next (fourth) stage.

Stage 4, Psychoeducational and Traditional Family Therapy Approaches

You know you have entered Stage 4 when the various environmental stressors have settled down and there is a good working alliance between the birth family, the foster family, the agency, and you. Everyone is less defensive, less distracted by momentary "brush fires," and more in agreement with regard to the larger issue of the family's capacity to be an adequate custodial environment. In the fourth stage, we are concerned with the parents' capacity to provide their children developmentally appropriate and necessary care—in other words, there is an increased probability of children looking to their parents for guidance and nurture, and those parents must be sensitive to their children's needs and meet those needs in an appropriate, timely, and complete fashion. It is in this stage that we turn at last to psycho-educational approaches, where we work with the parents and their children together, encouraging positive expectations and limit-setting that is appropriate to the developmental level of the children. This is an excellent time for you to coach parenting skills and provide information about child development, nutrition, hygiene, assertiveness, and the fine points of communication during your family sessions. Experience has taught us that issues of the prospective physical environment can be directly addressed at this time.

Although a systems orientation has been present from the very beginning, Stage 4 incorporates traditional family therapy for both the birth (again, see Chapter 6, "The Case for Relational Therapy with Young Children in Foster Care") and the foster families (see Chapter 12, "Intervening with Foster Infants' Foster Parents: Attachment and Biobehavioral Catch-Up"). Your role now is to focus on those things that the birth and foster families do well, and on those things that keep them from adequately adapting to changing circumstances. At this stage, the birth family is expected to accept responsibility for the situation that led to the children being placed in foster care, and to address and resolve those things that elicited and maintained the unsafe environment.

Structural family therapy is often a good fit for working with birth families (DeMaio, 1995). Children in these families may be parentified, recruited into taking sides, and scapegoated. Structural therapy is designed to help parents assume functional positions of authority while relieving children of unhealthy roles. Other major models of marriage and family therapy, especially those that track and resolve patterns across generations, are appropriate with birth families (see Chapter 14, "'It Isn't Right!' The Need to Redress Experiences of Injustice in Child Abuse and Neglect"). There are several good presentations of these theories available (see, for example, Becvar & Becvar, 2002; Goldenberg & Goldenberg, 2003; Nichols & Schwartz, 2003).

When children have been abused, they will need your help to separate the safe present from the dangerous past. They need to learn that the rules have changed, abuse is not allowed, and the perpetrators are either gone or transformed. However, there is one final need (Davies, 1991): The children need the corrective emotional experience of seeing the former failing-to-protect parent stand up to former and prospective perpetrators, even if that perpetrator is ostensibly a "changed person."

Stage 5, Transitions to Permanent Placement

In the last stage we are concerned with what needs to be done with the birth family, the foster family, and the adoptive family when the case is ready to be resolved—when the children are to be returned to the birth home or placed for adoption. For details, see Chapter 19, "'Ready or Not, Here I Come!' Equipping Families for Transitions," and the work of Lau and her associates (2003).

In summary, there are stages within foster care, and each individual involved must be ready in order for the next step to succeed. When this doesn't happen, biological families are likely to fail in getting their children back and all parties involved may lose their sense of direction. This is called "foster care drift." When it occurs, children and adults are inhibited from making lasting emotional investments and relationships, and there may be immediate and long-term emotional, social, and cognitive problems for the children (Milner, 1987; Sprey-Wessing & Portz, 1982). The children's problems likely began with whatever maltreatment they experienced in their birth families, but if they linger in foster care these children are increasingly likely to:

- be unable to trust adults, peers, and the world;
- have problems in their physical, psychological, and social development;
- be behind in physical, cognitive, language, self-regulation, and social skills; and

- demonstrate learning and social problems in school, hostility, substance abuse, and delinquency.

Therefore, it is important that birth parents visit the children early, frequently, and constructively, and that the various stages are used as opportunities for interventions, as well as for diagnosis and assessment. Each stage presents certain tasks, and family therapy professionals are in a position to discover and report progress. Formal reports will be made to the court over the course of foster care. Finally, there will be a recommendation for the ultimate disposition of the case, either reunification of the family—with recommendations about what it continues to need if it is to be a successful custodial environment—or termination of parental rights.

The main challenge for those of us working with children and their families is to decide whether or not the current nuclear and/or extended birth family is a "good enough" custodial environment. We may find that some families are unwilling or unable to change the situation that led to the child being removed from the home. For example, some parents don't have sufficient emotional investment in their children to compete with their other interests. Others may not be able to overcome deficits such as extreme intellectual dullness, impulsiveness, addiction to substances, or psychopathology, including destructive acting out associated with their parental roles. (For example, a mother may deprive or punish her infant lest the child be "spoiled.")

In some cases you may uncover a multiplicity of reasons why the parents are not able to do what they must do to get their children back. For example, different combinations of the above traits, as well as unwillingness or inability to use environmental supports, might lead to a continuing lack of adequate shelter, nurture, and/or supervisory capacity. When you see parents engage in goals and interventions, stage by stage, you are able to identify those critical parental issues that emerge at each stage. You can more confidently identify those parents who can and cannot be expected to do what is necessary to have their children return home. When the children are to be returned home, you can specify more clearly

what the family still needs (in terms of support) to have a successful custodial environment. When you recommend that it is in the
child's best interests to be placed somewhere other than their birth
family, you can specify with confidence why this is so.

Appreciating and Using Foster Care as a System

As you have learned by experience, the same foster care that is
meant to rescue children can sometimes harm them. All of us hate it
when placing children in foster care becomes actually harmful. Our
goal is to increase the probability of desirable things happening.
Therefore, first pay attention to your families' readiness for interventions and to what is standing in their way. The impediments to
progress at each stage must be recognized and consistently removed.
Second, consider the larger system in which your children are situated and consider interventions with multiple impacts.

We know that child abuse and neglect often occur when a family is socially isolated. There may be no witnesses to the abuse and
neglect, and therefore no adequate response from the larger community. The walls between the birth family and its larger environment need to come down and stay down. One of your major jobs
as a therapist serving child welfare agencies is to track and address
the relationships between all of the entities that comprise the
child's ecosystem: birth family, foster families, diverse agencies,
court, schools, health care system, neighborhoods, and workplaces.
You want to discover how all the players interact—roles, hierarchy,
relationships, "ways of doing business"—and you want to make
that known, so that the larger system and the family within it experience and practice new—successful and positive—ways of living.

Who are actually in your consulting room and what power do
they have? Even if these folks are not physically present, they are
present nonetheless. And it is a very crowded place! It probably
includes the birth mother and her extended family, the birth father
and his extended family, the child welfare agency worker and the
agency's supervisory and administrative people, the foster parents,
the court system—judge, parental attorneys, prosecutor, and the

children's guardians ad litem—and the parents' and children's therapists. Then, too, there are all the significant members of the birth and foster families' social systems. So many players, so many systemic complications! Let's think about the influence of some of these (and see Imber-Black, 1991).

Potential Role Problems

There may be role problems. All of the parties involved in the life of any foster child, including you, most likely have overlapping roles. For example, I'm pretty sure that the caseworker, agency, birth parents, foster parents, officers of the court, and you, the therapist, all view your jobs as planning for the child. Each of you has pretty much the same responsibility ("the best interests of the child") and each of you have various degrees of influence in determining how it all turns out. Therefore, since all of you have the same job, or important parts of that job, to what extent do you agree on the solution?

Does the agency and/or its care workers generally want to rescue the children to a better home? Does the court, perhaps influenced by the legislature, primarily intend to reunify children with their birth families? Do your foster parents see themselves as the adoptive parents of choice and in competition with the birth parents? (Some states originally did not allow foster parents to be considered for adoptions so as to avoid this conflict. However, to remedy the shortage of foster parents, this policy has been reversed. Prospective adoptive parents are urged to begin by fostering.) Does the case manager favor one parent and you another?

Do the various parties have beliefs about one another that are conducive to a working alliance? We have mentioned that many birth parents may derisively regard everyone involved in the foster system as "do-gooder social workers in the service of the court, who neither understand nor like poor and unlucky folks." I have often overheard urban caseworkers refer to "crack mamas" and "crack babies." All of us have socioeconomic and other kinds of prejudices. With so much distrust, how can a working alliance take place? (See Jivanjee, 1999.)

In addition, do all of you in the foster care system agree on the criteria that determine whether or not to return the children home? Is it enough that an adult maintains some period of sobriety, a parent moves geographically away from an abusive partner, housing with adequate room is obtained, or that the adults attend parenting classes? Do all of you agree on what is needed? If so, do you also agree on what yardstick is used for measuring these things? Are some of the parties looking for ideal, perhaps unrealistic, attributes of the custodial environment? Can everyone agree that "good enough" is all that is required—and what constitutes "good enough?" When I did parent evaluations I often was sobered by what I discovered about the families. A cross-examining attorney taught me to think about what other households on that urban or rural street were like, and to consider if the family in front of me were any different.

There are many influential members in any child's foster care system, and they may be at odds with one another about a variety of things. The foster care system, like other social systems, has its way of resolving these conflicts. One of the most common is to form unholy alliances, in which a party who feels weak makes an alliance with someone stronger. For example, a birth family, sensing dislike by the caseworker, seduces the judge. Now the birth family is stronger. Of course, the caseworker addresses this new imbalance by recruiting the children's therapist and, perhaps, their guardian ad litem. Once again one-down, the birth family brings in *(To Be Announced)*. And so it goes, an escalating power struggle in which constructive collaborative approaches in the best interests of the child are unlikely to occur.

So what are you to do? Raise the consciousness of all the players in the group about their mutual involvement in your case. You can do this directly at case planning meetings, and during consultations in person and by phone, by asking "what other parties" are involved in the case. You can construct and share a diagram with the child in the middle and all of the other players indicated by labeled circles around the child. The thickness of the line between the child and the other entity might indicate the amount of influence. Loops around different entities could indicate alliances, zigzag lines conflict, and a line with a slash across it a breakdown of communication.

Once all the parties to a case are identified, you can ask about role redundancy and explore the mutuality of goals and their measurement. *The goal is for everyone to be on the same page.* You can look at where conflict may exist among the players and ask the whole group to consider how it might be resolved in order to keep the case moving forward beneficially. In effect, you are acting as the "family therapist" to the group involved in the case. And, of course, a major question is whether or not you have enough personal rapport with the other parties.

If you have a good enough working relationship, then you can address more subtle factors promoting conflict—for example, rivalry between parties, anxiety about making decisions, and so on. Your primary role for the group is to raise their awareness of the process. Sometimes this is easier when you are a therapist housed in a child welfare agency, because you have the personal relationships and credibility you have built. Sometimes it is easier to get a group to look at its process when you are perceived as an outsider. Then you can say: "I'm new to you all, so I don't have your understanding. But as I watch and listen, I think this is what I may be seeing getting in our way (describe it.) Do you think I am correct in this? If so, can you see how it is a problem? What would you like to do about that?"

As a relational therapist you understand that children exist in family systems and they and their families are now living parts of a foster care system. You probably also worry about "self-fulfilling prophecies." For example, if someone with influence over them is consistently grilling them like a prosecuting attorney, the defendants probably will be nervous, angry, and/or avoidant—they may act in ways that reinforce the negative stereotypes of the prosecution. To correct for this, it is important to remind the members of the foster care system that:

- interventions need to be for the whole family,
- interventions need to be strength-based,
- interventions need to be respectful,

- interventions need to be collaborative and not adversarial, and
- interventions need to be tailor-made. One size does not fit all.

In short, we want to act to maximize the probability of desirable things happening, minimize the probability of undesirable things happening, and address the court's and other agencies' doubts and fears. All of us are involved in the relationship-building business—relationships between the birth parents and their children, between the birth parents and the agency, and between all the members of the foster care system. We want to use what we know about building healthy relationships to see if we can help the birth family experience new ways of being and doing (see Haight, Kagle, & Black, 2003; Marvin, Cooper, Hoffman, & Powell, 2002; also see Chapter 6, "The Case for Relational Therapy with Young Children in Foster Care"; Chapter 9, "An Integrative Approach Involving the Biological and Foster Family Systems"; Chapter 10, "Kinship Placements: An Integrative Approach"; and Chapter 11, "Creative Ways to Strengthen Family Bonds").

We also want to help all of the parties to the case—birth families, foster families, caseworkers, agency supervisors, judges, lawyers, therapists, and educators—experience new ways of perceiving the birth family. To the extent that this group can do that, foster children generally will feel more secure and will behave better in the foster home and in day care, demonstrate more positive relationships with adults and other children, require a fewer number of replacements, and demonstrate more normal developmental trajectories. Their birth parents will visit more frequently and constructively, show more faith in the foster care system, describe themselves in more positive terms, more realistically inventory their parenting needs, more quickly complete their parent–agency agreements, and show less recidivism.

Summary and Recommendations

We have recommended what child welfare innovators have termed multiple impact (Fraser, 1995), multilevel (DeMaio, 1995), and stage-wise (Bicknell-Hodges, 1995) interventions. Our birth families' problems are intra- and interpersonal. Intrapersonal problems exist inside a person's own psyche. The interpersonal problems exist within the family and between the family and other social entities. Some problems are more urgent and need to be solved before others can be effectively addressed, and often these problems involve the family's place in and relationship to the larger ecosystem. Birth families often see all child welfare people as "agents of the court" and can be utterly defensive to their own and their children's detriment. Although individual and family therapy eventually might be needed, family support—including advocacy and casework—are needed up front. The goals initially are crisis intervention and life stabilization and eventually include more traditional family therapy outcomes, including changes in family roles, communication, and the way the family typically conducts its business. However, in all cases, at every stage, we need to consider birth families as they are situated in larger systems.

References

Bavolek, S. J. (1989). Assessing and treating high-risk parenting attitudes. *Early Child Development and Care, 4,* 99–112.

Becvar, D. S., & Becvar, R. J. (2002). *Family therapy: A systemic integration* (5th ed.). Boston: Allyn & Bacon.

Bicknell-Hodges, L. (1995). The stages of the reunification process and the tasks of the therapist. In L. Combrinck-Graham (Ed.), *Children in families at risk: Maintaining the connections* (pp. 326–349). New York: Guilford.

Browne, D., & Maloney, A. (2002). "Contact irregular": A qualitative analysis of the impact of visiting patterns of natural parents on foster placements. *Child & Family Social Work, 7,* 35–45.

Colapinto, J. A. (1995). Dilution of family process in social services: Implications for treatment of neglectful families. *Family Process, 34,* 59–74.

Courtney, M. E. (1994). Factors associated with the reunification of foster children with their families. *Social Service Review, 68,* 81–108.

Crittenden, P. M. (1993). An information-processing perspective on the behavior of neglectful parents. *Criminal Justice and Behavior, 20,* 27–48.

Davies, D. (1991). Intervention with male toddlers who have witnessed parental violence. *Families in Society: The Journal of Contemporary Human Services, 72*, 515–524.

Davies, D. (2004). *Child development: A practitioner's guide* (2nd ed.). New York: Guilford.

Dawson, K., & Berry, M. (2002). Engaging families in child welfare services: An evidence-based approach to best practice. *Child Welfare, 81*, 293–317.

DeMaio, R. X. (1995). Helping families become places of healing: Systemic treatment of intrafamilial sexual abuse. In L. Combrinck-Graham (Ed.), *Children in families at risk: Maintaining the connections* (pp. 125–149). New York: Guilford.

Family Resource Coalition. (1996). *Guidelines for family support practice.* Chicago: Author.

Fraser, L. H. (1995). Eastfield Ming Quong: Multiple-impact in-home treatment model. In L. Combrinck-Graham (Ed.), *Children in families at risk: Maintaining the connections* (pp. 83–106). New York: Guilford.

Goldenberg, I., & Goldenberg, H. (2003). *Family therapy: An overview.* Belmont, CA: Wadsworth.

Haight, W. L., Kagle, J. D., & Black, J. E. (2003). Understanding and supporting parent–child relationships during foster care visits: Attachment theory and research. *Social Work, 48*, 195–233.

Hannan, K., & Luster, T. (1991). Influence of parent, child, and contextual factors on the quality of the home environment. *Infant Mental Health Journal, 12*, 17–30.

Imber-Black, E. (1991). A family–larger system perspective. In A. S. Gurman & D. Kniskern (Eds.), *Handbook of family therapy* (Vol. 2, pp. 583–605). New York: Brunner/Mazel.

Jivanjee, P. (1999). Professional and provider perspectives on family involvement in therapeutic foster care. *Journal of Child and Family Studies, 8*, 329–341.

Lau, A. S., Litrownik, A. J., Newton, R. E., & Landsverk, J. (2003). Going home: The complex effects of reunification on internalizing problems among children in foster care. *Journal of Abnormal Child Psychology, 31*, 345–359.

Laufer, Z. (1994). The "no man's land" of home weekends for children in residential care. *Child Abuse and Neglect, 18*, 913–921.

Lee, R. E., & Lynch, M. T. (1998). Combating foster care drift: An ecosystemic treatment model for neglect cases. *Contemporary Family Therapy, 20*, 351–370.

Lerner, R. M. (1991). Changing organism–context relations as the basic process of development: A developmental contextual perspective. *Developmental Psychology, 27*, 27–32.

Lewis, K. G. (1995). Sibling therapy: One step in breaking the cycle of recidivism in foster care. In L. Combrinck-Graham (Ed.), *Children in families at risk: Maintaining the connections* (pp. 301–325). New York: Guilford.

Littner, N. (1975). The importance of natural parents to the child in placement. *Child Welfare, 54,* 175–181.

Mapp, S. C. (2002). A framework for family visiting for children in long-term foster care. *Families in Society: The Journal of Contemporary Human Services, 83,* 175–182.

Marsh, P. (1986). Natural families and children in care: An agenda for practice development. *Adoption and Fostering, 10,* 20–25.

Marvin, R., Cooper, G., Hoffman, K., & Powell, B. (2002). The Circle of Security project: Attachment-based intervention with caregiver–pre-school child dyads. *Attachment & Human Development, 4,* 107–124.

Maslow, A. (1962). *Toward a psychology of being.* New York: Van Nostrand.

Mech, E. V. (1985). Parental visiting and foster placement. *Child Welfare, 64,* 67–72.

Milner, J. L. (1987). An ecological perspective on duration of foster care. *Child Welfare, 66,* 113–125.

Minuchin, P. (1995). Foster and natural families: Forming a cooperative network. In L. Combrinck-Graham (Ed.), *Children in families at risk: Maintaining the connections* (pp. 251–274). New York: Guilford.

Nichols, M. P., & Schwartz, R. C. (2003). *Family therapy: Concepts and methods.* Upper Saddle River, NJ: Pearson Education.

Oyserman, D., & Benbenishti, R. (1992). Keeping in touch: Ecological factors related to foster care visitation. *Child and Adolescent Social Work Journal, 9,* 541–554.

Rabin, C. (1995). The use of psychoeducational groups to improve marital functioning in high-risk Israeli couples: A stage model. *Contemporary Family Therapy, 17,* 503–515.

Schatz, M., & Bane, W. (1991). Empowering the parents of children in substitute care: A training model. *Child Welfare, 70,* 665–678.

Sprey-Wessing, T., & Portz, P. (1982). Some aspects of identity problems in foster families. *Journal of Contemporary Family Studies, 13,* 231–235.

U.S. Department of Health & Human Services, National Center on Child Abuse & Neglect. (1996). *Child maltreatment 1994: Reports from the states to the National Center on Child Abuse and Neglect.* Washington, DC: U.S. Government Printing Office.

Whiting, J. B., & Lee, R. E. (2003). Voices from the system: A qualitative study of foster children's stories. *Family Relations, 52,* 288–295.

3

Cultural Issues: Diversity and Child Welfare

Edgar Tyson, Scott Ryan, Tomi Gomory, and Martell Teasley

*I*n child welfare, as in any other area of clinical practice, the cultural, ethnic, or racial backgrounds of both the service recipients and the providers plays an important role. Often, these characteristics determine what may be done to or with the individuals involved and how these interventions may be perceived.

Cultural competence "refers to the process by which individuals and systems respond respectfully and effectively to people of all cultures" including races, ethnic backgrounds, social class, languages, religions, and other diversity factors. This is done in a manner that "recognizes, affirms, and values the worth of individuals, families, and communities and protects and preserves the dignity of each" (National Association of Social Workers [NASW], 2001, p. 11). The NASW (1999) also addressed the professional obligation of its members regarding cultural diversity in its code of ethics—and it easily applies to members of all other child-serving professions. We should:

- understand culture and its function in human behavior and society, recognizing the strengths that exist in all cultures;

- have a knowledge base of our clients' cultures and be able to demonstrate competence in the provision of services that are sensitive to clients' cultures and to differences among people and cultural groups; and

- obtain education about and seek to understand the nature of social diversity and oppression with respect to race, ethnicity, national origin, color, sex, sexual orientation, age, marital status, political belief, religion, and mental or physical disability.

As child welfare professionals we should be particularly concerned about the provision of culturally aware interventions. The striking fact is that children and families of color are overrepresented in all stages of the child welfare process. Data retrieved from the National Data Analysis System (http://ndas.cwla.org) indicate that, although African American children make up approximately 15% of all children in the United States, they make up 40% of the children in the child welfare population, 49% of the children in foster care, and 28% of founded allegations of abuse or neglect. White children may be 61% of the total population of children, but they constitute only 38% of children in foster care.

In addition, child welfare outcomes are also different for African American and white children. Fifty-six percent of African American children are provided child welfare services in foster care and 44% receive them in their own homes, compared to 28% of white children obtaining such services in foster care and 72% in their own homes.

In contrast to their clientele, those who assess and intervene in child welfare settings are overwhelmingly—83%—white (Rosenthal, Groze, & Curiel, 1990). This means that many families of color are being provided professional services by white workers. Given the rapid rate of growth among minority populations, the number of minority children served by the child welfare services system is likely to increase. This considerable cross-racial/ethnic service provision raises questions about the continuation and effectiveness of these interactions.

Unfortunately, information and knowledge relating to the efficacy of cross-racial assessment and intervention remains limited, and few child welfare workers have received adequate formal training in serving minority clients. Because of their age-specific legal minority status, all children in the child welfare system are vulnerable to discrimination, coercion, and control. Minority children are at additional risk because of racial/ethnic discrimination, limited training of child welfare professionals, and the attendant differential socioeconomic and psychocultural factors common in society.

Assessment and Intervention Issues and Strategies

In 1999, 826,000 children nationwide entered the child welfare system because of maltreatment (U.S. Department of Health and Human Services, Administration on Children, Youth and Families, 2001). The majority of these children had persistent and severe mental health and behavioral problems. The fate of these young people is an important societal concern. Without immediate and adequate assessment and intervention, these vulnerable children may be at risk for chronic behavioral and mental health problems. Early and accurate assessment of children and adolescents is a fundamental prerequisite for appropriate and effective intervention; however, assessments and subsequent intervention decisions are often made through informal and unsystematic procedures (Martin, Peters, & Glisson, 1998).

Assessment

If we are to be culturally competent during the assessment process of racial and ethnic minority children, we must consider the cognitive framework that individuals use to understand and interpret reality (Guerra & Jagers, 1998). Cultural competence has been described as a developmental process along a continuum of six stages (Cross, Bazron, Dennis, & Isaacs, 1989; Diller, 2004). These are:

- *cultural destructiveness*—policies and practices that are destructive to individuals and communities;
- *cultural incapacity*—recommended policies and practices that unintentionally promote racial/ethnic bias;
- *cultural blindness*—attempting to avoid bias issues related to racial and ethnic groups, while at the same time adopting a mainstream approach to services;
- *competence precompetence*—failing at attempts towards cultural competence due to limited knowledge;

- *basic cultural competency*—promoting competence standards with a given agency to include the hiring of unbiased staff; and,

- *cultural proficiency*—exhibiting basic cultural competence and actively advocating for multiculturalism throughout systems and practice domains, while engaging in research on how to better serve racial and ethnic minority groups.

In many ways, our understanding of the limitations of mainstream assessments and interventions for use with African American children and youth may be only at the level of precompetence. Few of the most used assessment tools have been rigorously tested for measurement equivalence across different ethnic groups in the United States (Tyson, 2004). There has been some work involving the popular Child Behavior Checklist (Lambert, Rowan, Lyubansky, & Russ, 2002) and the Youth Outcome Questionnaire (Wells, Burlingame, & Lambert, 1999). However, only the Short Form Assessment for Children (Tyson & Glisson, 2005) has been tested in large systems that serve children, such as child welfare. Since African American youth are a significant proportion of youth referred to and assessed by child welfare systems, more research is needed on the usefulness of conventional assessment and intervention methods for African American children and youth. For example, a child may be identified as having a specific disorder when, in fact, he or she does not. This gap in knowledge with regard to behavioral assessment research is particularly troubling because ethnic, racial, or cultural biases present in behavioral or psychological assessment measures may have grave implications regarding client treatment, including placement decisions (Doueck, English, Defanfils, & Moote, 1993).

Finally, "it is important to realize that cultural sensitivity cannot [simply] be an afterthought based on inclusion of children from different cultures, but must be interwoven into the entire research process" (Guerra & Jagers, 1998, p. 168). With regard to psychometric testing, cultural competence means that (McLoyd & Steinberg, 1998):

- the providers are skillful and comprehensive in their knowledge of how cultural differences effect environmental perceptions, interaction, behavioral choices, and cognitive processes; and

- the providers can provide comprehensive documentation of findings that—through the use of both quantitative and qualitative data—explain developmental norms within the context of the cultural milieu of pertinent racial and ethnic groups (McLoyd & Steinberg, 1998).

Intervention

There has been considerable discussion of the importance of culturally sensitive treatment models, but few interventions have been well tested in this regard. "Hip-hop therapy" (Tyson, 2002; Tyson, 2003) is an exception. Hip-hop therapy incorporates a highly engaging and salient aspect of youth culture, captures several important treatment principles, and builds on existing models of intervention. It incorporates youth strengths by using an important resource that many listen to and interact with on a daily basis, namely, rap music. It also includes the basic principles of poetry therapy (Mazza, 1999).

In hip-hop therapy, the client and therapist listen to, discuss, deconstruct, reconstruct, and interpret lyrics from rap songs that are relevant to particular issues that the youth is currently facing. The therapist may also ask clients to write their own lyrics and then to discuss, deconstruct, reconstruct, and interpret them (Tyson, 2003). One of the most useful aspects of hip-hop therapy is that it quickly establishes a strong therapeutic relationship, which is thought to be perhaps the most important aspect when working with young clients from different cultural backgrounds (Nalavany, Ryan, Gomory, & Lacasse, 2005). And other practitioners (for example, De Carlo, 2001; Elligan, 2004) have begun to document their use of similar models and claim to have enjoyed some degree of success.

Case Example

The family has given us permission to profile their case in this chapter. All names have been changed and all identifying information has been deleted.

Case Background

Ms. D. is a 59-year-old mother of four children. Three are foster children and one is adopted. The family consists of two foster sons, Tahir, 10 years old, and Issau, who is 16, one foster daughter, Monique, aged 17 years, and an adoptive daughter, Africa, who is 19 years old. Africa was adopted shortly after her first birthday. Issau is the identified client.

Ms. D. has been a foster mother for more than 20 years and was once a Child Protective Services worker herself. Besides the four children currently in her home, Ms. D. has had over 12 different foster children during the past 20 years, and most of them have stayed with her for a minimum of two years. Monique has been with Ms. D. for 10 years, Issau for eight years, and Tahir for five years.

The therapist was experienced in the provision of home-based counseling with kinship and conventional foster families, as well as with adopted, single parent, and otherwise nontraditional families. In addition, the therapist had experience working with high-risk, adolescent, African American males—the subject of this case. A child welfare case manager at the local child welfare agency referred the family to the therapist three days after Issau had been suspended from school.

1st Session

Issau was in the tenth grade. He had been suspended for 10 days because he had seriously injured another student during a fistfight on school grounds. Moreover, since the end of his ninth grade year, his negative behavior had been increasing. He was increasingly physically aggressive with other students at school, and would shove and grab them whenever he became upset. He also had begun defying teachers' instructions, not turning in homework, and failing tests. By the end of his ninth grade year, Issau's classroom behavior and performance had deteriorated so severely that he had actually failed one course and received a D in two others. On the day of the incident, Ms. D. concluded that she needed professional assistance and asked her case manager for advice.

Ms. D. appeared to be a strong and nurturing parent figure. She was well informed about the child welfare system and assertively talked about what she had been through. She spent nearly 30 minutes telling her story, describing her past and some of the things she had been through with Issau. This early opportunity to talk about her experiences, while the therapist just listened, enabled Ms. D. to feel more comfortable in publicly sharing sensitive aspects of her relationship with Issau, including some of the reasons why she thought he had begun to travel on a different and more troubled path than other teenagers she had raised.

During this initial visit Ms. D. was very candid and stated that although she has helped raise more than a dozen children and was currently the mother of four, she was getting old and had not been able to reach Issau. She then told the therapist that "the worst part about it is that he just listens to that rap music garbage all the time and he thinks he is a rapper. I hate that stuff—it is poisoning the minds of our young kids."

Ms. D. went on to say that she bought Issau a set of earphones so that she did not have to "listen to that crap." The therapist explained to Ms. D. that he was among a new wave of urban-trained therapists (see, for example, Elligan, 2004) who used rap music constructively to work with youth. He explained that this approach was uniquely relevant to many high-risk youth who, like Issau, listened to rap music. Ms. D. was excited, intrigued, and comforted to hear that this "hip-hop therapy" (Tyson, 2002, 2003) might help Issau.

2nd Session

The first visit with Ms. D. enabled the therapist to develop a more complete picture of the family dynamics. Ms. D. had been widowed a few months after Issau's 10th birthday. She and her husband had worked together running a boxing gym, where they both coached a team of boxers. Ms. D. stated that Issau took her husband's death very hard and that, looking back, she thinks he began "going downhill" a little over a year later. Ms. D. thinks Issau would have been one of their best boxers. "He was always big. He is strong and, boy, is he a smart one." Ms. D. had already informed the therapist that Issau had just begun boxing with the team, but had not been in a tournament, when her husband died. After that, Issau no longer wanted to box. The therapist could see that he would have to explore with Issau how he felt about his foster father's death.

It was during this second visit that the therapist was to meet Issau. Although Ms. D. had told Issau to come downstairs, it was about 10 minutes later that he finally complied. Issau was wearing his headphones and he walked right past the therapist who was sitting in the living room. The therapist stood up, Ms. D. introduced him to Issau, and they both shook hands. The therapist told Issau that most young guys called him "Doc." Issau smiled and said, "What's up, Doc?" and then went into the kitchen, and said he was getting something to drink. After a minute or so in the kitchen, Issau asked the therapist if he wanted something to drink. The therapist went into the kitchen and said, "Sure." While Issau was getting two glasses of juice, the therapist asked him whom he was listening to and Issau said, "The Game and 50 Cent." The therapist said, "Cool," and told him that The Game's CD was the hottest in the country right now. Issau replied, "Yeah, it is. It's hot." They walked into the living room where they both sat down and continued talking.

The therapist told Issau that he had the same CD and asked if he would mind if they listened to the CD together. Issau seemed surprised by the request. He then turned off his portable CD player and put *The Game* CD in the CD player that was in the living room's entertainment center. After Issau played his favorite song, "How We Do," the therapist asked him what other song on the CD he liked. Issau replied, "All of them are all right to me." To which the therapist replied, "Yeah, me too—hey, flip it to #18," and Issau did so without hesitation. This particular song is about the range of emotions (love, excitement) that the artist, "The Game," had when his only son was born. The name of the song is "Like Father, Like Son." The chorus of this song was relevant to Issau. It states:

> I hope you grow up to become everything you can be,
>
> That's all I wanted for you. Like father, like son.
>
> But, in the end I hope you only turn out better than me.
>
> I hope you know I love you, young'in. Like father, like son.
>
> (Aftermath/G Unit/Interscope Records, 2005)

They listened to it and then, in a very lengthy conversation, explored various ways in which Issau related this song to his life. Towards the end of the session, he began telling the therapist that he also wrote lyrics. They agreed to discuss some of these in subsequent sessions.

3rd Session

Concrete and measurable goals were mutually set which focused on improving Issau's school performance both academically and behaviorally. Specifically, it was agreed that by the end of treatment, Issau would (1) not have any unexcused absences from school for 12 consecutive weeks and (2) not have any (self or other) reports of physical aggression for 12 consecutive weeks.

By the third session, Issau began talking about his foster father in a very healthy way—and his grades and behavior at school had begun to improve dramatically. And the therapist had asked Issau to write a few short rap lyrics about what he would say to his foster father as an assignment for this third meeting. Issau shared a song he titled, "I Miss You Man":

> I miss you, man—I miss you, man.
>
> I could kiss you, man—when I reminisce you, man.
>
> I know a man ain't supposed to kiss a man.

But you're not just a man, you're my dad, man.

You're my heart, man —I loved you from the start, man.

You taught me how to be a man. And I'll be a better man.

In front of me, nobody would eva dis you, man.

You're my father, man. That's why I miss you, man.

I won't stop, man—'til I get to the top, man.

You're my Pop, man. And I'll always miss you, man.

Issau stated this song said everything he wished he could say to his father. When he shared it with Ms. D., she cried and they hugged and both started crying. At that moment, Ms. D. looked Issau in the eyes and told him "I think your father hears you and he is smiling at you right now." This was such a powerful moment, the therapist also got teary-eyed and he turned away to wipe his eyes. Ms. D. said in a joking manner "You can see us cry, but you don't want us to see you cry. We don't care if you cry, Doc." All three burst out in laughter.

7th Session

Over the course of the subsequent weeks, Issau had several sessions similar to those above. He had not had any unexcused absences or any (self or other) reports of physical aggression since treatment started six weeks earlier. He was now generally doing very well. He often wrote lyrics about several school-related issues and showed them to the therapist:

His classroom experiences:

"… My classroom is loud and

everyone's shouting at each other

the teacher gets disrespected, but I wonder if

this is how they would treat their mother …"

Things that happened in the hallways at school:

"… The sucker kids be grabbing the hotties

all over their bodies,

not givin' a damn if they got a man,

but only focusin' on getting what they can

when they can, damn man,

we gotta change this plan."

Most importantly, his hopes and dreams:

"What's the point of living life

and will I one day get a wife?

What's the point of having a life

and will I eva get a wife?

It's the thought of a bride

that makes my mind wide.

I got pride

I'm tryin' to make all of my dreams manifest,

I cannot rest

Can I do my worst or can I do my best,

it's not real, it's just a test

Some say it sounds strange,

that I'm trying to make a life-change

I make the means justify the ends,

where does death end and life begins

What's the point of living life

and will I one day get a wife?"

Issau had written this rap the week before his last session. Clearly, treatment with this client ended with the attainment of both goals. The medium of communication and forum for treatment used were both culturally relevant and therapeutically effective.

Discussion

Many therapeutic approaches promote "color-blind" practice (ignoring obvious race/ethnicity differences between client and worker) as the best way to provide equitable services. This view may be based on the traditional view of American society as a "melting pot." In contrast, we believe that interpersonal racial dynamics can be used to strongly impact helping relationships. Part of any culturally sensitive intervention should be to explore and evaluate their probable impact (Davis & Gelsomino, 1994). Both white and minority workers need to attend to and acknowledge potential racial biases in their perceptions and treatment of clients.

Rap music has become the most popular form of music among youth in the United States (Farley, 1999) and possibly the world. Yet this music remains a severely underutilized resource in working with youth. Although this intervention has been primarily used with African American and Latino youth, it is very likely that—given the popularity of rap music among white American youth—rap music intervention can be useful with many of these young people as well. What is clear is that youth appreciate, respect, and are engaged by the use of "their" music in the therapeutic process.

Hip-hop therapy is one intervention. To the extent that you value cultural sensitivity together with a strengths-oriented and empowerment approach to individuals and families, you will appreciate the hip-hop therapy intervention presented in this chapter. We believe that a structured process that uses certain themes in rap music can help youth develop good social skills, positive self-images, and increased capacity to communicate their beliefs, values, and concerns. Not only therapists but also other human service professionals involved in direct practice with youth should find this model useful.

Speaking more generally, if agencies are to provide more culturally appropriate services, they need to place a high priority on the recruitment and hiring of more culturally competent workers, particularly racial and ethnic minorities (Courtney, Barth, Berrick, Brooks, Needell, & Park, 1996). We need to use professional development and skills training programs to develop practitioners who are increasingly competent to work with racial and ethnic minority families. Another useful approach might be to contextualize various treatment approaches to the language, values, and social milieu of the communities and families of the children who are being treated by the child welfare system (Tharp, 1991). If institutionalized service providers were to pay close attention to this and improve in this area, they would have an immediate and positive impact on the development of their minority child clients' identities, self-esteem, and connectedness to their communities (Haynes, 1993).

The authors of this chapter (two whites and two African Americans) are also attempting to role-model a multicultural approach to knowledge development which goes counter to much of the current intellectual efforts in both research and service delivery. Current approaches generally involve individuals studying and writing primarily about their own racial/ethnic groups. We believe in a fully integrated process, namely, one where some authors draft assigned portions that are fully reviewed and critiqued by all the other authors. These are then revised through a reiterative process and culminate in a final version to which every author agrees. Such an integrated approach allows each of us to articulate our specific points of view from our own ethnic and cultural perspectives. It also allows us to challenge and further stretch our own thinking in these crucial areas, through the critical feedback we give one another. Perhaps more individuals of varied racial/ethnic backgrounds should consider such cross-cultural partnerships representing both insider (within group) and outsider (external to group) knowledge in practice development. This openly critical approach may prove to be highly valuable in the development and evaluation of future modalities of culturally competent intervention strategies.

While many of the promising strengths of this approach have been explained, it is important to note a few important limitations regarding our case presentation. First, as a single illustrative case example, this is but one therapist and one child's experience and the results cannot be generalized. We also don't know to what extent other internal or external forces may have impacted this youth's change over the time period described. Further, because therapist and child in this case example are both African American, we don't know if such an intervention might work with other therapist-client combinations. Could a white therapist have had similar results, even if versed in rap music? Intervention research using this model with youths and therapists of different racial/ethnic backgrounds, while controlling for other possible explanations for change, is the fundamental next step in empirically validating this intervention.

In summary, it is important that social and behavioral science researchers reexamine assessment tools and interventions that are frequently used in child welfare practice with minority children and youth. If it is shown that specific instruments lack cross-ethnic equivalence, then researchers should begin to develop and validate new instruments and methods that have greater sensitivity to the differences that may exist among ethnic groups. These issues have practical significance, particularly for policymakers and administrators of large service systems throughout the United States. Policymakers and service system administrators in child mental health services must identify effective evidence-based assessment tools in this "age of accountability" and of outcome-based services. Taking an evidence-based approach to cross-ethnic assessments and interventions will ultimately lead to more effective treatment and placement outcomes for racial and ethnic minority children and youth.

References

Cross, T., Bazron, B., Dennis, K., & Issacs, M. (1989). *Towards a culturally competent system of care.* Washington, DC: Georgetown University Child Development Center.

Courtney, M., Barth, R., Berrick, J., Brooks, D., Needell, B., & Park, L. (1996). Race and child welfare services: Past research and future directions. *Child Welfare, 75,* 99–137.

Seneca | LIBRARIES

| Books | Articles | Videos | Subject Guides | Course Readings | Other |

Find a book:

_____ Search

or use the Library Catalogue directly.
- ⦿ All book types
- ○ Books only
- ○ eBooks
- ○ Audiobooks only

How do I?
Find Textbooks | Renew Items | Request Items / Place Holds | Find Course Readings | View My Library Account

Borrowing Items Outside Seneca
Interlibrary Loans or Direct Borrowing

More on Borrowing
FAQ | Loan Periods | Library Cards | Fines | Your Library Account

online research help

About the Library
- Our Hours
- Group Study Rooms
- Borrower Services
- Audio-Visual Services
- Information for Faculty
- About Us | Contact Us

➕ BOOKMARK   or follow us on 📘 📷

What's Happening?
> OverDrive eAudiobooks Now Available!
http://seneca.lib.overdrive.com

> Stream films directly with Films on Demand
http://lcweb.senecac.on.ca:2048/login?url=http://
digital.films.com/featuredVideos.aspx

New at Seneca Libraries

< Prev Next >
More new books

Need help with your research?
Start with the research guide or choose one of the following options:

| Citing (APA, MLA) | Tutorials | Quick Reference Tools | Academic Honesty | Copyright | Technical Help |

Featured Links

MLA giving you a headache?
We have everything to help you get started.

http://library.senecacollege.ca

Davis, L., & Gelsomino, J. (1994). An assessment of practitioner cross-racial treatment experiences. *Social Work, 39*(1), 116–123.

De Carlo, A. (2001). Rap therapy? An innovative approach to group-work with urban adolescents. *Journal of Intergroup Relations, 28,* 40–48.

Diller, J. (Ed.). (2004). *Cultural diversity: A primer for the human services* (2nd ed.). Belmont, CA: Brooks/Cole.

Doueck, H., English, D., Defanfils, D., & Moote, G. (1993). Decision-making in child protective services: A comparison of selected risk-assessment systems. *Child Welfare, 72,* 441–451.

Elligan, D. (2004). Rap therapy: A practical guide for communicating with youth and young adults through rap music. New York: Dafina Books.

Farley, J. (1999, February 8). Hip-hop nation. *Time 153*(5), 54–64.

Guerra, N., & Jagers, R. (1998). The importance of culture in the assessment of children and youth. In V. McLoyd & L. Steinberg (Eds.), *Studying minority adolescents: Conceptual, methodological, and theoretical issues* (pp. 167–182). Mahwah, NJ: Lawrence Erlbaum Associates.

Haynes, N. (1993). *Critical issues in educating African-American children.* New York: IAAS Publishers.

Lambert, M., Rowan, G. T., Lyubansky, M., & Russ, C. M. (2002). Do problems of clinic-referred African-American children overlap with the Child Behavior Checklist? *Journal of Child and Family Studies, 11,* 271–285.

Martin, P., Peters, C., & Glisson, C. (1998) Factors affecting case management recommendations for children entering state custody. *Social Service Review, 72,* 521–544.

Mazza, N. (1999). *Poetry therapy: Interface of the arts and psychology.* Boca Raton, FL: CRC Press.

McLoyd, V., & Steinberg, L. (Eds.). (1998). *Studying minority adolescents: Conceptual, methodological, and theoretical issues.* Mahwah, NJ: Lawrence Erlbaum.

Nalavany, B., Ryan, S., Gomory, T., & Lacasse, J. (2005). Mapping the characteristics of a "good" play therapist. *International Journal of Play Therapy 44,* 22–50.

National Association of Social Workers. (1999). Code of ethics. Washington DC: NASW Press.

National Association of Social Workers. (2001). *NASW standards for cultural competence in social work practice.* Washington, DC: Author.

Rosenthal, J. A., Groze, V., & Curiel, H. (1990). Race, social, class, and special needs adoption. *Social Work, 35,* 532–539.

Tharp, R. (1991). Cultural diversity and treatment of children. *Journal of Consulting & Clinical Psychology, 59,* 799–812.

Tyson, E. (2002). Hip hop therapy: An exploratory study of rap-music intervention with at-risk delinquent youth. *Journal of Poetry Therapy, 15,* 121–184.

Tyson, E. (2003). Rap music in social work practice with African American and Latino youth: A conceptual model with practical applications. *Human Behavior in the Social Environment, 8*(4), 1–21.

Tyson, E. (2004). Ethnic differences in using behavior rating scales in child mental health assessment: A conceptual and psychometric critique. *Child Psychiatry and Human Development, 34,* 1167–1201.

Tyson, E., & Glisson, C. (2005). A cross-ethnic validity of the Shortform Assessment for Children (SAC). *Research on Social Work Practice, 15*(2), 97–109.

U.S. Department of Health and Human Services, Administration on Children, Youth and Families (2001). *Child maltreatment.* Washington, DC: Author.

Wells, M. G., Burlingame, G. M., & Lambert, M. (1999). Youth Outcome Questionnaire (Y-OQ). In M. E. Maruish (Ed.), *The use of psychological testing for treatment planning and outcomes assessment* (2nd ed., pp. 497–534). Mahwah, NJ: Lawrence Erlbaum.

4

The Perspective of the Consumer: Foster Children Tell Us What They Need

Jason B. Whiting and John Seita

The foster care system is created to protect and serve at-risk children. Unfortunately, the children who enter it are often left without any say in what happens to them, and are often uninformed as to why they are in care. These children's stories can provide valuable information about the experience of foster care, as well as illuminate common therapeutic issues for these children.

In this chapter, we provide a forum for foster children's voices. These voices come from the authors' research and experience. We believe that listening to such voices will help all of us be more attuned to the unique needs of foster children.

> You're an orphan, right? Do you think I'd know the first thing about how hard your life has been, how you feel, who you are, because I read Oliver Twist? Does that encapsulate you?

This quote from the movie *Good Will Hunting* (Damon, Affleck, & Van Sant, 1997) was part of a conversation between a therapist and a young man who had lived a difficult life in foster care. This exchange poignantly captures the difficulty of understanding foster care from the outside. Both scholarship and professional practice can help us better understand what children experience in care, but our viewpoint needs to be informed by insiders' experiences. We recognize that most professionals who work with the vulnerable families and children in foster care have not personally experienced being in care. That is why we can better empathize and appreciate the unique experience of foster care by closely listening to those who are in care. As professionals we need to do a better job, both in listening to and talking to the children in foster care.

> You have to keep moving, and moving, and moving, until finally someone keeps you. That kind of sucks.
>
> —Brian, age 11

Few administrators and workers in the foster care system have ever been a consumer of services or have formally partnered with those who have experienced the system as consumers. The lack of consumer representation in foster care leadership suggests that much of the agency policy, practices, and culture are developed without formal consumer input (Seita, 2004). Unfortunately, time constraints and multiple systemic pressures on professionals make it difficult to adequately hear from children. Also, these children do not always present as eager and willing clients. Foster children often enter care with issues that are not amenable to quick fixes, and many do not seek opportunities to talk with professionals.

Although it may be difficult to do, there are two fundamental reasons for eliciting the perspectives of the foster children entrusted to our care. First, most foster children benefit psychologically from talking about their experiences. And listening carefully to children is therapeutic and respectful, and it acknowledges their individuality (Coles, 1989; Whiting, 2000). Second, when we hear from foster children we are not only engaging in a therapeutic act, but we also are wisely allowing them to be consultants to the care we intend to provide them.

By obtaining the perspectives of our respective foster children we are giving ourselves an opportunity *to better understand their diverse therapeutic needs.* Each child is unique and will have specific issues and experiences that are important for all of us to understand as we make decisions regarding his or her treatment. It is also respectful and clinically helpful to inform children what is happening to them, why they are in foster care, and what might happen to them in the future.

Foster care professionals who are committed to empowering clients should "certainly avoid drowning out the voices of the children" (Festinger, 1983, p. 297). These children often feel powerless in the child welfare system. Seeking feedback from them can be a very empowering experience for them. We also know that foster children are more satisfied with placements that they helped choose, and feel more in control of their lives when they are included in decisionmaking (Curtis, 1999; see also Chapter 14, "'It Isn't Right!' The Need to Redress Experiences of Injustice in Child Abuse and Neglect"). "Children in foster care, who are among the nation's neediest, merit the improved care that may result from a more complete understanding of their characteristics, needs, and experience in foster care" (Goerge, Wulczyn, & Harden, 1999, p. 20). There also is a need for more attention to the children's and their families' voices when creating agency policy (Curran & Pecora, 1999).

Foster children may be profoundly affected by the traumatic and stressful events they have experienced, even after they have "aged out" of the foster care system.

> I try not to think about it, but I can't help it. Sometimes I pretend that I am someone else in my dorm, some other girl whose life I admire. I go to sleep at night dreaming about that, but I wake up in the morning and I am still me. Then for just a minute, I am still angry with my parents for screwing up so badly, but I forgive. I have a saying that I use when I am mad: "forgiveness is giving up the hope of a better past." That always helps me. But that fantasy of being someone else and having their life is still close to the surface, still on my mind. I wonder how it would be to have my parents come to visit me, maybe take me out to lunch, buy me some clothes, or pay for gas in my car. I wonder how it feels to hug my mom, dad, and that kind of thing. I don't want anything too much, I don't think. Do I? Is that asking too much? To feel normal, like everyone else?
>
> —Anna, age 20

The Perspectives of Foster Children: A Separate Reality

Each foster child makes sense of his or her experiences in his or her own way. However, there also are common tendencies among foster children that are important to understand. We will first discuss how their thinking processes shape the reality of foster children. We will then review how the experiences of foster care are often confusing, traumatic, and emotionally provocative. Finally, in the last part of this chapter we will share some of the most important things foster children have told us they want in our dealings with them.

Private Logic

Foster children have experienced things that are outside the realm of most other children. This includes whatever maltreatment may have existed in the birth family, and also includes the removal from their homes and the losses that resulted. Each child processes these experiences in ways that may not be obvious or even rational to others. Each child ascribes meaning to his or her experiences in a process called "private logic."

Private logic is a way of understanding based upon assumptions about self and others (Adler, 1930/1963). This view is shaped through experiences and interpretations and can be an adaptive mechanism to protect against hurt and perceived slights. Adler framed private logic in the following schema: "I am ... others are ... the world is ... therefore." Seita draws from his own experiences in foster care and shares his own private logic when he notes:

> I denied who I was because I felt that I was different. Not good different, not unique-in-a-positive-way different, not proud different (as in marching to my own drum), but shameful different. I felt as if I was not strong, somehow less in nearly every way than others of my age. I created a fantasy, born of my hope that this was all a bad dream, in which I would wake up in our old apartment—the one I shared with my mom and dad when I was very young. The sun would be shining and everything would be perfect—or as perfect as it

ever had been. I came to understand that a "bad" family was better than no family at all (Seita, Mitchell, & Tobin, 1996, p. 12).

Common Views

Besides their unique ways of making sense of their life experiences, foster children have many important perspectives in common.

The wish to be "a normal person"

In his research with those who formerly were in foster care, Seita (2004) discovered that the theme of denial of their own reality— "Maybe I can live the life of someone else"—is not unusual. Respondents noted that they did not want to live the life of a famous person. They just wanted to be like someone they perceived to be "normal." This tendency to want to be like someone "normal" demonstrates how a child's thinking might reflect adaptation to difficult circumstances.

Wariness about the world

The maltreatment that foster children have experienced profoundly shapes their worldview. Many will have missed out on the many subtle, yet important, physical, psychological, and social benefits associated with being raised in a high functioning family. These combined benefits, called "family privilege," include safety, belonging, unconditional love, high expectations for children, parental and familial modeling, and the practice of positive prosocial values (Seita & Brendtro, 2005). Family privilege also consists of opportunities to develop meaningful skills and pursue interests and goals, and includes practical benefits such as seeing the success of an older sibling or parents, and observing what efforts it takes to be successful. Being able to learn about a career from an uncle, aunt, cousin, grandparent, or other relative are all benefits of family privilege. Family privilege helps a child to hope and dream. Such privilege also provides buffering from risk factors.

Lacking the family privilege of most adults in the system, foster children are likely to be mistrustful of therapists, caseworkers, or foster parents (Benzola, 1993; Brown, 1983; Fisher, 2001; Seita & Brendtro, 2005; Toth, 1998). They may even sabotage any potential therapeutic relationships with caring adults. This mistrust is adaptive. It is intended to protect foster children against further disappointments and pain. It is crucial for us and other child welfare professionals to expect and understand these tendencies. Otherwise, we may be likely to take them personally and further drive the children away through insensitive or ineffective methods.

The effects of maltreatment and being removed from their homes

The stories of foster children demonstrate that many are not only upset by what happened prior to being removed from their homes, but also by the removal itself. The following story of maltreatment and fear in the birth family is not unusual.

> Like, she would be mean in the morning, like all the time, and then she had this man and he used to beat us ... yeah, you know like a piece of a table, the leg, it had nails in it, and he used to beat us with that ... but he said that when you get back, if you go, then you is going to get beat again. He didn't say "beat" but he said "you know what is goin' to happen."
>
> —Deondre, age 12

> Yeah, and [the police] said hurry, hurry up, get out of the tub. So we got our clothes on, and my mamma was crying and we was too, so they just rushed us out of the house ... it was scary but I was just crying.
>
> —Wilt, age 8

However, no matter how difficult life may have been in the birth home, for many children the removal from birth parents and transition into a foster home may be traumatic (Folman, 1998). Many children enter foster care upset and confused, and blame the agency, foster parents, or themselves for their removal (Whiting & Lee, 2003).

> Yeah, foster care is just sick! I don't want to hear about it at all. You get taken away from your parents. It ruins your life! Your heart is totally destroyed, and the only thing that is left working in your body is your brain … That is why I want out of this foster care right now!
>
> —Keith, age 11

Professionals and foster parents are often astounded at the intensity of foster children's emotions (McFadden, 1996). The shock of removal and fear of what is coming next can produce intense feelings of anger, fear, sadness, or despair. These often accompany externalizing or internalizing behavior, which are difficult for foster parents, therapists, and caseworkers to accept and manage. It is important to recognize that these behaviors are manifestations of trauma, and that the trauma needs to be treated if the behaviors are to change (see Chapter 7, "Parent–Child Therapy for Traumatized Young Children in Foster Care," and Chapter 14 "'It Isn't Right!' The Need to Redress Experiences of Injustice in Child Abuse and Neglect").

> I did not really know what a foster home was, and no one took the time or cared enough to explain. I just knew that I did not want to go to one. The only thing that "the workers" made clear was that I would never live with my mother again. This was so horrifying, I became sick and vomited. The thought of not seeing my mom again devastated me. I was empty inside, dazed, and in a fog.
>
> —John, age 13

The loss of parents, siblings, friends, toys, and school, leaves children highly traumatized and distrustful of adults or authority figures. Children fear what will happen to their parents or their siblings, and often are unsure if they will ever see family members again (Folman, 1998). The losses continue, if there are multiple placements or new workers because of agency turnover. Each loss of an adult confirms to foster children that the world is a scary, unstable place that will hurt them.

It is also tough for a baby, because they grow up with foster parents, thinking they are his real parents, and once he goes back to his real parents, he is like "what the heck, who are they?"

—Keith, age 11

Tips for Professionals in Talking with Children

It's good to talk about it, because if I keep all this stress in me I'll start getting gray hairs.

—Patrice, age 11

Foster children have three to seven times more health problems, developmental delays, and emotional problems than do other children, even when their economic situations are similar (Orme & Buehler, 2001; Rosenfeld et al., 1997). Although most child welfare professionals are well aware of the complex issues associated with foster children, some are not always sure what to do about them. One common tendency is to self protectively distance oneself from the children, preferring not to become too close. Another is to pathologize children by seeing them as a set of diagnostic criteria and risk factors in search of placement. How much better it would be if we all could see and value these children for whom they are, namely, unique individuals with needs, fears, and experiences to share.

Professionals who work with children in care come with their own set of skills, expectations, and reality. These factors will influence how they interact with the children in care. Relationship-wary children are alert for insincere techniques and overly packaged therapy approaches. Having been through the gauntlet of abuse, foster care, and various so-called helpers, their antennae are fully extended and they are likely to be suspicious of manipulative efforts to draw them out. Therefore, it is important for professionals to be genuine in seeking a relationship. It is not always a simple, straightforward process.

This section consists of several tips on how professionals can facilitate communication with foster children in a way that creates a climate for trust and genuine connection. When approaching foster children, it may be helpful to consider the metaphor of "gardening." You cannot force a delicate flower to open up and thrive after it has been beaten down. But you can create a nurturing climate for its growth and recovery. This sometimes requires patient, small, focused efforts in clearing out weeds and debris, while continually nourishing and encouraging growth. Here are some ideas on creating this type of fruitful environment.

Take Time to Listen to Your Client

> Some of the bad things? I don't get to see my brothers and we're all split up ... yeah, I don't know what they remember. I wish I knew where they were.
>
> —Brian, age 11

In his autobiography about growing up in foster care, Brown (1983) writes about feeling disregarded by his therapist. "Our eyes never met" (p. 223). Feeling powerless, voiceless, alone, and angry may be a recipe for behavioral problems and failed placements. To counter this, both professionals and foster parents should create a climate that is inviting of and safe for expression. We can encourage our foster children to speak up and give them a chance to do so. Helping foster children express the losses they have experienced may help healing (Worden, 1996). Those children who are feeling scared and helpless may experience being asked for feedback as especially empowering. Foster children may also appreciate being consulted regarding their own placement and treatment plans.

When a child is not acting out or otherwise being difficult, it may be tempting to assume that he or she is doing well and does not need to be heard in the same way as do those referred for therapy. But foster children generally appreciate the chance to just share their opinions about their lives in foster care (see, for example, Gil & Bogart, 1982; Rice & McFadden, 1988; Whiting & Lee, 2003). Not all of them may be able to verbalize their stories. However, alternate forms of communication can be employed, such as storyboards, workbooks, drawings, and toys. For example, hip-hop therapy is described in Chapter 3, "Cultural Issues: Diversity and Child Welfare," and a variety of age-appropriate storying methods are given in Chapter 11, "Creative Ways to Strengthen Family Bonds."

Validate Your Client's Feelings and Experiences

> [The children at school] tell me I am too country and too black like the ground.... They tell me that is why I am in foster care and they tease me.
>
> —Junius, age 7

Foster children who do not have their feelings validated are more likely to discount their own experiences and create false realities or exaggerated senses of self (Folman, 1998). Foster children experience both intense and conflicting emotions. Many are sad about being in care, some are happy, some angry, and most feel a mixture of all of these (Whiting & Lee, 2003). Ambivalence about a single event is common. For example, the children may miss their parents and be angry with them. Our job is to validate the children's expressions and help them process the multitude of events and emotions they have experienced. We thereby send a message to the child that it is appropriate to feel all of those things. This can reduce the guilt associated with such circumstances as ambivalence toward parents, and it helps the children identify and accept their feelings. When they become more comfortable expressing their strong emotions, they are less likely to become overwhelmed by them.

Get to Know Your Client

> I was sick of getting hit, so I told [a friend], and he told his mom, and his mom called the people, and they came over and asked us to get our shoes on and get off of the bed. They asked us about our mom and dad, and we told them, and my mom and dad were gone getting the car. So the cops came over and knocked open the door, but nobody was answering because we were all watching a movie, so they just like, somehow got the door open, and walked in there and just said "get your stuff ready to leave."
>
> —David, age 12

In this example, it is important to note that David was the instigator for reporting his parents and was then removed from his home. As his therapist, upon hearing David tell this story, we would want to be sensitive to David's guilt for having reported his parents and his belief that he "broke up the family." Foster children benefit when we understand their specific experiences of confusion, fear, and ambivalence. However, we also should be careful that we do not assume too much because of what we have observed in other clients or have read. (This caveat includes this chapter.) If you are to really know the child in front of you, you need to elicit and hear that child's unique story. It will involve discovering what this child believes has caused his or her situation and what will happen next. This chapter offers a list of things to be aware of, but it is probable that your children will be experiencing thoughts and feelings that we have not discussed here. Better awareness of each child can improve joining, empathy, and positive outcomes.

Be Honest with Your Client

> What I want to know is why doesn't the judge keep his promises? He promised me that he would talk to me in person and never did! I wanted to bust the judge!
>
> —Keith, age 11

All of us who are working with foster children need to better inform them of the reason for their placement and what is currently happening with their families. Sometimes we mean well and withhold information from children because we do not know what will happen, or because we want to protect the child from upsetting information (Ward-Wimmer, 1998). Unfortunately, withholding truth can keep children in situations of ambiguous loss (Boss, 1999), where they cannot process their grief or form attachments to new caregivers (Fahlberg, 1991; Lee & Whiting, 2007, in press). Moreover, secrets are often more harmful to foster children than is knowledge of a bleak reality. Without accurate information, foster children are more likely to be confused or to make up fantasy stories (Gil & Bogart, 1982). When we deny our foster children information we may exacerbate the feelings of disempowerment and helplessness so pervasive in these children (Hughes, 1997).

> They was like, well, it was for the best and all this. They don't know what they talking about.
>
> —Bobby, age 11

> They [told me I would be going home the next day] so you'll stop crying. They shouldn't have lied. They shouldn't have told me.
>
> —Michael, age 10

These remarks (see Folman, 1998) illustrate how children who are given misinformation in an effort to reassure them ("things will all work out") are further victimized and frustrated as their distrust of adults is confirmed. "Whether the children conjured up their own perceptions because they were given no information, were given inaccurate information by caseworkers or family members, or were not able to hear the information given to them, the impact was the same: confusion, apprehension, and a sense of themselves as helpless and vulnerable" (Folman, 1998, p. 23).

Ambiguities may be unavoidable in the foster care process, but children benefit from knowing the status of their foster care placement, even when there are still uncertainties (Keefer & Schooler, 2000). When there is uncertainty regarding future reunification, we nevertheless can reassure children about the process or efforts being made. Many foster children recognize that there were family problems leading up to their placement. Direct information and conversation about these problems help the children avoid distorting the problems or blaming themselves for them. Children should be continually reassured that they are not to blame for their foster care placement (McDonald, Allen, Westerfelt, & Piliavin, 1996).

Be Appropriate

> Sometimes I feel scared that my mom is in trouble.
>
> —Krystal, age 10

Although it is important to talk frankly with foster children about the situations in their lives, it is important to do this in developmentally appropriate ways (Keefer & Schooler, 2000, and see Chapter 8, "Providing Developmentally Appropriate Family Therapy"; Chapter 11, "Creative Ways to Strengthen Family Bonds," and Chapter 18, "Teaching Developmentally Appropriate Parenting"). Common sense, along with knowledge of the child's emotional state, should guide decisions about how much to reveal about placement details.

It is also important to be sensitive when eliciting information from children. Interviewing children gives this "socially silenced group ... [whose] opinions are not heard in the public sphere" an opportunity to have a voice (Alldred, 1998, p. 148). However, children do not interview in the same way as adults (Zwiers & Morrissette, 1999). Guidelines for child interviews are few, but some common suggestions include being adaptable, respecting the child, and being aware of child development issues (Garbarino & Stott, 1992).

Professionals who understand how maltreated children view adults are less likely to be surprised or put off by angry or resistant behavior (see Chapter 7, "Parent–Child Therapy for Traumatized Young Children in Foster Care" and Chapter 14, "'It Isn't Right!' The Need to Redress Experiences of Injustice in Child Abuse and Neglect"). Care should be taken to not pressure children to speak or give the "right" information. Children who have been maltreated are in a powerless position and we need to follow moral and ethical guidelines to prevent further damage (Alldred, 1998). The child is more important than the possible information.

Physician Heal Thyself

> I was really insulted once by my therapist. She wanted to talk to me about going to college. She told me that a single mom had raised her, and that if she could make it, so could I. I asked her if her mom loved her, "Of course" she replied, "very much." That, I told her, is the difference, the big difference. My mom never loved me. In fact, she not only did not

love me, she abused me and abandoned me, and then I ended up in the system. I told her not to compare her life, living with a single mom who loved her, to my life with an abusive mom who did not love me and then abandoned me. Our lives were completely different. I wish people would not even try and compare their lives to me. She had no idea what she was talking about. If someone is going to talk to me about my life in care, I wish it would be someone who had been in care themselves. Otherwise I don't want to hear it. She was really preachy for someone who did not know what she was talking about. I wonder who will really hear me?

—Yolanda, age 19

We do not know if this therapist was attempting to share her story with Yolanda out of genuine desire to connect, or a defensive need to "prove something" to the child. What we do know is that the client perceived the therapist to be prescribing out of her own life, instead of being willing to listen to her (Covey, 1990).

The idiom "physician heal thyself" in this context indicates how important it is that we professionals understand who we are, what forces have shaped our lives, and what values we have. If we acknowledge and understand our biases and assumptions, it may prevent these from getting in the way of productive therapy (Whiting, Nebeker, & Fife, 2005). Sometimes we get frustrated with foster children's behavior. But we need to take responsibility for our own issues and reactions with the child, and not blame the child for them.

Embark on a Talent and Interest Search with Your Client

I'm gonna grow up to be a full-grown basketball player and make millions and billions of dollars, and then I'm gonna get a big, big house, and then I'm gonna run for president.

—Devin, age 7

While getting to know the child, look for his or her best self. It is easy to see problems, but finding strengths is helpful for a number of reasons (Brendtro, 2001). Everyone likes to be acknowledged for his or her talents and abilities, and these can be built upon in overcoming difficulties. Additionally, the therapeutic alliance is much more likely to succeed if a child feels acknowledged as a whole person, rather than just a package of problems. All young people have interests and strengths. Talking about strengths, interests, and "fun" things may feel nontherapeutic to a professional, but it may be one of the most appreciated interventions by the child (Hubble, Duncan, & Miller, 1999).

Sometimes it is hard to locate the strengths underneath the anger, and sometimes children hide their talents because they are fearful of losing one more thing. Kindness and patience usually prevail in finding strengths and talents. If we look, we will always find a story of survival, resilience, and struggle against negativity. Sifting through the events of a child's life to locate the strengths helps both you and the child be more positive.

Go Slow

> Me and my mama used to go places when my mom would pick me up at school and we would go everywhere before we go home and it was fun.
>
> —Patrice, age 11

> [I was] mad at first, but then I was happy about foster care.
>
> —Daniel, age 10

When seeking to help youth, our tendency is to want to quickly build a relationship. Although we do not attempt instant rapport in our social circles, we often seek it when working with challenging youth. Adult-wary youth will not assume that you care about them in the absence of concrete evidence otherwise. They have been disappointed and hurt too often.

Decode Behaviors

> Then I went to [a group home] and [a worker] … threatened to tie me up with a rope … and then I left because the

people couldn't deal with me. I kept going into the hospital because of my behavior. If I was bad there they would give me a shot in the butt ... and I got one too.

—Brian, age 11

When working with foster children we need to understand behavior on two levels simultaneously: The immediate behavior and the forces that continue to elicit and maintain that behavior. Because you need to immediately respond to maladaptive behavior, you need the skills to defuse any immediate crisis. At the same time you must search for the underlying causes and continued supports of the behavior.

Provide Your Client Opportunities to Belong

They took us away, and we went to foster care, came back, and now I am going to get adopted [and] I'm happy.

—Daniel, age 10

Children who benefit from family privilege have a built-in fan club that youth in foster care typically lack. Therefore, children in foster care may seek unhealthy ways of connecting to others, such as through gang behavior or promiscuity. All of us who work with foster children should be alert for opportunities to help them find connections within more desirable social systems. In addition to solidifying relationships with foster parents, therapists, and caseworkers, the children can be encouraged to become involved in forums and groups for children in foster care. We can also help these children strengthen their social skills and help them find opportunities for friendship networks.

Conclusion

[In foster care] you don't get beat, um, they teach you the right way to do stuff, they teach you not to lie, stuff like that, they don't try to harm you. Like if you be good, our foster parents take you out to the comic book store, they sometimes take us out the whole day, like we never come home.

One time they took us to [a restaurant], and after that we went to the comic store, then we went to the show, and then we went to the mall. After that we went out to dinner, and back, and then we finally came home. And we got this older brother, he plays with us, and my dad, he comes outside and throws a couple of passes to us. He tries to teach us how to play football, basketball, and how to have a good attitude if you want to play on a team. Sometimes if we do good for the week or something, we ask if we can go to the store or something, and they say yes. They really never say no.

—Deondre, age 12

As demonstrated by Deondre's experience, foster care can succeed in forging healthy new family relationships or reforming existing ones. Yet the process that children go through as they work towards this is usually tumultuous and traumatic. As professionals, we can help foster children make sense out of these experiences through careful listening and communicating with them. We believe that listening to these children's voices will remind us why we spend our time in the work with them.

References

Adler, A. (1963). *The Problem Child* (G. Daniels, Trans.). New York: G. P. Putnam's Sons. (Original work published 1930)

Alldred, P. (1998). Ethnography and discourse analysis: Dilemmas in representing the voices of children. In J. Ribbens & R. Edwards (Eds.), *Feminist dilemmas in qualitative research* (pp. 147-170). London: Sage.

Benzola, E. (1993). *Temporary child—A foster care survivor's story.* Fremont, CA: Real People Publishing.

Boss, P. (1999). *Ambiguous loss: Learning to live with unresolved grief.* Cambridge, MA: Harvard University Press.

Brendtro, L. (2001). Worse than sticks and stones: Lessons from research on ridicule. *Reclaiming Children and Youth, 10,* 47–53.

Brown, W. K. (1983). *The other side of delinquency.* New Brunswick, NJ: Rutgers University Press.

Coles, R. (1989). *The call of stories.* Boston: Houghton Mifflin.

Covey, S. R. (1990). *The seven habits of highly effective people.* New York: Fireside.

Curran, M. C., & Pecora, P. J. (1999). Incorporating the perspectives of youth placed in family foster care: Selected research findings and methodological challenges. In P. A. Curtis, G. Dale, & J. C. Kendall (Eds.), *The foster care crisis: Translating research into policy and practice* (pp. 99–128). New York: University of Nebraska Press.

Curtis, P. (1999). The chronic nature of the foster care crisis. In P. A. Curtis, G. Dale, & J. C. Kendall (Eds.), *The foster care crisis: Translating research into policy and practice* (pp. 1–16). New York: University of Nebraska Press.

Damon, M., Affleck, B., & Van Sant, G. (1997). *Good Will Hunting: A screenplay.* New York: Miramax/Hyperion.

Fahlberg, V. I. (1991). *A child's journey through placement.* Indianapolis, IN: Perspectives Press.

Festinger, T. (1983). *No one ever asked us … A postscript to foster care.* New York: Columbia Press.

Fisher, A. (2001). *Finding fish: A memoir.* New York: William Morrow.

Folman, R. D. (1998). I was tooken': How children experience removal from their parents preliminary to placement into foster care. *Adoption Quarterly 2*(2), 7–33.

Garbarino, J., & Stott, F. M. (1992). *What children can tell us: Eliciting, interpreting, and evaluating critical information from children.* San Francisco: Jossey-Bass.

Gil, E., & Bogart, K. (1982, January–February). Foster children speak out: A study of children's perceptions of foster care. *Children Today, 7*–9.

Goerge, R. M., Wulczyn, F., & Harden, A. (1999). Foster care dynamics. In P. Curtis, G. Dale, & J. Kendall (Eds.), *The foster care crisis: Translating research into policy and practice* (pp. 17–44). Lincoln, NE: University of Nebraska Press.

Hubble, M. A., Duncan, B. L., & Miller, S. D. (1999). *The heart and soul of change: What works in therapy.* Washington, DC: American Psychological Association.

Hughes, D. A. (1997). *Facilitating developmental attachment: The road to emotional recovery and behavioral change in foster and adopted children.* Northvale, NJ: Jason Aronson.

Keefer, B., & Schooler, J. E. (2000). *Telling the truth to your adopted or foster child: Making sense of the past.* Westport, CT: Bergin & Garvey.

Lee, R. E., and Whiting, J. B. (2007, in press) Foster children's expressions of ambiguous loss. *The American Journal of Family Therapy.*

McDonald, T. P., Allen, R. I., Westerfelt, A., & Piliavin, I. (1996). *Assessing the long-term effects of foster care: A research synthesis.* Washington, DC: CWLA Press.

McFadden, E. J. (1996). Family-centered practice with foster parent families. *Families in Society, 66,* 545–557.

Orme, J. G., & Buehler, C. (2001). Foster family characteristics and behavioral and emotional problems of foster children: A narrative review. *Family Relations, 50,* 3–15.

Rice, D. L., & McFadden, E. J. (1988). A forum for foster children. *Child Welfare, 3,* 231–243.

Rosenfeld, A. A., Pilowsky, D. J., Fine, P., Thorpe, M., Fein, E., Simms, M. O., Halfon, N., Irwin, M., Alfaro, J., Saletsky, R., & Nickman, S. (1997). Foster care: An update. *Journal of American Academy of Child and Adolescent Psychiatry, 36,* 448–457.

Seita, J. R. (2004). Strength based approaches expand into leadership. *Reclaiming Children and Youth: The Journal of Strength Based Interventions 13*(1), 22–25.

Seita, J., & Brendtro, L. (2005). *Children who outwit adults.* Bloomington, IN: National Educational Service.

Seita, J., Mitchell, M., & Tobin, C. (1996). *In whose best interest? One child's odyssey, a nation's responsibility.* Elizabethtown, PA: Continental Press.

Toth, J. (1998). *Orphans of the living: Stories of America's children in foster care.* New York: Touchstone.

Ward-Wimmer, D. (1998). *Grief as a metaphor for healing.* Unpublished manuscript. St. Francis Center, Washington, DC.

Whiting, J. B. (2000). The view from down here: Foster children's stories. *Child & Youth Care Forum, 29* (2), 79–95.

Whiting, J. B., & Lee, R. E. (2003). Voices from the system: A qualitative study of foster children's stories. *Family Relations, 52,* 288–295.

Whiting, J. B., Nebeker, R. S., & Fife, S. T. (2005). Therapists' moral responsiveness and the role of discontinuity: A preliminary qualitative study. *Counseling and Values, 50,* 20–37.

Worden, J. W. (1996). *Children and grief: When a parent dies.* New York: Guilford.

Zwiers, M. L., & Morrissette, P. J. (1999). *Effective interviewing of children.* Philadelphia: Taylor & Francis Group.

5

Ambiguous Loss: A Key Component of Foster Care

Robert E. Lee and Jason B. Whiting

T*he notion of ambiguous loss is useful in understanding the experiences and challenges of all those who are involved in the foster care system: Foster children, birth and foster parents, and court and agency personnel. Ambiguous loss shapes the experiences of everyone involved in a case. As a result, many behavioral indicators of cognitive and emotional discomfort in foster children and those responsible for their care are normal and to be expected. Therefore, our interventions with these children, their institutionalized caretakers, and the foster care system itself should be guided by this knowledge. Even though the lens of ambiguous loss may clarify the experiences of all of the members of the foster care system, in this chapter we only will focus on foster children themselves.*

Thinking About Loss, Grief, and Adjustment

Psychologists have thought a great deal about how people adjust to the stressful things that happen to them. Most theories suggest that how well people adapt depends on the nature of the stressful events (for example, their size and duration), what resources the people have, and how the people perceive and label their circumstances. Because how foster children and their caretakers make sense out of their experiences is so important to their respective adjustments, in this chapter we focus on just this one thing.

As you may know, the idea that perceptions and beliefs determine how people feel, decide, and act has been central to rational-emotive

(Morris & Kanitz, 1975) and cognitive-behavioral psychotherapies (see Freedman & Dattilio, 1994). Similarly, "reframing" has been a powerful therapeutic tool from the beginnings of family therapy (for example, Weeks & L'Abate, 1979), and the power of social constructions have been appreciated and used by the diverse postmodern relational therapies (for example, Friedman & Combs, 1996).

However, these models are limited to the extent that potentially stressful situations involve loss. Such models fail when losses are not clear-cut, such as when children are removed from their homes and placed with surrogate families. If their parents are dead, children have a firm, uncontested reality to which to respond, and grief work can begin (see, for example, Kubler-Ross & Kessler, 2005). However, in most foster care situations no one knows whether or not the parents are permanently gone. Furthermore, many times family members may be experienced as psychologically present even though they are physically absent. As a result, many foster care loss situations do not allow closure; instead, they are so ambiguous that people cannot decide how to think, feel, and act. This confusion adds to the stress experienced by the individuals involved.

Ambiguous Loss and the Foster Care System

Ambiguous loss, so useful in understanding complicated perceptions, emotions, and behaviors associated with unresolved losses (see Boss, 1999 and 2004), should be extended to the experiences of individuals involved in the foster care system. Children are removed from their homes because caregivers allegedly were *physically present but psychologically absent,* in that they did not consistently provide love, nurture, and protection. Moreover, once children have been placed with foster families there is often a lack of information about the loss or the status of family members, disagreement regarding family membership of a missing person, and lack of social validation of the losses (see Chapter 4, "The Perspective of the Consumer: Foster Children Tell Us What They Need").

Ambiguous loss may provide insight into the experiences of all members of the foster care system, namely, the birth family, foster family, and agency and court personnel. Individuals may be confused in their thinking, feelings, and actions because family members—parents and children—may be physically absent but psychologically present. They are not living in the same household, but they remain members of the family and influence each other (Whiting & Lee, 2003).

At times, family members may be physically present, for example, during family visitation, but psychologically absent because of emotional distress and/or preoccupation with the challenges in their lives (Lee & Lynch, 1998). In addition, even when individuals are currently perceived to be active members of the birth family, or of the foster family, those positions are not permanent. Courts can ultimately reunite or disband birth families and, in the case of foster families, children may or may not be adopted. In many situations, the children do not know if they ever again will see the individuals—birth parents, siblings, foster parents—removed by the court order.

Finally, many foster placements are made within children's extended families. Such "relative placements" may further muddy the boundaries about "who is in and who is out" (see Chapter 9, "An Integrative Approach Involving the Biological and Foster Family Systems," and Chapter 10, "Kinship Placements: An Integrative Approach"). Therefore, ambiguous loss is a problem for stakeholders in the foster care system because the various families' continued existence, and their membership, roles, rules, and ways of doing business are inconsistently recognized and their future undecided. Such ambiguity is thought to create psychological problems in the affected individuals, namely, feelings of confusion, hopelessness, and ambivalence, which, in turn, result in depression, anxiety, guilt, and immobilization (Boss, 2004).

These ambiguous situations may interfere with the birth family members' grief resolution and progress toward case goals. If agency personnel are not aware of the profound influence that ambiguous loss has on those in the foster care system, they may not appreciate the ambivalence and confusion of the children and parents in their care. A better understanding of ambiguous loss may improve their decisions regarding which individuals need to be included in case planning, and their understanding of why cases do not proceed in expected ways (again see Chapter 9, "An Integrative Approach Involving the Biological and Foster Family Systems").

Ambiguous Loss and Foster Children

Although the lens of ambiguous loss may clarify the experiences of all of the members of the foster care system, as a first step we would like the reader to consider the foster children themselves. Many components of ambiguous loss are exhibited by foster children of various ages and these symptoms have serious clinical implications for them and those involved with them.

Our examples of how ambiguous loss may be experienced and manifest in foster children come from two data sets provided by racially diverse and low-income urban foster children aged 2 to 12. The first set (Whiting & Lee, 2003) includes transcripts and field notes of semi-structured interviews of 23 foster children, aged 7 to 12 years old, where they described their experiences of the foster care process. The second set (Lee & Whiting, 2006, in press) contains the responses of 182 foster children, aged 2 to 10, to the Blacky pictures (Blum, 1950). These pictures depict a puppy in relationship to its family.

According to clinical researchers (Boss, 1999; 2004), ambiguous loss leads people to think, feel, and act in very predictable ways:

- "frozen" (unresolved) grief, including outrage and inability to move on,
- confusion, distress, and ambivalence,
- uncertainty leading to immobilization,
- blocked coping processes,
- the experience of helplessness, and therefore depression, anxiety, and relationship conflicts,
- responding with absolutes, namely: denial of change or loss, denial of facts,

- rigidity of family roles (maintaining that the lost person will return as before) and outrage at the lost person being excluded,
- confusion in boundaries and roles (for example, knowing who the parental figures are),
- guilt, if hope has been given up, and
- refusal to talk about the individuals and the situation.

We looked to see if such "symptoms" characterized our two samples of foster children and, of course, they did.

Illustrations

We used open coding to sort the children's responses according to the signs listed above. We found that the stories of the foster children, from toddlerhood through adolescence, contained or centered on many of the symptoms said to be characteristic of ambiguous loss. We are separating the two samples, since they had different tasks. All quotations have been taken from the children's transcripts but we changed all names to preserve anonymity.

Semistructured Interviews

Many individuals described horrific stories of their lives before being moved into foster care, and comments illustrative of ambiguous loss were plentiful. Although we have placed examples under each of the expected signs, the reader will appreciate that many of them are illustrative of more than one indicator.

"Frozen" (unresolved) grief, including outrage and inability to move on

Some children expressed anger about being in foster care, and others directed their anger at other children or authority figures. Brian and Chris were both angry about not seeing their siblings. Keith was particularly livid about foster care: "Yeah, foster care is just sick! I don't want to hear about it at all. You get taken away from your parents. It ruins your life! Your heart is totally destroyed, and the only thing that is left working in your body is your brain …

that is why I want out of this foster care right now!" He also was angry with the judge: "What I want to know is why doesn't the judge keep his promises. He promised me that he would talk to me in person and never did! I wanted to bust the judge!"

Others expressed anger toward other children. Patrice said, "this girl in my class, she bugs me and I just want to rip her guts out." Some children mentioned being angry because they were teased about being poor and in foster care, such as Chad, who said children made fun of his "haircut and shoes." Krystal was angry with the judge, but also identified conflicting emotions regarding her mother: "I get angry when I think she could have taken care of me better."

Foster children experience severe losses (Fahlberg, 1991), and these children mentioned many, such as family, siblings, cousins, foster families, friends, pets, and possessions. Bryan's comments about missing his siblings were typical: "I don't get to see my brothers and we're all split up … yeah, I … wish I knew where they were." The children frequently described the loss of their biological families, especially their mothers. Junius said, "I don't think I'm ever going to see her. They said I was going to be seeing her, but …" He later remarked: "I was about to cry when we were talking about my mom."

Seven-year-old Cherise had many family losses which she commented on, such as the loss of a cousin who died after being bit by a rat, a brother who smothered in a couch, and a deceased father whom she had never known. She recalled a family funeral: "I started crying too. I was screaming out loud," and mentioned missing her two pet dogs, an aunt, and a good friend: "I miss her!" When asked if she would ever see her birth mother again, she said, "Never ever … that's what the court said."

Confusion, distress, and ambivalence

Nearly every child was confused about one or both of the following: the reasons for being in care, and what would happen in the future. There were numerous responses of "I don't know," when asked about the past and the future. Keith explained the difficulty this way:

"It is also tough for a baby, because they grow up with foster parents, thinking they are his real parents, and once he goes back to his real parents, he is like 'what the heck, who are they?'" Chad thought his birth parents were "probably going to die." Wilt's memories of a confusing and distressful removal from his parents were typical: "They said 'hurry, hurry up, get out of the tub.' So we got our clothes on, and my mamma was crying and we was too, so they just rushed us out of the house … it was scary but I was just crying."

Uncertainty leading to immobilization

The speculations about the future in these children's stories often were vague or uncertain. When asked whom they would be with or what would happen next in their lives, several just shrugged or said, "I don't know." Some children mentioned that they would see their mothers or fathers again after they were 18, and several mentioned the possibility of adoption. Brian described the painful ambiguity of having one's future left in the hands of others: "You have to keep moving, and moving, and moving, until finally someone keeps you. That kind of sucks." The younger children tended to have less clarity of their future than did the older children.

The experience of helplessness, and therefore depression, anxiety, and relationship conflicts

Often the fears expressed were related to the negative experiences attendant upon being a foster child. David remembered a frightening incident of someone breaking into his house. "I hid in the bedroom and this guy smashed the door in." Both Junius and Jessie remembered being scared when locked in a closet. According to Junius, "… my momma didn't get me out." Devin reported being disturbed by "scary movies" and Krystal worried about how her mom was doing.

About half of the children mentioned getting in trouble at home or at school. For example, Brian described both: "Well, I like to read, and I am getting better at it … I am in special ed because of my behavior … I am really bad in everything." He further described challenges getting along in foster care placements:

"Then I went to [a group home] and [a worker] ... threatened to tie me up with a rope ... and then I left because the people couldn't deal with me. I kept going into the hospital because of my behavior. If I was bad there they would give me a shot in the butt ... and I got one too."

Responding with absolutes, namely: denial of change or loss, denial of facts

Although many children were explicit about why they were in foster care ("Because [mom's boyfriend] beat us ... " "My momma, she had to go to jail"), many of the children were less sure about why they were in care, and many said so. It is possible that the children chose not to share events due to a reluctance to implicate a parent for whom they still felt loyal. However, the anger of many children about being placed in a foster home suggested that they were denying the maltreatment that led to placement. Cage said that he didn't like his foster family for the simple reason that "it wasn't my mama, my real mama." Brian only described maltreatment in the foster home: "I was always getting yelled at, these people ... [did] drugs and everything ... She threatened to tie me up with a rope, she threw me outside, [and] it was wintertime, freezing cold." In contrast, other children implied that they had resolved losses and were forming new attachments to their foster families: "We had some parents that we could trust [and] ... they care about me." "They're fine ... they are like a family."

Guilt, if hope has been given up

Several children exonerated their parents and took the blame for the home breaking up. Miles thought he had to leave his family "Because I was bad ... we set fires." Although Morris's mother was in jail, he did not think he would see his mother again until he could "fix my behavior."

Refusal to talk about the individuals and the situation

One child chose not to be interviewed and three children chose not to answer specific questions.

Stories to the Blacky Pictures

The Blacky pictures are very cute, but are meant to be provocative. You can review some of them at www.psych.usyd.edu.au/museum. Although there are 11 Blacky pictures, we used only four because we expected them to be most sensitive to issues of ambiguous loss. The first shows Mama lying on her side, with pronounced mammary glands, and Blacky in a nursing posture. The second picture shows Blacky in an angry posture, with teeth bared, clenching Mama's collar. A third picture depicts Mama and Papa in love, holding hands and touching noses, with hearts radiating between them, while Blacky looks on with an angry expression. The fourth picture we used depicts Blacky looking on while Mama and Papa are petting another puppy, ostensibly Blacky's sibling. Blacky is shown from the rear making it impossible to ascertain Blacky's expression. There were prominent indications of ambiguous loss.

"Frozen" (unresolved) grief, including outrage and inability to move on

None of the pictures explicitly depict sadness, sickness, or death. Nevertheless, the children often expressed themes related to loss or grieving in response to them. "He ... can't find his mother." Sometimes Mama was said to be permanently gone. For example, one child said that Mama was dead from being "run over." There were other such stories: "She's flipping her over—because she thinks Mama is dead." "His mama run away, I think she killed." Sometimes the sadness was ascribed to a lack of nurturing. "Sad, because Mama don't want to play. Just want to sleep." "Blacky's head under Mama and Mama sleeping on it." And, in one case, the sadness was tied to an absent father. "Sad! He wants to go to his house and play with the daddy. He don't want to sleep with the mama." Sometimes Blacky's sadness was associated with feeling abandoned by Mama. "... His mama don't want to live with him no more."

The first two pictures elicited the best illustrations of the children's outrage. Despite the first picture's pastoral scene—Mama sleeping peacefully and Blacky nursing—Blacky was often described as wanting to fight or bite his mother. "He knocked the mama down ... because he didn't like the mommy!" "He hates her." The second picture, depicting an angry Blacky chewing up Mama's collar, often tied Blacky's rage to feelings of betrayal, unfairness, and frustration. "He hate mama ... because she left." "Maybe he mad because mamma don't want to live with him no more." "He don't like his mom. He wants another mom." "Mama hates dogs." "She did something to embarrass him." "Mad ... 'cause I think his mama gone. I think his mama run away." Several descriptions of the anger were associated with hunger. "He's mad and hungry." "Mad because she ain't milking him no more." "Didn't get enough." "They having a fight because Blacky wants some food. She sleeping."

Many children apparently felt uncomfortable by having Blacky being angry at Mama. They therefore had it displaced upon an inanimate object thing or person. "Tear the collar up—because he can't have things his way." "Biting the collar. Because he found this and he can't find his mother." "Mad at other dog because he took Mama or killed her." "He's mad at another dog—or cat." "Another dog—his brother—hurt him."

Confusion, distress, and ambivalence

Several stories indicated confusion about the children's situation, namely, the family to which the child belonged, who the parents were, and what could be expected of them. "Blacky ... wish he had a mommy that look like him and Daddy. Look like him to protect him. Then he can visit the other kids, but have his mother and father." "His mom and dad trying to trick him about that dog. Thinks it's a real dog but it's a play—foster—dog." "They already have a kid. All of 'em. Made a joke on him."

Uncertainty leading to immobilization

Some children told stories wherein Blacky was confused and didn't know what to do. For example, given a picture of Blacky looking at the other family members standing together, one child observed "It's like he can't do nothing. Like he's looking at it and he don't know what to do."

The experience of helplessness, and therefore depression, anxiety, and relationship conflicts

Like the last story in the paragraph above, many stories implied feelings of helplessness "Blacky getting mad because he can't beat up him. He's too big." Conversely, sometimes Blacky denies helplessness in a display of bravado, for example, "He just so mad he wanna do what he wanna do, hitting people, doing all the stuff he wants." "He's growling. So he can scare everybody." However, in many stories the grandiosity does not persevere: "His dad is liking another dog, he's getting angry. Cause that ain't Mama. He gonna bite that dog in the legs and she will go howling home. And the owner will come and shoot him and his owner will shoot her and all be dead because there are killers around." "When Blacky saw them in love, Blacky tried to kill one of them, a Daddy drove him away. Daddy has scared him away."

As expected, the children described an impotent Blacky experiencing low self-esteem. Some children reasoned that Mama's absence was because Blacky was unlovable, for example, "Maybe he's got fleas." "All three laughing at Blacky." "Blacky is mad, and Papa and Mama is happy, because he couldn't find some food." Other children tied Blacky's unhappiness to Blacky's youth (for example, "OK, he wishes he was a big dog and he was in a good mood.") or loneliness ("He don't got nobody to play with." "... his mother found a lover and he never with them." "Cause he don't have no mama to play with.")

This discontent was also manifest in insecurity and jealousy in relationships.

"The mother is meeting a friend and he saying 'grrrr' 'cause he don't like it when she meets people." "Blacky mad because the other dog is trying to take his girlfriend, his mom." "Blacky's mad 'cause the dad kissed the mom. 'Cause he hates the dad." "Mad because his mama is giving Papa love! Because he hates his Papa. I don't know! He must hate him! He must hate him!" "He angry ... because another dog took his girlfriend. No, it looks like his Mama and Papa. Yeah, he jealous because his mother and father are together and he feel they don't pay enough attention to him."

Many stories included relationship conflict, namely, hostility toward and fighting with parents, siblings, and peers. Sometimes Blacky was described as the perpetrator and sometimes the other parties were. Mama was included as perpetrator: "She went outside and played with her mom. Her mother knocked her over and she was afraid." "He's going under there. Mama just trying to squish him up." However, often Blacky was said to be the perpetrator: "He's scratching her. Biting her. That means he's getting milk from his mom." "He wanna fight. He jump on Mama. 'Cause he wanna fight." "Blacky biting Mama. Right here." "Blacky is hurting Mama. Kicking and peeing." "He knocked the mama down. Because he didn't like his mommy!" Finally, several children described Mama and Blacky fighting with each other. "They fighting. He's biting her. I don't want to be bit by that dog!" "They having a fight. Yeah, and Mama dead." Sometimes the fighting was said to be over food. "Trying to fight. Trying to get the bone. He killed her." "They're having a fight because Blacky wants some food."

Responding with absolutes, namely: denial of change or loss, denial of facts

In some cases a child seemed to be trying to reverse the negative tone of the external stimulus. Sometimes a clearly aggressive Blacky was described as being playful. "Blacky jump over her and knock Mama down!" In other cases, where Blacky was clearly depicted in a foul mood, there was no recognition that Blacky was upset and estranged from his family. "Blacky and his family are nice—all dogs are nice." Other stories had a compensatory tone. Blacky was described as precociously self-sufficient and no longer vulnerable to the acts of others. "He's dreaming he's bigger and he can scare everyone now more." "Dreaming of his self as a big dog. He gonna start his own family soon." Another story reverses the roles so that Blacky is leaving as opposed to being left. "Blacky's sleeping and looks like he's thinking about self walking away from Mama and brother."

Rigidity of family roles (maintaining that the lost person will return as before)—outrage at the lost person being excluded

Both of these ideas appeared to be the dominant theme of some children's stories. For example, some children described Blacky and Mama as yearning for each other, and looking forward to being reunited. "Blacky's dreaming about his Mom. His Mom is thinking about Blacky and wants to go over because she hasn't seen him in a long time." Other children described Blacky as being outraged because, despite social support, Blacky is not being allowed to be with Mama. "… His friends are over. And Blacky's mad at 'em because he's not with his Mama and Papa." In such stories, Blacky is not interested in substitutes. In both cases, the connotation of Mama is positive and Blacky is preoccupied with her loss.

Confusion in boundaries and roles

Occasionally Blacky was described as confused about how to relate to the family in which Blacky finds him- or herself. "Blacky … wish he had a mommy that look like him and Daddy. Look like him to protect him. Then he can visit the other kids but have his mother and father." Sometimes, Blacky demonstrated role reversal with a parent. "Blacky is being mad and mean. Because somebody probably killed his mother and took her collar off … Blacky chased the person. And he probably bit him in the leg." "Mad. Mad. Mad. Mad. Mad. That's *his* son and his mom is loving *his* son." Finally, one child described Blacky reacting to the loss of his mother with gender confusion. "He dreaming he want to be a girl! A girl dog! He don't want to be a boy! He just want to be like his mama."

Guilt, if hope has been given up

Several children scolded Blacky for turning against his mother. "Blacky got mad at Mama and might get into trouble. Because he's getting a big temper." "He gonna be a devil. He's having a dream because he be mean." "Blacky having a nightmare—about what he did." "He had a dream about his self. Because he's mean, he don't deserve nothing." "He's dreaming about being good."

Refusal to talk about the individuals and the situation

Two individuals, aged 5 and 6, made no verbal responses to the Blacky pictures. They sat uncomfortably through the presentation and said nothing. Moreover, it was not uncommon for any of the children to say "I don't know" in response to one or more pictures and despite encouragement. This did not seem to reflect lack of imagination. Often a child would give a negative content and then refuse to continue. For example, several children responded to the ostensibly nursing mother and child as "Fighting." They then would pause and eventually say, "I don't know."

Clinical Implications of These Examples

Two constellations of symptoms are very impressive with regard to both the older and younger children: First, "frozen" (unresolved) grief, including outrage and inability to "move on;" and second, the experience of helplessness and therefore depression, anxiety, and relationship conflicts. These illustrate the characteristic externalizing and internalizing behaviors found to be so detrimental to constructive life in surrogate families (see Chapter 4, "The Perspective of the Consumer: Foster Children Tell Us What They Need").

- *Externalizing behaviors.* These children, old and young, have ready access to outrage. The older children can more readily direct it toward the birth parents who are not doing what is necessary to bring their children home. Many of the younger children may be displacing this anger from their psychological caretakers to others, for example, male adults, judges, foster family members, and the foster care system as a whole.

- *Internalizing behaviors.* All of the children, especially the younger ones, poignantly describe feelings of helplessness and attendant depression and anxiety. In some cases, the children appeared to be counteracting impotent feelings with grandiose statements of self-agency and power. More often, they described themselves as unlovable and inept. Sometimes this anxiety and depression may have led to learning difficulties in school, which, in turn, exacerbated the anxiety and depression. Lack of self-esteem and insecurity in relationships appear to result in distrust of others and misconduct at home and in school.

Implications for Practitioners

As a result of reading this chapter, and considering our illustrations, we hope that you will agree that the model of ambiguous loss has clear clinical utility when applied to your cases. If you use this lens when you seek to understand the people involved in your cases, and if you create appropriate interventions, it will provide valuable insights to inform both your individual and contextual interventions.

Individual

Intense anger may be normative for foster children of all ages. Often it may be focused on people other than the primary caretaking parents, including strangers. Ironically, anger may be displaced upon those—foster care workers, therapists, judges, and care managers—who perceive themselves to be rescuing the children. This anger may be tied to unresolved grief or it may be a protracted tantrum tied to the experience of impotency. Shattered self-esteem also may lead to characteristic coping strategies. On the externalizing side of things, a child may attempt mastery and competence by attacking institutionalized authorities, bullying peers, and demonstrating precocious "self-sufficiency" with regard to emotional and logistic need for others. On the internalizing side, children may decide that if they were more lovable, their parents would not have treated them as they had. This depressive posture allows children two important illusions: Their parents are capable of nurturing the children and this happenstance is in the hands of the children themselves.

Therapists, case managers, officers of the court, and foster family members need not see these externalizing and internalizing behaviors as pathology, but as active coping strategies appropriate to the children's circumstances. Attempts to squelch these behaviors in the interest of tranquil foster placements are unrealistic and may exacerbate underlying psychosocial conditions. Initial interventions need to be psychoeducational and involve all stakeholders in a placement plan. The immediate goal is to smooth out those things that are disruptive to the foster placement. The diverse stakeholders, including the children, need to appreciate how unresolved grief leads to ambivalence about and fears of interdependency, relationship testing, and self-fulfilling prophecies of unlovableness.

In short, all invested members must move from deficit detecting to appreciating that many of these otherwise disturbing behaviors are signs of ego strength. For example, the presence of loyalty conflict implies the continuing capacity to want to relate. Perhaps most importantly, while setting important limits on externalizing behaviors, all need to move away from blame, shame, and punitive behavioral management strategies that exacerbate underlying outrage, insecurity, and depression. For example, when a child misbehaves the tendency is to scold the child and to set them apart from the other family members (for example, "Go to your room"). Instead, one could remind the child that he or she has performed in more desirable ways in the past and the adult would like to see more of that. Instead of exile to a bedroom, the child could be required to spend more time in the company of the parents, perhaps helping them while they are doing some household chore.

According to ambiguous loss concepts, there are several overarching strategies that are helpful to keep in mind while working with these challenging situations (Boss, 2004). These include a need to:

- attempt active listening while withholding judgment,
- offer all the stakeholders psychoeducation about the confusion inherent in their situation, and

- give the children permission to be angry with parents who don't visit consistently, fulfill promises, or do what they need to do in order for the children to return home.

Contextual

Besides these psychological considerations, there are systemic ones. The children's confusion about what losses have occurred and may occur, and what compensations there may be, can be mitigated by contextual improvements (see Chapter 9, "An Integrative Approach Involving the Biological and Foster Family Systems").

- As observed above, those who are working with foster children and their birth and foster families need to assume the presence of ambiguous loss and its influence on all stakeholders. Using this lens, many individual and systemic features are less likely to be pathologized and treated with unhelpful responses and interventions.

- Also, as observed above, all of you may need to better inform your foster children of the reason for their placement and what is currently happening with their families. Sometimes we mean well and withhold information from children because we ourselves do not know what will happen, or because we want to protect children from upsetting information. Unfortunately, withholding information may elicit, maintain, or exacerbate ambiguous loss. In such cases, the foster children have difficulty processing their grief and forming attachments to new caregivers. Sometimes foster children, especially very young ones, use fantasy to escape the confusion engendered by the unknown (Gil & Bogart, 1982). Furthermore, when we deny our foster children such information, we may exacerbate the feelings of disempowerment and helplessness so pervasive in these children (Hughes, 1997).

- Given the importance and pervasiveness of ambiguous loss in foster care, Kim Sumner-Mayer highlights three transition points in Chapter 9: Joining the foster family, visiting with the birth family, and leaving the foster family. She sees these as critical because of how the shifting family memberships at each transition contribute to ambiguous loss on the part of all stakeholders. Sumner-Mayer observes that establishing rituals related to comings and goings of family members may be a helpful practice for adoptive and foster families (Lieberman & Bufferd, 1999; Pavao, 1999).

Finally, "shuttle diplomacy" is an important tool in minimizing the stakeholders' experiences of ambiguous loss (again see Chapter 9). It makes good sense to group and regroup the stakeholders with an eye to bridging the foster care subsystems—birth family, foster family, agency—and effecting developmentally appropriate collaboration.

References

Blum, G. S. (1950). *The Blacky pictures: A technique for the exploration of personality dynamics.* New York: Psychological Corporation.

Boss, P. (1999). *Ambiguous loss: Learning to live with unresolved grief.* Cambridge, MA: Harvard University Press.

Boss, P. (2004). Ambiguous loss research, theory, and practice: Reflections after 9/11. *Journal of Marriage and Family, 66,* 551–566.

Fahlberg, V. I. (1991). *A child's journey through placement.* Indianapolis, IN: Perspectives Press.

Freedman, A., & Dattilio, F. (Eds.) (1994). *Cognitive-behavioral strategies in crisis intervention.* New York: Guilford.

Friedman, J., & Combs, G. (1996). *Narrative therapy: The social construction of preferred realities.* New York: Norton.

Gil, E., & Bogart, K. (1982). Foster children speak out: A study of children's perceptions of foster care. *Children Today, 11*(1), 7–9.

Hughes, D. A. (1997). *Facilitating developmental attachment: The road to emotional recovery and behavioral change in foster and adopted children.* Northvale, NJ: Jason Aronson.

Kubler-Ross, E., & Kessler, D. (2005). *On grief and grieving: Finding the meaning of grief through the five stages of loss.* New York: Scribner.

Lee, R. E., & Lynch, M. T. (1998). Combating foster care drift: An ecosystemic treatment model for neglect cases. *Contemporary Family Therapy, 20,* 351–370.

Lee, R. E., & Whiting, J. B. (2006, in press). Young foster children's voices: Narratives about the relationship of a puppy to its mother. *Child & Youth Care Forum.*

Lieberman, C. A., & Bufferd, R. K. (1999). *Creating ceremonies: Innovative ways to meet adoption challenges.* Phoenix, AZ: Zeig, Tucker.

Morris, K. T., & Kanitz, H. M. (1975). *Rational-emotive therapy.* New York: Houghton Mifflin.

Pavao, J. M. (1999). *The family of adoption.* Boston: Beacon Press.

Whiting, J. B., & Lee, R. E. (2003). Voices from the system: A qualitative study of foster children's stories. *Family Relations, 52,* 288–295.

Weeks, G. R., & L'Abate, L. (1979). A compilation of paradoxical methods. *American Journal of Family Therapy, 7*(4), 61–76.

Part 2

Family Therapy Approaches

6

The Case for Relational Therapy with Young Children in Foster Care

Robert E. Lee and Ann M. Stacks

*I*n whose arms should the "healing" of the maltreated infant or toddler occur, the therapist's or the parents'? If reunification of a biological family is a reasonable goal in a foster care case involving infants and toddlers, relational therapies may be the psychotherapeutic treatments most indicated. Working within the context of family relationships addresses many of the perils of contemporary foster care for children in the earliest years of life, including lengthy stays and loss of supportive family bonds. An illustration is given in which court-ordered family visitation provided an opportunity for relational assessment and interventions.

The process of foster care begins when a court decides that it is too dangerous for children to live in their home. As a result of this decision, the children are housed in a safe place while they, their parents, and their household are assessed for special needs to be remedied while the children are outside the home or upon their return. A contract specifies what needs to be done if the children are to return home. This may include change of housing, increase of income, removal of an adult, cessation of substance use, and acquisition of additional parenting resources. These additional parenting resources are expected to come from some form of traditional counseling and attendance at didactic parenting classes.

There may be basic problems with all of this. Except in cases of heinous abuse, prolonged lack of meaningful contact between parents and children (while the children are in foster care) can be destructive to the children (Littner, 1975; Marsh, 1986; Mech, 1985; Milner, 1987; Sprey-Wessing & Portz, 1982). Moreover, obligatory counseling and parent education often are mechanical, the focus of the therapy and parenting classes may not be specific to the immediate needs of the family, and neither of these things may be capable of producing the relationship changes necessary to good enough parenting (Lee & Lynch, 1998). Finally, if we only focus on the individual child or parent, then all of us, birth family, agency personnel, and court system alike, may be relatively insensitive to family system and larger systems issues (Imber-Black, 1991; Lee & Lynch, 1998).

Clearly, the biological parents of children of any age, especially infants and toddlers (studies summarized in Davies, 1999; Gaensbauer & Siegel, 1995), need to work as soon as possible on meeting the goals which would result in reunification with their children. Experts (Bavolek, 1989; Crittenden, 1993) observe that parental traits common to all forms of child maltreatment include insensitivity to children's cues, inappropriate expectations, lack of empathy, and reliance on physical discipline. This is true whether or not the parents are impoverished, abusing psychoactive substances, or highly stressed (Casady & Lee, 2002). Moreover, contemporary understanding of parent–child relatedness is that it is a process that goes "both ways"; that is, parents and children stimulate or inhibit each other (Belsky, Taylor, & Rovine, 1984; Greenspan, 1999; Lindsey & Mize, 2001). Therefore, all of our foster care therapeutic interventions need to focus on the parent–child *relationship* itself. We want parents to be more aware of their children's needs. We want to remove those things that keep the parents from being appropriately responsive. We want to foster realistic expectations of their children. Finally, we want to give the parents insight into the connection between their own relationship histories and their relationships with their children. If we can do this with the birth parents, we think there will be an increased probability that their children will reach out and respond to them in positive ways.

Previous Methods and Programs

Historically, dyadic approaches to negative parent–child related-ness have employed either filial therapy (Guerney, 1964) or meth-ods informed by the infant mental health model (for example, Fraiberg, 1980; Zeanah, 2000). Filial therapy teaches mothers to engage their children in therapeutic play. Infant mental health inter-ventions focus on the psychological qualities of mothers, including lack of knowledge, that interfere with quality nurturing. Both approaches appreciate that emotional distress in a child is elicited and maintained in relationship to primary caregivers. Accordingly, both approaches are based on the transactive interplay of parent and child while incorporating "best practice" models of parenting (see, for example, Baumrind, 1977; Belsky, 1984; Lieberman & Zeanah, 1999; Zeanah, Larrieu, Heller, & Valliere, 2000).

Currently, treatment of parent–child dyads varies along two dimensions. The first is the theory that informs the therapy. It can range from psychodynamic forms of psychotherapy (for a review, see Lieberman, Silverman, & Pawl, 2000), through expressive-supportive therapy (Muir, 1992), to psychoeducational interventions (McDonough, 2000). The second dimension involves the role of the child in the therapy. The focus can be on the mother, with the child used as an *agent provocateur* (Fraiberg, 1980). Or the focus can be on the relationship between parent and child and the child can be seen as a responder, instigator, and therapeutic agent (Lojksek, Cohen, & Muir, 1994). Goals may range from pro-found transformation of the individuals' capacity to relate in positive ways to helping the individuals interact in more enjoyable and developmentally appropriate ways.

Research has found that dyadic family therapy focused on the relationship between mothers and children at risk for maltreat-ment can make that relationship more nurturing (Bavolek, 2002; Lieberman & Zeanah, 1999). Many of these are adaptable to fami-lies whose infants and toddlers are in foster care (Craven & Lee, 2006). Nevertheless, only a few service–research programs have explored this possibility. These include: our own (to be described below), that of Zeanah and his colleagues in New Orleans (Larrieu & Zeanah, 1998), the "Good Fit" program (Groppenbacher, Hoard, & Miller, 2002), that overseen by Joy Osofsky and her colleagues in Miami, and the ABC intervention project (Dozier, Dozier, & Manni, 2002). Unlike the other programs, Dozier and her associates focus on attachment-based interventions for foster parents rather than birth parents (see Chapter 12, "Intervening with Foster Infants' Foster Parents: Attachment and Biobehavioral Catch-Up").

Once you think about it, it is hard to escape the conviction that relational therapy is the treatment of choice in foster care, where infants, toddlers, and young children are involved. If you treat parents and children together, you go straight to the heart of the presenting problem, namely, what is and is not happening between them that results in the parents' lack of appropriate nurturing. Moreover, infants are too young to be worked with individually, and timely parental contacts are necessary if babies are to keep their birth mothers in mind. Finally, relational therapy is important to the recovery of maltreated toddlers and preschool children. If these children are to recognize that their present and future are changed from the past, and that the world is now a secure place, they need the contemporary experience of their primary caregivers engaged in appropriate protective behavior (Davies, 1991).

Visitation-Centered Foster Care

Visitation, when the family members come together, provides a valuable and unique opportunity for family therapy. It is a setting in which all the participants can appreciate firsthand the family members' roles, hierarchy, alliances, relationships, boundaries, rules, and beliefs (Minuchin & Fishman, 1981). Supervised visitation also may afford you, a systems-savvy therapist, an opportunity to consult to the larger system—court, foster care agency, schools, mental health agencies—of which the biological family is a part (see Chapter 2, "An Ecosystemic Approach to Foster Care"). Such consultation would recognize and seek redress of overlapping areas of responsibility ("planning for the child"), incompatible goals (for example, family reunification vs. termination of parental rights), and unrealistic if not impossible concurrent requirements on our birth families (for example, the requirement to work while also satisfying several appointments a week, often in the absence of personal and reliable transportation). Similarly this affords you a chance to teach the biological family how to advocate effectively for themselves within a system from which they often feel estranged.

In short, family therapy during supervised visitation is a setting in which all parties—birth parents, caseworkers, supervisors, and foster parents—can experience new perceptions of themselves, discover strengths, and rehearse "best practices" in what they do. At the very least, we believe that supervised visitation provides an unparalleled opportunity to build positive relationships—between parents and their children, and between parents and the agency—while also teaching developmentally appropriate parenting skills in the live family group.

In our own program, we offered parents with infants and toddlers extra sessions of family visitation each week at a site away from the supervising state agency. Our family therapists had specialized knowledge of early child development. They engaged the children and parents in a family therapy program that included self-reflection and integrative use of the psychotherapeutic interventions employed in the contemporary infant mental health movement (for example, see Zeanah, 2000). Part of each session taught developmentally appropriate expectations and throughout there was an emphasis on recognizing and appropriately responding to child cues. These family therapy sessions were mixed with individual adult, couple, and extended family therapy sessions as needed. Developmental screening, with an eye to early intervention for these at-risk children, was ongoing. Finally, the therapists made monthly visits to the foster parents to facilitate their resourcefulness to the birth family.

Families involved with the foster care system have a variety of issues that impact the structure and process of treatment. These are elaborately detailed in Larrieu & Zeanah (1998). However, when it comes to structuring sessions, the therapist must consider the age of the child or children, the number of children in the family, each child's developmental level, the parent's cognitive ability, and the number of adults in the family system. In addition, the parent's history of abuse and or neglect and the circumstances under which the children were placed into foster care must be considered. When children are over 18 months old, it is imperative that you structure sessions so that you can have time with the parents alone. Parents need to be able to work through feelings and mechanisms that perpetuate abusive relationships (for example, see Fraiberg, 1980). Often you will discover that as parents begin to recollect and work through some of their own maltreatment, they become more empathic with their children.

Typically, we asked parents to come in twice a week for at least the first three months after they were referred to the program. However, we were very careful about our own expectations of them. Many of these parents were perplexed, frustrated, and even overwhelmed by the many weekly appointments—often in the absence of reliable transportation—that agencies expected them to consistently keep if they were to get their children back. They had to go to work, visit their children at the foster care agency, go to parenting classes, obtain personal psychotherapy, give urine samples, attend 12-step substance abuse treatment groups, and attend anger management classes, among other demands. However, beyond these logistical concerns, our scheduling also had to incorporate the times when parents and children were functioning at their best, that is, a time when the parents were tranquil and the children were awake and had been fed. Some parents preferred to be seen for an hour, two days a week, while others preferred to spend two hours in one day. When children were over 18 months of age, we typically reserved one hour as an individual therapy or couple session, and the other for the parent–child therapy.

A typical session involved a foster parent bringing children to our clinic where the birth parents were waiting. All our sessions were videotaped from behind a one-way mirror. Often the first 15 minutes of each session involved a short lesson taken from a parent education curriculum specifying what might be expected of a child this age and ways in which parents could constructively interact with such a child. If the child was an infant, we made sure that the child was in a parent's arms or in a transportation seat facing them. A toddler usually was given free play. Age-calibrated toys allowed a concurrent gross assessment of children's development. When children appeared to needed more intensive developmental screening and treatment, they were referred for it.

The remainder of a typical parent–child therapy session was an integrative application of contemporary infant mental health psychotherapeutic techniques. The goal of each session was to have the parents become sensitive to their children's cues and to respond in a timely and appropriate manner. Toward this end, parents were coached while they closely watch their children. Sometimes the therapists spoke for themselves. ("Notice how your baby looks away. She probably is feeling too excited.") They also spoke for the baby. ("Mom, I really like it when you do that.") However, often the parents did not accurately interpret their children's behavior because the parents' expectations were rooted in their own maltreatment as children.

To get at such "baggage"—unconsciously ascribed meanings and under- and overreactions—our therapists asked leading questions. "Tell me about your baby." "What do you think your baby is thinking/feeling?" It was not unusual to have parents of (for example) a 3-month-old infant talk about the baby's "willful," "aggressive," "punitive," or "manipulative" ways. And, as you will readily appreciate, a 90-day-old child is not capable of any of this. What was happening is that the baby was a blank screen upon which were projected the parents' needs and fears. Often videotapes of the parents and children in gratifying interchanges were used for awareness and reinforcement. If necessary, we viewed negative interactions to raise consciousness. This was done infrequently because we wished to create a health, resources-oriented ambience so as to maintain the cooperation and enthusiasm of the parents.

Therapy continued until the authorization by the supervising agency ran out (often 24 sessions, renewable for an additional 24; 6 months to a year), or sooner if the courts reached a determination. Our program has been popular with the birth families. It allowed more time together, did not take away from the parents' time alone with their children, was strengths-based, and incorporated foster care's traditional requirements to go to parenting classes and obtain counseling into one meaningful session. The program was popular with the agencies because, besides addressing long-standing agency personnel concerns, it required no new funds. We were paid from the funds traditionally budgeted for psychotherapy services for those foster children who were thought to need them.

Case Example

Renee, age 17, and Eric, age 19, were referred to our program when their 15-month-old baby daughter was taken away from Renee and placed with a relative because of physical and emotional neglect. Renee herself had been living in foster homes since she was 11 years old. She had been neglected and finally abandoned by her mother and the latest in a succession of men who lived with and abused her mother. Renee subsequently had been moved from one foster home to another because of a defiant attitude, under-achievement, and cannabis use. Eric was a high school dropout who ran away from home at 14. He had an uneven employment history and found lodging with friends. Eric and Renee fell in love when she was 15 and she quickly became pregnant with their daughter Morgan, who was 15 months old at the time of the referral. Renee then began working part time at a fast food restaurant and attending night school. She now was six months pregnant with their second child, who would be named Eric after his father.

According to the referring agency, Renee would sneak out of her foster home at night to be with Eric, leaving Morgan asleep in her bed, unattended. While with Eric she would drink alcohol and have an occasional "joint." Moreover, when Eric visited her at the foster home and they had an argument, they would curse, hit, and shove each other in front of the baby. However, Renee and Eric told the program therapist that they loved each other very much and intended to get married when Renee turned 18. They said that they wanted parent–child therapy because they wanted to be better parents to their children than they themselves were parented. They also were afraid that the new baby would be taken away from them upon his birth.

From the outset the therapist was impressed that Renee and Eric loved each other and that much of their difficulty represented their youth on the one hand, and the "porcupine love" of "burnt" children on the other. (How do porcupines make love? Very carefully.) Renee also appeared to be emotionally available to Morgan; she perceived her cues, and responded in a timely and satisfying manner. Eric, in contrast, appeared to have some difficulty appreciating when Morgan was being overstimulated and he would increase whatever he was doing. He thought he was "teasing" her. Both parents expressed interest in learning new behaviors to engage their daughter and to better understand her cues.

Concurrent with Eric's commitment to finding steady employment, a reliable car, and adequate housing, the couple committed to a therapeutic contract that prohibited physical aggression in the relationship and required two therapeutic visitation sessions each week, one of which would focus on couple issues.

The therapy took place in a large playroom. The furniture had been removed so that the family and children would be on the floor. In the early stages of treatment, the therapist primarily used an array of psychoeducational tools. Reflective listening helped the parents become more aware of their thoughts and feelings. Videotapes of family sessions and worksheets alerted the parents to developmental accomplishments and challenges. The therapist "coached" developmentally appropriate expectations and responses. Often she spoke for the children. (*"The baby is saying 'Oh, Daddy, I like it when you do that!'"*) She used circular questioning to help the parents see the interrelatedness of their behavior. (*"When the baby does that, what does Eric do? When Eric does that, what does Morgan do? Then, what does Renee do?"*).

Sessions 1 to 24

The couple faithfully attended all of their therapy sessions except when transportation difficulties made this impossible. Shortly into the treatment, Eric got a stable job and soon bought a used automobile. This thrilled both parents since they often felt frustrated by their dependence on others for transportation at a time when the agency required them to do so many things. Since Eric Jr. had not been born yet, Renee and Eric pursued a clear interest in themselves and in Morgan. They explored the negative impact of physical and emotional violence on themselves and their child. While playing and caring for Morgan in the session, they—more or less enthusiastically—sought information about child development and parenting techniques. Morgan, for her part, seemed to respond well to her parents and demonstrated adequate attachment. Renee and Eric spoke of having a good life for the whole family upon being married. At the same time they spoke with bitterness about the referring agency. In their view, the staff members enthusiastically looked for personal and parenting deficits with the goal of terminating their parental rights. At this juncture, both parents were working full time while simultaneously trying to satisfy court mandates to keep their jobs, get adequate housing, get reliable transportation, supply urine specimens, go to anger management classes, didactic parenting classes, and individual psychotherapy. The therapist at first supported that anger and then helped them get beyond it to deal more effectively with their impossible situation. Using the dictum of "Do it *for* them, then do it *with* them, and then cheer while *they do it,*" the couple was moved toward a more constructive interaction with the agency. Things were going well, and the couple became increasingly animated and optimistic. This came to a drastic end right after Eric Jr. was born.

Sessions 24 to 48

Eric Jr. went straight from the hospital into foster care. Renee and Eric could see him only at therapy sessions, and the couple was outraged, while also feeling helpless. With therapeutic support the two of them eventually channeled their emotions into a conviction to prove their adequacy as parents and win their children back.

Events remained stormy, however. Renee repeatedly attacked Eric. She said she could not entrust herself and the children to him. He allegedly was insensitive, self-indulgent, and irresponsible. These accusations occurred when she was feeling frustrated by the lack of fun in her life or overwhelmed by all the things life was requiring of her. *("I've never had a childhood and now all I do is work and, with the kids, that's all I'll EVER do.")* In response to these attacks, Eric busied himself with Morgan and seemed content in that. The therapist observed that while Renee was complaining about Eric, she was preoccupied with Eric Jr., and intrusively lavished care that was not in accordance with his infant cues. However, as alert she was to the baby's presence, Renee was now insensitive to Morgan. She now seemed to have no interest at all in their little girl, who would babble and gesture in attempts to engage her mother. Morgan clearly was the province of Eric.

The therapist was worried that Renee, while not consciously thinking about her own history of abuse ("it was no big whoop"), was in fact acting it out. Renee was coming to fear that Eric had many of the hated qualities of her parents, and she was treating him in ways that influenced him to act in accordance with those fears. She herself seemed to be repeating her parents' neglect of her in favor of her younger half brother.

Prodded to think about her family of origin, Renee described a childhood where the parents often were drunk and were unaware of the children's needs, and Renee was required to fend for herself and her little brother. When her parents were attentive to their children, the little boy was indulged and Renee would be punished for his messes. Renee especially remembered mealtimes as being awful affairs. If she didn't like what she was served, she went hungry and was given the offensive entrée cold at the next meal. If she rejected it again, the food reappeared at the following meal, this time taken from the trash container. Renee opined that parents were wrong to do these kinds of things, but said that she had forgiven them because they didn't know any better. Besides, she said, it was over now and she did not want to talk about it. Eric described a similar family of origin, which was why he ran away from home and why, he said, he was most comfortable with little children.

The primary orientation of the therapist during this painful time was to create a safe setting for the family, a place where the parents could experience their fear and anger, explore the reality of what they were thinking and feeling, and consider the implications of things for themselves and the children. They could do all this in light of their goals for a new life, and find constructive ways to act. Observation and provocative questioning uncovered inappropriate perceptions and expectations of the children *("What do you think Eric Jr. is doing"? Reply: "He's such a little manipulator!").* Often such interventions were followed by attempts at differentiating the reality of baby and toddler development from the unrealistic stereotypes. Typically the therapist would explore the source of the parents' interpretations while giving correct developmental information. Similarly, the therapist would explore distortions in how the parents saw themselves and each other, and ask differentiating kinds of questions *("How is Eric similar to your mother? In what ways is he quite different?").* The therapist also was alert for opportunities to help the parents recognize how they and their lives were different now from how they may have been in the past. Finally, reframing helped the parents see themselves in a different, less negative way *("You called yourself 'bitchy' and now say that Morgan is being 'bratty.' Both times I see someone expressing her needs.").*

Over time, the couple developed humor and insight into themselves and their family relationships. They demonstrated a wide range of appropriate expectations and emotions. As they separated past from present, they identified strengths in themselves as well as growing edges upon which to work. (For example, they appreciated how Morgan used her mother as a safe base from which to explore. However, they also could see how they too quickly used Morgan's quasi-independent forays as a respite opportunity for themselves.) They discussed what they would like for their children relative to their own childhood experiences, and committed themselves to providing that. They were increasingly alert to each other's cues and more timely and appropriate in their responses to their mate and to each child. Renee worried about a propensity toward corporal punishment and her own poor anger management. Both parents noticed a connection between Renee's anger at the children and her disagreements with Eric. Accordingly they contracted not to spank the children while continuing couple counseling, until this no longer would be a problem. Renee looked into a GED and community college. Eric settled into construction work. Periodic urine screening for drug use continued to be negative.

At the time of this writing, Renee is aged 18, a legal adult, and no longer a foster ward of the state. She and Eric have rented a home and announced their engagement. They have been allowed extended overnight, unsupervised visits with the children. Renee appears to be more appropriate with Morgan, meeting her needs for nurturing and play. Although Renee has consistently worried that she is unable to care for two children at the same time, in the family therapy sessions both parents have seemed very relaxed in dealing with both children simultaneously. Morgan and Eric Jr. actively and happily engage both parents for help, affection, and play. In response to Renee's reasonable concern, both adults have soberly considered what will be required of each of them if they are to adequately take care of each other and their children.

Discussion

When children are placed in foster care, it is important to build positive and constructive family bonds where they do not exist, and to strengthen and maintain them where they do exist. Our overarching vision is synchronous and developmentally appropriate parent–child interaction. This can be accomplished through a sensitive application of interaction guidance and support (McDonough, 2000), live ("on the floor" with one's child) developmental education and, where possible, object relations–informed "uncovering" psychotherapy (see, for example, Scharff & Scharff, 1995). Relational therapy recognizes that the infant or toddler is an influential member of the parent–child system. Parent–child synchrony is developed within a relationship where children's cues are read quickly and appropriately and are consistently responded to in a sensitive manner (for example, see Ainsworth, Blehar, Waters, & Wall, 1978). In response to changes in their parents—in the context of a sensitive and responsive relationship—children are likely to send more consistent, less ambivalent cues, and to provide a more gratifying relationship.

Of 24 families referred to date, only two have dropped out. Both were teen mothers who had easy access to their children because they had been placed with relatives, and the mothers did not want to curtail their immature behavior. Another mother-child dyad showed significant improvement. The mother was more consistently "there" for her 8-month-old infant and the infant became less avoidant toward her. But the child was not returned home because the mother continued contact with an abusive male. In the remaining 21 cases, the children were returned to their biological parents. However, we have no way to know if the changes accomplished in our therapy were robust enough to characterize these families' lives outside the treatment sessions.

The agency caseworkers tell us that when this kind of psychotherapy is provided to maltreating parents and their children in supervised family visitation sessions, the workers see substantial and beneficial relational changes. We believe that this is because of the specific goals of relational therapy, and the fact that such sessions keep parents and children positively connected while the children are in the foster care environment. The workers also report that they feel more comfortable in their recommendations to the court with regard to the final disposition of the cases. Unlike traditional assessment procedures, which may involve as little as one assessment session with a psychologist or panel, the procedures described in this article provide biological parents perhaps their best opportunity to acquire and demonstrate parenting resources and competencies.

References

Ainsworth, M. D. S., Blehar, M. C., Waters, E., & Wall, S. (1978). *Patterns of attachment: A psychological study of the strange situation.* Hillsdale, NJ: Erlbaum.

Bavolek, S. J. (1989). Assessing and treating high-risk parenting attitudes. *Child Abuse and Neglect: Theory, Research and Practice, 42,* 99–112.

Bavolek, S. J. (2002). *Research and validation report of the Nurturing Parent Programs.* Park City, UT: Family Development Resources.

Baumrind, D. (1977). Some thoughts about childrearing. In S. Cohen & T. J. Comiskey (Eds.), *Child development: Contemporary perspectives* (pp. 248–258). Itasca, IL: F. E. Peacock.

Belsky, J. (1984). The determinants of parenting: A process model. *Child Development, 55,* 83–96.

Belsky, J., Taylor, D. G., & Rovine, M. (1984). The Pennsylvania Infant and Family Development Project II: The development of reciprocal interaction in the mother–infant Bowlby dyad. *Child Development, 55,* 706–717.

Casady, M. A., & Lee, R. E. (2002). Environments of physically neglected children. *Psychological Reports, 91,* 711–721.

Craven, P. A., & Lee, R. E. (2006). Therapeutic interventions for foster children: A systematic research synthesis. *Research on Social Work Practice, 16,* 297–304.

Crittenden, P. M. (1993). An information-processing perspective on the behavior of neglectful parents. *Criminal Justice and Behavior, 20,* 27–48.

Davies, D. (1991). Intervention with male toddlers who have witnessed parental violence. *Families in Society: The Journal of Contemporary Human Services, 72,* 515–524.

Davies, D. (1999). *Child development: A practitioner's guide.* New York: Guilford.

Dozier, M., Dozier, D., & Manni, M. (2002, April/May). Attachment and biobehavioral catch-up: The ABC's of helping infants in foster care cope with early adversity. *Zero to Three, 22(5),* 7–13.

Fraiberg, S. (Ed.). (1980). *Clinical studies in infant mental health: The first year of life.* New York: Basic Books.

Gaensbauer, T. J., & Siegel, C. H. (1995). Therapeutic approaches to posttraumatic stress disorder in infants and toddlers. *Infant Mental Health Journal, 16,* 292–305.

Greenspan, S. I. (1999). Building healthy minds: The six experiences that create intelligence and emotional growth in babies and young children. Cambridge, MA: Perseus.

Groppenbacher, E., Hoard, C. & Miller, S. (2002, April/May). Providing mental health services to young children in foster care: A family-by-family, moment-by-moment approach to change. *Zero to Three, 22(5),* 33–37.

Guerney, B. G. (1964). Filial therapy: Description and rationale. *Journal of Consulting Psychology, 28,* 303–310.

Imber-Black, E. (1991). A family-larger system perspective. In A. S. Gurman & D. Kniskern (Eds.), *Handbook of family therapy* (Vol. 2, pp. 583–605). New York: Brunner/Mazel.

Larrieu, J., & Zeanah, C. H. (1998). An intensive intervention for infants and toddlers in foster care. *Child and Adolescent Psychiatric Clinics of North America, 7,* 357–391.

Lee, R. E., & Lynch, M. T. (1998). Combating foster care drift: An ecosystemic treatment model for neglect cases. *Contemporary Family Therapy, 20,* 351–370.

Lieberman, A. F., Silverman, R., & Pawl, J. H. (2000). Infant-parent psychotherapy: Core concepts and current approaches. In C. H. Zeanah (Ed.), *Handbook of infant mental health* (2nd ed., pp. 472–484). New York: Guilford.

Lieberman, A. F., & Zeanah, C. H. (1999). Contributions of attachment theory to infant–parent psychotherapy and other interventions with infants and young children. In J. Cassidy & P. Shaver (Eds.), *Handbook of attachment: Theory, research, and clinical applications* (pp. 555–574). New York: Guilford.

Lindsey, E. E., & Mize, J. (2001). Measuring parent–child mutuality during play. In P. K. Kerig & K. M. Lindahl (Eds.), *Family observational coding systems: Resources for systemic research* (pp. 171–185). Mahwah, NJ: Erlbaum.

Littner, N. (1975). The importance of natural parents to the child in placement. *Child Welfare, 54,* 175–181.

Lojksek, M., Cohen, N. J., & Muir, E. (1994). Where is the infant in infant intervention? A review of the literature on changing troubled mother-infant relationships. *Psychotherapy, 31,* 208–220.

Marsh, P. (1986). Natural families and children in care: An agenda for practice development. *Adoption and Fostering, 10,* 20–25.

McDonough, S. C. (2000). Interaction guidance: An approach for difficult-to-engage families. In C. H. Zeanah (Ed.), *Handbook of infant mental health* (2nd ed., pp. 485–493). New York: Guilford.

Mech, E. V. (1985). Parental visiting and foster placement. *Child Welfare, 64,* 67–72.

Milner, J. L. (1987). An ecological perspective on duration of foster care. *Child Welfare, 66,* 113–125.

Minuchin, S., & Fishman, H. C. (1981). *Family therapy techniques.* Cambridge, MA: Harvard University Press.

Muir, E. (1992). Watching, waiting, and wondering: Applying psychoanalytic principals to mother–infant intervention. *Infant Mental Health Journal, 13,* 319–338.

Scharff, J. S., & Scharff, D. E. (1995). *A primer of object relations theory.* Northville, NJ: Jason Aronson.

Sprey-Wessing, T., & Portz, P. (1982). Some aspects of identity problems in foster families. *Journal of Comparative Family Studies, 13,* 231–235.

Zeanah, C. H. (Ed.). (2000). *Handbook of infant mental health* (2nd ed.). New York: Guilford.

Zeanah, C. H., Larrieu, J. A., Heller, S. S., & Valliere, J. (2000). Infant–parent relationship assessment. In C. H. Zeanah (Ed.), *Handbook of infant mental health* (2nd ed., pp. 222–235). New York: Guilford.

7

Parent–Child Therapy for Traumatized Young Children in Foster Care

Douglas Davies

*S*ometimes timely trauma-focused treatment in the context of a reunification plan is not possible. In those cases, relational therapy needs to be offered while the child is in foster care, using the potential of the foster child–foster parent relationship. The goal is to help the child develop a coherent narrative perspective on the traumatic experience—one that explicitly locates the trauma in the past—while providing reassurance that the child is protected from trauma in the present.

It is likely that traumatized children who subsequently have been placed in foster care have critical therapeutic needs for which they need a therapist's care as soon as possible. Here are several important things to understand regarding these children's experiences.

- Children typically cope with trauma by establishing post-traumatic defenses ranging from avoidance of intimacy and counterphobic aggression to dissociative numbing. Often the children are emotionally constricted and hard to reach. It is likely that their new relationships in foster care will be negatively influenced by these defenses. Physically abused young children who act aggressively toward their foster parents may be punished for it. It is helpful for foster parents to understand that the children's aggression is a way of coping with trauma (Dozier, Albus, Fisher, & Sepulveda, 2002). Moreover, the foster parents' angry and punitive reactions feel "abusive" to the children, and reinforce their already-established models of what caregivers are like.

- Because foster parents will most likely misunderstand their difficult behavior, these traumatized young children may be moved from one foster home to another. They must then cope with these new disruptions of relationships and environments.

- It is likely that traumatized children have been maltreated in other ways, including negative and inconsistent relationships with caregivers (see Klee, Kronstadt, & Zlotnick, 1997, and Maluccio & Ainsworth, 2003, with regard to the disorganizing effects of substance abuse on parenting). There is a high probability that all of these experiences have affected their development and their capacity for establishing positive relationships. For example, these children may be terrified of being dependent (for example, see Barnett, Ganiban, & Cicchetti, 1999; Fanshel, Finch, & Grundy, 1990) and may struggle to find ways to deal with the important adults in their lives (James, 1994). For these children, the imagery of trauma is inseparable from their models of attachment relationships. Since young children are so dependent on their caregivers, abuse trauma will be remembered and symptomatically reenacted, not as discrete events in the child's individual life, but rather as *relational events* (Scheeringa & Zeanah, 2001). Their working models of attachment will have been shaped around expectations of pain, harshness, and inconsistency that are sometimes mixed with appropriate and loving caregiving. These working models contribute to a prevailing mistrust of relationships and a picture of oneself as bad, unworthy, and to blame for abuse (Toth, Maughan, Manly, Spagnola, & Cicchetti, 2002).

- Abused children are likely to have been the objects of negative attributions by their parents, and have internalized these attributions—"mean," "bad," "to blame for parents' anger"—as part of their view of self (Lieberman, 2000). These working models and attributions will transfer into these children's new relationships with their foster parents.

- By being placed in foster care, these same children suffer a loss of parents, families, and familiar environment. No matter how nurturing their new homes, these children now face problems of adaptation to new people, family styles, behavioral expectations, and routines.

When timely trauma-focused treatment in the context of a reunification plan is not possible, relational therapy needs to be offered while the child is in foster care. This therapy will use the potential for healing and new learning contained in the foster child–foster parent relationship. In the relational treatment of traumatized young children in their foster parents' care, the following elements are essential:

- education of foster parents about the symptoms and dynamics of trauma in the young child,
- encouraging foster parents to establish high levels of stability, routine, and security in the child's daily life, and
- child–foster parent therapy focusing on the child's trauma history, using the child's ability to represent trauma in play or behavior.

Just as relational therapy holds the potential for promoting adaptive reunification, it can offer foster parents and young foster children a chance to establish a positive relationship that becomes a protective factor against placement disruption.

Issues in Preparing Foster Parents for Parent–Child Therapy

Young children who have been chronically abused or neglected enter foster care with negative expectations of caregiving relationships. In addition to posttraumatic symptoms and adaptations, they often show difficulties in self-regulation (Cicchetti & Rogosch, 2001; Perry, 2002; Thomas & Guskin, 2001) and engage in precocious self-reliance as a defense against getting close in relationships. Being egocentric, they may blame themselves for having been abused and feel responsible for being removed from their parents. They may be mistrustful in relationships with caregivers and peers, and may be ready to respond to perceived provocation with intense aggressive behavior.

Research has shown that an important predictor of foster parents' satisfaction with the fostering experience is "feeling competent to handle the types of children placed" (Denby, Rindfleisch, & Bean, 1999, p. 298). When children have significant posttraumatic behavior problems, support from a therapist and foster care agency can be critical factors in preventing placement disruption. The effects of successive placement disruptions are well known—the children's behavior problems continue while their capacity for establishing attachments diminishes (Newton, Litrownik, & Landsverk, 2000). When young traumatized children enter care, their foster parents' feelings of competence are likely to increase if they understand the behavioral symptoms and dynamics of trauma and how they influence the child's view of self in relationships. Education about the nature of trauma is a crucial role for those who work with traumatized children and their foster parents.

Before beginning parent–child therapy, there should be some preparatory sessions with the foster parents alone. In these sessions, the therapist can elicit and often reframe the parents' experience of the child, stress the importance of providing stability and nurturance for the child, educate the parents about posttrauma symptoms and relationship dynamics, and outline the process of relational therapy. These preparatory sessions are important because they help the foster parents begin to view the child in terms of his or her past history, provide them with a framework for observing the child's current behavior, and provide a tentative road map of how relational treatment of trauma works. Equipped with these perspectives, as well as a supportive relationship with the therapist, the foster parents are more likely to invest in the child and the therapy, and less likely to reactively terminate the child's placement in response to his or her difficult behavior.

Preparation 1:
Explore the Foster Parents' Perceptions of the Child

In the first session with the foster parents, the therapist elicits their perceptions of the child. Frequently, foster parents will report behavior that is both perplexing and disturbing. For example, the foster mother of the 4-year-old boy in this chapter's case example recalled, "Two days ago, Andrew disappeared. I looked for him everywhere in the house for about 20 minutes. I was in a panic, and when I finally found him in the hall closet, he couldn't tell me why he did it. He'd been sitting in there quiet for the whole time I was calling him. I can understand a kid hiding for a while, like it was hide and go seek, but this is weird and scary." The therapist can validate the foster parents' affective experiences, while helping them understand that there are hidden causes for such unusual behavior that are related to the child's life before coming to foster care. A beginning goal of the parent–child sessions will be to get to know the child and to learn about experiences in his or her family of origin that may shed light on the child's difficult behavior, and open a pathway for changing it (see Chapter 4, "The Perspective of the Consumer: Foster Children Tell Us What They Need").

The therapist also can encourage the parents to look for patterns in the child's behavior at home. For example, foster parents can be asked to pay attention to antecedents to unusual behavior, asking themselves, "What was happening before s/he did that?" (O'Neill, Horner, Albin, Storey, & Sprague, 1996). When Andrew's foster mother realized that he hid fairly often, she began to note that there was always some tension in the household that preceded Andrew's disappearance. On one occasion, she had yelled at her biological son; on another, her husband had come home complaining loudly about a problem at work. Looking for antecedents often leads to an important shift in the foster parents' view of the child's behavior. Observation of patterns helps the foster parents begin to discover that the behavior has meaning. It is not strange, random, or inexplicable.

It is also crucial in preparatory sessions to explore each foster parent's perception of his or her relationship with the child. Often the foster parents will report inconsistency between their own self-images and the child's reactions to them. Andrew's foster father said, "Last night I told him that it was time to get ready for bed, and I said it calmly. I wasn't mad or upset, and he flipped out, started screaming at me like I was an ogre." Such incidents can be used to point out that the child seems at times to respond to the foster parent as if he or she were someone else. This opens up a discussion of working models and learned responses derived from the child's relationships with abusive parents. In Andrew's case, I suggested, "His reaction didn't make any sense to you, because you simply told him it was time for bed. But to him an expectation from an adult feels coercive and even abusive. I'm guessing a bit, but maybe in his family there was almost no lag time between being told to do something and getting hit. So it seems like his reaction could be a carryover from his abuse. His reaction has nothing to do with your intention, and everything to do with his fear of being abused. That's a fear he'd carry into a relationship with any foster parent, not just you, because that's what he learned to expect."

Preparation 2: Promote Stability and Nurturance

Because young foster children have been exposed to inconsistent and often chaotic family relationships, they may adopt a self-reliant stance that conveys that they do not need relationships. Foster parents may need help in understanding that the child's distancing behavior represents a defense. Consequently, "… an important focus of interventions for foster parents of young children is to help caregivers provide a nurturing environment, even though foster children may not appear to need nurturance," and may actually reject nurturing overtures (Dozier, et al., 2002, p. 855)

Trauma treatment presupposes that the child is no longer exposed to trauma. If a child feels a current sense of threat in his or her environment, he or she will not be able to process past trauma in treatment. By definition, of course, people with post-traumatic stress disorder (PTSD) continue to be highly sensitive to perceived or imagined threats. However, young foster children may be particularly reactive because, in addition to trauma, they have experienced so many destabilizing changes in their lives. A precondition to children being able to work on trauma is the background of a stable environment. This has implications for work with foster parents.

- Foster parents should be advised to establish clear, regular routines for the child.

- They should be advised to provide verbal preparation for changes in routine or new experiences.

- Particular attention should be paid to the issue of limit setting. Foster parents should make simple, clear, and unambiguous statements about their expectations for the child's behavior. Although setting clear limits on behavior helps the child contain impulses, it is important for therapists to clarify that traumatized children associate harsh or angry limit-setting statements with the abuse they have experienced. Therefore, foster parents should be advised to make limit-setting statements in calm and warm tones. Limits should also be enforced when the child's play becomes reckless or aggressive. Such aroused behavior, even though it may reflect attempts to deny trauma, is likely to frighten the child because it brings up affects and memories associated with trauma. Clear limit setting communicates to the child that the parent will maintain control of situations that evoke feelings associated with the trauma. This helps the child feel safer and protected and provides the background of safety that allows the child to work on the trauma issues in therapy.

- Foster parents should make direct statements that they will keep the child safe, as well as making clear that they are available to help the child contain anxiety and hyperarousal. They can say,

"If you get worried or scared, you can tell me, and I'll try to help you feel better." The foster parents can help the child draw lines between past trauma and current experience by saying, "We're not going to let those same scary things happen here."

- As a corollary of this, especially for young children who lack verbal skills, the foster parents should be encouraged to learn what situations (see, for example, a group of noisy children, separation in the morning at day care) provoke anxiety or difficult behavior, and to intervene proactively with support when the child is going into such a situation.

- Foster parents should be advised to limit the young child's exposure to overstimulating or arousing situations. These include television shows or movies depicting violence, or specific places or events associated with the child's trauma history.

- Children need to be helped to perceive their away-from-home environments as safe and stable. Childcare providers should be made aware of child's vulnerability to stress and need for a sense of safety. They need to ready to intervene supportively when the child's behavior at school seems reactive to feelings and memories of trauma. Childcare providers will value consultation because the therapist can clarify issues related to trauma and make suggestions how to intervene with the child (Davies, 2004).

Preparation 3: Educate About Trauma

Abuse is traumatic, as is exposure to frightening events where the child feels helpless and without protection. Once traumatized, children begin to reactively view their experiences through the lens of trauma. They are hypersensitive to situations that resemble the traumatic situation, and vigilantly scan the environment with the unconscious goal of avoiding future trauma. A therapist teaching a foster family about their traumatized foster daughter might say: "She doesn't see things the way most of us do. She's always looking for threats, and her fears are always there. That makes her see little

threats as big ones, and then she's got to do something to defend herself, either by becoming aggressive or withdrawing. A lot of the time,
it will be hard to tell what will set her off. To you, it may look like
here extreme behavior is coming out of the blue, but she is reacting
to her own thoughts or feelings connected to her past trauma."

As these issues are defined for them, most foster parents can
recall instances of the child's overreactions related to hyperarousal.
For example, Andrew's foster mother said, "My son has had to
learn that you can't tease or joke around with Andrew. Jimmy's a
sweet kid and doesn't tease in a mean way, but Andrew can't take
even a hint of teasing, and there were several times that he started
hitting my son."

It is also useful to discuss the major symptoms of trauma in
young children, particularly with reference to the symptomatic
behaviors the foster parents have observed. The therapist can be
guided by the Diagnostic Classification 0-3R (Zero to Three,
2005), which provides clear descriptions of PTSD symptoms in
young children. Andrew's foster parents noted, for example, that he
had trouble going to sleep and woke frequently in the middle of
the night. I discussed this behavior as symptomatic of hyperarousal, saying that Andrew's need to remain on guard made him
resist giving himself up to sleep and kept him from sleeping deeply.
I normalized, from the perspective of previous trauma, behavior
that the foster parents did not understand, offering a framework
for viewing it. I also suggested in the short run that they have different expectations for Andrew than they might for a nontrau-
matized child. Rather than expecting him to stay in his bed and
simply deal with his fears on his own, they should allow him to call
for them and go and comfort him physically. Throughout these
initial educational sessions, the therapist can offer hope that parent–child treatment and the foster parents' home interventions
will gradually reduce children's symptomatic behavior and
improve their relationship with the foster family.

Trauma education will continue as the child–parent sessions
proceed and the children reveal more details via play about their

pre-placement experiences. During treatment, the therapist will help foster parents understand the children's play and behavior, both during and out of sessions. For example, one child repeatedly had a dinosaur kill and eat small child figures. The foster parents found this raw play shocking and wondered if it proved the child's aggressive nature. The therapist said, "It's disturbing to watch this, but we know that he must have experienced his stepdad's beatings as if they were attacks by a monster. I know his play looks aggressive, but I think he's beginning to show us what was so frightening to him. As we learn about his perception of what happened to him, we can figure out how to help him feel more secure." The therapist's contextual statements and empathic support helped the foster parents tolerate their anxious reactions to the child's violent and seemingly hopeless play. Lieberman (2004) underscores the value of this stance in parent–child therapy for trauma: "The therapist serves as a mediator between the child's play and the parent's understanding of it, providing a steady presence that speaks for the legitimacy of the child's play as it moves through the inevitable periods of chaos." (p. 111)

Parent–Child Therapy

Parent–child sessions often help the foster parents understand the child better and relate to him or her in more adaptive ways, including in relation to the child's trauma symptoms. As the foster parents and the therapist learn together about the children's behavior and play, opportunities arise to clarify developmental questions, articulate the children's perspectives and experiences, and make connections between their current symptoms and their histories of trauma. The goals of this work include helping the foster parents take a view of the child that is at once more empathic and objective, helping the child experience the relationship with foster parents as understanding and supportive, and helping the child process the trauma.

Parent–child therapy with toddlers and preschoolers extends the principles of infant–parent psychotherapy developed by Selma

Fraiberg and her colleagues (Fraiberg, Adelson, & Shapiro, 1975). In this model, parents and infants are seen together and the therapist and parents watch, wonder about, and attempt to understand the baby's affects and behavior. The therapist may "speak for the baby," in order to help the parents see the world from the baby's perspective (Weatherston, 2002). When negative interactions have evolved between a parent and an infant, the therapist helps the parents think about how current stressors, the baby's characteristics, the history of their relationship with the baby, their working models of relationships, and their personal histories contribute to the interactional difficulties. The goal is to help parents see the baby realistically and empathically, and to separate the baby from projective, attributional biases informed by the parents' own histories.

In work with toddlers and preschoolers, developmental attachment theory continues to offer a rationale for parent–child therapy together, rather than seeing either the young child or parent alone (Lieberman, 2004; Lieberman & Zeanah, 1999) (see also Chapter 6, "The Case for Relational Therapy with Young Children in Foster Care"). A recent study of intervention with maltreated 3- and 4-year-olds demonstrated that parent–child therapy based on attachment theory was superior to a parent-only intervention focusing on teaching parenting skills. Young children treated in the parent–child therapy model showed more positive self-representations and more positive views of their parent over the course of intervention (Toth et al., 2002). From a developmental perspective, attachment-based treatment of toddlers and preschoolers is particularly timely. It can improve the parent–child relationship and alter the child's representational models of caregiving and of the self in a positive direction before the young child's working models have become stabilized (Davies, 2004).

Even though the 2- to 6- year-old child is developing an autonomous self, he or she continues to need the attachment relationship to provide a sense of protection and support. Difficulties in attachment are observable as the child interacts in therapy. An important contrast with infant work, however, is that toddlers and preschoolers, because of their advancing representational abilities, become more active participants in the therapy (Bennett & Davies, 1981; Lieberman, 1992).

Although young children may not be able to express complicated thoughts and feeling in words, they can increasingly represent their experiences, including traumatic events, through symbolic play and reenactment. The play of toddlers and preschoolers often provides a more complex story about their experience than they can describe in words. As early as ages 18–24 months, symbolic play and behavioral reenactments allow parents and therapists to learn about a child's perspective.

After age 18–20 months, children's developing language facility also becomes available for therapeutic uses. Words and narratives are increasingly used to understand and construct images of the world. By age 2-1/2, most children are well on the way to thinking in words rather than in imagery, and this continues to develop through the preschool age. Awareness of a young child's receptive language skills is important in conceptualizing parent–child treatment. The child's growing ability to understand the explanations of adults can be used to help the child process trauma. Language offers the traumatized young child a means of cognitively reorganizing the experience of trauma through narrative and clarification of cause and effect. The therapist and the parents can name the toddler's feelings and describe stressful experiences in simple terms so that the toddler is helped to make sense of them.

Parent–child therapy begins by orienting the child to the treatment situation. The therapist says to the young child, "We want to help you feel better about your worries and the scary things that happened before you came to live with your foster mom and dad. The way we learn about what scares kids is by playing." In early sessions, it is often striking how readily young children represent the trauma they've experienced through symbolic play or reenactment. For example, a 2-year-old had witnessed domestic violence many times. On one occasion, he and his mother had been showered by breaking glass when his father kicked in a door. In therapy, the child almost immediately presented that scene by repeatedly having the dinosaur break down a Lego door and bite the baby who was hiding on the other side. Another young boy reenacted his father's frightening actions of turning over furniture and throwing dishes against the wall by doing exactly the same thing in the clinic playroom.

These examples are common rather than exceptional. They demonstrate how quickly young children can understand the function of therapy, as well as how much they are motivated to gain mastery over their traumatization (Lieberman, 2004). Play allows the child to represent trauma with specificity. It allows the therapist and the foster parents to convey to the child that they understand what happened and how frightened the child was, and that they intend to protect him or her from new scary experiences.

However, foster parents may be taken aback by such startling behavior, especially because it appears so aggressive and raw. The therapist should point out that the play of young children is surprisingly transparent. The play should be described as reflecting the child's need to represent and master trauma. To counter the foster parents' anxiety that is aroused by the child's violent play, it is important to interpret it as a representation of what has frightened the child. When the boy described above threw dishes, and his mother confirmed that he had seen his father do the same thing, I said, "He's showing us what scared him. Frightening scenes like that stick in the mind of a kid. He's not being aggressive. His play tells us how scary it was to see those dishes crashing."

As treatment unfolds, "dialogues" between (a) the child's play and (b) the foster parents' and the therapist's words become the vehicle for processing the child's trauma experiences. For example, when the little boy repeatedly broke down the door with the dinosaur, his play representation helped his mother see beyond his symptomatic aggression to the fear and anxiety that were fueling it. The therapist and mother put words to the events and emotion expressed in his play: "It was so scary when daddy broke the glass. The glass hit you. Mom's not going to let daddy do that again."

Putting the story expressed in play into words helps the child begin to contain and master the trauma at a verbal level. Reassurance by the parents that they are aware of the child's fears and intend to act protectively is equally important (Davies, 1991).

As the children's play is interpreted to the foster parents, the children feel understood, and this encourages them to elaborate the experience of trauma. Often they will add new elements to their stories. It is especially important to attend to traumatized foster children's elaboration of play themes, because the children may begin to represent events that no one knows about (Davies, 2004).

In parent–child therapy, attention to play themes not only allows for more specific processing of trauma, but also can lead to significant changes in the relationship between the foster parents and the child. When young children enter foster care with people who are unaware of the traumas they have experienced, their sense of isolation from and mistrust of the new relationship may intensify. Effective parent–child therapy makes sense of children's current symptomatic behavior by clarifying its historical context. In the presence of the foster parents, the therapist facilitates connections between the children's current behavior and their pre-placement trauma histories. This helps the foster parents become more empathic towards these children and increases the chances that a mutual attachment can be established (Dozier et al., 2002).

Essentials of Trauma Treatment

I have alluded to a number of procedures in trauma treatment of young children. In this section I want to briefly make these approaches to trauma explicit. These principles are common to treatment of trauma in general and can easily be integrated into parent–child therapy.

Traumatized children—especially when the trauma is abuse by caregivers—usually were not helped by adults to process the experience verbally when it occurred (Fivush, 1998). Early intervention can interrupt the development of rigid adaptations to trauma. The children continue to live with intrusive trauma imagery after entering foster care. The experience of trauma may overpower their coping capacities and supplant thinking and words with raw and overwhelming affect. The sense of personal continuity and narrative memory are also severely disrupted, so that children's representations of traumatic events are imagistic and distorted rather than organized narratives. This is particularly likely when trauma has been chronic (Terr, 1991). Even if young children have clear memories of traumatic events, the fear associated with the traumatic memory causes them to suppress or avoid the memory. This often is accomplished through acting out behavior that is perplexing and disturbing to their new caregivers.

The main goals in the treatment of traumatized children are to help them develop a coherent narrative perspective on the traumatic experience—one that explicitly locates the trauma in the past—and to provide reassurance that they are protected from trauma in the present. A basic assumption of trauma treatment is that increasing a child's ability to make sense of stressful and traumatic events is an important protective and curative factor, which mitigates the impact of trauma. The therapist and the foster parents must collaborate to help the child create a trauma story that contains and reduces the affective power of the memories of traumsa.

Treatment procedures and goals with traumatized children include the following:

- *Help the child express what happened and help the child develop a coherent story.* Very often the play of traumatized children is disorganized and lacking in narrative. They simply repeat over and over an image of the traumatic events. It becomes the job of the therapist and the foster parents to help the child structure this seemingly chaotic play by interpreting it and casting it into a narrative. The narrative should clarify what happened, establish the sequence of cause and effect, and describe the child's affective reactions (Gil, 1991).

- *Process the traumatic experience, both cognitive and affectively,* by exploring the details of what occurred in the context of a safe relationship. Young children's play in sessions is often the best entry point for this process. Especially with young children, this work involves parent–child psychotherapy, with the parent being the primary provider of the safe relationship. Together the therapist and foster parent serve as chroniclers and interpreters of the trauma experience. Then the child can process the trauma from his or her current, more advanced, cognitive perspective. This takes advantage of the fact that egocentrism declines and objectivity improves as cognitive development proceeds. This is particularly important for the child who was very young at the time of the trauma (Salmon & Bryant, 2001).

• *Identify and correct trauma-based distortions in the child's thinking.* This is a particular concern in work with young children because of their cognitive immaturity, namely, egocentrism, magical thinking, personalism, and confusion of cause and effect. These cognitive traits likely perpetuate trauma symptoms and are based on misunderstandings about the child's role in the traumatizing event (Davies, 2004). For example, it is common for children to believe that, if an attachment figure abuses them, they must deserve to be abused. It is important to look for such distortions and explicitly counter them: "Kids think that if a grownup hurts them, it must be because it was their fault. But that's a mix-up. Really it's the grownup's fault. Because no grownup should hurt a kid, even if the kid does something the grownup doesn't like."

• *Locate the trauma in the past, while drawing a firm distinction between past and present.* "It was such a scary thing that happened. But it's already happened, and you're just remembering it. We won't let it happen again. Children worry that the bad thing could happen all over again, but we're going to keep you safe." The aim is to help the child think of the trauma as an incident or series of incidents in the narrative of the child's past life, and not a fearful lens for viewing the world at present.

- *Promote mastery and a sense of safety* by offering explicit suggestions for coping with fears: "Your (foster) mom understands how scared you were when your dad hurt you. She knows you still get scared sometimes. If you're feeling scared, you can come and tell her and she will be able to help you feel better."

Clinical Example

Andrew was removed from his mother and stepfather and entered foster care at age 3 years, 10 months. He began treatment at age 4 years, 2 months. His presenting symptoms included aggression towards peers in day care, sleep difficulties and nightmares, hiding/disappearing at home, subdued affect, and emotional distancing from his foster parents.

Precipitant for Removal

Andrew's stepfather punished him for misbehavior by holding onto his ankles and hanging him headfirst out a second-story window. A passerby heard Andrew's terrified crying, saw what was happening, and called the police. When the police arrived, they found that both parents were high on drugs and that Andrew had fresh bruises on his face and back. His 4-month-old infant sister appeared malnourished and lethargic. The police report, though sparse in details, did note that the officers could not find Andrew when they arrived, and that they discovered him wedged in a narrow space between the couch and the wall. The children's mother also had a black eye and bruises on her jaw. She acknowledged that the stepfather had been abusive to Andrew and her. She denied abusing the children. Both parents were arrested for crack cocaine possession. Andrew was placed in foster care. His sister was hospitalized for evaluation and subsequently placed in a separate foster home.

Early History

Andrew's early years were marked by parental substance abuse, chaotic and neglectful parenting, physical abuse, and witnessing of domestic violence. This spare enumeration of risk experiences does not do justice to what the daily texture of Andrew's life must have been like but, as in many cases of traumatized children removed to foster care, the details of his pre-placement life were not fully known. Since the parents did not follow through on treatment mandated by the reunification plan, we did not learn from them how long Andrew had been exposed to stressful and traumatizing circumstances, nor did we learn details of his developmental history. Protective Services did gain access to Andrew's hospital birth records. No father was listed. He had been born healthy following a normal, full term pregnancy, with no evidence of drugs in his system. Observations of his development based on his current functioning at age four suggested the following: Andrew's overall self-regulatory abilities were not seriously impaired, although he was easily aroused by stress; his language ability and ability to play symbolically were intact; he showed a capacity respond to warmth, especially from his foster mother. These observations allowed me to speculate that his mother's crack addiction had not begun until he was at least age two, because the relational, regulatory, and symbolic abilities that develop during the first two years were less compromised than would be expected if he had spent his entire life in a disorganized, traumatizing environment.

Treatment

After two preparatory sessions attended by both foster parents, once-weekly parent–child sessions began. Andrew's foster mother, Mrs. McGowan, attended all the sessions, while her husband came only occasionally because of his work schedule. Treatment lasted eight months. During this period, Andrew was entirely in the care of his foster parents, except for three half-days each week at day care while his foster mother worked part time. Andrew was the only foster child in their care. The McGowans were fairly new foster parents. They had fostered two children previously for short periods. Mrs. McGowan felt that caring for Andrew would be challenging, and she was eager to begin treatment. They had two children of their own, Jimmy, 10, and Allison, 12. I am selectively focusing the treatment themes on the issues of parent–child treatment of trauma and promotion of positive attachment.

In the first session I told Andrew that I knew he had been removed from his parents and taken to live with his foster parents so he'd be safe. I said, "I know your stepdad hurt you and scared you. Even though that isn't happening now, a kid can still feel worried and scared. Your foster parents and I want to help you feel better. Sometimes kids can show their feelings by playing."

Theme 1: Trauma representation

Andrew's initial play was not clearly representational, but did seem to reflect intense affect. He threw a ball against the wall many times. He also climbed on a chair and threw the ball hard to the floor with an angry expression on his face. He seemed caught up in the throwing and remote from his foster mother and me. Although the content of the play was unclear, its driven repetitiveness suggested posttraumatic play.

Partway through the session, when it appeared Andrew would keep throwing the ball endlessly, I asked his foster mother to play with him. Mrs. McGowan engaged him in building with blocks and his affect calmed. I told Andrew that I could see that his foster mother knew how to help him play in a way that was fun and not upsetting. In asking Mrs. McGowan to play with him, I had two aims:

- I wanted to help Andrew shift from aroused play to pleasurable or at least more affectively neutral play. It is important for the traumatized child to learn experientially that intense affects can be both expressed and contained in sessions. Specifically, I did not want Andrew to leave our session in a state of posttraumatic arousal, because that might cause him to associate treatment only with trauma and not with safety. This could lead to resistance and avoidance.

- I wanted to help Andrew begin to perceive Mrs. McGowan as someone who could help him regulate his affects and I wanted to help Mrs. McGowan feel competent in that role. My overall aim was to help them develop mutual strategies of regulation of affect and arousal.

In the next session, I attempted to help Andrew give clearer meaning to his play. I showed him the dollhouse and suggested that children could show worries and feelings with the doll people. Andrew ignored the people. But he began pushing furniture out of the windows of the house, and chairs and beds fell a few feet to the floor. Andrew looked at me with apprehension. I asked what was happening and he said anxiously, "It's falling down and cracking up." I said, "You're pretending they're cracking, but they're really not. It's OK for a kid to show his worries by pushing things out the window. But you know that your mom and I are here to keep you safe, and we won't let scary things really happen." Such clarifications of pretend and real are helpful to young traumatized children. Their limited ability to keep fantasy and reality delineated when they are affectively aroused requires us to make explicit distinctions between play representations and the reality of the current situation (Samuels & Taylor, 1994).

A moment later Andrew pushed one of the dolls out the window and then looked at me very anxiously. I said, "This scary play makes me remember that your stepdad held you out the window, and you thought you'd fall and crack up." Andrew looked frightened but did not respond. I said to Mrs. McGowan, "Andrew's showing us what scared him so much." She said, "Oh, Andrew, I'm so sorry that happened to you." Andrew resumed the play, making it more explicit by having a larger doll push the child doll out repeatedly. I said, "It's good you can show us that you thought you'd be dropped out the window. I know that other times your stepdad hit you. You were taken away from him and your real mom because kids have to be kept safe." I asked Mrs. McGowan to tell him the differences between her house and Andrew's old house. She said, "We don't hurt or scare you at our house. We're going to keep you safe." I asked her to pretend the dollhouse was her house and to show how she and her husband took care of children. While Andrew watched, she played out having the mother doll fix dinner for the children and then tuck them into bed.

In subsequent sessions, these themes were reprised and elaborated both in Andrew's play and our interventions. In addition to representing his stepfather's abuse, Andrew showed the father and mother hitting each other while the child hid in the closet. As these events were represented, I said, "I'm glad you can show us the scary things you remember. Those things happened before, when you were with your stepdad and mom, but they aren't happening now." At such times Mrs. McGowan would chime in reassurance that Andrew was safe and that she would not let hurting things happen at her house. Then she would play out rituals of caregiving with the dolls.

In the 10th session, after Mrs. McGowan had tucked all of the doll children into bed, Andrew picked up a child doll and dropped it out the window. I said this reminded me that children remember scary things when they're going to sleep and that they may dream about them too. I said, "Andrew, your mom told me that you've been having scary dreams. Dreams are not really happening. But they are a way that kids remember scary things that happened before." I pointed out that his foster mom helped him feel better when bad dreams woke him up. Mrs. McGowan creatively added a new element to the nighttime ritual. As she tucked the doll into bed she would say, "Now if you have a bad dream, call for me, and I'll come and help you feel better." She then generalized this behavior to the foster home. Mrs. McGowan and I discussed the value of reassuring Andrew of her availability to help with bad dreams when she tucked him in, and she integrated this into their actual nighttime routine.

Cognitive distortions are common in the aftermath of trauma. Young children who normatively think in egocentric and magical ways are particularly at risk for distortions that reflect misunderstandings of events and reversals of cause and effect.

As I labeled the stepfather's abuse as wrong, as something no grownup should do to a child, Andrew's play began to alternate between representing his stepfather's abuse and directing anger and punishment towards him. For example, Andrew would have the child doll push the father doll out the window. I said "The kid is so angry at the dad for hurting him, he wants to throw the dad out the window." Andrew continued to push the dad out, yelling, "You little prick, I'll teach you!" I asked what the child was teaching the dad, and Andrew said, "Because he wasn't supposed to drink his diet Coke." I said "Is that what happened before your stepdad held you out the window?" Andrew said, "I shouldn't do it." I clarified Andrew's apparent belief that he was responsible for what had happened to him. "Even if a kid drinks the diet Coke when he's not supposed to, that's not a reason for a grownup to hit a kid or hold him out the window. But a kid might think it was his own fault that he was being hurt and scared. But that's a mix-up, because it's really the grownup's fault. Because no grownup should do what your stepdad did. If a grownup does that, it's always the grownup's fault, even if the kid did something he shouldn't." I asked Mrs. McGowan what she would do if Andrew took something from the refrigerator without permission. She said, "Andrew, I'd tell you not to do it again, and if you did it again, you'd have sit down for while and think about what you did." I asked if she would ever hit Andrew in the face or hold him out the window, and she said with much feeling, "Andrew, I would never do that to you!"

Mrs. McGowan reported the next week that Andrew had tested her by taking bags of chips that his foster father packed in his lunches. Twice she made Andrew sit down in a time-out. It is important for foster parents to be aware that such testing may occur in response to issues that come up in treatment, and to see them as positive. The young child is misbehaving as an unconscious attempt to master previous trauma by repeating the precipitating incident, but without traumatic results.

Theme 2: Hiding

Early in treatment Andrew introduced the theme of hiding. Gradually, it became clear that hiding had been his only defense against abuse.

After we had begun to talk directly about his stepfather's abuse, Andrew asked to turn out lights so that he could hide. I said there weren't many places to hide in my office, and suggested he hide a little Fisher-Price figure while his foster mother and I pretended it was dark by closing our eyes. Andrew hid the figure and then began play that seemed unrelated to the theme of hiding. In the hiding play of 4- and 5-year-olds, children typically ask the adults to search for the hidden object. They then respond with pleasure, both when the adults are unable to find it and when they show them where it is. Such play often reflects themes of exerting power over the adult. It may also represent anxiety about separation, which is mastered by a reunion when the figure is found. Andrew, by contrast, hid the little figure and did not ask us to look for it. A ritual developed in which, early in each session, Andrew would say "Close your eyes, I have to hide my guy." At first I interpreted this behavior as reflecting self-reliance, and tried to suggest the possibility that his guy might feel better if someone could take care of him and help him feel safe. Andrew said "No, he likes to be by himself." During this period, Mrs. McGowan expressed frustration that Andrew begun to hide again at home for up to half an hour and would not respond to her increasingly worried calls to him.

Andrew's dollhouse play gradually helped us understand what "hiding" meant to him in the context of his experience in his family. He began to hide a little rubber baby in a closet, in the oven, under the bed, or under the mattress in the crib. When the baby was hidden, a much bigger dinosaur would search for him. Sometimes the dinosaur would find the baby and try to eat him and the baby would run away in terror. At other times the dinosaur could not find the baby and would go away. I began to summarize this play. "That baby is a good hider. It's his way of keeping himself safe from the monster. I think that might be what a kid does if a grownup gets mad at him and hurts him a lot. The kid tries to hide where the grownup can't find him, so he won't get hurt. I bet that's what you did, when you got worried your stepdad was going to hurt you or when he would hurt your mom." Mrs. McGowan said,

"I understand about hiding when you were at your old house. But you don't have to hide at our house, because nobody's going come after you and hurt you. I don't want you to hide unless you tell me you're going to, and then maybe we can play hide and seek."

Theme 3: Developing attachment

As treatment progressed, Andrew and Mrs. McGowan's attachment deepened and became increasingly adaptive. Mrs. McGowan's consistent responsiveness at home and her empathic understanding and reassurance in sessions helped Andrew begin to experience her as a reliable caregiver. Initially she reported that he often seemed withdrawn and uncommunicative. But this began to change as he developed positive attachment tendencies. This also became clear through some of his behaviors in day care.

Andrew was in placed in part-time childcare only a week after entering foster care. The staff described him as alternating between withdrawing from peers and being aggressive towards them. They also observed that he kept himself distant from adult caregivers and seemed to maintain a self-reliant and watchful stance. During the first three months Andrew showed no obvious resistance to going to day care. He would separate from his foster mother stoically. However, a few months later, after he had been in parent–child therapy for about three months and in foster care for five months, Andrew began to resist separation each morning. This was surprising to his foster mother and caregivers, because he had begun to seem more comfortable in day care and his aggression there had decreased.

In a parent–child session, I suggested that this new behavior might reflect his growing attachment. "We've been seeing that he's really begun to feel safer with you and to believe you'll help him if he's scared. So maybe now he wants to stay with you instead of going to day care." Andrew's foster mother asked him if he didn't want to go to day care because he wanted to stay with her. He did not respond directly, but said in baby talk, "No go center, no go." I said, "I can understand why you want to stay with your mom, because she takes good care of you. So maybe you'd rather stay with her." Andrew's removal from day care was neither desirable nor possible. Being in preschool carried some important benefits for Andrew's social development, and the foster mother wanted to keep her part-time job. I suggested some ways to ease his separation anxiety. Andrew's "preferred provider" could talk regularly with his foster mother, so that he could see they were allied on his behalf. He could bring a picture of himself and his foster mother to day care so that he could look at it when he was missing her. His foster mother could assure him each day that she would pick him up at the end of the day.

Andrew's separation anxiety was a positive sign of his developing attachment. As his confidence in the attachment grew, his hiding behavior in sessions underwent important transformations. He continued the ritual of hiding the figure, but then he would say to his foster mother "Let's find him" and he would give her hints where to look. He also began to hide himself. The places a four-year-old could hide in the treatment room were quite limited. But this was not important because now Andrew wanted to be found. He would laugh with pleasure when his foster mother found him behind a chair.

At the end of treatment, Andrew's symptoms were much less in evidence. His intrusive memories had diminished. He had fewer bad dreams, and his play in sessions was more flexible and imaginative and did not center on trauma themes. His day care teachers reported that he was playing more with other children and that he was much less aggressive. This suggested that Andrew's threshold for anxious arousal was higher now. He felt much more secure in his relationship with his foster parents. This was indicated by his ability to let them know when he was distressed and needed their understanding and comforting. Mr. and Mrs. McGowan felt much more confident in their ability to parent Andrew. They were ready to adopt him if, as seemed likely, the mother's rights were terminated. At the termination of our family therapy I suggested to the foster parents, as well as to the foster care worker, that traumatized children retain an ongoing vulnerability to stress. They may need to reprocess trauma as development proceeds. Therefore, it would be important to bring Andrew back for treatment if he became symptomatic. It is helpful to tell parents that more treatment may be needed in the future for a couple of different reasons— unexpected events may reactivate traumatic memories and affects, or the child may need to understand the experience from the perspective of a later developmental level.

Discussion

Parent–child therapy has two major goals: To provide direct treatment of the child's traumatization, and to enhance the relationship between the child and foster parents. These goals are realized in tandem when foster parents are able to empathize with and give words to the children's traumatic experiences as represented in play. With the help of a therapist, foster parents can put into words their understanding that specific frightening things have happened to the child, and they can then take a protective stance to reassure the child that those scary events will not be repeated in their relationship.

In Andrew's treatment, exploring a nodal traumatic event— being held out the window—became the basis for learning about other events that were emotionally and experientially similar for him. There undoubtedly were other abusive incidents that we did not know about and that Andrew did not represent in his play. However, Andrew's representation of an event that was known allowed his foster mother and me to help him develop a more generalized schema for processing posttraumatic affects and memories. We repeatedly responded to Andrew's play representations by acknowledging what had happened and how he had felt, making explicit distinctions between past and present realities, and offering reassurance that Mr. and Mrs. McGowan would keep him safe.

Engaging foster parents directly in trauma treatment may increase their investment in the child placed with them. By understanding the child's behavior in the context of the child's trauma history, foster parents may become more empathic and less likely to take negative behavior at face value or in a personal way. As foster children become aware that their foster parents empathize with their experiences and are able to act protectively, they become less mistrustful and less likely to act out because of hyperarousal. Such strengthening of the relationship and the foster parents' understanding of the child are likely to be strong preventatives against placement disruption while promoting the child's adaptive development.

References

Barnett, D., Ganiban, J., & Cicchetti, D. (1999). Maltreatment, negative expressivity, and the development of Type D attachments from 12 to 24 months of age. *Monographs of the Society for Research in Child Development 64*(3), 97–118.

Bennett, J. W., Jr., & Davies, D. (1981). Intervention and adaptation in the third year: The mother-child dialogue. *Journal of Child Psychotherapy, 7,* 19–32.

Cicchetti, D., & Rogosch, F. A. (2001). The impact of child maltreatment and psychopathology on neuroendocrine functioning. *Development and Psychopathology, 14,* 783–804.

Davies, D. (1991). Intervention with male toddlers who have witnessed parental violence. *Families in Society, 72,* 515–524.

Davies, D. (2004). *Child development: A practitioner's guide* (2nd ed.). New York: Guilford.

Denby, R., Rindfleisch, N., & Bean, G. (1999). Predictors of foster parents' satisfaction and intent to continue to foster. *Child Abuse and Neglect, 23,* 287–303.

Dozier, M., Albus, K., Fisher, P. A., & Sepulveda, S. (2002). Interventions for foster parents: Implications for developmental theory. *Development and Psychopathology, 14,* 843–860.

Fanshel, D., Finch, S. J., & Grundy, J. F. (1990). *Foster children in life course perspective.* New York: Columbia University Press.

Fivush, R. (1998). Children's recollections of traumatic and nontraumatic events. *Development and Psychopathology, 10,* 699–716.

Fraiberg, S., Adelson, E., & Shapiro, V. (1975). Ghosts in the nursery: A psychoanalytic approach to the problems of impaired mother–infant relationships. *Journal of the American Academy of Child Psychiatry, 14,* 387–421.

Gil, E. (1991). *The healing power of play.* New York: Guilford.

James, B. (1994). *Handbook for treatment of attachment–trauma problems in children.* New York: Lexington Books.

Klee, L., Kronstadt, D., & Zlotnick, C. (1997). Foster care's youngest: A preliminary report. *American Journal of Orthopsychiatry, 67,* 290–298.

Lieberman, A. F. (1992). Infant–parent psychotherapy with toddlers. *Development and Psychopathology, 4,* 559–574.

Lieberman, A. F. (2000). Negative maternal attributions: Effects on toddlers' sense of self. *Psychoanalytic Inquiry, 19,* 737–757.

Lieberman, A. F. (2004). Child–parent psychotherapy: A relationship-based approach to the treatment of mental health disorders in infancy and early childhood. In A. J. Sameroff, S. C. McDonough, & K. L. Rosenblum (Eds.), *Treating parent-infant relationship problems: Strategies for intervention* (pp. 97–122). New York: Guilford.

Lieberman, A. F., & Zeanah, C. H. (1999) Contributions of attachment theory to infant–parent psychotherapy and other interventions with infants and young children. In J. Cassidy & P. R. Shaver (Eds.), *Handbook of attachment: Theory, research, and clinical applications* (pp. 555–574). New York: Guilford.

Maluccio, A. N., & Ainsworth, F. (2003). Drug use by parents: A challenge for family reunification practice. *Children and Youth Services Review, 25,* 511–533.

Newton, R. R., Litrownik, A. J., & Landsverk, J. A. (2000). Children and youth in foster care: Disentangling the relationship between problem behaviors and number of placements. *Child Abuse and Neglect, 24,* 1363–1374.

O'Neill, R. E., Horner, R. H., Albin, R. W., Storey, K., & Sprague, J. R. (1996). *Functional assessment and program development for problem behavior: A practical handbook.* Belmont, CA: Wadsworth.

Perry, B. D. (2002). Neurodevelopmental impact of violence in childhood. In D. H. Schetky & E. P. Benedek (Eds.), *Principles and practice of child and adolescent forensic psychiatry* (pp. 191–203). Washington, DC: American Psychiatric Publishing.

Samuels, A., & Taylor, M. (1994). Children's ability to distinguish fantasy events from real life events. *British Journal of Developmental Psychology, 12,* 417–427.

Salmon, K., & Bryant, R. (2001). Posttraumatic stress disorder in children: The influence of developmental factors. *Clinical Psychology Review, 22,* 163–188.

Scheeringa, M. S., & Zeanah, C. H. (2001). A relational perspective on PTSD in early childhood. *Journal of Traumatic Stress, 14,* 799–815.

Terr, L. (1991). Childhood traumas: An outline and an overview. *American Journal of Psychiatry, 148,* 10–20.

Thomas, J. M., & Guskin, K. A. (2001). Disruptive behavior in young children: What does it mean? *Journal of the American Academy of Child and Adolescent Psychiatry, 40,* 44–51.

Toth, S. L., Maughan, A., Manly, J. T., Spagnola, M., & Cicchetti, D. (2002). The relative efficacy of two interventions in altering maltreated preschool children's representational models: Implications for attachment theory. *Development and Psychopathology 14,* 877–908.

Weatherston, D. J. (2002). Introduction to the infant mental health program. In J. J. Shirilla & D. J. Weatherston (Eds.), *Case studies in infant mental health: Risk, resiliency, and relationships* (pp. 1–14). Washington, DC: Zero to Three.

Zero to Three (2005). *Diagnostic classification 0-3: Diagnostic classification of mental health and developmental disorders of infancy and early childhood* (revised ed.). Washington, DC: Author.

8

Providing
Developmentally Appropriate
Family Therapy

Lenore M. McWey and Patricia D. Donovan

Foster children have different needs and capacities at different developmental stages, as do their parents and foster families. This chapter describes the special needs of infants, toddlers, preschoolers, early elementary and middle childhood children, and early-, middle-, and late adolescents. We then discuss how to use relational therapy to create a milieu that meets these needs. Other chapters give clinical examples of families with younger children. This chapter will focus on middle adolescents.

Developmental theories and ideas about interventions can be integrated to form treatment plans that are specific for individuals and families, and are based on their abilities and needs (Cohen, 1995; Myers, Shoffner, & Briggs, 2002). Specifically, therapy should reflect a current understanding of child development and the developmentally appropriate approaches that can facilitate change (Cohen, 1995). However, because foster children exist in environments heavily influenced by the significant adults in their lives, we also need to consider the developmental levels of these adults. Just like with children, the developmental levels of the adults determine their abilities and what is important to them (Erikson, 1993). Our treatment plans need to be developmentally appropriate if they are

to adequately provide nurture, engage all parties, facilitate beneficial growth for all of these people, and thereby optimize treatment
outcomes (Lee & Lynch, 1998).

The Developmental Paths of Children

Regardless of age, all children have the same basic needs. Above
being fed, clothed, and sheltered, they need to feel loved and valued, believe that they are protected from harm, and be given
opportunities to grow physically and emotionally. Beyond these
universal needs, children have specific developmental needs, and
our interventions should reflect an awareness of them all. For
example, our interventions should reflect a current understanding
of development across the life span, developmental psychopathology, and potential approaches to altering behavior and facilitating
development (Kazdin, 1987, 1988; Kendall & Morris, 1991).

Attachment Theory and the Development of Children

The quality of children's bonds to their parents has been related to
their subsequent ability to attach to others. If a child with an insecure attachment experiences more rejection with time, the possibility for that child to form secure attachments to others becomes
less and less likely (Bowlby, 1977; Weinfield, Sroufe, & Egeland,
2000). Attachment theorists assert that infants organize lessons
learned about their primary caretakers' responsiveness in the form
of internal working models (Bowlby, 1980). These models include
expectations about the predictability of the caregivers' responsiveness and the infants' own ability to elicit reactions (Bretherton &
Munholland, 1999). These models then become templates by
which the children construct expectations in other relationships.

What infants learn about people and the world in infancy
becomes the lens through which the rest of their lives are viewed
and a primary determinant of how they will interact with significant others. This sometimes becomes a self-fulfilling prophecy.
Infants who expect caretakers to be appropriately nurturing and
who experience their world as secure tend to act in ways that their

significant others like. In contrast, children who expect disappointment typically engage in negative attention seeking. They are stand-offish, irritable, or ambivalent, and their significant others probably react to them accordingly.

This idea is central to understanding and planning for the foster children in your care. A number of studies have demonstrated that maltreated children exhibit insecure attachment styles (Crittenden, 1988; Egeland & Sroufe, 1981; Finzi, Ram, Har-Even, Shnit, & Weizman, 2001; McCarthy & Taylor, 1999; McWey, 2004; McWey & Mullis, 2004; Wekerle & Wolfe; 1998). Their attachment style may depend on whether the children were neglected, abused, or both (Finzi et al., 2001). Neglected children often are anxious in their attachment to others, whereas abused children may be more avoidant (see also Crittenden, 1988; Egeland & Sroufe, 1981; McWey, 2004; Wekerle & Wolfe, 1998). How these maltreated children have learned to interact with their caretakers may very well determine how the children act once they are in foster care (Cantos, Gries, & Slis, 1997; Marcus, 1991). Foster children with secure attachments typically do not act out (Marcus, 1991) and are generally better adjusted in their foster placements (Cantos et al., 1997). In contrast, children with insecure attachments often are socially withdrawn, mistrustful, oppositional, and have low self-esteem (Cantos et al., 1997; Finzi et al., 2001). Insights into the attachments of foster children and the self-protective strategies used by them are described in Chapter 10, "Kinship Placements: An Integrative Approach."

Age Specific Developmental Concepts

Although attachment is one way of looking at developmental patterns of children involved in the foster care system, there are age-specific developmental expectations that also may be useful. It is quite likely that children in foster care are not at the level of their chronological peers—the normative expectations listed below—and they may require specialized treatment. You need to consider the capacities and orientations of your unique clients as you create treatment plans for them and their families. The following descriptions of developmental stages introduce some of the main issues to consider for children of various ages (for example, see Berk, 1997; Davies, 2004; Papalia, Olds, & Feldman, 2004).

Infancy (Birth–2 Years)

In the first few weeks of life and beyond, babies learn vast amounts of information. Babies explore their environment by reflexively using their arms, legs, hands, feet, and mouths. Then, around the fourth month of life, they begin to learn how to reproduce desired outcomes originally discovered by chance. Babies will soon learn, for example, that kicking their legs at the toy on the side of the crib produces music. Babies build on this learning throughout the first year of life so that by the end of the 18th month, they have relatively sophisticated plans of action in order to accomplish tasks. At this age they have typically learned several ways to try to get a toy that they can see.

Infants learn to adapt quickly to their environment in the first months of life, and they begin to experience their world emotionally as well. Soon after birth, babies show contentment, interest, and distress. In the next six months, babies also develop the ability to show joy, surprise, sadness, disgust, anger, and fear. The ability to show these emotions is either helped or hindered by the child's own temperament, which is largely influenced by heredity.

One of the major issues faced by children in their first months and years is developing trust (Bowlby, 1977, 1980; Erikson, 1993). From the beginning, infants gain a sense of reliability in the people in their world. Children who cry when hungry soon learn whether or not their caretakers will respond to cries in a timely and appropriate way. Attachments to caregivers develop and they lay the foundation for how children will relate to others over their lifetimes. Once children have reached their second birthday, their developmental focus typically shifts from exploring the external world to exploring their internal world of cognition and emotion.

Toddlers (2–4 Years Old)

Children in this age group are walking and actively exploring their environments, using the people to whom they are most attached as a secure base (Sroufe, 1979). At this point in their development, children typically use symbols to represent people, places, and events. As they face challenges, toddlers also develop a "balance of independence and self-sufficiency over shame and doubt" (Papalia et al., 2004, p. 26). Using these benchmarks, it is important to note what a toddler is capable of and more importantly how a child expresses him- or herself.

Play is the language of children. Toddlers' play is best described as constructive play, where objects or materials are used to create something (Papalia et al., 2004). Four-year-olds in preschools or day-care centers may spend more than half their time in this kind of play (Johnson, 1998). Children in this age group will use play to construct their world, and this will often reflect their understanding of their roles and relationships. Observation of toddlers at play will show beginning understanding of his or her self-concept, which is "a cognitive construction … a system of descriptive and evaluative representations about the self" (Harter, 1996, p. 207). The children begin to incorporate how others see them into their growing self image and can begin to express emotional understanding as well.

Children's emotions also begin to fully develop in the preschool years, and are shaped by family relationships. Preschoolers can talk about their emotions and can often discern the feelings of others. They have a harder time recognizing emotions that are self-directed, like pride and shame. Although children in this development stage are able to understand that others have emotions, they are not yet able to see things through another's point of view. Egocentrism is heavily present in these younger children. However, as children are exposed to others and gain an understanding of other people's thoughts and emotions, empathy begins to develop. These changes in worldview help prepare children for the next major milestone in their lives, entrance into formal education.

Early School Age (5–7 Years Old)

When children enter school, many things begin to change for them in their environment, in others' expectations of them, and in their own cognitive and emotional processes. Early school-age children build on their representational ability that has been developing over the last few years. These children gain the ability of an autobiographical memory, a process that begins around age four and continues through age eight. Autobiographical memory refers to specific and long-lasting memories that form a person's life history. These children are able to tell their own stories of their lives. They use this information, as well as input that they get from others, to develop their self-concept. During this time, children begin to explore their individual worlds and their personalities become visible. However, these are also tenuous years. Negative input from the children's environment, as well as early trauma, can have devastating effects on their self-concepts and their ability to have a full understanding of their own memories.

Children in the early school years continue to use play as both a recreational activity and as a way to express themselves and process their worlds; however, entering school has a major impact on how children play. Children move from using pretend play in preschool to playing games with formal rules in the early part of elementary school. Traditional models of education reinforce this learning process by instructing children that there are right and wrong ways to play. This inchoate morality begins to show itself in other areas of the child's life. Children are now more conscious of rules and fairness in regard to their peers and family, and will carry this awareness into the next developmental stage, where logic will play a large part in their cognitive abilities.

Middle and Late Childhood (8–11 Years Old)

Children in this age group have reached another milestone in their cognitive development. They now should have the ability to solve problems logically, use rudimentary inductive and deductive reasoning, and have a clearer understanding of cause and effect. They also can perform simple mathematical problems.

Children's social skills and their ability to have conversations with others will more fully develop during this time period. You can imagine the difference this makes in your work with them! The youngest children of this period will typically respond with only a few words when asked questions, but somewhat older children will often greatly expand on the details of their stories. The oldest children will be able to offer detailed descriptions of people, places, and events and engage in causal thinking (Myers et al., 2002).

As children improve their ability to provide detailed descriptions, their capacity to tell accurate stories about themselves also improves. Many can see their own strengths and weaknesses and make accurate statements about themselves. For example, a child in this stage will be able to tell someone that he or she is really good at writing and math, but not very good at science.

The challenges of this life period can be very influential on children's self-concepts and how they see themselves in relation to others. This is the time when children typically are expected to learn the skills of their culture in order to thrive in society. However, they also struggle with feelings of incompetence while they try to master these expected skills.

At this stage children typically develop a more sophisticated sense of moral reasoning. You probably will see it reflected in their decisionmaking ability. It is better illustrated than described: for example, imagine that a child is asked to watch two short video clips. The first child in the video is seen sneaking a cookie and breaking the cookie jar, which costs $25.00. The second clip shows a child dusting the living room—the child then bumps and breaks a $100 vase. The child watching the videos is then asked who is in more trouble. Children younger than 7 years old will often state that the child who broke the vase should be in more trouble because what she broke costs more. Older children will see that the child who broke the cookie jar was doing something sneaky and should be punished more than the child who is helping her parents by dusting. Immature moral judgments center only on the degree of the offense, while more mature judgments consider intent. As children learn more about consequences of their own actions they not only develop an understanding of intent but also a greater sense of equity, and are able to take specific circumstances into account. A child of 11 might say that a 10-year-old child who broke a cookie jar should know better and be held to a higher standard than a 4-year-old who did the same thing. This heightened sense of morality will help carry children into adolescence where they will be expected to make increasingly tougher moral choices.

Early Adolescence (12–15 Years Old)

Adolescence is generally considered to begin with puberty—the process that leads to sexual maturity. Puberty causes many changes in children's bodies and their hormonal fluctuations can wreak havoc with their emotions. Cognitive changes also are happening, but they are overshadowed by the more radical physical changes. In early adolescence, the capacity for abstract thought typically develops and solidifies. Adolescents increasingly are able to describe their own feelings and can sometimes describe their patterns of feelings (Myers et al., 2002). This is a very important trait for those of us who work with these children. Once patterns are identified, our adolescent clients may be presented with the choice to either continue in the identified pattern or to make a change (Sweeney, 1998).

Early adolescence also is the time in which young people are struggling with the questions of "Who am I?" and "What is my place in society?" Constructing an identity involves defining who you are, what you value, and the directions you choose to pursue in life. Adolescents begin to understand the consequences of choices. This is both exciting and confusing. Adolescence also brings about the emergence of autonomy, where young people establish themselves as separate, self-governing individuals. Autonomy has both an emotional component, which allows for a stronger reliance on oneself and less reliance on parents for support and guidance, and a behavioral component, which involves making decisions independently by carefully weighing one's own judgment and the suggestions of others to reach an informed decision. However, as you well know, peers have a great influence on how adolescents behave. What friends may think of a particular decision weighs heavily on adolescent minds. Early adolescents are more likely than younger children to give in to peer pressure (Brown, Clasen, & Eichler, 1986). But older adolescents continue with this struggle throughout their teenage years and well into adulthood.

Late Adolescence (16–18 Years Old)

Older teenagers continue to expand their capacities for abstract thinking and struggle with issues of identity and autonomy. They are also redefining their relationships with their parents. Adolescents who have explored and committed to an identity will often experience better overall communication and more of an open relationship with their parents (Bhushan & Shirali, 1992). Unfortunately, adolescents often have trouble finding their identity and this can cause problems in their families and peer relationships.

Beginning in early adolescence, children develop stronger peer relationships as a way of letting go of their parents and developing their identities. During this stage, peer relationships become more cooperative, and peer groups and cliques become more tightly knit and exclusive. These peer relationships can be positive influences on a adolescent's self-esteem and can help develop a sense of belonging— or they can have negative effects. As teenagers grow into their later adolescence, they are confronted with choices like whether or not to drink, smoke, do drugs, and have sex. In the United States, despite recent declines, teenage alcohol and drug use is more per-vasive than in any other industrialized nation (Newcomb & Bentler, 1989). The poor decisionmaking associated with the use of drugs makes this a very dangerous time for these children.

Virtually all theorists agree that adolescence is an especially important time for the development of sexuality. Adolescents typ-ically are very concerned about how they manage sexuality in social relationships. It also is during this time that differences in sexual orientation become evident. Adolescents who are coming to terms with their homosexuality often face a profound sense of isolation and loneliness because of pressure from both parents and friends to date heterosexually. Family rejection and social stigma contribute to high rates of psychological distress and problem behaviors among homosexual teenagers, including depression, suicide, substance abuse, and high-risk sexual behaviors (Baumrind, 1995; Hershberger & D'Augelli, 1995).

High-risk sexual behaviors—both in GLBTQ and heterosexual teens—can lead to exposure to sexually transmitted diseases. According to the Centers for Disease Control and Prevention, 2002 gonorrhea rates among 15- to 19-year-olds were estimated at 476.4 per 100,000 population; 834,555 women had chlamydia; and 45,599 individuals under the age of 24 were diagnosed with AIDS. Teenagers engaging in unsafe heterosexual sex also risk pregnancy. According to the U.S. Department of Health and Human Services (2002), about 900,000 pregnancies occur each year among American teenagers aged 15–19.

While it may not seem like it, parents have a great deal of influence over the choices their adolescents make (Sebald, 1986). This makes it that much more important that parents understand the developmental aspects of their children's growth, the struggles their children are facing, and the influence of parental guidance.

Adult and Family Development

Understanding the stages of child development is essential in working with children. However, the adults in their lives and in their families also go through developmental changes that determine what may be most important to them at any one time, and what personal and social adaptive resources they may have. When we are talking about the developmental progress of adults, two things are different than when we describe the growth of children. First, we can describe the developmental stages that children go through separately from that of their families. No matter what family they are in, children typically go through the same steps of biological, psychological, and social growth. This may be colored somewhat by their religious and ethnic subcultures, but generally all children are seen as traveling a single developmental path. In contrast, the stages that adults and families go through are hard to describe separately. Second, a number of influences—poverty, mental and physical illness, divorce, remarriage, death, religious and ethnic subcultures—determine whether adult individuals go through a few or all of same stages (see the discussions in Falicov, 1991).

The stages that adults go through are typically described in terms of their relationships: Becoming a self-sufficient individual, getting married (or cohabiting), having children, dealing with family matters when the children go off to school and when they reach adolescence, adjusting to the last child leaving the nest and, perhaps, navigating through retirement and the deaths of partners. If we think about our dealings with our nuclear client families— mother, father, and children—only the first three of these stages seem important. But if you consider the children's entire custodial environment, including their extended birth- and stepfamilies, then all of these stages need to be considered. The illustrations given in Chapter 2, "An Ecosystemic Approach to Foster Care," indicate how important diverse kin can be to the successful resolution of a case.

Consideration of these adult stages is very important to your treatment planning. For example, what does it mean if a father or mother has not yet adequately separated emotionally from his or her family of origin? Or if he or she has not yet acquired the capacity to be self-sufficient in more tangible ways? Similarly, what if the parents have not yet been able to find a way to move from self-sufficient adulthood into the challenges and tasks of married life— that is, share, resolve conflicts, arrive at a division of labor satisfactory to each, and make mutual decisions about resources? Then, if two adults are in a household and are able to live together successfully, can they move from their couple-centered relationship into a child-centered one? As we think about the various families we meet in the foster care system, we can think of many adults who—despite living together and having children—have not yet come to terms with the financial and psychological aspects of committed relatedness or accepted the importance of the needs of children in the household.

When we think in terms of developmental "stages," the implication is that these parents will not be successful at any stage until they have accomplished what is required psychologically and socially in the preceding stages. How can a father be a good husband or, indeed, something other than a sperm donor, until he has become psychologically and socially self-sufficient and is emotionally invested in his relationship with partner and children? Taking all this into consideration, it is important, when working with families, to identify which stage the family is currently in, as well as which developmental tasks they have completed. Gaps and delays may need to be resolved, in order for the family to move on to the next stage of development.

Having said all this, we admit that these stage models are an oversimplification of what we know about people, how they grow, and what is important to them, relative to their resources. In the past, researchers have attempted to track the personality development of adults with several longitudinal studies (Bengtson & Schaie, 1999; Helson & Wink, 1992; Neugarten, 1964), in which cohorts of adults were studied to track changes experienced by the groups. Tracking people as they age is an interesting way to learn about adult development. But it is important to recognize that just because people are the same age chronologically, they may not be experiencing the same developmental changes at the same rate. Context is extremely important when looking at the development of adults.

And the importance of historical events that shape social expectations and influence how individuals move through their life spans cannot be overlooked. A group of people who lived through the Great Depression will have most likely developed at a different rate, and value different things, than those who were coming into adulthood during the late 1960s or even 1980s. Gender is also an important component of adult development. Many of the stage theories of adult development focus on career choice and work achievement, which have historically been male-dominated arenas (Santrock, 2002). Where do women fit in these theories of development? Stage theories also have often been criticized for assuming that there is a normative sequence of development and that everyone must go through every stage in a certain order. This becomes problematic when women, who were once at home with their children, are now re-entering the workforce or going back to school in order to start on a new career.

One approach—one that allows for the influence of different kinds of families and the complex roles of both men and women in modern society—is to emphasize the role of life-events as contributors to an individual's adult development (Santrock, 2002). This view emphasizes that the influence of events on a person's development depends not only on the life event itself, but also on mediating factors (physical health, family support, etc.), the individual's adaptation to the life event, the life-stage context, and the sociohistorical context. In this model, there are a number of factors that contribute to the impact of any one event on a person's life and therefore his or her development. When working with adults, it is important to assess their perspective of the impact of stressful events on their lives, rather than make assumptions about it.

Despite this complexity, which may make such considerations overwhelming, it is important for us to include developmental assessment of all of the adults in the custodial environment, as well as the children. Only in this way can we create developmentally appropriate treatment plans and therapy.

Treatment Considerations

Many experts consider clinical work with families involved in the foster care system to be virtually incomparable to work that occurs with more "traditional" families (Crenshaw & Barnum, 2001). Nevertheless, if we are going to intervene in a way that increases the health of the social systems of which our child clients are a living part, we need to do family therapy. To do this effectively we must take into consideration the family context, as well as the abilities of the children and parents, including their capacities to understand themselves and to understand the process of what we are trying to do (Kazdin, 2003).

Capacities to Mutually Participate

All of the family members need to be ready for our intervention. They need to be able to understand their circumstances, recognize specific problems and strengths, appreciate what needs to be accomplished, and be capable and willing to use the help provided. This may be complicated. Your children and their parents may be inhibited by developmental deficiencies, avoidant and anxious relatedness, and conflicting agendas. The parents also may be distracted by competing personal and/or court-mandated goals, for example, self-sufficiency, relational health with their adult partners, and sobriety, to name a few (see the stage-wise approach to relational therapy with birth families in Chapter 2, "An Ecosystemic Approach to Foster Care").

As you craft your treatment plans, you should maximize interventions that are comprehensible by each member of the family at his or her level of cognitive and emotional development. For example, everyone's language, questions, and explanations should be kept simple. One way to accomplish this is to use nontalking therapies, such as family play therapy (see Chapter 11, "Creative Ways to Strengthen Family Bonds").

However, when therapists have opportunities to work with at-risk families, there are a number of things to consider besides developmental theories. It is important to remember that each child's experience of abuse is unique (Gil, 1991, 1996; Whiting & Lee, 2003). For example, in cases of abuse there may be a temptation for therapists to use "yardsticks," such as the type, duration, or severity of the abuse, to judge the impact that the trauma will have upon a child (Gil, 1991). But children react differently. What impacts one child may not impact another in the same way, even if the children are the same age and operating at the same developmental level. Therefore, it is important to understand each child individually and to provide each a voice (Whiting & Lee, 2003; see also Chapter 4, "The Perspective of the Consumer: Foster Children Tell Us What They Need").

Limitations on Your Therapy

Before agreeing to conduct therapy with abusive families, it is important to assess at what point family therapy is appropriate, what the gender of the therapist should be, and what limitations are to be placed on the therapy itself. Many suggest that in cases of sexual abuse, concurrent therapy replace conjoint therapy (for example, see Bentovim, 2004; Hildebrand, 1988; Hooper, 1992). Consider, for instance, a family where there have been recent allegations of sexual abuse committed by a father upon his adolescent daughter. Conducting family therapy at the beginning of the investigative process may jeopardize the investigation, may cause even more trauma to the child, and may be counterproductive to positive therapeutic outcome. Before therapy begins, therapists should weigh the impact the abuse has had on the child, the family's level of dysfunction, the age and developmental stage of the child, and the child's relationship to the offender (Gil, 1991).

Another aspect to consider is the gender of the therapist. Children who have experienced abuse may have idiosyncratic responses to persons of the same gender as their perpetrators (Gil, 1991). In such instances, all that might be needed is an awareness of the potential impact gender may have upon treatment. However, in other situations, where there are strong reactions, it might be appropriate to consider transferring a case. You also could offer co-therapy as a means of providing a safe opportunity for the child to experience a positive relationship with a member of the gender by whom they were abused.

Treatment for families involved in the foster care system is multidimensional. It involves individuals, parent–child dyads, families, and groups, all delivered within the context of the social service and legal systems (Gil, 1991; Lee & Lynch, 1998). The involvement of every aspect of the system is needed for successful treatment outcomes. Yet, the multidimensional aspect of treatment can also provide unique limits on the therapeutic relationship. Specifically, when working with families involved in the foster care system, it is important to clearly identify limits of confidentiality and issues surrounding communication with social services agencies. Many of the families you are seeing are ordered by the court to receive treatment. Therefore, your client may not only be the family, but also the social services agency (Bentovim, 2004). No doubt you have already been made unpleasantly aware of the conflicts attached to your dual roles. The only way to establish effective therapeutic relationships with families and agencies involved in the foster care system is to be very overt about to whom you will disclose what information and when. If everyone involved in your case cannot reach agreement, it is unlikely that optimal relational therapy can be accomplished.

Goal Setting

One critique of much of the therapeutic services provided to at-risk families is that both the treatment and treatment goals are mandated by social services agencies. This is thought to create a "negative contextual framework of coercion in family work" (Bentovim, 2004, p. 124). Therefore, it may be valuable to begin your family therapy by assessing issues of motivation. You can ask questions such as "What do you think needs to change before social services feels comfortable with you regaining custody of your children?" The probability of successful treatment outcomes is heightened when, early in your relationship, the family as a system becomes co-responsible with you for the treatment goals and is actively involved in shaping and assessing the treatment process.

It is also important to set realistic goals for families based on their level of functioning (Gil, 1991). The goal of treatment should be to provide "corrective and reparative experiences" for children and their families, and to "demonstrate through intervention the potentially rewarding nature of human interaction" (Gil, 1991, p. 52). Some (for example, see Lee & Lynch, 1998) have advocated for structural goals, where issues such as parentification, triangulation, or scapegoating are addressed. Structural goals are important and often isomorphic to what is happening at the larger system level (Colapinto, 1995; Lee & Lynch, 1998). Helping families recognize patterns and themes may be one way to alter not only family systems, but the ways in which they interact with larger systems as well.

Assessing Treatment Progress

Treatment plans should not focus solely on symptoms. Of course, there is a wealth of research demonstrating the behavioral problems manifested by children involved in the foster care system (for example, see Dozier, Albus, Fisher, & Sepulveda, 2002; Harman, Childs, & Kelleher, 2000; Kaplan, Pelcovitz, & Labruna, 1999), but these behaviors must be considered in context (Kazdin, 2003). Simply because a symptom has diminished does not mean that there is no longer a need for therapy. We should not focus solely on parental behaviors either. Although abusive behaviors may have ceased, it is important to directly address those factors that led to the maltreatment. They may still have toxic potential. For example, if stress was a probable factor that led a mother to physically abuse her son, it would be important not only to ensure that the physical abuse cease, but that she also have coping strategies in place to manage the stress she experiences. It is crucial that we assess our parents' abilities to cope with outside stressors. In doing so, we need to assess parents' physical, emotional, and cognitive development, as well as personality factors which might lead to increased risk for children in their homes.

There may be specific factors that are predictive of outcomes for at-risk families (Bentovim, 2004). One such factor is parental acceptance of responsibility for the abuse or neglect. If parents deny responsibility for what has occurred, or if they minimize the impact of their actions upon the family system, the prognosis for the family may be poor. Accepting responsibility means that parents understand the origins and the process of the abuse and the negative impact their actions have had on their children. Treatment may not be over until the parents are able and willing to do that.

Family Play Therapy

One critique of family therapy with young children is that it often involves the therapist and parents engaged in conversation while the children play with toys in a corner of the therapy room (see Chapter 6, "The Case for Relational Therapy with Young Children in Foster Care"; also see Gil, 1991; Scharff & Scharff, 1987). In contrast, family play therapy is a means of involving the whole family in treatment (see Chapter 11, "Creative Ways to Strengthen Family Bonds"). Since play is the language of children, family play therapy can provide a voice for younger children within the family system. Helping children express their emotions not only can provide understanding, but also can facilitate healing. Children in foster care who have their feelings ignored may discount their own feelings and experiences (Whiting & Lee, 2003). Thus, it is therapeutic for children to have their voices heard, particularly children who have experienced abuse or neglect (Gil, 1991; Whiting, 2000). Family play therapy is a means to facilitate that expression. Children can symbolically depict people, places, and events in their play.

Family play therapy gives each family member an opportunity to engage in constructive play. This provides two areas of intervention. We can work with how the family members interact as they play or don't play together. We also can explore what the individuals may be saying about their family, their situation, and their hopes through their creations.

It is difficult to conduct family play therapy with children under the age of two. However, any decisions about treatment should be based on the individual development of the children at hand (Gil, 1991; Ruble, 1999). In fact, some older maltreated children have lost or have not developed the ability to engage in symbolic forms of play (Davies, 2004). You may have to teach some children how to "do" symbolic play and encourage its expression in others.

However, if you decide that family play therapy is a good idea for your client family, a cache of age-appropriate toys, puppets, and drawing materials is important.

Traditional Family Therapy

Although family play therapy can be a useful supplement to any treatment plan, older children might appreciate the various forms of traditional ("talking") family therapy. Older children are likely to be operating from a higher level of cognitive development and they can more readily engage in therapeutic interventions that ask them to observe themselves in interaction with others and to describe what they see, think, and feel. This is especially true of adolescents, since most are capable of abstract thought and can describe their own feelings (Myers et al., 2002).

Developmentally Appropriate Treatment of Attachment Issues

Attachment theory may be a useful guide for developmentally appropriate family therapy for children and parents involved in the foster care system (Bentovim, 2004; Dozier, 1990; McWey, 2004). A developmentally appropriate, attachment-based model provides a way to interpret the behaviors exhibited by children and the parental responses to them.

When the children range from infancy to age four you see the parents together with their children and you look at each parent's relationship to the individual children (Leiberman, 2003). You provide developmental guidance to the parents and work with them on ways to respond to the expressed needs of their young children (see Chapter 18, "Teaching Developmentally Appropriate Parenting"). Studies (for example, see van Ijzendoorn, Juffer, & Duyvesteyn, 1995) have shown that increasing parental sensitivity through psychoeducation, modeling, support, and recognition of the parents' own attachment history and internal working models can positively influence the parent–child attachment.

When the child is approximately age five, you will want to focus more directly and overtly on the overall insecurity and lack of trust in the parent–child relatedness (Leiberman, 2003). This is the age at which parents complain most about children's perceived misbehavior, so you will also need to address that. When the children are acting up, you can profitably explore what their parents might be doing in response that is exacerbating the children's misbehavior (Keiley & Seery, 2001; Leiberman, 2003). Many parents overlook or misinterpret what their children are expressing in their behavior. They then respond in ways that reinforce attachment injuries; namely, they yell at or hit the children. Therapy that uses both concrete developmental guidance for parents and attachment-based treatment can be very effective (Keiley & Seery, 2001; Leiberman, 2003). Some would argue that attachment-based therapy, combined with psychoeducation regarding child development, is the "essential cornerstone" to treatment with families involved in the foster care system (Leiberman, 2003).

When working with families with adolescents, there are other issues to consider when employing an attachment-based treatment model. As stated above, adolescents are working towards identity formation and autonomy, and this may strain the parent–adolescent relationship. Family members may respond to this strain with anger and hostility (Keiley & Seery, 2001). In such situations, the treatment plan is to help parents influence their adolescents' affect by first controlling their own. When this is done, both adolescents and parents report stronger positive relationships with one another.

Clinical Illustration

Janis, a 16-year-old female, is an only child. Janis is in high school and is an honor-roll student. She is very articulate but also seems very introverted. Janis's mother is a nurse. She has a bachelor's degree and has aspirations to go back to school for her master's degree. The father is a Gulf War veteran who had been unemployed for approximately one year. Janis's parents had been married for 20 years.

One day at school, Janis disclosed to her guidance counselor that her father was "sneaking in her room at night" and molesting her. She reported that this abuse had been going on for approximately two years. Social services became involved, and the father admitted to the accusations. When interviewed by social services, Janis's mother denied knowing about the abuse. She attributed her husband's alleged behavior to his military service in the Gulf War, September 11th, and his subsequent drinking problem. The mother also defended her husband's actions. She said that he "was just expressing his love for his beautiful daughter." Social services reported that they did not trust that the mother understood the severity of the abuse, and Janis was removed from the home. Since there was no extended family residing in the immediate area, Janis was placed in foster care.

While the criminal investigation was being conducted, the father was court-ordered to undergo inpatient substance abuse treatment for his addiction to alcohol. He was also court-ordered to have no contact with his daughter during the investigation. The mother, however, was court-ordered to participate in family therapy with her daughter.

There were a number of people and agencies involved in the case. There was a victim advocate, a guardian ad-litem, law-enforcement officers, social services personnel, and individual and family therapists. It was important to identify how each of the agencies involved were working to help the family, so that there would not be competing or conflicting goals. In addition, the therapist was overt in discussing limits of confidentiality and what types of reports and communication would be exchanged with specific agencies throughout the course of treatment.

The initial considerations of treatment were the developmental level of Janis, her relationship to her father, the mother's interpretation of the occurrences, and the impact the abuse had on Janis. Initially, sessions were held with the mother and daughter because Janis's mother was in denial of the abuse. After information was gathered, it seemed that family therapy would be beneficial, so the mother and daughter were brought together for family sessions.

Social services designated the following therapeutic goals: "Ensuring the mother acknowledges the severity of the abuse, and establishes a safety plan to be used if Janis is returned to the home." The therapist assessed the mother's motivation level by asking questions such as "What do you think needs to change before social services feels comfortable with you regaining custody of Janis?" The mother described a primary goal of helping to create a safe place for Janis to live. The mother stated that her goal was to regain custody of her daughter.

Developmentally speaking, both Janis and her mother had reached the final stage of cognitive development and therefore had the ability to think abstractly and express their own feelings directly—which they both did in session. However, although both Janis and her mother were at similar stages cognitively, they were worlds apart with regard to emotional development. Janis was struggling with her identity development, but her mother was preoccupied with whether or not she had done a good job parenting. In this context, accepting the reality of the incestuous relationship would have significant impact on both Janis's and her mother's emotional development.

A primary goal of therapy was to create a safe place for constructive communication to occur. After this occurred, Janis and her mother began to question each other with an eye toward understanding their situation. For example, Janis's mother recognized that Janis was becoming withdrawn over the past two years, but said she thought it was because Janis was becoming an adolescent and more autonomous from her parents. Therefore, one psychoeducational aspect of therapy involved educating the family about adolescents' need for autonomy while remaining connected with their parents through positive communication (Bhushan & Shirali, 1992). Janis and her mother also discussed sexuality. Janis described how she felt guilt because sometimes she enjoyed her father's touch.

Anger was a pervasive theme in the initial sessions. Janis believed that her mother should have protected her. When she described the anger she felt, her mother would be angry in response, and their mutual hostility would escalate. The therapist facilitated the expression of these emotions. She asked Janis's mother to observe how she responded when Janis described her feelings. In time, Janis's mother recognized that she felt intense guilt and this caused her angry reaction when her daughter expressed pain. Once these patterns were identified and explored, there was a more open discussion of feelings and a de-escalation of the emotional tension (Keiley & Seery, 2001).

As is the case with many adolescent girls, Janis was beginning to develop physically. She also had begun wearing low-cut shirts and short shorts. This initially caused Janis's mother to shift the blame away from her husband. She accused Janis of seducing her father. Their mutual emotional distance and lack of trust were typical of mother/daughter dynamics in incestuous families. There often is deep resentment and hostility directed at the mothers by daughters who see their mothers as abandoning and nonprotective (Finkelhor, 1980; Furniss, 1983; Reiss & Heppner, 1993).

The therapist dealt with these feelings of blame in individual sessions with Janis's mother and then again in joint sessions with Janis. In that way, the blame and anger were worked through and communication improved. This allowed the mother and daughter to address other issues common to incestuous families, including the extent to which Janis was a buffer in a weak marital relationship (Ingram, 1985; Katz, 1983). Young girls like Janis typically have been depicted as pseudomature in their caretaking responsibilities and, at the same time, they are often emotionally immature and constricted (Mayer, 1983).

An apology session may be indicated for parents and older children with higher cognitive abilities. In such sessions, children can be "freed from their own sense of confusion and guilt and attribution of abuse to their own actions" (Bentovim, 2004, p. 129). Although Janis's mother was not the perpetrator in this case, Janis attributed a great deal of responsibility to both her mother and her father for what had happened to her. The therapist facilitated an apology session: Janis wrote questions to her mother; the mother then came for an individual session in which she could deliberate her responses. Next, in a family session, the mother and daughter exchanged questions and answers. At the end of the session, the two embraced.

With time, Janis's father was prosecuted, and the social services agency decided to work toward reunification of Janis with her mother, provided that Janis have no further contact with her father. Janis's mother agreed to this arrangement. Before reunification, however, there were a number of issues that needed to be addressed in therapy. First, a safety plan needed to be created. The therapist and Janis worked together to devise a plan that Janis could implement any time that she not feel safe in her home. Second, feelings associated with reunification needed to be discussed. In the end, Janis was reunified with her mother.

References

Baumrind, D. (1995). Commentary on sexual orientation: Research and social policy implications. *Developmental Psychology, 31,* 130–136.

Bengtson, V. L., & Schaie, K. W. (Eds.) (1999). *Handbook of theories of aging.* New York: Springer Publishing.

Bentovim, A. (2004). Working with abusing families: General issues and a systemic perspective. *Journal of Family Psychotherapy, 15,* 119–135.

Berk, L. E. (1997). Child development (4th ed.). Boston, MA: Allyn and Bacon.

Bhushan, R. & Shirali, K. A. (1992). Family types and communication with parents: A comparison of youth at different identity levels. *Journal of Youth and Adolescence, 21,* 687–697.

Bowlby, J. (1977). The making and breaking of affectional bonds: Aetiology and psychopathology in the light of attachment theory. *British Journal of Psychiatry, 130,* 201–210.

Bowlby, J. (1980). *Attachment and loss: Vol. 1. Attachment* (2nd ed.). New York: Basic Books.

Bretherton, I., & Munholland, K. A. (1999). Internal working models in attachment relationships. In J. Cassidy & P. R. Shaver (Eds.), *Handbook of attachment: Theory, research and clinical implications* (pp. 89–111). New York: The Guilford Press.

Brown, B. B., Clasen, D., & Eichler, S. (1986). Perceptions of peer pressure, peer conformity dispositions, and self-reported behavior among adolescents. *Developmental Psychology, 6,* 139–154.

Cantos, A. L., Gries, L. T., & Slis, V. (1997). Behavioral correlates of parental visiting during family foster care. *Child Welfare, 76,* 309–329.

Centers for Disease Control and Prevention. (2002). STD Surveillance, 2002. Retrieved November 3, 2004, at www.cdc.gov/std/stats/adol.htm.

Cohen, D. J. (1995). Psychosocial therapies for children and adolescents: Overview and future directions. *Journal of Abnormal Child Psychology, 23,* 141–161.

Colapinto, J. A. (1995). Dilution of family process in social services: Implications for treatment of neglectful families. *Family Process, 34,* 59–74.

Crenshaw, W., & Barnum, D. (2001). You can't fight the system: Strategies of family justice in foster care reintegration. *Family Journal: Counseling & Therapy for Couples & Families, 9,* 29–36.

Crittenden, P. (1988). Relationships at risk. In J. Belsky & T. Nezworski (Eds.), *Clinical implications of attachment* (pp. 136–174). Hillsdale, NJ: Erlbaum.

Davies, D. (2004). *Child development: A practitioner's guide* (Rev. ed.). New York: Guilford.

Dozier, M. (1990). Attachment organization and treatment use for adults with serious psychological disorders. *Development and Psychopathology, 2,* 47–60.

Dozier, M., Albus, K., Fisher, P., & Sepulveda, A. (2002). Interventions for foster parents: Implications for developmental theory. *Development and Psychopathology, 14,* 843–860.

Egeland, B., & Sroufe, L. (1981). Developmental sequel of maltreatment in infancy. In R. Rizley & D. Cicchti (Eds.). *Developmental perspectives in child maltreatment* (pp. 77–92). San Francisco: Josey-Bass.

Erikson, E. H. (1993). *Childhood and society.* New York: W. W. Norton.

Falicov, C. J. (Ed.). (1991). *Family transitions: Continuity and changes over the life cycle.* New York: Guilford.

Finkelhor, D. (1980). Risk factors in the sexual victimization of children. *Child Abuse and Neglect, 4,* 265–273.

Finzi, R., Ram, A., Har-Even, D., Shnit, D., & Weizman, A. (2001). Attachment styles and aggression in physically abused and neglected children. *Journal of Youth and Adolescence, 30,* 769–786.

Furniss, T. (1983). Family process in the treatment of interfamilial child sexual abuse. *Journal of Family Therapy, 5,* 263–278.

Gil, E. (1991). *The healing power of play: Working with abused children.* New York: Guilford.

Gil, E. (1996). *Treating abused adolescents.* New York: Guilford.

Harman, J., Childs, G., & Kelleher, K. (2000). Mental health care utilization and expenditures by children in foster care. *Archives of Pediatrics and Adolescent Medicine, 154,* 1114–1117.

Harter, S. (1996). Developmental changes in self-understanding across the 5 to 7 shift. In A. J. Sameroff & M. M. Haith (Eds.), *The five to seven year shift: The age of reason and responsibility* (pp. 207–235). Chicago: University of Chicago Press.

Hershberger, S. L., & D'Augelli, A. R. (1995). The impact of victimization on the mental health and suicidality of lesbian, gay and bisexual youths. *Developmental Psychology, 31,* 65–74.

Helson, R., & Wink, P. (1992). Personality changes in women from the early 40s to early 50s. *Psychology and the Aging, 7,* 46–55.

Hildebrand, J. (1988). The use of group work in treating sexual abuse. In A. Bentovim, A. Elton, J. Hildebrand, M. Tranter, & E. Vizard (Eds.), *Child sexual abuse within the family* (pp. 150–168). London: Wright Publishing.

Hooper, C. A. (1992). *Mothers surviving child sexual abuse.* London: Reutledge.

Ingram, T. L. (1985). Sexual abuse in the family of origin and unresolved issues: A Gestalt/systems treatment approach for couples. *Family Therapy, 12,* 175–201.

Johnson, J. E. (1998). Play development from ages four to eight. In D. P. Fromberg & D. Bergen (Eds.), *Play from birth to twelve and beyond: Contexts, perspectives, and meanings* (pp. 145–153). New York: Garland.

Kaplan, S., Pelcovitz, D., & Labruna, V. (1999). Child and adolescent abuse and neglect research: A review of the past 10 years. Part 1: Physical and emotional abuse and neglect. *Journal of the American Academy of Child and Adolescent Psychiatry, 38,* 1214–1222.

Katz, E. E. (1983). Incestuous families. *Detroit College of Law Review, 1,* 79–102.

Kazdin, A. E. (1987). *Conduct disorders in childhood and adolescence.* Newbury Park, CA: Sage Publications.

Kazdin, A. E. (1988). *Child psychotherapy: Developing and identifying effective treatments.* New York: Pergamon Press.

Kazdin, A. E. (2003). Psychotherapy for children and adolescents. *Annual Review of Psychology, 54,* 253–276.

Keiley, M. K., & Seery, B. L. (2001). Affect regulation and attachment strategies of adjudicated and non-adjudicated adolescents and their parents. *Contemporary Family Therapy, 23,* 343–366.

Kendall, P. C., & Morris, R. J. (1991). Child therapy: Issues and recommendations. *Journal of Consulting and Clinical Psychology, 59,* 777–784.

Lee, R. E., & Lynch, M. T. (1998). Combating foster care drift: An ecosystemic treatment model for neglect cases. *Contemporary Family Therapy, 20,* 351–371.

Leiberman, A. F. (2003). The treatment of attachment disorder in infancy and early childhood: Reflections from clinical intervention with later-adopted foster care children. *Attachment and Human Development, 5,* 279–282.

Marcus, R. F. (1991). The attachments of children in foster care. *Genetic, Social and General Psychology Monographs, 117,* 365–394.

Mayer, A. (1983). *Incest: A treatment manual for therapy with victims, spouses, and offenders.* Holmes Beach, FL: Learning Publications.

McCarthy, G., & Taylor, A. (1999). Avoidant/ambivalent attachment style as a mediator between abusive childhood experiences and adult relationships. *Journal of Child Psychology and Psychiatry, 40,* 465–477.

McWey, L. M. (2004). Predictors of attachment styles of children in foster care: An attachment theory model. *Journal of Marital and Family Therapy, 30,* 439–452.

McWey, L. M., & Mullis, A. (2004). Improving the lives of children in foster care: The impact of supervised visitation. *Family Relations, 53,* 293–300.

Myers, J. E., Shoffner, M. F., & Briggs, M. K. (2002). Developmental counseling and therapy: An effective approach to understanding and counseling children. *Professional School Counseling, 5,* 194–202.

Neugarten, B. L. (1964). *Personality in middle and later life.* New York: Atheron.

Newcomb, M. D., & Bentler, P. M. (1989). Substance use and abuse among children and teenagers. *American Psychologist, 44,* 242–248.

Papalia, D. E., Olds, S. W., & Feldman, R. D. (2004). *A child's world: Infancy through adolescence* (9th ed.). Boston: McGraw-Hill.

Reiss, S. D., & Heppner, P. P. (1993). Examination of coping resources and family adaptation in mothers and daughters of incestuous versus nonclinical families. *Journal of Counseling Psychology, 40,* 100–108.

Ruble, N. (1999). The voices of therapists and children regarding the inclusion of children in family therapy: A systematic research synthesis. *Contemporary Family Therapy, 21,* 485–503.

Santrock, J. W. (2002). *Lifespan development* (8th ed.). Boston: McGraw-Hill.

Scharff, D. E. & Scharff, J. S. (1987). *Object relations family therapy.* Northvale, NJ: Aronson.

Sebald, H. (1986). Adolescents' shifting orientation toward parents and peers: A curvilinear trend over recent decades. *Journal of Marriage and the Family, 48,* 5–13.

Sroufe, L. A. (1979). Socioemotional development. In J. Osofsky (Ed.), *Handbook of infant development* (pp.462–516). New York: Wiley.

Sweeney, T. J. (1998). *Adlerian counseling: A practitioner's approach.* Philadelphia: Accelerated Development.

U.S. Department of Health and Human Services. (2002). Fact sheet on preventing teen pregnancy. Retrieved on October 26, 2004, at www.os.dhhs.gov/news/press/2002pres/teenpreg.html.

van Ijzendoorn, M., Juffer, F., & Duyvesteyn, M. (1995). Breaking the intergenerational cycle of insecure attachment: A review of the effects of attachment-based interventions on maternal sensitivity and infant security. *Journal of Child Psychology and Psychiatry, 36,* 225–248.

Wekerle, C., & Wolfe, D. A. (1998). The role of child maltreatment and attachment style in adolescent relationship violence. *Development and Psychopathology, 10,* 571–586.

Weinfield, N., Sroufe, L. A., & Egeland, B. (2000). Attachment from infancy to early adulthood in a high-risk sample: Continuity, discontinuity and their correlates. *Child Development, 71,* 695–702.

Whiting, J. B. (2000). The view from down here: Foster children's stories. *Child and Youth Care Forum, 29,* 79–95.

Whiting, J. B., & Lee, R. E. (2003). Voices from the system: A qualitative study of foster children's stories. *Family Relations, 52,* 288–295.

9

An Integrative Approach Involving the Biological and Foster Family Systems

Kim Sumner-Mayer

his chapter focuses on facilitating positive and productive birth family–foster family relationships in the interests of preferred outcomes for children—as well as, but secondarily, for birth and foster families. This requires consideration of what each party brings to the table, as well as issues of timing and transitions across the course of foster placement. Effective birth family–foster family work requires a combination of work with each family system and bridging between family systems, an acute awareness of the larger systems within which both families operate (especially the agency and state child welfare authority), and a choreography of sorts that recognizes the different goals and strategies necessary for facilitating these relationships at different stages of placement.

Ideally, foster and birth families have a common goal: To reunify children with their birth families and, if reunification is not possible or preferable, to provide children with nurture and a sense of family connection as other plans are made and enacted for the children's permanent care (Maluccio, Warsh, & Pine, 1993). However, the gap between this ideal and reality is the area in which most readers of this book operate.

We will first consider the importance of collaboration in pursuit of these common goals. Next, we will look at some central organizing perspectives for birth family–foster family work. From there, we will explore what each major party—the agency, the birth family, and the foster family—brings to the relational equation, and how we can most effectively work within and between systems to maximize chances of positive and productive relationships. Finally, we will consider the critical importance of transitions in foster placements. In doing so, we will look at how goals and interventions should change to reflect the changing needs of the entire foster care system—of which all stakeholders are dynamic parts—as this system moves from its early "getting to know you" phase through later phases, including postreunification. This chapter focuses on nonrelative foster family placements. Kinship foster placements, although similar to nonrelative placements on some dimensions, differ significantly in other ways. For a comprehensive review of clinical issues involved with kinship care families, see Crumbley and Little (1997), Weinstein and Takas (2001), and Chapter 10 in this book, "Kinship Placements: An Integrative Approach."

Why Collaborate?

Not all birth families should reunify with their children. Some parents abandon their children and are not able or willing to provide a physically and emotionally safe home. Others cannot work productively with foster families. They continually attempt to disrupt the children's stability in alternate caregiving environments. In contrast, some birth families are easy to work with; they are motivated to gain their children's return, are respectful of foster family boundaries and authority, express gratitude toward the foster family, and are willing to learn and change. However, there are many birth families in between these two extremes. These are families who could become partners with foster families in meeting their children's needs, or they could go the other way. They could disappear or they could become antagonistic toward the foster placement. Our approach toward these families may be a determining factor in their attitude about the process.

There is no time to waste once a child is placed. We need to challenge ourselves, the foster families, and our agencies to create a climate that is ripe for collaboration. Regardless of how birth families present, the longer the parents are alienated from their parenting role—while their children are in placement—the more difficult reunification will be. Parent–child bonds weaken, parental ambivalence increases, and the birth family develops a new homeostatic balance around the child's absence.

Any clinician who has attempted to work collaboratively with foster and birth families knows that it is difficult and time-consuming work. That is why many agencies don't attempt much collaboration— in the short run, it seems easier and more efficient to manage foster children's behavior (and the foster families' anxiety and hesitance to engage with birth families) by excluding the birth family from the picture. This strategy often leads to tragic consequences with which you are probably familiar:

- termination of parental rights where reunification might have been possible, given the right help,
- reunifications that disrupt due to inadequate preparation and support,
- tortuous separations between foster families and children that have ripple effects on the families' ability to appropriately nurture future foster children, and
- postadoption disruptions in which birth family relationships were inadequately resolved before finalization.

The Primacy of Birth Family Connections

Children need to feel positively connected with their birth families in order to feel good about themselves. Foster children frequently feel abandoned and rejected by their birth families on some level, no matter how loyal they still are to them. And, at some level, almost all foster children harbor doubts about their own worthiness of love, care, and protection. Foster children must be able to retain some sense of their parents as positive and worthy people, if they are to maintain a positive self-image. Moreover, most foster children do eventually return to the care of their birth parents.

Family connections are broader than just parent–child relationships. They include siblings and extended family members as well. The child welfare system does not always consider that children and teenagers grow into young adults who are connected with parents, siblings, and other family members—and they are likely to become parents themselves. Commonly the birth family becomes the support network for youths who age out of the foster care system— no matter how disconnected they may have become. This is true even if ties have been severed legally or because all of us—families, agencies, courts, and therapists—have neglected these relationships. However, it is incumbent on those of us working in the system to be mindful of these connections and to do everything possible to strengthen family ties of placed children. Given the historical legacy of the child protective system as a vehicle for saving children from bad families, the system still struggles to understand the importance of positive birth family connections (Fahlberg, 1991; Kosonen, 1996; Young, Gardner, & Dennis, 1998).

Foster parents often do not think about helping children and their birth families work toward reunification. They also may receive little or no guidance from the child protective agency regarding the attitudes and skills necessary for this important work. As a result, one of your most critical roles is to encourage the foster and birth families to unite and cooperate on behalf of the children. There is much research showing that positive birth family– foster family connections support sustained reunification and better life outcomes for children (Hess & Proch, 1988; Minuchin, Colapinto, & Minuchin, 1998; Palmer, 1996; Pine, Warsh, & Maluccio, 1993; Tiddy, 1986).

Reconceptualizing Reunification

Reunification does not need to be all or nothing. You should strive to facilitate an exploration of the *optimal level of child–birth family connection.* In some cases, one way to maintain children's family membership (in the safest way possible) might be to continue their birth family connection through visits, letters, and phone calls, but not to return them to live in that household (Maluccio et al., 1993; Maluccio, Ambramczyk, & Thomlison, 1996). This can be an important but challenging task. Continued contact with the members of the birth family may be in the adoptive child's *and* the foster family's best interests. However, the child welfare system increasingly looks to foster parents as potential adoption resources, and foster families who hope to adopt a child may find it difficult to negotiate a continuing role for the birth family in the child's life.

The child welfare system generally assumes that all birth parents should want full-time custodial reunification. However, some birth parents cannot meet the criteria for this, and others are ambivalent about full reunification. For example, some parents would prefer to disappear from their children's lives rather than experience failure again. Others may believe that their disappearance will allow their children to have a better life (Lee & Nisivoccia, 1989). You should address the parents' potential ambivalence about reunification early and consistently. (Guidelines appear later in this chapter.) If full-time custodial reunification is not to occur, kinship care or adoption, voluntary relinquishment, open adoption, long-term foster care for older children, and other options safeguard children while preserving important birth family connections (Hess & Folaron, 1991; Maluccio et al., 1993). Facilitating optimal connections between children, their birth families, and their foster families could lead to more creative, stable, and child-affirming permanency arrangements, and perhaps even to lower rates of placement and postadoption disruption.

Organizing Perspectives

Fostering is a unique family context and it is important to appreciate how clinical work with foster families is different from work with intact birth families.

- It is the only parenting arrangement purposefully designed to end in a parent–child separation before the child is ready to launch.

- Loss is a central organizing principle for all parties.
- There are few models and rituals for handling the family boundaries and transitions that are typical of foster families.
- Our society thinks about family units defined by blood relations.

Therefore, it is useful to view foster families from two important perspectives: We need to consider how each of our foster families is influenced by the larger systems in which they are situated, and we need to always be aware of the pervasive influences of grief and loss.

Ecosystemic Framework

Foster families operate amidst an extremely complex web of larger systems. These larger systems influence dynamics both within and between foster and birth families as well as the other systems involved. An ecosystemic framework is most useful in understanding these dynamics. For elaboration of this perspective, see Chapter 2, "An Ecosystemic Approach to Foster Care."

The Centrality of Grief and Loss

Loss is *the* central organizing dynamic in foster care work for everyone. Unmourned grief and loss, regarding the placement of the child or children, drives much problematic birth parent behavior. For example, birth parents often report how devastating it is to see the pain in their children's eyes at visits, and to face their inevitable questions: "When can you take me home? Why can't we be together? Are you doing what the judge says you have to do?" One possible solution is to avoid contact. Another is to criticize the agency or the foster family. In this way, the birth family's unresolved grief and loss get in the way of their empathy for their children's experiences. As a result, the agency staff and foster parents then perceive the birth parents as selfish and uncaring. Tragically, this perception may be used as evidence to reduce contact between the children and their birth parents and, as birth families become excluded, alienation between the birth parents and their children increases.

Foster families must also contend with many types of loss (Edelstein, 1981; Edelstein, Burge, & Waterman, 2001; Sumner-Mayer 2003, 2006; Urquhart, 1989). During placement, foster children often make disclosures about their histories of maltreatment and loss; these stories may horrify members of the foster family, and also may trigger painful memories of the foster parents' own childhoods. Such situations can trigger strong negative feelings about the birth family (Duclos, 1987; McFadden, 1996). Especially when they hope to adopt, many foster families fear the child being returned to the birth home, and they mourn the child's loss when that happens. Foster families may defensively distance themselves from the birth families simply because of the possibility of such a loss. These families also experience grief and loss if they are not able to maintain gratifying contact with the foster children once they have been returned to their birth parents (Edelstein, 1981).

Sometimes foster families are wary of birth families because of unresolved grief and loss from previous foster placements. In fact, unresolved loss from previous placements can lead the family to adopt a subsequent foster child, just so the family can avoid another painful loss. However, this motivation alone does not ensure a stable and positive adoption experience for that child or for the foster family (Sumner-Mayer, 2003).

Ambiguous loss (Boss, 1999) is a useful concept for fostering. It occurs when there is a lack of information about the loss or the status of a family member, disagreement regarding family membership of a missing person, and lack of social validation of the loss. Family members don't know what to think or do when their losses are not clear. This ambiguity—wondering "To what extent are they here or not?"—leads to problems with grief resolution and interferes with progress toward case goals. For a detailed discussion of the role of ambiguous loss in foster care, see Chapter 5, "Ambiguous Loss: A Key Component of Foster Care."

Understanding the nature and dynamics of these multiple and intertwined losses is vital for effective therapy with birth and foster families. The roles of both clear and ambiguous loss will arise and be addressed throughout this chapter.

Parental Ambivalence

Ambivalence regarding the desirability of reunification plays a major and underappreciated role in the foster care drama. It is normal for birth parents to have mixed feelings about parenting and uncertainty about what to do (Hess & Folaron, 1991; Bicknell-Hentges, 1995). However, when this ambivalence remains unresolved, it has serious potential to disrupt family reunification plans and birth family–foster family relationships. Ambivalence can be discerned through direct statements describing indecision about permanency, or indirectly, through behavior that is inconsistent with an articulated interest in reunification (such as noncompliance with a service plan, or missing visits).

Ambivalence is complicated by societal expectations about the desirability of reunification. Parents, foster parents, courts, and case managers tend to believe that parents should want to reunify with their children. As a result of this prevalent idea, other permanency options are not discussed until parents have failed at reunification. When grief and loss are suffered, the birth parents' unresolved ambivalence may result in their unresponsiveness to the children's needs, and may cause them to appear antagonistic and defensive regarding the foster family. And when birth parents are viewed as uninterested or disruptive, the idea of severing parent–child ties gains momentum.

Ambivalence needs to be addressed early and throughout the treatment process. Helping birth parents identify and address their ambivalence and educating the other members of the foster care system about ambivalence can contribute to improved relations with foster families and to improved parent–child relationships.

The Critical Role of Transitions in Foster Care

Transitions are a part of life in all families. They are critical in foster care. Transitions disrupt usual routines, require adaptation to new realities, and may increase susceptibility to positive or negative influence (Minuchin, 1990). The entire foster care system is a transitional and, by definition, unstable system. These foster care transitions usually occur in a climate of crisis attended by confusion and anxiety, instability, moodiness, and regression. Disturbed functioning may follow such a crisis. It will need to be addressed in positive ways. Unfortunately, this is a time when many of the participants seek immediate stabilization in the foster placement. However, this may be an inappropriate goal. In fact, the word "stable" may infer "stuck" and not moving toward resolution of the placement (Colapinto, 2005).

Both birth and foster families are affected by transitions during the placement process. The children literally move between the two families throughout the foster placement and carry baggage from one into the other. These movements require foster and birth families to adjust their family boundaries, routines, rituals, and hierarchies in different ways at different phases of placement (Minuchin, 1995; Minuchin, et al., 1998).

Differing Values, Attitudes, Lifestyles, and Beliefs

All of us—therapists, birth and foster families, and agency personnel—are interdependent. Therefore, we all must negotiate differences in customs, beliefs, values, language, communication styles, dress, and many other variables. Individual attitudes about racial, ethnic, and socioeconomic traits (Dillon, 1994) must also be examined and challenged. In the area of childcare, there is much diversity in thought regarding conscious and unconscious expectations for children's behavior and achievement; approaches to understanding, communicating with, and disciplining children; and handling children's emerging sexuality. Therapists need to be alert to tensions, attributions, and defensiveness, and must be ready to identify and defuse problematic interactions throughout the foster care system. For example, disagreements about a child's manner of dress and speech may reveal deep differences and judgments about appropriate behavior—and these differences and judgments may be based on ethnicity or social class.

Elements of Cooperative Foster Family–Birth Family Relationships

The needs, concerns, beliefs, feelings, and behaviors of all four parties—agency, therapist, birth family, and foster family—are at the foundation of a constructive collaborative approach.

Agency/Therapist Contributions and Guidelines for Action

Whether you work directly for a foster care agency or you contract with one, you have a critical role to play in maximizing the chances that the larger social system surrounding birth and foster families supports a cooperative relationship between them. You exert that influence through your:

- stance toward birth families and foster families,
- advocacy for and support of policies and practices that facilitate cooperative relationships, and
- work with and between members of both systems.

Therapeutic stance

Your stance toward foster and birth families is critically important, *especially* if you are working for or with an agency whose policies and practices are not very supportive of them. Your view must include humility, respect, a sincere belief that both birth and foster families bring valuable expertise and perspectives to the work of parenting, understanding and validation of both families' experiences of grief and loss, and an unwavering commitment to uncovering and using strengths to ameliorate or counterbalance problems. Your therapeutic stance should also recognize that the relationships between you, case managers, the agency, and birth parents, and the relationship between birth family and foster family are secondary in importance to, and need to serve the interests of, the relationship between birth parents and children (Colapinto, 2005).

The story you read in the case record about any given birth or foster family is only part of the whole story. In the case of birth families, it is almost invariably skewed toward the negative. Part of your job is to uncover the rest of the story; that is, the parts of the story that have to do with strength, commitment, good intentions, and resilience. Strengths always exist, but they may not become apparent unless you look for them. Your clients may have survived as a family against great odds. They may have extended family or fictive kin relationships that have been vital to the family's success. There may be high levels of caring and commitment. Most birth families in "the system" have had so many experiences of having their stories told for them by others, and told in such negative and pathologizing ways, that they need help (1) believing that you see them differently and (2) recognizing and utilizing their strengths.

> The first time I spoke with Janet, it was after having skimmed through a two-inch-thick case record provided by her child protective manager. Janet came with dual diagnoses of a mood disorder and alcohol dependence, and the record was full of notes from previous psychiatric hospitalizations and details of her many failings as a parent. For example: she had passed out and her children had to call 911 to revive her; there was not enough food in the apartment where they lived; both of her younger children had academic, developmental, and/or emotional problems; an older child had suffered sexual abuse at the hands of her partner. During the initial

staffing meeting (to which Janet was not invited), I learned that the child protective case manager was highly dubious that a successful reunification was possible.

During our first phone conversation, I told Janet that I had seen her case record, but that I knew that the record is only one sliver of her story, and not even one she had written for herself. I asked her to tell me what she thought was important for me to know about her and her children. I learned that she had a stable job and that she had recently requested a move into a less stressful position in the interest of maintaining her sobriety; that she had voluntarily arranged to continue attending her aftercare group, even after formally completing her treatment program; that she owned the apartment in which the family had lived; and that when she learned of her oldest child's sexual abuse many years earlier, she believed the child and initiated the process that resulted in her now ex-partner's eventual conviction and imprisonment. None of this was in the case record.

Janet later said she was relieved to be asked about these other parts of her story because she was acutely aware that her psychiatric record probably painted a very different portrait of her than the one she had of herself. She also had had a volatile relationship with the child protective manager, and I am certain that my deliberate effort to start out our relationship on a different foot was instrumental in gaining the trust and leverage needed to help her begin to interface differently with the case manager. Nine months later, Janet reunified with her two youngest children.

Once these strengths are uncovered you, the birth family, the case manager, and the foster family need to consider these assets relative to the grave problems that brought the family into the foster care system in the first place. Those who are involved with the birth families are commonly given limited and negative information about them. Because they witness the effects of parental neglect and abuse, it can be extremely difficult for them to view birth parents in a positive light without assistance.

If foster families are to think about birth parents differently than this, they need to know that you and the agency really appreciate how challenging it is to care for children who have been hurt or neglected by their birth families. Their concerns and grief must be acknowledged and validated. Often they perceive the agency as interested only in the children's well-being and not their own. Only after they have been reassured of everyone's understanding and respect, can you realistically ask foster parents to view birth families in the same way.

In the case described above, I met with the foster mother early on. I asked about her motivations for fostering, previous fostering experiences (especially with birth families of placed children), fostering-related losses, and her children's adjustment to becoming a foster family. I then asked her what traits or behaviors she saw in Janet's children that she thought reflected well on Janet's parenting. She identified the children's manners, how nicely they played with her own young son, and how one of the children was particularly sensitive toward others. This was an important step in setting the stage for a cooperative relationship to blossom between these sets of parents.

Policies and practices

Agency policies and practices can facilitate or hinder positive relationships between themselves, birth families, and foster families. Important areas to notice are foster parent training, who is invited to case conferences, and how the agency financially supports foster placements.

Recruitment of prospective foster families who are open to working cooperatively with birth parents is an important precursor to training. Their subsequent training should include preparation for birth family reunification and their role in that process. Such training will facilitate their understanding of and empathy for the children's birth families; will help develop essential skills for interacting with birth families; and will identify attachment, grief, and loss manifestations in children's, birth families', and even the foster families' own behavior. Foster parents will learn to join with the birth families; to search for their strengths; to map out and create room in interactions for birth families' competence and contributions to come out (Minuchin, 1990, 1995; Minuchin et al., 1998). I highly recommend consulting Minuchin's (1990) excellent training manual for foster parents for these purposes. Training should also include education regarding common presenting issues in placement, including parental addiction and recovery, trauma, and major mental illness.

How you and your agency view collaboration between all of the parties will be reflected in your practices with regard to case conferences and meetings. Both birth and foster parents should be included in most meetings concerning a particular child. There should be discussion among case managers, therapists, and foster parents beforehand about how to access the birth parents' competence and how to encourage their participation during the meeting. You and the case managers should endeavor to facilitate positive interaction between the foster parents and the birth parents. One way to do this is by strategically holding back and creating space in the conversation so that foster parents will take the lead during parts of meetings. Both sets of parents should be encouraged to share their perspectives and expertise. For example, you can ask them for suggestions about how to handle difficult behavior or situations.

Flexible visitation arrangements are often beneficial to a collaborative approach. Visitation should be natural, comfortable, and in a home-like environment—to the degree that this is possible. Some agencies are hesitant to give foster parents' addresses to birth parents. They are fearful that the birth parents will violate the foster families' privacy. However, visitation in foster homes is often a wonderful concept when it is handled correctly. The advantages are: foster families do not have to disrupt their family lives to transport the children, the children can stay in a familiar caregiving environment during the visit, and they can extend their sense of security by including their birth parents in that environment. Likewise, the birth parents can be reassured of the quality of their children's caregiving environment. In addition, if they are properly prepared, foster parents potentially may be the best visit coaches and supervisors available. Policies and practices concerning transportation and other visit logistics should also facilitate this cooperation between birth families and foster families. Visitation should occur on days and time convenient to both birth and foster families, and money should be available to provide transportation assistance, respite care, and visitation-related supplies for whoever has need of them.

Birth Family Contributions and Guidelines for Action

Birth families differ in their capacity to develop a working relationship with foster parents. Many initially defensive birth families could move toward such an alliance under the right conditions. The purpose of this relationship is to grease the wheels of the birth parents' relationship with their children. Ultimately, it is not important that foster and birth families like each other. But they must develop functional ways of relating in order to meet their children's needs.

Joining with birth parents

Unrecognized grief, loss, guilt, and shame drive much of the negative behavior by birth parents that affects their relationships with foster families. Of all the adults in the foster care drama, it is the birth parents who are required to make the largest changes in their lives in order to resolve their children's placement. At the same time, they face both overt and tacit reminders that they have failed and have been proven inadequate—in the only adult role that may have given them a sense of efficacy and status, that of parent. The loss of a child to foster care is a devastating blow to most birth parents. But society rarely validates their loss as real and as a reason to grieve.

As a result, work with the birth parents begins with their grief, loss, guilt, and shame. It goes on to address ambivalence as it influences the relationship between birth and foster parents. Finally, clinical work should increase the birth parents' self-awareness and their interaction skills, especially as the latter involve members of the foster families.

Expanding birth family stories

Instead of fully accepting the story provided about the birth parents at intake, you invite the family to share aspects of their stories that are not told in the official records. In so doing, you carefully gather evidence of birth family strengths. You are inviting the birth family to amend the record held by that system. This strategy achieves multiple objectives, and it is your first opportunity to join with the birth family and assume a position that is somewhat *outside* the system. It conveys your awareness that the birth family comes into the equation at a disadvantage and offers them an opportunity to level the playing field somewhat. Finally, by communicating your vision of the family's strengths and resilience, you offer them building blocks toward solutions from within the family's *existing* history and organization. Your vision can help the birth family begin to see itself as more functional, and indeed to become more functional because of the changed self-perception.

This strategy can be enhanced by letting birth parents consult on and read—and even co-author—progress notes and reports. This is a powerful antidote to the devaluation and exclusion these individuals often experience with the child welfare system.

Validating grief and loss

Because the way birth families respond to loss can heavily influence their relationships with foster families, it is necessary to validate and work with those feelings and responses. Educating birth parents regarding the nature of grief and loss, and explicitly naming the placement as a major loss, opens the door to consider feelings they may never have previously experienced or even acknowledged. Birth parents often comment on how liberating and humanizing this process is, and how powerfully it counters feelings of guilt and shame. Birth parent psychoeducational support groups are extremely effective in this regard. However, the same results are possible working with individual birth families.

Promoting awareness of links between feelings, thoughts, and behavior

Therapists can also use grief and loss as a vehicle for teaching skills to birth parents—skills that will enable understanding of the connections between feelings, thoughts, and behaviors. The first step is to encourage birth parents to tell the story of the loss of their child, and to explicitly name and explore the feelings associated with it. The next step is to trace out the thoughts that emanate from those feelings, and the behaviors that follow from the feelings and thoughts. Finally, we ask parents to then consider the consequences of those actions: *"How does that behavior help or hurt your relationship with your child? With their caregiver? With your case manager?"* As birth parents become better observers, they learn how their responses to grief and loss affect their children and the foster family, and they are more able to make conscious decisions about how to participate in those relationships.

Helping birth parents appreciate the connections between feelings, thoughts, behaviors, and other peoples' actions is especially helpful when substance abuse is a contributing factor in the placement (see Chapter 17, "'We're in It Together': Family Therapy Where Substance Abuse Is a Problem"). This lack of awareness is destructive to the relationships between birth parents, their children, and the foster families. Of course, active participation in an addiction treatment program is also extremely helpful.

Addressing Parental Ambivalence

Birth parent ambivalence is usually attributable to one or more of three sources (Brudenell, 1997; Hess & Folaron, 1991; Marcenko & Striepe, 1997):

- lack of a bond, with resulting lack of investment, in the parent–child relationship;
- concern that the parent lacks the skills to care for the child adequately; and
- concern that stress associated with parenting will cause or contribute to parental relapse and a preference not to endanger themselves or their children in this way.

Because parental ambivalence is potentially so destructive—especially to the relationship between the birth and foster families and to foster care outcomes—clinical intervention must recognize and resolve it.

Name and normalize ambivalence

The first step in addressing ambivalence is to name and normalize it. For example, parents who do not desire reunification with their children usually encounter heavy negative judgment. Because of this, without explicit permission and encouragement from others these parents are unlikely to acknowledge their doubts about their desire or ability to parent. It is helpful to remind them that, even though most parents do reunify with their children, almost all of these parents harbored doubts about their desire or ability to do so at some point. It is even more helpful if you can network the birth parents in your office with other birth parents who have either successfully reunified or who made other plans for their children's care in a conscious and caring way.

Resolve ambivalence

Once the existence of ambivalence is out of the closet, you can work on addressing its source(s). If the concern is lack of an emotional bond, then a purposeful visitation plan with appropriate parent coaching is appropriate. If the concern is lack of skills, or the inability to handle simultaneous reunification with multiple children, then the case plan can be adjusted to allow gradual reunification and appropriate support of parenting skills. If the concern is over parenting-induced relapse, then enhanced relapse prevention planning (coordinated with the parent's treatment provider) and enhanced parenting-specific posttreatment support services can be arranged. Foster parents can play pivotal roles in each of these scenarios.

However, if this is to happen, parental ambivalence must be out in the open and consciously addressed. If it is ignored it will resurface later and wreak havoc on the relationship between the birth and foster families. Also, when you overtly explore ambivalence, permanency planning may speed up. In some cases the birth parents may decide that they genuinely do not desire reunification. You and they can then turn your attention to alternative permanency planning and appropriate parent–child closure.

Improving self-awareness of behavior with the foster family

Birth parents often harbor resentment and defensiveness toward foster parents. However, they may be unaware of how they communicate this verbally and nonverbally. They may also be so angry at the system, and so fearful of being replaced by foster parents, that they are hesitant or unable to express gratitude to caregivers. Therefore, promoting awareness of their behavior and improving their communication skills with the foster parents and other caregivers is important.

Again, groupwork with birth parents is very useful in achieving these goals. You also can do this work individually. I often invite birth parents to make a list of their criticisms and praise regarding the foster parents. I specifically ask them about praise or appreciation, because I want to encourage them to move beyond their gripes and find aspects of the caregiver that they can connect with in positive ways. I then validate the birth parents' criticisms, explore their praise, and expand on that if possible. Finally, I invite the birth parents to use the *Inventory of My Behavior with My Child's Caregiver* (appended at the end of this chapter) to evaluate their relationship with the foster parents. Discussion of specific inventory items usually sparks lively conversation about both foster parent and birth parent behavior. If you use a group format, invite one set of parents to dramatize or role play interactions with foster parents—you will find that the other parents are often excellent sources of feedback about verbal and nonverbal behaviors. When birth parents identify legitimate complaints about foster family behavior, you can coach them about how to raise their concerns in a respectful way, even rehearsing their approach as needed.

It is also helpful to encourage birth parents to respect foster family rules and boundaries, and to express gratitude to the foster family. You can use the criticism/praise exercise above to coach birth parents to offer genuine thanks and appreciation for specific foster family acts. Many reluctant birth parents find that, when their expressions are genuine, appreciation will go a long way toward softening foster parents and garnering more support and flexibility from them in return.

Foster Family Contributions and Guidelines for Action

Whenever you have the privilege to work with foster parents—during recruitment, in training, or after a child is placed—there is much you can do to encourage the attitudes and skills necessary to working productively with birth families. Whether they are new to fostering or have years of experience, it is always helpful to develop a substantial relationship with foster families from the earliest point of contact. If you are not prompt in connecting with a foster family, you may have to do a lot more work to enable them to view birth family reunification as the primary function of fostering and not just the birth family's and agency's responsibilities. It is very important that all members of the team (foster family, agency, birth parents) are working toward the same goal.

Such a foundation of understanding requires therapists to work consistently with foster parents from the very beginning of treatment (Sumner-Mayer, 2003, 2006). It also requires that dialogue and discussion with foster families be broader than the immediate concerns of managing the foster child's behavior. When foster parents are given the opportunity to discuss and reflect on their fostering experiences, they tend to spontaneously develop greater self-awareness and the ability to include themselves in the relational equation. You can take advantage of the recruitment and initial training processes to shape inchoate role conceptions among the foster parents, and even consult on the prospective foster families' certification assessment. Are the family members willing and able to adopt the necessary mindset? This must include acceptance of the idea of preserving birth family relationships during placement, outreach to the extended birth family, and working toward identifying and creating space for birth family strengths to emerge.

Foster parents do not often think of themselves as therapy clients, and we need to be mindful of this, as we work to cultivate more willingness in the foster family to examine their own ideas and practices. We need to convey respect for the foster families as fellow team members with special expertise. In doing so, we need to maintain an ongoing dialogue with them in order to understand more about who they are, how they approach fostering, and how previous fostering experiences are informing their expectations and concerns about the current placement. Out of these interactions also comes knowledge about what needs might be met by fostering, how roles are conceived, tolerance for boundaries, and what they have learned from their experience of earlier placements—especially fostering-related losses. Such information allows us to draw on foster families' personal and systems resources when difficult times inevitably arise (Hughes, 1997).

While some foster parents implicitly understand the importance of helping children maintain connection with their birth families, others need more help in adopting the necessary mindset. Foster parents who don't see the value of these connections are often acutely aware of the hurt and damage caused by the birth family, and they view their role as protecting foster children from the birth family. It is possible to work with this child-saving mentality and use it to cultivate more willingness to collaborate with the birth family. We do this by appealing to the foster parents' skills and inclinations as nurturers and teachers. We can point out that most foster children, especially teenagers in the foster care system, do maintain relationships with their birth families after their stay in foster care. If foster parents truly wish to save children, the best way may be to take the birth families under their wing, and provide care and mothering for them as well as for their children. We don't do this in a patronizing way. We recognize and honor birth families' desire to provide good parenting for their children.

Developing understanding of and empathy with the birth family

It is extremely helpful when foster families empathize with the birth families with whom they are connected. This empathy often results from a more widely contextualized understanding of the birth families' circumstances. To encourage this, our job is to help foster parents understand the behavior of the children and their birth families within the larger contexts of the families' history, social networks, developmental challenges, and the grief and disorientation associated with the experience of child removal. Foster parents are not likely to easily understand the profound disempowerment, discouragement, and perceived condemnation that birth parents experience when their children are placed in foster care. If we ask foster parents to consider the ways in which birth family behavior may be an expression of those feelings, we can help them break through some of the negative attributions that foster parents often hold about birth parents.

If you are working with foster parents during their initial training, or if you have cultivated a wide-ranging dialogue and good rapport with foster families, you may have earned permission to ask them to reflect on significant losses or challenges in their own lives. It is often helpful to ask the foster parents to think about a time in their own lives when they faced a significant challenge or loss. They may want to consider the following questions: *What was happening in the family? How did family members react? Did people act out of character? How did they work through this time? To whom did they turn for support? How did family roles and routines change during this time?*

Then ask foster parents to imagine how they would feel if the state removed one of their children, and then told them that they would have to prove their worthiness to get the child back. How would they feel upon first meeting the family caring for their child? How might these feelings influence how they behave toward that family? How could that family make it easier or better for them? Our goal is to get foster parents to look to the broader context for explanations of birth family behavior. This helps to depersonalize what the birth parents are seen as doing and to move toward thinking about how the foster family contributes to dynamics in the relationship.

The importance of knowledge about common birth family problems

Foster families find it helpful to understand the circumstances that brought the birth family into the system and to learn about attachment dynamics. Learning about addiction, depression and other mental illnesses, domestic violence, the dynamics in sexually abusive families, and other common presenting issues is very important. When foster parents understand that behavior in families is patterned and follows rules, they are also better able to identify potential strengths. In addition, knowledge of attachment dynamics can help foster parents normalize the children's reactions to birth family contact and also may suggest ways to comfort and guide them. This is important because foster parents often complain that birth family visits are associated with misbehavior, moodiness, and other negative episodes. The apparently adverse events are frequently considered to be evidence that there should be less birth family contact. Instead, the misbehavior and emotional liability probably reflect normal attachment dynamics, such as separation protest. Sometimes *increasing* rather than decreasing contact is most helpful in managing difficult child behavior. Therapists are in a powerful position to help foster parents, case managers, and court personnel appreciate attachment dynamics and respond more appropriately (a good presentation of attachment issues in foster care can be found in Fahlberg, 1991, and in Chapter 8, "Providing Developmentally Appropriate Family Therapy").

Developing skills for interacting with the birth family

It is important that foster parents develop these birth family interaction skills: joining with them, mapping the birth family system, looking for strengths, making room for birth parents to demonstrate and build their competence during visits, and developing awareness of their own attributions and ways of understanding birth family behavior (Minuchin, 1990; Minuchin et al., 1998; Sumner-Mayer, 2003, 2006).

Joining. Just as you need to join with new clients, foster parents need to join with birth parents. You can help foster parents join with birth parents by encouraging them to show respect and interest toward them. Encourage foster parents to

- compliment birth parents on qualities they appreciate about them or the children,
- ask questions about routines and the ways things were done in the birth family before placement,
- reassure birth parents that they are not trying to take their place in the child's heart,
- ask birth parents if they are pleased with how the foster parent is caring for the child,

- respect the need for parent and child to have privacy during visits (within the limitations set by the court),
- welcome the birth parents to their home, assuming the agency does not actively oppose this practice, and
- demonstrate interest in gathering information about the birth family and its resources.

"You're going to visit your children in somebody else's home. They are doing what you should be able to do for them. The guilt complex is overwhelming. You just can't describe it—walking into a house and having your children call somebody else Mommy and Daddy. You want them to be treated as their own children. You want them to call them Mommy and Daddy, to feel this much relaxed with them, to go to them with their problems. But you don't want it. You are their mother. They are nothing but caretakers for the children, and this is very difficult to face. But I walked in the house anyway … Bless this woman, bless Lucille. I knocked on the door and the kids opened the door because they were expecting me, and they went, 'Mommy, Mommy,' and they jumped all around me, and I stood there stiffly afraid to walk in the front door.

"She was in the kitchen … She said, 'Hi, come right in. The coffee's on the stove, the cups are up here—grab a cup. Sit down and we'll talk.' Like I was a neighbor, not like I was company coming to visit her home. Like this was something I did every day. I walked in and grabbed a coffee cup off the shelf, poured myself a cup, and it totally relaxed me.

"I think it might have scared me away, if they had been dressed up for a Sunday afternoon visit, ushered me into the parlor where I sat there very stiffly, and said to my children, 'How do you do?' But here I was taken as a friend. We talked about the weather and I don't really remember vividly, but I remember the conversations were very general. It was like two neighbors sitting down and talking.

"She suggested to the children that they bring me outside to show me some pets that they had in the backyard, to give me a chance to be with my children without her making some excuse, 'Well, I'll go upstairs and powder my nose.' Bless this woman, Lucille."

—U.S. Department of Health, Education, & Welfare, 1976, cited in Lee & Nisivoccia, 1989, p. 35–36

Mapping. A basic family map brings family patterns, important relationships, and history into clear focus in a way that words rarely do. It also may uncover potential resources. You can teach receptive foster parents how to create a basic family map for themselves and how to invite birth families to create their own family map with them. Such maps would include information about family members, their ages, and where they live; it may include individuals who are significant family resources and convey basic information about the quality of relationships. The curiosity and respect conveyed by asking into and sharing wider family and community connections can counteract birth parents' suspicion and hostility, uncover information about family strengths, and provide stories that support the children's identity. Maps also encourage foster parents to think about the wider context of their own attitudes and behaviors, and about birth family problems and resources.

Searching for strengths. A focus on birth parents' problems is both necessary and inevitable in foster care. However, an exclusive focus on problems and pathology often leads to overly negative, trait-based attributions about birth parents. Such characterizations neither recognize their complexity nor nurture their ability to better care for their children. If foster parents were inclined to look for, point out, and build on birth family strengths, they would instead demonstrate respect for and foster confidence in birth parents' abilities to care for their children. Searching for strengths is not sugarcoating problems—it is a reframing of events that recognizes positive intent and focuses on things the parents already are doing well. This orientation builds optimism while realistically amplifying competence. In short, we uncover what the parent can do now in a way that encourages better performance in the future (Lee & Nisivoccia, 1989). We can ask foster parents to review their interactions with birth parents and think about opportunities to point out strengths and how to frame constructive criticism in ways that support birth parents' efforts to provide care for their children.

> A birth parent who had been reluctant to hold her 6-month-old baby, and who did not often try to engage the baby in play, was visiting the child in the agency visitation room. She laid the baby on the carpeted floor on her stomach, and showed the baby two or three toys she brought for the visit. She waved them in front of the baby to get her attention and handed the baby each toy. Rather than rushing in to reposition the child and to criticize the parent for placing the child on the floor, the foster parent noted out loud how responsive the baby was to her mother's attempts to engage her. She praised the mother for learning how to play with her child and bringing toys the child enjoyed. Then she suggested that the mother put something on the floor underneath the baby, since the visit room was a heavy traffic area, and to put the toys just out of the baby's reach so as to encourage the baby to move toward them. This would help the baby develop her motor skills.

Making room for parents to act like parents. Also referred to as "working with complementarity" (Minuchin, 1990; Minuchin et al., 1998) and "playing second fiddle to parents" (Felker, 1974, cited in Lee & Nisivoccia, 1989), this refers to recognizing that when one party in a relationship overfunctions, the other will tend to underfunction. Therefore, foster parents should consciously look for ways to create situations where birth parents can exercise parental skills and responsibilities. Once children are placed into foster care, often everyone—the agencies, foster parents, and the birth parents themselves—acts as if the birth parents are incapable of caring for their children. This allows those outside the birth families to literally take over responsibility for the children's lives, even in areas where the birth parents may have the capability to do so if they were allowed and encouraged. Ironically, the birth parents will be required to prove that they are capable of providing such care before they will be allowed to resume responsibility for their children.

Creating the opportunity for parents to act like parents can be as simple as handing the parent the diaper bag at the beginning of a visit rather than the foster parent changing the diaper. The foster parents can ask birth parents their preferences on a child's haircut or solicit their help in solving a problem with the child's behavior. When a foster parent asks "Angelina, how did you handle it when Juan had trouble settling down to sleep, and staying in his bed at night?" it sends a powerful message to Angelina. It implicitly recognizes her experience with Juan and her interest in helping to solve the problem. Within the parameters set by the court for supervision of parent–child contact, therapists should encourage foster parents to invite birth parents' involvement in all possible areas of a child's life. This includes doctor visits, clothes shopping, haircuts, school-related events, and participation in important family celebrations. Honoring the birth parents' rights and respecting their abilities to exert influence in appropriate areas of their children's lives counteracts the tendency toward parent–child alienation during foster care. It also may increase their receptivity to foster parents' coaching on other parenting practices, such as the need for children to have structure, routine, and predictability. In short, by allowing birth parents more influence in their children's lives, foster parents can often increase their own influence on the birth parents' behavior.

Attending to grief and loss issues. There are several things we can do when foster families' problematic responses to the grief and losses associated with fostering get in the way of optimal birth family relationships. We can ask about the previous losses and validate the family members' feelings. We can explore possible links between the strategies the families have used to manage previous losses and current placement difficulties. In so doing, we can help foster family members become more consciously aware of the impact of the loss in the current fostering situation and develop more awareness of their behavior. We can encourage foster family members to do the grief work that remains undone. We can also encourage them to use rituals to heal from past losses and soften the blow of impending ones. We can facilitate connections with other foster families who can provide support. We can encourage the use of spiritual supports.

> "After being in a state of shock and withdrawal over the sudden removal of three siblings from her home, Rosita reported that she spent the first several months of the next foster child's placement consciously attempting to withhold contact, attention, and affection from him. After her mother confronted her about this tactic, Rosita constructed a ritual to help her face and recover from the loss of the previous foster children. She asked family members to join her in sharing memories of these children and talking about their feelings about the end of the placement (which they had all avoided until this time). She gathered all of her photos and mementos of the children, and said the 'good-bye' she wished she could have said in real life. She then put those objects away and decided not to look at them for a period of time. Shortly thereafter she hugged the newer foster child for the first time and, to her surprise, it felt good. With regard to the entire process of recovering from the loss of the previous children, she later reported, 'It put a backbone on me.'"

Improving foster parents' awareness of attributions about birth families. How foster parents think about birth families determines how they feel about and treat them. When foster parents (1) reflect on their impressions of and reactions to birth family behavior and (2) consider how their impressions and behavior influence interactions with birth families, good things tend to happen. The foster parents are more likely to assume a nondefensive stance, less likely to personalize negative birth family and foster child behavior, and often are more willing to alter their behavior in order to increase chances of positive birth family relationships. I refer to this as *Self-Inclusion in the Relational Equation,* or *SIRE* (Sumner-Mayer, 2003, 2006). Foster parents are most likely to SIRE in birth family relationships when they have opportunities to discuss and reflect on interactions with birth families, and when therapists ask questions aimed at uncovering attributions and including themselves in the relational equation: *How do you understand that behavior? What other experiences have led you to believe that [birth parent] will do that? What do you think you could do in this situation to make a difference in the way [birth parent] reacts?* Of course, this process is much easier if, as suggested earlier, you have established a substantial and wide-ranging dialogue with foster parents before placement crises arise.

The value of foster parent support groups. Most foster parents will tell you that no one really understands what it is like to foster better than another foster parent. Foster parents will accept feedback from another foster parent that they might reject from a therapist. If possible, we should advocate for and facilitate foster parent support groups that use the foster parents' own experiences and successes to encourage exploration of their feelings about working with birth families, provide validation of the difficulties involved, and support development of the skills and mindsets (including SIRE) that are so beneficial.

Choreographing the Dance

If there are to be positive, collaborative connections, we need to work with each birth and foster family separately (see reciprocal coaching below), while we also facilitate contact between them. In both the intra- and interfamily work we act as choreographers and dance instructors. We want to teach our families how to work effectively together, while we also identify and discourage tendencies that might keep them from reaching their full potential. In this regard, it is always a good idea to meet separately with birth and foster families before facilitating joint contact. This is true even if they have already met each other. Separate meetings allow us to assess each family's thoughts and feelings regarding the other parties, and to begin to work on the skills and attitudes discussed in earlier sections of this chapter. However, joint meetings should start as soon as possible. Ideally, the first time the families meet should not include the child. However, a parent–child visit can follow this meeting immediately.

Placement Phase

Early meetings with foster and birth families should focus on everyone getting to know each other, establishing goals for parent–child contact, and developing understanding and agreement regarding what form the planned parenting time might take and how it is to be scheduled. These early meetings are for joining, learning about each other—mapping is a good tool at this phase—and developing an alliance in support of the children. Once the children recognize this alliance, they can feel secure in the knowledge that both of their families are on the same page. Again, it is not important for the foster and birth family to like each other, or for the foster family to take the birth family under its wing. Although this may be helpful, it is more important that both families agree that frequent communication and contact need to occur for the child's sake.

Once the framework is established, ongoing contact and visits should be structured purposefully to meet case goals. For more detail on planning purposeful and therapeutic visitation, see Chapter 6, "The Case for Relational Therapy with Young Children in Foster Care"; Chapter 8, "Providing Developmentally Appropriate Family Therapy"; and Chapter 18, "Teaching Developmentally Appropriate Parenting" (also see Bicknell-Hentges, 1995; Hess & Proch, 1988; Warsh, Maluccio, & Pine, 1994). Depending on how the supervision of family visits takes place, foster parents may be reporting what transpires to case managers. This process should be as transparent as possible and reports should be about birth parent behavior rather than character. Recognition of strengths would be beneficial.

The foster and birth parents should have time before and after visits to discuss logistics and relationships with the agency. This communication should not take place during the visits themselves because the time with the children is precious. Before, during, and after the visits we can coach case managers and foster parents on how best to invite and facilitate birth parent participation and competence in these sessions. We should also be alert to how we ourselves participate in these joint meetings. We want to create as much room as possible for the birth and foster parents to communicate directly rather than through us.

Early on in this process, we can expect to engage in substantial "reciprocal coaching;" that is, we need to go to each family in turn and resolve any impediments to a collaborative process. For example, both families will probably need to process their reactivity to each other, explore their attributions, depersonalize interactions, and redirect their focus to the child's needs. This process will be highlighted in a case example to follow below.

Later phases involve more concentrated preparation for reunification or movement toward another permanency option. Accordingly, our work with birth and foster families is largely focused on the children's responses to those things associated with ending their current placement, and how to negotiate continued contact after a new placement has been made (see Chapter 19, "'Ready or Not, Here I Come!' Equipping Families for Transitions").

Ritualizing Transitions

There are three critical transition points that deserve special attention because of the unique dynamics involved with shifting family memberships in foster families (Minuchin et al., 1998):

- joining the foster family,
- visiting with the birth family, and
- leaving the foster family.

Rituals are particularly useful in helping individuals and families manage life transitions and cope with losses (Imber-Black, 1989; Imber-Black & Roberts, 1998; Jewett; 1982). The absence of rituals is associated with the deleterious effects of ambiguous loss (Boss, 1999). Accordingly, establishing rituals related to comings and goings of family members is a helpful practice for adoptive and foster families (Imber-Black, Roberts, & Whiting, 1988; Lieberman & Bufferd, 1999; Minuchin et al., 1998; Pavao, 1998).

As we observed earlier, during visitation foster children literally travel between two families of which they are a meaningful part. Each family has its ways of being, doing business, and enforcing membership. Foster parents frequently complain about the children's behavior before and after visits. Ritualizing visitation is helpful because it makes the transition process more transparent, congruent, and concrete. Transitioning out of a placement is another major stress point. All foster family members must come to terms with the impending loss and negotiate the anxiety caused by living "in between" families. This is a prime time for crises to develop. A crisis enables the children and foster parents to avoid grappling with grief and loss by becoming preoccupied with the immediate problem or escaping into anger and distance. Ritualizing impending changes and losses enables all family members to explore their mixed feelings and anxiety regarding the changes.

> "When Sharita began visits with her birth family, we used sessions to discuss differences in the ways her foster and birth families worked. We focused on how routines, rituals, rules, and boundaries varied between the two families. Her foster and birth parents discussed what routines were most helpful to Sharita, and how these could be preserved in the birth family's home during visits while still honoring that family's uniqueness and autonomy. I encouraged the foster and birth parents to have contact in the days before a scheduled visit and at the end of visits to discuss Sharita's mood and any 'baggage' she may be carrying into either home from the previous days, the visit plan, and ways to make the transition smoother. Although Sharita and her two sets of parents enjoyed the time they spent together, there were bumpy moments during the transition process, especially around differences in rules between the two homes.

> "Sharita had just learned to ride a bicycle with different speeds. So I observed that switching between homes was like

changing the gears of her bicycle. She had to figure out which gear she needed to be in to handle the road she was on at the time. (The foster and birth parents could also relate to this metaphor as car drivers.) Sharita really got into the metaphor and asked to make a 'Visit Gear Changer.' In a session with her birth mother Sharita constructed a gear changer out of cardboard, grommets, and art supplies. Sharita decided to include 'school' on the gear changer as well, since there was a different schedule and different rules there as well. She and her birth and foster parents developed a ritual around taking out the gear changer at the beginning of a visit (or upon Sharita's return), turning it to the right 'setting,' and reviewing some of the house rules for that setting. When Sharita had difficulty following a rule or routine in either setting, her foster or birth parents would first ask her, 'What gear are you in?' By normalizing the difficulty of adjusting to new rules and routines, they also contextualized Sharita's behavior. This reduced their frustration with her adjustment difficulties and their tendency to blame the other parents."

Special Issues

So far we have discussed the course of foster care as if it follows a single developmental trajectory from beginning to end. We recognize that this often is not the case. Nonnormative events involving one or more of the parties—employment changes, geographic moves, illness, couple problems, economic problems, incarceration, and relapse, to name a few —may change the course of a case. We want stability for our foster children, but flux may be more typical. Crises often are made worse for the children by the loss of a positive relationship between the birth family and the foster family. At such times everyone on the team—birth parents, foster parents, children, case managers, and extended families—may find reason to feel disappointed, discouraged, angry, and perhaps frightened. The investment of hope and energy may seem all for naught. With regard to the relationship between birth and foster families, we worry that the various parties may cut off contact with each other and give up on a collaborative approach.

There is a great deal that we can offer in these difficult circumstances. We can validate and empathize with the adults' and children's disappointment, worry, and concern. We can separate the actions experienced as betrayal from an individual's intent and caring. We can regroup the members of the system, including replacement members, and with them reaffirm the need for a collaborative alliance in the best interests of the children. We can identify and address new obstacles, such as renewed distrust, pessimism, and defensiveness. As mentioned, this may require individual and joint sessions attended by reciprocal coaching.

Case Example

The following case example illustrates the process of building a cooperative relationship between birth and foster families. The clinical work necessary takes place at multiple system levels. The vignette also highlights the roles of reciprocal coaching, bridging foster and birth families, and rituals in easing transitions between homes and families.

"Trevor and Tracy, 9- and 10-year-old siblings, had been in foster care for over a year, while their mother, Annette, completed drug treatment and continued therapy to manage symptoms of a mood disorder. Annette was making good progress in her treatment and was working toward reunification with Trevor and Tracy. Starr, or 'Auntie Starr' as they called her, was Trevor and Tracy's second foster parent. Starr's teenaged daughter, Stacy, and nine-year-old son, Deshawn, were also part of the foster family. Starr and Annette had met twice at the agency, but they had little contact outside of these encounters except for occasional phone calls. In my first in-person meeting with Starr (without Annette present), I asked her how she might feel about Trevor and Tracy having family visits in her home. She was wary, but open-minded.

She worried that Annette might criticize her care of Trevor and Tracy, worried about privacy issues, and wasn't sure how it might affect the placement if the visits didn't go well. On the other hand, she heard a lot of positive things about Annette from Trevor and Tracy, and she credited Annette for them being 'nice kids from the beginning.'

"When I first asked the child protective services case manager if Annette could visit her children in the foster home, she stated that this was against the usual policy. She questioned the wisdom of such an arrangement, especially given Annette's guarded prognosis for sustained recovery and reunification. I worked with the case manager and her supervisor to convince them of the benefits of in-home visiting and to allay their concerns regarding risk to the foster parent. They subsequently gave their permission.

"Before the first planned visit, a terrible tragedy occurred. Trevor and Tracy's older sister died unexpectedly in an auto accident. The first in-home visit, already scheduled, would be the time and place for Annette to tell them about it. Individual and joint discussions with Annette and Starr before the session helped them work out what their respective roles would be and how they might respond to the children. Annette expressed worry to me privately about not being able to handle her grief, and not being strong enough for her children. She also worried about Starr's impression of her as a parent if these traits became apparent. Starr worried privately about how Annette would feel if the children turned to her instead of Annette for comfort. After encouraging Starr to share this concern with Annette and broaching it myself during a conjoint meeting to create an opening, Annette admitted that this would hurt, but she would also feel good knowing that they could rely on Starr for comfort at a time like this. Starr appreciated Annette's thoughtfulness about this possibility.

"The children experienced both their birth and foster families' presence when they learned of their sister's death, and Annette and Starr vowed to the children to work together to help them get through this time in their lives. Over the next several days, frequent phone calls, brief visits from Annette, and funeral preparations brought the families closer together. In the weeks that followed, the increased phone contact continued and helped the children grieve and adjust to the loss.

"The increased contact also created opportunities for friction to arise between Annette and Starr, requiring another round of reciprocal coaching and bridging work. Starr felt burdened by Annette's phone calls and complained to me about them in an individual session. She began by saying that the calls were too frequent and disruptive. Careful questioning revealed that it was not the frequency of calls that was problematic, but their timing. Annette's frequent phone calls often came in the after-school hours, when Starr was busy with homework help, dinner preparations, and caring for a new arrival, a foster baby. In addition, Starr assumed that the frequency and timing of the calls was designed to check up on her parenting, which she resented. After I validated Starr's resentment, I asked what led her to assume that Annette was checking up on her. She said she could not understand why the calls needed to be so frequent now, since the immediate crisis of the death had passed several weeks before. I encouraged her to consider the children's attachment needs at a time like this, and we discussed the need to discuss these problems with Annette. I encouraged her to communicate her concerns to Annette in a respectful way and we discussed how to do so, and what might get in the way.

"Meanwhile, Annette had begun to sense Starr's impatience on the phone, and she personalized it, accusing Starr in an individual session of impeding her progress toward reunification. 'How am I supposed to get them back if I can't be a part of their everyday lives?' she ranted. I helped Annette separate out her anger at Starr from her anger at the system, and she was able to see how her previously adversarial relationship with her caseworker was contaminating her otherwise good relationship with Starr.

"During the joint session, Starr brought up the phone calls and disarmed Annette by stating up front that she welcomed frequent contact, but they needed to work on the timing. In response to careful probing by me, Annette explained that when she, Trevor, and Tracy lived together, they had an informal ritual of spending time right after school recounting the day's events, and that she was trying to preserve this ritual now that she and the children were separated. Annette apologized to Starr for not appreciating how difficult the after school hours were for her, and her anger about being 'kept from her children' dissipated quickly when she realized that Starr was interested in working with her on a solution. She agreed to call in the after-dinner hours more often. During this conversation, Annette also expressed appreciation for Starr's caring and sensitivity toward her children. I encouraged Starr to respond to Annette's explanation of the timing of calls and her expression of gratitude, both of which counteracted Starr's negative attribution about the frequency and timing of the calls. Starr said that she was pleased that Annette approved of her caregiving.

"An additional and unanticipated benefit of this exchange was that, in addition to Annette altering her calling patterns, Starr began calling Annette as well, in order to keep her up to date on the kids' daily lives. At a scheduled unsupervised visit during which Annette was to take the children out, the children asked if Deshawn could come along, and Starr agreed. Annette later commented that Starr's entrusting her son to her care felt like a turning point in their relationship and in her sense of herself as a competent parent.

"Trevor, Tracy, and Annette reunited six months later. They planned an elaborate 'Going Home Day' ceremony to be held in Starr's home and including Annette's mother and the caseworker. Starr, Stacy, and Deshawn decorated the house with banners and balloons. Trevor and Tracy made cards expressing gratitude and identifying the role each family member, their case manager, and I played in them going home. They shared their cards aloud and told stories of the placement, and of the family's progress. Annette thanked Starr for caring for her children. Starr responded that it was Annette's hard work that made this day possible. The case manager admitted her initial skepticism about encouraging the relationship between Annette and Starr. She then expressed her admiration for Annette's hard work, and her gratitude for having this experience and learning to work differently. Everyone shared cake and they talked about how they would maintain their connections after that day, especially in light of the affection Trevor, Tracy, and Deshawn had for each other. Starr vowed to remain a supportive contact to Annette, Trevor, and Tracy. She offered to have the children stay with her occasionally on weekends or in emergencies to offer Annette respite. We videotaped the entire ceremony and both families received copies to retain for future viewing."

Conclusion

Working within and between foster and birth families requires commitment, skill, and humility, but the rewards are rich. When optimal outcomes are achieved, everyone feels the success. Even when the permanency plan changes, or when foster or birth families are not able to function in optimal ways, we can be satisfied knowing that we have done everything possible to help children and families along their journey. Regardless of the outcomes, when we honor individuals and relationships the entire foster care process has greater integrity and the likelihood of positive long-term outcomes is increased. Foster children and their families deserve nothing less.

Inventory of My Behavior
with My Children's Caregiver(s)

Directions: Place a check mark in the space next to each behavior that you have done, even once, in the past or in the present.

Some checkmark lines are on the right and some are on the left. If you have done that behavior, place your checkmark wherever the line is for that item. Be truthful with yourself—no one else will see this paper. When you are done, read the instructions at the end of the inventory.

_____ Thank caregiver for taking care of my child

_____ Express appreciation for specific things caregiver
does for child or for me

_____ Make every scheduled visit or call at least one day
in advance to reschedule

Miss a visit occasionally without giving more
than one day's advance notice   _____

Miss visits more than occasionally   _____

Miss a visit without calling afterward to say why
or say hello   _____

Show up for visits at days/times not scheduled,
or without advance permission or notice   _____

_____ Ask caregiver what is new with my child/ask
about changes and progress

_____ Ask caregiver how I can help make his or her job easier

Refuse to be flexible with caregiver on visit date
or time because I am unhappy with something
caregiver did or said   _____

Say negative things about caregiver where child
can hear me   _____

Give negative messages about caregiver in front of
child without actually saying anything negative out loud   _____

_____ Make a plan for visits—activities, etc.

_____ Share plan for visit with caregiver beforehand

_____ Come to visit prepared with something for child—food, or supplies for an activity, or something like that

Bring a gift to every or almost every visit   _____

Bring a large or expensive gift to some or most visits   _____

_____ Know the caregiver's rules for child (about behavior, food, schedules, etc.)

_____ Cooperate with caregiver's rules during visits, even when caregiver is not there (for example, don't give child food that caregiver doesn't approve of; follow caregiver's rule about bedtime, or no playtime before homework is done, etc.)

_____ Tell child to follow caregiver's rules and respect caregiver

Tell child he/she does not have to follow caregiver's rules while on a visit with me   _____

Tell child he/she does not have to follow caregiver's rules when in caregiver's home   _____

_____ Check with caregiver for permission before doing something that might be against his or her rules (even if it's not against your rules)

_____ Try to follow caregiver's schedule for child (re: bedtime, etc.) during longer visits

Bring up old beefs with caregiver without admitting to the part I played   _____

Use a third party (someone else) to communicate with caregiver about my child instead of talking directly with caregiver   _____

Avoid listening to things caregiver says about the effects of my behavior on my child (past or current)   _____

Dismiss what I hear about my child because I don't like who's saying it   _____

Dismiss what I hear about myself from the
caregiver because I feel angry or hurt by him or her   ____

Answer disrespect from caregiver by showing
disrespect toward caregiver   ____

____ Tell my child it's okay to love both me and
the caregiver

Tell my child it's not okay to love the caregiver
(either direct or indirect)   ____

Directions

Behaviors with a blank on the left are usually helpful to caregivers,
your child, and in the long run, to you. Behaviors with a blank on
the right are usually NOT helpful to your caregiver or your child—
so they create problems for them and for you.

Add up the number of behaviors on each side and write them
in below:

Helpful behaviors (left side): ____
Unhelpful behaviors (right side): ____

Go back to the list and pat yourself on the back for all the
behaviors you are already doing that are helpful (left side). Decide
which of these you can do even more. Circle at least one helpful
behavior that you can either do more of (if you are already doing
it), or that you can start doing if you are not already.

NOW, go back to the list and look at the behaviors you checked
on the right side of the page. Circle at least one unhelpful behavior
that you can work on—either do it less, or stop doing it all together.
Think about what might get in the way of changing this behavior,
and what you will need to do in order to make good on your decision to change it.

Congratulations. You have just made an honest self-assessment
of behaviors that are helpful and behaviors that are not so helpful
with your child's caregiver. Helping your child's caregiver helps
your child AND yourself in the long run.

References

Bicknell-Hentges, L. (1995) The stages of the reunification process and the tasks of the therapist. In L. Combrinck-Graham (Ed.), *Children in families at risk: Maintaining the connections* (pp. 326–349). New York: Guilford Press.

Boss, P. (1999). *Ambiguous loss: Learning to live with unresolved grief.* Cambridge, MA: Harvard University Press.

Brudenell, I. (1997). A grounded theory of protecting recovery during transition to motherhood. *American Journal of Drug and Alcohol Abuse 23*, 453–466.

Colapinto, J. (March 19, 2005). *Playing it straight in the foster care system.* Workshop presented at the 28th Annual Psychotherapy Networker Symposium, Washington, DC.

Crumbley, J., & Little, R. (Eds.). (1997). *Relatives raising children: An overview of kinship care.* Washington, DC: Child Welfare League of America.

Dillon, D. (1994). Understanding and assessment of intragroup dynamics in family foster care: African American families. *Child Welfare, 73,* 129–139.

Duclos, A. (1987). Clinical aspects of the training of foster parents. *Child and Adolescent Social Work, 4*(3–4), 187–194.

Edelstein, S. (1981). When foster children leave: Helping foster parents to grieve. *Child Welfare, 58,* 564–570.

Edelstein, S. B., Burge, D., & Waterman, J. (2001). Helping foster parents cope with separation, loss, and grief. *Child Welfare, 80,* 5–25.

Fahlberg, V. (1991). *A child's journey through placement.* Indianapolis, IN: Perspectives Press.

Felker, D. W. (1974). *Building positive self-concepts.* Upper Saddle River, NJ: Pearson Custom Publishing.

Hess, P. M., & Folaron, G. (1991). Ambivalences: A challenge to permanency for children. *Child Welfare, 70,* 403–424.

Hess, P. M., & Proch, K. O. (1988). *Family visiting in out-of-home care: A guide to practice.* Washington, DC: Child Welfare League of America.

Hughes, D. A. (1997). *Facilitating developmental attachment: The road to emotional recovery and behavioral change in foster and adopted children.* Northvale, NJ: Jason Aronson.

Imber-Black, E. (1989). Idiosyncratic life cycle transitions and therapeutic rituals. In B. Carter & M. McGoldrick (Eds.), *The changing family life cycle: A framework for family therapy* (2nd ed., pp. 149–163). Boston: Allyn and Bacon.

Imber-Black, E., & Roberts, J. (1998). *Rituals for our times: Celebrating, healing, and changing our lives and relationships.* Northvale, NJ: Jason Aronson.

Imber-Black, E., Roberts, J., & Whiting, R. A. (Eds.). (1988). *Rituals in families and family therapy.* New York: Norton.

Jewett, C. L. (1982). *Helping children cope with separation and loss.* Boston: Harvard Common Press.

Kosonen, M. (1996). Maintaining sibling relationships—Neglected dimension in child care practice. *British Journal of Social Work, 26,* 809–822.

Lee, J., & Nisivoccia, D. (1989). *Walk a mile in my shoes: A book about biological parents for foster parents and social workers.* Washington, DC: Child Welfare League of America.

Lieberman, C. A., & Bufferd, R. K. (1999). *Creating ceremonies: Innovative ways to meet adoption challenges.* Phoenix, AZ: Zeig, Tucker.

Maluccio, A. N., Ambramczyk, L. W., & Thomlison, B. (1996). Family reunification of children in out-of-home care: Research perspectives. *Children and Youth Services Review, 18*(4/5), 287–305.

Maluccio, A. N., Warsh, R., & Pine, B. A. (1993). Family reunification: An overview. In B. A. Pine, R. Warsh, & A. N. Maluccio (Eds.), *Together again: Family reunification in foster care* (pp. 3–20). Washington, DC: Child Welfare League of America.

Marcenko, M. O., & Striepe, M. I. (1997). A look at family reunification through the eyes of mothers. *Community Alternatives: International Journal of Family Care, 9*(1), 33–48.

McFadden, E. J. (1996). Family-centered practice with foster-parent families. *Families in Society, 77,* 545–557.

Minuchin, P. (1990). *Training manual for foster parents based on an ecological perspective on foster care.* New York: Family Studies, Inc.

Minuchin, P. (1995). Foster and natural families: forming a cooperative network. In L. Combrinck-Graham (Ed.), *Children in families at risk: Maintaining the connections* (pp. 251–274). New York: Guilford.

Minuchin, P., Colapinto, J., & Minuchin, S. (1998). *Working with families of the poor.* New York: Guilford.

Pavao, J. M. (1999). *The family of adoption.* Boston: Beacon Press.

Palmer, S. E. (1996). Placement stability and inclusive practice in foster care: An empirical study. *Children and Youth Services Review, 18,* 589–601.

Pine, B., Warsh, R., & Maluccio, T. (Eds.). (1993). *Together again: Family reunification in foster care.* Washington, DC: Child Welfare League of America.

Sumner-Mayer, K. (2003). The inner workings of foster families: Implications for family therapists. *Dissertation Abstracts International: Section B: The Sciences and Engineering, 64* (2-B), 976.

Sumner-Mayer, K. (2006). Children in foster families. In L. Combrinck-Graham (Ed.), *Children in Family Contexts* (2nd ed., pp. 190–222). New York: Guilford.

Tiddy, S. G. (1986). Creative cooperation: Involving biological parents in long-term foster care. *Child Welfare, 65*(1), 53–62.

U.S. Department of Health, Education, and Welfare (1976). *Don't condemn me till you know me* (film transcript) Washington, DC: Author.

Urquhart, L. R. (1989). Separation and loss: Assessing the impacts on foster parent retention. *Child and Adolescent Social Work, 6,* 193–209.

Warsh, R., Maluccio, A., & Pine, B. (1994). *Teaching family reunification: A sourcebook.* Washington, DC: Child Welfare League of America.

Weinstein, N., & Takas, M. (2001). *The ties that bind: Kinship care and parental substance abuse.* New York: Phoenix House.

Young, N. K., Gardner, S. L., & Dennis, K. (1998). *Responding to alcohol and other drug problems in child welfare: Weaving together practice and policy.* Washington, DC: Child Welfare League of America.

Kinship Placements: An Integrative Approach

Patricia McKinsey Crittenden and Steve Farnfield

oster care can be used in helpful or harmful ways. In this chapter, we consider the many challenges associated with successful placement in foster care, and address the developmental needs that are common in foster children. Kinship care, which involves fostering, especially fostering by relatives, is explored as an important alternative to standard foster home placements, and it may be used in the most advantageous ways. We offer guidelines to help case managers make decisions involving relative and nonrelative foster placements that will not only protect children in the short-term, but also promote their long-term development and the availability and goodwill of those adults who rear them.

When children must be removed from their parents, most communities now have a policy of placing them with relatives, if possible; with nonrelative foster parents, if suitable relatives are not available; and in residential care, only if all else fails. Kinship placement can provide advantages that traditional foster home placement cannot. Potential benefits may include less disruption for the child, improved long-term outcomes for families, and support for the needs and strengths of the children, depending on the organization of the kinship networks and the availability of support services. Given the many challenges inherent in removing children from their birth parents and placing them with others, the potential benefits of kinship placements should be carefully considered. This chapter will discuss many of the general challenges and issues with out-of-home placement for children, and then explore how kinship networks may be helpful in addressing them. Consider the following case in light of these issues.

> A pair of preschool-aged twins is awaiting adoption. Three years ago, they and their siblings were placed in foster care with a couple willing to adopt the entire sibship. Adoption was not yet possible and, after two years, the couple wanted a vacation. The twins were placed temporarily in another foster home. These foster parents fell in love with them and were permitted to adopt them, in part because it kept them away from their very troubled older sibling. The original couple complained—and were blacklisted by the local authority. The adoption failed when the children's initially sweet behavior turned to aggression, bedwetting, and tantrums. They were moved to a new foster home. A social worker, deemed an attachment expert, assessed the children, determined that they were "unattached" and recommended that they stay in this foster placement until they learned to attach, then be made available for adoption (to yet another family). Within weeks, when the third foster mother complained of increasing behavior problems, one of us (PMC) carried out formal assessments of attachment. The twins were anxiously caregiving of the foster mother—and equally so to the stranger. In fact, they behaved in ways characteristic of nonspecific, "promiscuous" attachment. They were not attached to any adult, but they were attached to each other. In the dangerous world created by adults, they each were the single, stable point of reference for the other sibling and they guarded one another both tenderly and fearfully. Ironically, in three short years, by following its written policies, the social service that had set out to protect these children had destroyed every relationship they had formed with adults, separated them from all other family members, and rendered them unadoptable. They also lost a competent foster family.

Short-Term Versus Long-Term Placement Goals

The short-term goal of placement is the safety of the child. Unfortunately, this immediate protection is frequently obtained at the expense of long-term planning. Current placement practice can have a divisive effect on parents and children. If service personnel or temporary caregivers believe that the child is being protected *from* the parents, then the needs of the child are placed in opposition to those of the parents. If the alternative perspective is taken—that the child's *family* needs protection and preservation—both professionals' and caregivers' perspectives change. Often foster children's interests more nearly coincide with their parents' (see Crittenden, 2006). We all agree that the long-term goals of foster placement are:

- *Promoting enduring relationships.* Any action that reduces children's ability to establish their own families as adults is inherently detrimental to children's welfare. Because children with multiple placements are less able to form enduring intimate relationships, reducing the number of broken attachment relationships is essential to the long-term welfare of children. And separation creates anxiety and doubt for *both* parent and child. This is true no matter how the situation is explained, and no matter what the parents did that required the children to be removed from the home. Once people have experienced painful breaks in relationships, they want to prevent the recurrence of that sort of pain. For parents, that may mean that they pull back from the relationship with the child. This makes it more difficult for parents to fully accept the child if he or she is returned. This invites a cycle of failed attempts at rehabilitation (Quinton, Rushton, Dance, & Mays, 1998) and sometimes serious maltreatment (English, Marshall, Brummel, & Orme, 1999; Reder, Duncan, & Gray, 1993).

- *Promoting children's identity.* In order for children to develop a healthy psychological self (in other words, a personal identity), they need to experience themselves in interaction with a committed adult over long periods of time. At about three years of age, children begin to develop an autobiographical narrative of their personal life experiences. A semantically defined self, one expressed in terms of values, beliefs, and ideals (an Eriksonian self-identity), does not develop until adolescence and, if these earlier forms of identity have been managed successfully, the adolescent self is in little jeopardy. However, if the adolescents are in foster care, it might take longer to form and stabilize. When there is no permanent interaction with a caregiver or when children's caregivers do not know one another, children cannot experience themselves as responding and feeling in predictable and familiar ways, and thus cannot become aware of their personal characteristics. They also cannot form a sense of agency; a sense where they believe that they have the ability to have predictable effects on others. Even in maltreating homes, children do form a self-identity in these two ways—even if that identity has some negative attributes. But when their primary caregiver has changed several times, the unity of identity is greatly jeopardized. This leads to a fragmented self or lack of a personally generated identity. The latter is an extremely serious condition that can lead to an *"externally assembled self"* (see Crittenden, 2006). Because this is an unintegrated form of self that lacks personally generated input, it bodes very poorly for later adaptation. Stable foster families can enable children to construct a varied and integrated self. Our strategy is continuity of experience as opposed to multiple placements.

• *Fostering children who are likely to become available for adoption.* The most urgent issue for all children is reducing the number of placements. Where adoption is likely, even two placements (the foster and adoptive placements) may seriously threaten a child's potential to form trusting and intimate relationships, as well as his or her ability to regulate feelings and behavior. Steps should be taken to speed decisionmaking regarding permanent termination of parental rights, because uncertainty in relationships always leads to anxiety in both children and adults. If our goal is to place children where they can grow into balanced and adaptive adults, then both they and their parents need the certainty that they are connected to one another permanently. If they do not feel secure in this, they cannot feel confident enough to trust the good times or test the bad times. Those who cannot trust the good times often show compulsive strategies (below). Other children will test the relationship continually. Their behavior asks for constant and repeated evidence that they will be kept and cared for (see coercive strategies below).

Children's Development: Strengths and Limitations

Understanding children's development is crucial to making appropriate placement decisions. In this section, we discuss some general issues regarding attachment, then consider how these issues affect very young children (birth–5 years), school-age children (6–12 years) and adolescents (13–18 years).

Attachment

Attachment refers to the propensity of humans of all ages to form lasting affectional bonds to one or more specific persons—people to whom they turn when they are in danger or feel threatened (Ainsworth, 1979). In childhood, this is usually filled by the child's parents, particularly the mother. Ideally, children have more than one protective figure available and they attach to two or three such figures (for example, mother, father, grandmother) in a hierarchy of closeness and importance (Howes, 1999). This promotes survival should the child lose one or both biological parents. When there are multiple attachments, each is uniquely organized around the sensitivity, responsiveness, and availability of the specific attachment figure. For example, a child can be anxious with his or her mother, but secure with a father or grandmother. The term "attachment" also refers to the strategies used to elicit protection and comfort, and to the mental processing that underlies such strategic behavior (Crittenden, 1997; Crittenden & Claussen, 2003).

It was once thought that adults had to be loving and protective for children to attach. However, it is now well established that children form attachments even to dangerous parents, and that these attachments are as tight (or possibly tighter) than those to protective parents. But they are not secure. Indeed, these attachments can be anxious to the point of displaying very substantial distortions that can be almost impossible to reverse. They typically are called "disorganized" attachments (see Main & Solomon, 1986), and are viewed as a negative development.

These somewhat traditional notions are applied to foster children in this book, namely, Chapter 8, "Providing Developmentally Appropriate Family Therapy" and Chapter 18, "Teaching Developmentally Appropriate Parenting." However, Crittenden (1995, 1997, 2002) has observed abused and neglected children in both home and out-of-home placement, and reframed their disorganized behavior as strategic attempts by the child to reduce the danger he or she has already experienced (and to prepare for it in the future). By adopting this model, you are able to view the world through the child's perspective in order to improve communication between children and the adults in their lives. You help the adults recognize that the children's behavior about which they are complaining is deeper than it appears—the behavior is in response to the perception of danger and is not something that should be suppressed. Adult-focused solutions may seek to rid children of the symptoms without first reducing their feelings of threat. This may make parent–child communication even less explicit and might lead the children to distort current strategies even further.

There are two basic and opposite forms of strategy: compulsive and coercively obsessive. Both compulsive and coercive children are very anxious and all anxious children are agitated, easily aroused, hypervigilant, excessively attentive to the behavior of important adults, and minimally attentive to other situations, for example such as, schoolwork.

Compulsive strategies

Children using compulsive strategies inhibit negative affect, often display false-positive affect, and do what powerful adults want. Children with a withdrawn depressed parent may engage in *compulsive caregiving*. They use role reversal to draw the parents' attention to themselves. This increases children's safety because an inattentive parent cannot be protective. With an aggressively angry parent, a child may be *compulsively compliant,* that is, do exactly as the parent desires without complaint and even before the parent requests it. Needless to say, adults are generally pleased by children who behave in compulsive ways. Unfortunately, the child is improving short-term adaptability (which reduces parental neglect and abuse) at the expense of long-term adaptation. Compulsive children lose access to their own feelings and motivations and become excessively wary of self-revealing intimacy. This bodes poorly for the establishment of family life in adulthood.

If access to the attachment figure is lost altogether, through death or separation, the attached person may become *compulsively promiscuous* or depressed. Compulsively promiscuous children are socially facile with potential caregivers, but distant from the same people when they become a stable part of the child's life. Some school-age children and adolescents find it difficult to engage at all with other potential attachment figures and become *compulsively self-reliant.* This is especially true when multiple separations or losses occur in childhood. Having multiple successive—as opposed to concurrent—attachments makes acceptance and security in future relationships unlikely.

Coercive strategies

Coercively obsessive relationships are the opposite of compulsive relationships. Coercive children have learned that they can manipulate adults' attention and protection by acting aggressively or incompetently. They use exaggerated displays of negative affect to attract attention to themselves. They then reverse their display from angry to "charmingly disarming" when adults change their response. This functions to *maintain* the adults' attention. The shifts in affective display appear to adults to be unpredictable. These children seem demanding, self-focused, dependent, and moody one moment; engagingly sweet, delightful, and even comical the next. The more unsafe coercive children feel, the more likely that their behavior will escalate from merely agitated and clumsy to provocative, disruptive, or even self-harming. In the short-term, the coercive strategy elicits the attention that children need, but over the long-term, it promotes a self-centered, demandingly anxious approach that ultimately frustrates and angers their caregivers. This puts the children at risk for explosively punitive punishment and even rejection.

Children can manage multiple attachment relationships if their caregivers know one another and work together to raise them. Having a primary attachment figure know and approve of a new attachment figure helps children form the new attachment. This collaboration is necessary if the children are to form an integrated self. However, the nature of the new attachment depends not only on the behavior of the new attachment figure but also on the child's prior attachment experience. If children have had disruptions or unwelcome changes in prior attachments, they may resent the new attachment figure and form an anxious relationship. Substitute parents often experience rejection in which a child's responses indicate either worry about forming a relationship that might break, or displaced anger from a more important relationship that the child considers too vulnerable to attack directly (for example, with the birth mother).

Developmental Differences in Fostering

How these attachment issues get played out in foster care depends on the developmental level of the individual child.

Infancy and the preschool years

The quality of care that infants and preschoolers receive is of crucial importance because their minds, and the strategic behavior discussed above, are not yet formed. There is a window of opportunity in the first six months of life, even in cases of very severe parental threat. Children who are removed from their parents and placed in permanent homes within that timeframe are unlikely to experience long-term negative effects (Schaffer, 1971). However, change of caregiver occurring between six and 30 months are likely to be *maximally* disruptive. A person-specific attachment has formed and the children lack the language and cognitive competencies to understand why their parent is no longer available.

Between 30 months and 5–6 years of age, children learn to put thoughts and feelings into language and begin to construct a personal narrative. It is very important that their attachment figures understand their real feelings and give them the correct words for their negative feelings. If attachment figures do not recognize the inner state and label only what they see (or want to see), language may fail the child as a communicative tool. This leaves children without access to their inner selves. Instead they rely excessively on enacted, nonverbal communication (Crittenden, 1997). Older preschool-aged children need help telling both the happy and unhappy stories of their lives. Caregivers who know firsthand what the children have experienced are best able to help them speak from their own perspective. Otherwise, children may say what the adults want to hear or may have no personal perspective at all. Such children later may be vulnerable to a variety of abusive or manipulative influences that provide a ready-made self for the child—these influences may include intimate relationships, cults (religious or otherwise), or gangs.

It is crucial to recognize that only people who know a child's experience firsthand should try to help the child construct a personal narrative; otherwise, there is a possibility of harming the child. Even well-meaning professionals may try to fill in the blanks in such a narrative, especially about a maltreating parent, with feelings that they imagine the child may have or events they have read about in the record. This may become the source of an externally assembled self. Life story work (see Lacher, Nichols, & May, 2005; Rose & Philpot, 2005; Ryan & Walker, 1985, 1993) or some forms of attachment therapy (for example, Hughes, 2003) lend themselves to this sort of misuse. Giving adults' words and events to children can be considerably more harmful than helpful.

School-aged children

A change of home in the school years will be distressing and disruptive. School-aged children normally enlarge their network of protective figures to include teachers and peer best friends. Concurrently, they pull back from their previously close relationships with their parents. Placement in a new home probably means a change in neighborhood and school, and loss of these new protective figures. However, if the biological parents remain a frequent and meaningful part of their children's lives, and if they approve of the new caregivers, children are likely to feel supported through all of the changes.

Multiple changes in placement can do much more harm than good because children may come to believe that they have no control in the most crucial matters of their lives. Distressed school-aged children can be extremely difficult to manage. One problem is that they do not know why they are doing what they do. If they are to control their behavior, children need to be aware of its motivation, but some adults do not want to hear about children's negative feelings or past unpleasant experiences. When adults merely want compliance with their rules, children may only learn what to do and not why they must do it. Children can more easily learn to separate their internal states and motivations from their actions if the substitute parents help children talk about their mixed feelings and motivations without passing judgment. Foster caregivers who fail to understand the meaning of children's behavior sometimes feel overwhelmed because the children appear to be beyond their control. The foster parents' alarm over the behavior may tempt them to seek out quick but dangerous remedies, such as holding or attachment therapies.

Adolescents

Generally, adolescents begin to distance themselves from their parents. They perhaps think of parents more as "consultants" than as direct protectors. This means that adolescents are unlikely to profoundly attach to new caregivers. Because peers are the appropriate focus of adolescents' attachment, group homes with a fostering couple may be a viable context, one that can be preferable to a foster placement.

Many adolescents in care have not learned to differentiate their feelings and motivations from their behavior. As they near adulthood, their behavior may become quite extreme. Some may turn to substance abuse and others to negative peer groups. Girls may become promiscuous—fleeing genuine intimacy while engaging sexually— or pregnant (thus seeking both a partner and a baby to create an instant family). Boys may engage in delinquent behavior. It may be very difficult for substitute parents to provide the steady guidance that helps adolescents understand their behavior and choices without eliciting rebellious reactions. Placement with relatives offers the advantage of continuity while creating enough distance to permit adolescents to accept some guidance.

Making the Placement Decision

Deciding whether relatives or strangers should care for a child is complex. We recommend that you consider two things: 1) the merits of shifting your orientation from fostering *children* to fostering their *families;* and 2) appreciating your children's *kinship network.*

Fostering Families

With regard to your placement goals and your clients' developmental parameters, we suggest that all professional activity be reframed in terms of *fostering families,* not only the children. Fostering families requires that temporary caregivers, whether familial or not, accept support of the biological parents as a central part of their mission. This implies that foster families not think of themselves as rescuing children from their parents. Instead, they should seek contact with the birth parents and invite them to share as much as possible in the rearing of their children during the placement. This might seem radical. However, most maltreating parents who are expected to regain custody are not dangerous. And most parents who are offered support—support that is given with respect and compassion—will try to use it.

Fostering children's families—instead of just the children themselves—provides numerous benefits. This is even more beneficial when the children are placed with relatives. The biological parents become less absolute and the children are free to talk with all their caregivers about their lives. Then the children can be psychologically whole. In addition, because all the caregivers know one another, they can participate meaningfully in the children's dialogue. When the caregivers are relatives, it is likely that they already share a knowledge base with the child, and for young children who depend on adults to understand their meanings, this is a very substantial advantage. To the extent that parents remain an ongoing part of their children's lives while the children are in care, fostering whole families offers several additional advantages:

- The children will not experience separation and its detrimental effects on the establishment of secure relationships, both immediately and later in life.

- The parents will not experience separation and its detrimental effects on reunifying with their children.

- The parents will have their children present as an impetus and guide for learning to modify their parental behavior.

- Behavior changes will be transparent—children and parents will change together in known and congruent ways.

Appreciating Kinship Networks

When biological parents cannot care for their children, substitute care by blood relatives is the norm. Professionals usually are drawn into family systems only when the children's relatives are unable to resolve the problem themselves. Moreover, the benefits of kin over stranger care have been documented in a number of small studies (see Broad, Hayes, & Rushforth, 2001). These advantages include:

- Placements with kin are more stable.

- Siblings are more likely to be kept together.

- There is a continuity of cultural inheritance.

- Children appear to be more stable emotionally.

An initial question might be "What is preventing the family from protecting the child?" In fact, intrafamilial care is very complex. It requires close attention to the organization of the kinship network, particularly the relationships among various family members. And placement with relatives reduces the control that professionals typically enjoy when supervising foster parents. For example, parental visits and household activities may be outside the oversight of the overseeing agencies. There also may be unholy alliances between the parents and the relative caregivers. Let's look at some additional complicating issues.

Issues Regarding Kin Competency

In cases where parental maltreatment is the reason for out-of-home placement, grandparents may not be perceived to be a resource. In fact, we may consider them a contributing factor! Put bluntly: *They raised the inadequate parents so why should they do better with their grandchild?* Indeed, the empirical literature indicates that grandparents with kinship care of a grandchild often exhibit acute shame and a sense of failure at having failed their own children. This especially is true when their child has a drug problem or AIDS (Conway & Stricker, 2003; Hayslip, Silverthorn, Shore, & Henderson, 2000; Joslin, 2000; Minkler, Fuller-Thomson, Miller, & Driver, 2000).

In addition, grandparents involved in kinship care are more likely to suffer from depression and physical ailments than are other grandparents (Minkler et al., 2000). Their poor health is related to feelings of humiliation and the changes in their roles. Since troubled grandparents have difficulty asking for professional help, their less than optimal presentation may lead professionals to doubt their fitness (Waterhouse & Brocklesby, 2001). Although families applying for kinship care often do not meet the standards that are applied to other foster parents, they may still offer safety and continuity of care that out-of-family placement cannot.

However, we have found that individuals' ability to raise children responsibly is most affected by their capacity for self-reflection. They must be able to show flexibility when faced with new challenges and to develop the ability to integrate new information about themselves, the child, and the situation—so that they can generate caregiving strategies (Crittenden, Lang, Claussen, & Partridge, 2000; Fonagy & Target, 1997). One indicator for long-term success may be when grandparents report having learned from the past and when they appear to have reconsidered previous parenting behavior (Pitcher, 2001).

Motivation

Substitute parents who are biologically related to the child may have complicated and conflicting reasons for taking on parenting responsibility. Their motivations can include commitment to the child, prevention of the child's entry into state care, interfamilial obligations in which the caregiver owes a debt to family members, moral duty (but without a personal commitment to the children or their birth parents), and the desire to expiate prior failure as parents (see reviews in Greeff & Campling, 1999). Of these, guilt is the least desirable motivation.

Family Triangulation

Family systems theory offers a way to think about the impact of kinship care on the family network without pathologizing individuals. Although the children's parents are physically absent, they probably exist as a powerful presence in the minds of all family members. For children, idealization of and loyalty to the physically absent parent may prevent them appreciating their relative caregivers. As a result, the children may be doubly deprived because they are unable to access the love of either party (Henry, 1974).

Often the relative placement may be with grandparents, and these placements may invite special challenges. Grandparents may find it especially difficult if they are called upon to parent both their children and their children's children. Grandparents also may be bitter regarding what they perceive to be their own and their children's failings as parents. This bitterness may alternate with periods of hope, when yet another effort is made to hand back parental responsibility to their offspring. In some tragic cases, the AIDS epidemic has left grandparents caring for a dying child while trying to manage their own and the grandchildren's grief (Joslin, 2000).

Ideally grandparents will support both their grandchild and child, either as quasi-adopters where the grandparents have overall control, or in a pattern of shared care (see O'Brien, 1999). However, sometimes the grandparents' motivation is punitive.

> Linda first came to the attention of social services at the age of 13 when her mother brought her to them and demanded that "you teach her some discipline, as she is out of our control." At age 15, Linda was pregnant with Beth and her parents forbade her to have an abortion. Linda had been living with friends. A few months after her daughter Beth was born, Linda moved back in with her parents. Linda's father repeatedly told her she was not fit to care for a baby, and most of Beth's care was carried out by Linda's mother. The family was locked in a cycle of blame and retribution punctured by attempts at rescue. Linda functioned as the carrier of all that was bad in the family. Tired of being marginalized, she moved out. The role of family scapegoat then fell on baby Beth. Beth then was placed by her grandparents in foster care and, after a protracted struggle between Linda, her parents, and social services, she was adopted by nonrelatives. When young mothers like Linda are enmeshed in punitive relationships with their own parents they may benefit most by being helped to develop alternative support systems (Dukewich, Borkowski, & Whitman, 1996). In this way they can achieve emotional distance from the destructive parents. With regard to adoption, an older and supportive foster family willing to take a genuine interest in helping the mother should be the first option.

Triangulation is also an issue when professionals are drawn into an alliance with one family member against another. Conflict appears most likely when intrafamilial alliances shift easily or when the parents are in dispute with both grandparents and social workers (O'Brien, 1999). When professionals are unable to predict family behavior or feel they have lost control, they sometimes manage their own anxiety by placing the child in state care (Dingwall, Eekelaar, & Murray, 1983). Using a family group conference in decisionmaking can support family expertise and reduce problems caused by professionals (Lupton & Nixon, 1999; Nixon, 2001). Placements managed by families last at least as long as those determined by professionals.

The Child's Attachment Figures

When selecting a kinship placement, it is important to identify the child's existing attachment figures. Although biological parents are usually the primary attachment figures, other people may fulfill that role. Cultures vary in terms of who is most likely to parent a child. For example, Hispanic families rely on aunts and godparents more than grandparents (Fuller-Thomson & Minkler, 2000).

- *Grandparents and other relatives.* The current longevity and increased health of grandparents indicates that they will figure largely in cases of kinship care. An estimated 6 million American children (8.4% of children under the age of 18) live with nonparental relatives. Three-quarters were cared for by grandparents (U.S. Bureau of the Census, 2003). This represents a considerable increase in "skipped generation households" over a ten-year period and, together with demographic changes in family structure, has been attributed to poverty-related issues such as drug and alcohol abuse and parental death from AIDS (Fuller-Thomson & Minkler, 2000).

- *Fathers and biological relatedness.* When mothers are incapacitated, custody is sometimes sought by an adult who is not an attachment figure, but who has a biological relationship to the child. Most commonly this arises when fathers have not provided consistent care and, in some cases, may have had little or no contact with the child at all. Most legal jurisdictions give fathers an automatic right to be heard in these cases. It is worth highlighting that if the father has not been a continuous presence in the child's life, then he is not an attachment figure (Howes, 1999). However, his child does carry his genes and, from an evolutionary perspective, some say that he may have a greater investment in the child than nonfamilial caregivers (see Simpson, 1999).

Roles and Boundaries

A common concern in kinship placement is uncertainty regarding familial boundaries and limit setting (Minuchin, 1974). Grandparents typically approach welfare services either with difficulties in managing the behavior of boys using coercive strategies, or with problems in readjusting to the new parenting role (Hayslip & Patrick, 2003). Clarity concerning who does what and what can be expected of whom increases the chances of providing the child with a predictable environment and hence reducing the anxiety that fuels coercive behavior (Crittenden, 1997; Johnson-Garner & Meyers, 2003). This is particularly an issue when the child's parent has a drug or alcohol problem. Recovery is uncertain and the risks of additional children or even death are higher than otherwise (Hirshorn, Van Meter, & Brown, 2000).

Managing uncertainty is a key part of the professional role, and it is worth reflecting that in stranger care, children and adults frequently endure long periods of not knowing who will be caring for the child or how long a placement will last. Kin placement does not necessarily remove anxiety, but it can provide a structure based on familiarity. It also includes the possibility of the familial caregiver retaining contact, if rehabilitation is successful, and retaining care, if rehabilitation fails. However, clarity regarding boundaries is itself a matter of where one stands in the network. For example, professionals may press the grandparents to apply for legal custody of the children in order to ensure their safety. The grandparents may resist, not because they are unconcerned about their grandchildren, but because they think of themselves as acting for both the grandchildren and the grandchildren's parents—one of whom is the child of the grandparent (Conway & Stricker, 2003). In such cases, we professionals should tolerate a little ambiguity around boundaries, while keeping the needs of the child in focus.

Availability and competence may not be sufficient to ensure a successful placement; the life goals of the fostering adult are relevant as well. In the postindustrial West, the role of grandparents has become increasingly ambiguous. It is assumed that older people will maintain independence from their children for as long as possible. A reversion to functioning as part of an extended kin network will inevitably cause conflicts and confusion, and may account for depression in grandparents who become caregivers to their grandchildren (Minkler et al., 2000). In contrast, Mexican families value the extended family, and Mexican grandparents appear to find meaning and satisfaction in the custodial role, even when they report high levels of problems (Toledo, Hayslip, Emick, Toledo, & Henderson, 2000).

Conclusions and Recommendations

Substitute care of any kind must aim for continuity. Once children are severed from their families they are at immediate risk for psychological problems. In too many cases the child welfare system compounds this risk by moving children through a series of placements. This may harm the children they are trying to rescue. If we visualize our task to be fostering *families,* where it makes sense to do so, as opposed to rescuing children, the children have the benefit of maintaining family ties.

Kinship care offers a number of advantages: continuity of experience with familiar people, including siblings; reduction of the long-term damage caused by abandonment; and more regular contact with birth parents. However, when substitute care is offered by strangers, maintaining continuity of experience is still essential and the task of fostering families is broadly the same, even though social services may hold legal responsibility for the child.

If our intention is to foster families, we must focus on the children's available kinship networks as our first and most potent resource for long-term care. This orientation requires a systemic approach, coupled with close attention to the meaning of the children's behavior. Child behavior problems bother adults, but these problems usually reflect the children's response to feeling acutely unsafe. The compulsive and coercive strategies outlined above represent children's predictions about how safe they are. These behavioral patterns should be understood from the children's point of view and not that of the adults. From our orientation, certain practices should be avoided or used with great caution. Primary among these are multiple placements, discrete or "bridging placements," forms of holding or attachment therapy that use intruded forms of intimacy to eliminate difficult behavior, and narrative therapies that do not reflect children's actual experience.

At the point when professionals must consider the removal of children from their home, it is likely that those children have already lost the opportunity for a safe and happy childhood. Consequently, we must consider our actions very carefully so as to avoid further damage and to prepare the child to be able to take advantage of the opportunities for change that adulthood can offer. We are not merely protecting children; we are protecting their adulthood. If adaptive functioning in adulthood is used to organize immediate decisionmaking, all members of the childcare system will feel better about what they do and have greater optimism for the future.

Adaptive functioning in adulthood requires children to grow up and have families, because that is where life is lived. Instead of taking away their childhood families, we can bolster those families. We believe that supporting kin, and supporting their efforts to help their troubled relatives, will best help children in the long run. We can reduce the complexity of troubled families' lives by using placement with relatives more often and by fostering families and not merely children. We can enable children and parents to cope with complexity by selecting interventions that respect the mixed feelings and motivations that real people have and that promote reflection in a developmentally attuned manner.

Adaptive development accrues over a lifetime, but its direction can be distorted in a moment. Research suggests that quick fixes rarely work and often harm children and their parents. We therefore recommend that:

- professionals hesitate before moving children from one environment to another;

- kinship placements are the first choice for children, to minimize the disruption of relationships;

- extensive and empathic efforts are made to assist parents and foster parents; and

- interventions are done with a focus on long-term adaptation and the psychological processes that underlay these.

The list of guidelines in Figure 1 summarizes what we consider to be best practice for professionals working with these children and families.

FIGURE 1

Choosing a Placement

- Long-term placement planning should begin even before a decision to remove has happened and surely before the initial placement occurs.

- Breaks in the parent–child relationship should be avoided, even within protective care.

- Fostering families may mean supporting kinship networks or using professional help to keep families together at times of crisis.

- The network of adults caring for the child must be continuous and capable of thinking together around the needs of the child and the meaning of his or her behavior.

- Adults who can foster families may not be those who traditionally choose to foster children.

- Group home placements may better fit the needs of adolescents than nonkin foster families.

Making It Work

- Use professionals more as mediators between parts of the family and the community system, and less as sources of authority.

- Arrange frequent, relaxed contact and contact that includes the attachment function (in other words, protection), and not merely playtime.

- Provide continuing service to biological parents after placement, and include the children.

- Offer a range of services from parent education to counseling, parenting programs, and psychotherapy. Choose the services carefully, not wasting them by throwing everything at the most severe cases.

- Use educational approaches to inform both biological and foster parents how to understand the strategic meaning of children's behavior.

- Help parents to see that children who are apparently controlling feel that they have no control, and they need more, not less, opportunities to influence the behavior of important adults.

- Help parents to understand that very good, very quiet, and accepting children may be inhibiting anger because they are afraid of punishment or rejection and abandonment. They need to feel safer.

- Monitor how life story work is conducted. The aim should be to help children tell the varied stories of their lives without adults imposing feelings, words, or episodes upon them. The people who were present are best able to do this.

- Validate children's feelings about their current experience in care and being away from their parents, even if the feelings are upsetting or confusing.

- Teach reflective processes because they are essential to parenting success; videotaped viewing of the parent and child can be very helpful.

References

Ainsworth, M. D. S. (1979). Infant-mother attachment. *American Psychologist, 34,* 932–937.

Broad, B., Hayes, R., & Rushforth, C. (2001). *Kith and kin: Kinship care for vulnerable young people.* London: National Children's Bureau.

Conway, F., & Stricker, G. (2003). An integrative assessment model as a means of intervention with the grandparent caregiver. In B. Hayslip Jr. & J. H. Patrick (Eds.), *Working with custodial grandparents* (pp. 45–58). New York: Springer Publishing Company.

Crittenden, P. M. (1995). Attachment and psychopathology. In S. Goldberg, R. Muir, & J. Kerr (Eds.), *John Bowlby's attachment theory: Historical, clinical, and social significance* (pp. 367–406). New York: The Analytic Press.

Crittenden, P. M. (1997). Toward an integrative theory of trauma: A dynamic-maturational approach. In D. Cicchetti & S. Toth (Eds.), *The Rochester symposium on developmental psychopathology, Vol. 10. Risk, trauma, and mental processes* (pp. 34–84). Rochester, NY: University of Rochester Press.

Crittenden, P. M. (2002). If I knew then what I know now: Integrity and fragmentation in the treatment of child abuse and neglect. In K. Browne, H. Hanks, P. Stratton, & C. Hamilton (Eds.), *Early prediction and prevention of child abuse: A handbook* (pp. 111–126). London: John Wiley and Sons.

Crittenden, P. M. (2006). Why do inadequate parents do what they do? In O. Mayseless (Ed.), *Parenting representations: Theory, research, and clinical implications* (pp. 388–434). Cambridge, U.K.: Cambridge University Press.

Crittenden, P., & Claussen, A. H. (Eds.). (2003). *Organization of attachment relationships: Maturation, culture, context* (paperback edition). Cambridge, U.K.: Cambridge University Press.

Crittenden, P. M., Lang, C., Claussen, A. H., & Partridge, M. F. (2000). Relations among mothers' procedural, semantic, and episodic internal representational models of parenting. In P. M. Crittenden & A. H. Claussen (Eds.), *The organization of attachment relationships: Maturation, culture, and context* (pp. 214–233). New York: Cambridge University Press.

Dingwall, R., Eekelaar, J., & Murray, T. (1983). *The protection of children: state intervention and family life.* Oxford, U.K.: Basil Blackwell.

Dukewich, T., Borkowski, J., & Whitman, T. (1996). Adolescent mothers and child abuse potential: an evaluation of risk factors. *Child Abuse and Neglect, 20,* 1031–1047.

English, D., Marshall, B., Brummel, S., & Orme, M. (1999). Characteristics of repeated referrals to child protective services in Washington State. *Child Maltreatment 4,* 297–307.

Fonagy, P., & Target, M. (1997). Attachment and reflective function: Their role in self-organization. *Development and Psychopathology, 9,* 679–700.

Fuller-Thomson, E., & Minkler, M. (2000). America's grandparent caregivers: who are they? In B. Hayslip Jr. & R. Goldberg-Glen (Eds.), *Grandparents raising grandchildren: Theoretical, empirical, and clinical perspectives* (pp. 3–21). New York: Springer Publishing Company.

Greeff, R., & Campling, J. (Eds.). (1999) *Fostering kinship: An international perspective on kinship foster care.* Aldershot, Hampshire, U.K.: Ashgate.

Hayslip, B., Jr., Silverthorn, P., Shore, R., & Henderson, C. E. (2000). Determinants of custodial grandparents' perceptions of problem behavior in their grandchildren. In B. Hayslip Jr. & R. Goldberg-Glen (Eds.), *Grandparents raising grandchildren: Theoretical, empirical, and clinical perspectives* (pp. 255–268). New York: Springer Publishing Company.

Hayslip, B., Jr., & Patrick, J. (2003). Custodial grandparenting viewed from within a life-span perspective. In B. Hayslip Jr. & J. H. Patrick (Eds.), *Working with custodial grandparents* (pp. 3–11). New York: Springer Publishing Company.

Henry, G. (1974). Doubly deprived. *Journal of Child Psychotherapy, 3,* 29–43.

Hirshorn, B. A., Van Meter, M. J., & Brown, D. R. (2000). When grandparents raise grandchildren due to substance abuse: Responding to a uniquely destabilizing factor. In B. Hayslip Jr. & R. Goldberg-Glen (Eds.), *Grandparents raising grandchildren: Theoretical, empirical, and clinical perspectives* (pp. 269–288). New York: Springer Publishing Company.

Howes, C. (1999). Attachment relationships in the context of multiple caregivers. In J. Cassidy & P. Shaver (Eds.), *Handbook of attachment: Theory, research, and clinical applications* (pp. 671–687). New York: The Guilford Press.

Hughes, D. A. (2003). Psychological interventions for the spectrum of attachment disorders and intrafamilial trauma. *Attachment & Human Development, 5,* 271–277.

Johnson-Garner, M. Y., & Meyers, S. A. (2003) What factors contribute to the resilience of African-American children within kinship care? *Child and Youth Care Forum, 32,* 255–269.

Joslin, D. (2000). Emotional well-being among grandparents raising children affected and orphaned by HIV disease. In B. Hayslip Jr. & R. Goldberg-Glen (Eds.), *Grandparents raising grandchildren: Theoretical, empirical, and clinical perspectives* (pp. 87–105). New York: Springer Publishing Company.

Lacher, B., Nichols, T., & May, J. (2005). *Connecting with kids through stories: Using narratives to facilitate attachment in adopted children.* London: Jessica Kingsley Publishers.

Lupton, C., & Nixon, P. (1999). *Empowering practice? A critical appraisal of the family group conference approach.* Bristol, U.K.: Policy Press.

Main, M., & Solomon, J. (1986). Discovery of an insecure disorganized/disoriented attachment pattern: Procedures, findings, and implications for the classification of behavior. In M. Yogman & T. B. Brazelton (Eds.), *Affective development in infancy* (pp. 121–160). Norwood, NJ: Ablex.

Minkler, M., Fuller-Thomson, E., Miller, D., & Driver, D. (2000). Grandparent caregiving and depression. In B. Hayslip Jr. & R. Goldberg-Glen (Eds.), *Grandparents raising grandchildren: Theoretical, empirical, and clinical perspectives* (pp. 207–220). New York: Springer Publishing Company.

Minuchin, S. (1974). *Families and family therapy.* Cambridge, MA: Harvard University Press.

Nixon, P. (2001). Making kinship partnerships work: Examining family group conferences. In B. Broad (Ed.), *Kinship care: The placement choice for children and young people* (pp. 93–104). Lyme Regis, Dorset, U.K.: Russell House Publishing.

O'Brien, V. (1999). Evolving networks in relative care: Alliance and exclusion. In R. Greeff & J. Campling (Eds.), *Fostering kinship: An international perspective on kinship foster care* (pp. 113–134). Aldershot, U.K.: Ashgate.

Pitcher, D. (2001). Assessing grandparent carers: A framework. In B. Broad (Ed.), *Kinship care: The placement choice for children and young people* (pp. 105–114). Lyme Regis, Dorset, U.K.: Russell House Publishing.

Quinton, D., Rushton, A., Dance, C., & Mayes, D. (1998). *Joining new families: A study of adoption and fostering in middle childhood.* Chichester, Essex, U.K.: John Wiley and Sons.

Reder, P., Duncan, S., & Gray, M. (1993). *Beyond blame: Child abuse tragedies revisited.* London: Routledge.

Rose, R., & Philpot, T. (2005). *The child's own story: Life story work with traumatized children.* London: Jessica Kingsley Publishers.

Ryan, T., & Walker, R. (1985). *Making life story books.* London: BAAF.

Ryan, T., & Walker, R (1993). *Life story work.* London: BAAF.

Simpson, J. A. (1999). Attachment theory in modern evolutionary perspective. In J. Cassidy & P. R. Shaver (Eds.), *Handbook of attachment theory, research, and clinical applications* (pp. 115–140). New York: Guilford.

Schaffer, H. R. (1971). *The growth of sociability.* Middlesex, U.K.: Penguin Books.

Toledo, J. R., Hayslip, B., Jr., Emick, M. A., Toledo, C., & Henderson, C. E. (2000). Cross-cultural differences in custodial grandparenting. In B. Hayslip Jr. & R. Goldberg-Glen (Eds.), *Grandparents raising grandchildren: Theoretical, empirical, and clinical perspectives* (pp. 107–123). New York: Springer Publishing Company.

U.S. Bureau of the Census. (2003). *Grandparents living with grandchildren: 2000.* Retrieved June 6, 2005, from http://www.census.gov/prod/2003pubs/c2kbr-31.pdf.

Waterhouse, S., & Brocklesby, E. (2001). Placement choices in temporary foster care: A research study. *Adoption and Fostering, 25*(3), 39–46.

Creative Ways to
Strengthen Family Bonds

Larry Barlow and Sandra M. Barlow

T his chapter provides concrete guidelines for experiential activities that can be used with families to establish, maintain, and strengthen interpersonal connections, and also to identify important emotional issues. It will describe many creative "family play" interventions, including family games, role-playing, art, and diverse storytelling techniques.

Creative expressive techniques—games, music, art, psychodrama, or play—allow us to engage family members in ways that traditional talk therapy cannot. We use these techniques to facilitate the experience and expression of feelings, as well as to accomplish other therapeutic goals. One advantage of creative expressive approaches is that they afford comprehension by each member of the family at his or her level of cognitive and emotional development (see Chapter 8, "Providing Developmentally Appropriate Family Therapy"). Some therapists use creative expressive techniques when traditional talk therapy is not working well. Many use them as part of an integrated approach with most client families.

There are many ways to creatively strengthen therapeutic alliances with our families. The use of creative expressive approaches acknowledges that there is no one style that fits all clients and situations. Your personality, the dynamics of the family with whom you are working, and the theoretical model that informs the work—these factors will determine the choice of technique— and it is a choice that you and a client family make together. At times, you may choose an intervention to support a traditional talk therapy. At other times, a creative expressive therapy may be the primary method of treatment.

Creative expressive techniques have earned their place along-side more traditional therapy approaches. They are valuable tools in many individual and group approaches to mental and physical health care treatment. They are extensively used in music, art, speech, physical, and occupational therapies.

In this chapter we present several creative expressive therapies and describe how they can be used to connect with and treat families involved in the child welfare system. We have browsed several sources, including our personal experiences and those of our friends, for established activities that can provide examples of these techniques. And we indicate how each may prove effective.

Choosing What to Do When

First, we organize the creative expressive techniques developmentally. You will want to select therapeutic activities that are appropriate to the developmental levels of the individuals you want included in your intervention. We have organized these developmental stages as follows:

- infants and toddlers,
- preschoolers,
- early childhood,
- late childhood,
- early adolescents, and
- late adolescents.

After identifying the developmental levels of the participants, you will want to pick activities that have a high probability of maximizing your immediate therapeutic goals. Three possible goals are:

- *To improve relationships among family members.* This includes creating or building empathy and understanding among family members. Frequently in your work as an agency therapist you find tension, hurt feelings, and misunderstandings that need to resolve or improve before behaviors can change within the family context.

- *To teach parenting skills.* This goal is comprised of many therapeutic objectives—enhancing family communication, teaching the family how better to resolve conflict, modeling for parents how to improve their children's self-esteem, and teaching parents how to garner more compliance from their children.

- *Improve family problem solving.* Families need coping skills in order to grow past the ongoing crises and chaotic lifestyles that may have been developed. We want to teach parents how to improve their judgment and we want to help the entire family, including children, develop and use problem-solving skills.

See the following table for some exemplary activities that are organized according to the developmental stages of the participants and your immediate goal. We are aware that many of the activities could be used for individuals at other developmental stages and for achieving other goals. We encourage you to adjust the use of the techniques accordingly. The activities themselves are explained later in this chapter.

TABLE I

Therapeutic Goal

Developmental Stage	Relationship Building	Teaching Parenting Skills	Improve Family Problem Solving
Infants and toddlers	Smile and touch	Food game	Bedtime rituals
Preschoolers	Puppets	Family tea party Sock puppets	Family drawing exercise
Early childhood	Storytelling	Balloon game	Candy reach
Late childhood	Writing notes	Family treasure chest	Board games
Early adolescence	Parachute game Writing poems	Family sculpting	Over, under, and through
Late adolescence	Judge and jury	Role playing	Create a machine game

It is important to develop trusting relationships with your client families before undertaking creative approaches. In our work with incarcerated fathers and their families we discovered that if creative approaches were employed too soon, strong resistance would follow. We initially thought that something simple, like blowing bubbles, would facilitate rapport between the fathers and their children. However, we discovered that the inmates were not ready for those activities—there needed to be a bond of therapeutic trust in place. This was a lesson for us about parallel processes. We wanted to influence these fathers to learn about the importance of parental bonding through play, but we ourselves lacked the requisite amount of therapist–client bonding to bring about change. Once we reorganized and moved this part of our fifteen-hour program into the middle of the training, it was received much more successfully. Once trust was established, even 250-pound inmates with tattoos all over their bodies—men who needed to maintain a tough exterior presentation—would publicly blow bubbles or play with paper bag puppets with their children. If you meet resistance when you attempt creative expressive activities, particularly with some adult and adolescent family members, it may be that you haven't yet established the needed positive therapeutic alliance.

On the other hand, if you can get them started, the processes of play and other activities may help you establish your therapeutic alliance. This is particularly true when you are seeing children. Play is an innate and spontaneous process for children and an important part of their normal development. Play is sometimes viewed as the main approach to therapy with children because it allows for self-expression, communication, and a cathartic release of feelings (Gil, 1991). Play can be renewing and constructive, and it allows adults a way to observe and understand the child's thoughts, feelings, and experiences (see Chapter 7, "Parent–Child Therapy for Traumatized Young Children in Foster Care"). As you consider using play and other creative expressive approaches with families in the child welfare system, look for a balance among the emotional needs of all family members—and keep in mind that variables relating to building a trusting therapeutic relationship fluctuate according to the number of family members and their experiences (see Chapter 20, "'But I Don't Trust You'—Recognizing and Dealing with Parents' History of Trauma: The Story of Amy"). Families can find solutions to difficult problems and facilitate their own healing within the natural interactions of playfulness.

The history of creative expressive therapy stretches back to the roots of family therapy. Virginia Satir, a family therapy pioneer, employed a variety of creative expressive techniques in her work with families. Satir used them to guide, teach, and nurture families to new ways of understanding and behaving. For example, she used ropes and blindfolds to dramatize roles which constricted family members or which kept families trapped in unhealthy patterns. Satir created family sculpture techniques to demonstrate communication and relational patterns (this is described below). She also originated the method called "Family Reconstruction," a multigenerational family psychodrama through which family members identify the origins of family patterns, roles, and expectations (Griffin, 1993; Nerin, 1986). Satir's effectiveness with families was founded on the respect and positive regard she had for all family members. Satir never blamed the parents of troubled families, but she did hold them responsible for their actions.

Examples of Creative Expressive Techniques

Smile and Touch

Goal: To improve relationships among family members

Developmental stage: Infants and toddlers

This infant-level game is a happy, playful way to begin the process of communicating and connecting (Bavolek, 1989). The parent puts his or her face close to the baby's face and talks, sings, and smiles. The parent allows the baby to touch and explore the parent's face while singing, talking, and smiling. When two parents (and other children) are available, one can watch and notice how the other parent and baby interact. Possible observations could be how the baby mimics the parent's facial expressions and thereby increases the parent's connection with and understanding of the baby. Both parents can take turns interacting with the baby at various times. This infant game evolves to toddler games such as naming body parts and "This Little Piggy." The therapist's role is to help reluctant, unskilled parents recognize the baby's ability to interact as well as the importance of this early interaction.

Toddler–Parent Food Game

Goal: To improve parenting skills

Developmental stage: Infants and toddlers

In this activity, parents select a variety of foods on a plate for toddlers to experiment with while discussing the food. They are told to gather different textures of food, such as firm (but safe), soft, and liquid. They might also include a variety of food tastes such as tart, sweet, salty, or sour. However, they should limit the food to two or three varieties at a time. More would be overstimulating for a toddler. Once the parents have selected the foods they want to use, they allow the toddler to touch each food with his or her fingers, smell the food, and finally taste it. Even if the taste turns out to be unpleasant for the child, the game is still a success in that the parents can communicate about taste preferences, and share their likes and dislikes with the child.

Bedtime Rituals

Goal: Family problem solving

Development stage: Infants and toddlers

Toddlers have many reasons to be uncooperative at bedtime. One reason may be anxiety. Bedtime rituals are good ways to get toddlers ready for bed. "Rituals provide containers for uncertainty, bind anxiety, and provide reassuring bonds of human connection" (Lieberman, 1993, p. 164). Coach your parents to structure their toddler's evening. Encourage a routine mealtime, bath time, and perhaps quiet time with reading before bed. They can add enjoyable activities such as pajama games, singing, or prayer time, as long as these are soothing. Of course, they will want to refrain from activities that increase the child's arousal levels! The idea is to use these rituals to create a sense of family security and belonging. A father confided that if he tried to hurry the process, his toddler would fuss about the missed routine activity: "Daddy, you didn't wrap the towel around me after my bath." We cannot emphasize enough how reassuring it is for toddlers to have routine and predictable activities that also build relationships. Once toddlers learn these rituals, they gain mastery over this previously difficult time and go to sleep on their own.

Paper Bag Puppets

Goal: To improve relationships among family members

Developmental stage: Preschoolers through adults

The paper bag puppets game (Lowenstein, 1999) enables the therapist to engage and assess the family, while also creating a safe environment for work. Everyone in the family makes a paper bag puppet to represent him- or herself. We like this activity because the resources required are inexpensive and readily available. These include paper bags, decorative supplies, glue sticks, and child-safe scissors. The informal discussion and process arising during puppet creation can facilitate family assessment. Once the puppets are made, they are introduced, and then the therapist conducts a fun interview seeking pertinent information about the family. The use of puppets allows a safe distance for family members to express their feelings and thoughts (Lowenstein, 1999).

Family Tea Party

Goal: To teach parenting skills

Developmental stage: Preschoolers

A therapist friend with four daughters recounted the many times he joined with them in a tea party. He described how the children beamed with joy and self-confidence at serving dad imaginary cake and tea. It is especially important that children learn that fathers will allow them to play in ways that humanize the male image. A therapist working with a family where domestic violence and dysfunctional conflict patterns among adults have prevailed could model such an activity with fathers and children. It is important to coach the parent to allow the child the leadership role. Many times fathers will automatically "show" children the "right way to do it." Here the father needs to learn that however the child leads is the right way. This develops mastery for the children and teaches the parent how to enhance the child's sense of ability to lead.

Sock Puppets

Goal: Teaching parenting skills

Developmental stage: Preschoolers

The wonderful imaginations of preschoolers allow a simple, undecorated sock to become a puppet. While some parents and older children may need guidance from the therapist to find their own imaginations, all family members can join the puppet conversation. Sock puppets can be decorated using yarn, felt, patches of cloth, and other things found around the house (Barnes & York, 2001). During the family session, each puppet can tell the others what happened to him or her that day or the puppets can tell stories to each other. Parents can continue the use of the sock puppets in bedtime stories or in stories that address specific family issues.

The Family Drawing Exercise

Goal: To improve family problem solving

Developmental stage: Preschool and older

One way to assess and improve family communication patterns is to have the family complete a drawing without verbal or written expression. You provide the family art supplies and poster paper. You then ask each family member to visualize a drawing that depicts their family. Then, without discussion, they are to work together to create a single drawing for the whole family. They are to cooperate in whatever manner possible for them except by verbal or written instructions.

As the family works you can observe their patterns of communication, leadership, and cooperation. After allowing the family perhaps a half hour to complete the drawing, you ask them to talk about it. "Explain what that exercise was like for you. What was frustrating? How did you figure out what to do? What feelings did you experience? How did you wish it could have been different?"

You then can share your own observations made while watching the exercise. Try to use metaphor to explain and perhaps even diagram the patterns that were observed. Next, generalize this process to their life events. "How is it similar? What happens day-to-day that is similar to that activity? How can it be done differently?" Then you can use the metaphor to teach communication skills, interaction skills, or relationship dynamics.

Storytelling

Goal: To improve relationships among family members

Developmental stage: Preschool—early childhood

Parents who want to change their children in some way often talk at them or lecture them. This approach often fails. You could help these parents learn anecdotal storytelling (Brett, 1988). Children may better grasp and receive the desired lesson through a story about some other child or magical being. Anecdotal storytelling works because it speaks the language of children and enters into the child's own world of reality.

When our oldest son was about ten years old, he was acting out some anger and anxiety at school by running away and defiant behaviors. At that time, we were busy in both graduate school and work. The home environment was often stressful with many divided loyalties. A therapist told our son a story about a knight who was seeking to serve his king by leaving home to fight a monstrous dragon. Of course, the therapist embellished the story with exciting features and scary choices. Then he asked our son if the knight was choosing well to serve his country while leaving his family for a time. Our son, who loved fantasy stories, quickly chose to say "Sure!" Then the therapist asked him if he saw any comparisons from the story with our family at that time. He replied affirmatively. He could understand that his parents often went away to "fight dragons for the good of the people." His behaviors soon changed. Of course, we also understood that we needed to learn lessons from this story. Even well-intentioned servants must not neglect their own families for the good of others.

Balloon Game

Goal: Teaching parenting skills

Developmental stage: Preschool–early childhood

This technique requires medium to large balloons. You help the family members identify troublesome feelings, such as anger or frustration. Balloons are then blown up, and the individuals decide what they wish to do with the balloons. Children and parents might imagine themselves feeling angry, make an angry face, and then blow the anger into the balloon. Then they can let go of the balloon, allowing it and the anger to flutter away. This process allows parents to safely observe their children's expressions of difficult feelings.

Candy Reach

Goal: Family problem solving

Developmental stage: Early childhood

This is a fun and tasty game that teaches problem solving and cooperation toward a goal. It allows the family to practice helping each other and accepting help from others. Materials for the game include a bag of individually wrapped candies and a square of cardboard, wood, or carpet, big enough for two people to stand on at the same time. The game is set up by placing the board (playing field) on the floor, then spreading the candy on the floor all around it. Put the pieces of candy far enough away that they would be hard to reach if you were standing on the board by yourself. The family members take turns pairing into groups of two to stand on the board and work together to pick up the candy. The rules are as follows (adapted from Jones, 1998):

- Both people must be on the board at all times.
- No body part or piece of clothing may touch the floor.
- If you touch the floor, your pair has to lose your turn.
- You may not slide the board.
- You must pick up the candy, not drag it.
- You may not use any item (belt, clothing, etc.) to pick up the candy.
- Whatever candy you pick up, you and your partner may keep.
- Once you pick up one piece, you have ten seconds more before your turn is over.

It is a good idea to put some really desirable pieces of candy far away to make the game more challenging. For shorter or taller people the distance from the board may need to be adjusted. Allow time for the family teams to make a plan. It may take a while before the teams realize that if one person holds the other who reaches out to get the candy, they can expand their reach.

This game allows family fun while the family practices cooperation and problem solving. The therapist can use the process to generate discussion about challenges, feelings, and working together.

Writing Notes

Goal: To improve relationships among family members

Developmental stage: Late childhood

The therapist can remind parents to write notes to their children and each other. They are to leave them around the house in places the children frequent as well as in unexpected and creative places. Notes can simply say "Hi!" or "I love you" or "I'm thinking about you today." This can provide a concrete connection among the family members in spite of the busyness of daily living (adapted from Taffel, 2001).

Family Treasure Chest

Goal: Teaching parenting skills

Developmental stage: Late childhood

Everyone likes treasure hunts. This activity involves all of the family members in a game that sharpens communication skills, teaches respect for belongings, and enhances self-esteem (Lewis & Lewis, 1996). Each family member looks through the house and collects five or six personal treasures, namely, objects with special meaning. These will vary based upon the age of children. They may include cards, books, or games. Allow everyone about ten minutes to collect the belongings, and then gather the family members back in front of a chest or decorated box. The objects are then placed ceremoniously in the treasure chest for later play. As each member places the object in the chest, you may encourage him or her to talk about what makes it special. Family members learn about each other and what is valued.

Board Games

Goal: Improve family problem solving

Developmental stage: Late childhood

Playing board games helps children develop frustration tolerance, self-control, and the ability to follow rules (Webb, 1991). They let you observe the reactions of both children and parents to winning and losing. You can use those interactions to promote conversation about problem-solving methods both within individuals and among family members. Two commercial games frequently found in therapeutic playrooms are Chutes and Ladders and Sorry. Each of these games involves an element of chance. In Chutes and Ladders, there is no way to avoid the difficulty encountered and feelings must be dealt with. In Sorry, the players sometimes make choices regarding the self and its effect upon others. During game play, it is helpful to identify the feelings and choices members make, in order to help the family recognize and take responsibility for their actions.

The Parachute Game

Goal: To improve relationships among family members

Developmental stage: Early adolescents

The parachute game is one that you may have played at school in physical education class or at summer camp. You will need an old parachute from your army surplus store and a large area where the parachute can be fully spread out. The entire family and therapist can participate in this activity. One variation of the game involves spreading the parachute on the ground and having everyone pick a corner up. As the parachute is raised it will catch air and fluff up. After the parachute is fluffed, the family members fall into it and ride the air cushion down as it collapses. We used this game with a family in which a young adolescent and his father had not touched for years except through violence. The pair frequently fell into each other, laughing and playing in ways that they had not done for a long time. At the end of the game they did not want to stop. The therapist built on this positive interaction later in sessions.

Writing Poetry

Goal: To improve relationships among family members

Developmental stage: Early adolescents

In 1991, Janet Heller founded a poetry workshop for at-risk youths. She believed that creative self-expression has therapeutic value because it helps us confront difficult emotional issues and increases our self-esteem—her ideas can be adapted for use with children and their families. Begin by asking the children to write a poem about some traumatic event. Most will understand what you mean right away, and will not need lengthy explanations. Then, after the poems have been written, ask the authors if they might share their poems in the family therapy setting. You then help the family process what has been written. This creative expression activity, especially its processing, can help parents and other family members understand each other and build a better relationship (see, for example, Gardner, 1997). For an interesting variation, see "hip-hop therapy" in Chapter 3.

Family Sculpting

Goal: To teach parenting skills

Developmental Stage: Early adolescence

Family sculpting involves placing family members in poses that demonstrate an emotional or role experience. Usually family members take turns as the sculptor. When a tableau is created, the family members reflect upon it and their individual experiences in the pose. Sometimes in this exercise you can have members take other individuals' positions in order to experience how that position might feel. You can also have family members experiment with repositioning each other in ideal ways that change the experience and process of the family.

With one family we chose to use this activity to teach better communication skills. The family composition in treatment included two adolescent children and a single mother. Once the activity was explained to the family, we had the youngest child place the other two family members in a pose that symbolized the family experience she had of communication. She chose to have all three parties choking each other in a circle. We had them maintain the pose to heighten the experience. Then we processed their emotional reaction to it. After that, we asked them to share when their family communication most often seemed to end up at this conflicted point. This allowed us to suggest some positive changes and teach them some noncoercive ways with which to communicate their needs and desires.

Over, Under, Through

Goal: To improve family problem solving

Developmental Stage: Early adolescence

This activity is a rope game that involves all family members who must work cooperatively to get over, under, and through two pieces of rope tied between two stands (trees, poles). You tie the two ropes between the objects so that there is enough room for each family member to get his or her body between the ropes with help from others. The rules are:

- No one may touch the ropes at any time, or the family must start over.
- One person must go over the top of the highest rope and one under the lowest rope.
- The rest of the family members must go through the ropes.
- No one is allowed to go around the ropes.

As the family tackles this task, they must decide which family member goes where and how to assist each other. When processing the activity after completion, you can ask them questions such as "What was the hardest part? What did you have to do to be successful? How did the family team together? In your family life, when is teamwork needed?" Then you can coach the family on the mastery of teamwork and how it might be improved for this family (adapted from Jones, 1998).

Judge and Jury

Goal: Building family relationships

Developmental stage: Late adolescence

This game helps adolescents and their parents see other points of view and learn how to negotiate issues. The parents and children take turns acting as attorneys. You are the court reporter and write down evidence as it is presented. For example, a teenager wants to attend a party that the parents do not want their child to attend. One parent takes the role of attorney for the teen and enters into evidence as many reasons he or she can think of why the teenager should attend the party. The teenager acts as attorney for the parents and enters into evidence as many reasons that he or she can think of why the teenager should not attend the party. Rebuttals may occur and new evidence may be introduced. After all the evidence has been presented, the court reporter reads the summary. Then the parent(s) and teenager are able to discuss the issue with more information about the other's point of view and negotiate appropriately (adapted from Shelby, 2004).

Role Playing

Goal: To teach parenting skills

Developmental Stage: Late adolescence

It is not unusual for parents and teenagers to have conflicts over style, boundaries, and limit-setting. Parents may not like the dress, hair color, or music their adolescent chooses. Teenagers frequently believe they are more competent than their parents believe them to be. In order to improve parent–adolescent conflict resolution you might try role reversal role-playing. Have the parent play the role of the teenager who wishes to wear the inappropriate clothing or to come home later than is currently allowed. Have the teenager take on the role of the parents. However, you should caution the parents not to mimic their child in an overly satirical manner. Instead, everyone should try to support a rule of mutual respect so that the learning process is not lost. Challenge the child-as-parent to invent some realistic reasons why their former choices could lead to trouble. If prepared in this way, most teenagers are able to reflect on their parent's position, even though they may have a hard time admitting it in an argument. For example, they may point out that being out past a certain time leads to more scrutiny from law enforcement, or that alcohol-impaired drivers often leave bars late at night. While this is going on, a parent-as-teenager expresses his or her sincere desire why they need to be allowed the freedom to make these choices. Adolescents are stressed by these daily activities in ways that parents have long forgotten.

Once an understanding of the respective roles has been experienced, it is time for the family members to come up with new ways of resolving the conflict. As the family processes this experience, you find opportunities to reflect the parents' dilemma of wanting to protect their children, while also helping them transition into self-regulation and mature decisionmaking. This activity helps adolescents see how limit-setting by parents is important—and at the same time, it helps parents see the teenager's need for independent decisionmaking.

Create a Machine Game

Goal: To improve family problem solving

Developmental stage: Late childhood and adolescents

This game offers the family an opportunity to learn how to improve their problem solving and also asks them to be as creative as possible. The family is told to create a machine—it can be real or imaginary. Family members will be parts of the machine. Working in unison, the family members will produce the machine's sounds and movements. If the family is stumped by the assignment, you can demonstrate by modeling how they could create a locomotive. In such a case, they would act out the movement of the train and the sounds of the train, such as "choo-choo" and the whistle.

Patterns of family leadership will emerge as the members decide what machine to create, how to model the machine, and how to implement it. Once they have chosen the machine and have demonstrated it with you cheering and enjoying their efforts, then you lead the family members as they process the experience. How was it to work together? How did they decide what machine to create and how to model it? Was anyone left out of the process? Would you have liked for it to be done differently? How does that process generalize to other family choices?

Summary

The above techniques provided only a few examples of how to organize and apply creative expressive interventions. When you consider with whom you are working and the goals at hand, there are thousands of activities from which to choose. There are many helpful websites (for example, www.a4pt.org, www.arttherapy.org, www.childtherapytoys.com, www.ctherapy.com, www.sourceresource.com, www.therapyresourcesinc.com, to name a few organizational and commercial sites) and books (for example, Kaduson & Schaefer, 2000; Lowenstein, 1999; Nerin, 1986). Use your own and your families' imaginations to have fun and experience the healing power of creativity.

References

Barnes, B. A., & York, S. M. (2001). *Common sense parenting of toddlers and preschoolers.* Boys Town, NE: Boys Town Press.

Bavolek, J. D. (1989). *Nurturing book for babies and children.* Park City, UT: Family Development Resources, Inc.

Brett, D. (1988). *Annie stories.* New York: Workman.

Gardner, J. (Ed.). (1997). *Runaway with words: A collection of poems from Florida's youth shelters.* Tallahassee, FL: Anhinga Press.

Gil, E. (1991). *The healing power of play: Working with abused children.* New York, Guilford.

Griffin, W. A. (1993). *Family therapy: Fundamentals of theory and practice.* New York: Bruner Mazel.

Jones, A. (1998). *104 activities that build: Self-esteem, teamwork, communication, anger management, self-discovery, and coping skills.* Richland, WA: Rec Room Publishing.

Kaduson, H. G., & Shaefer, C. E. (Eds.). (2000). *Short-term play therapy for children.* New York: Guilford.

Lewis, S., & Lewis, S. K. (1996). *Stress-proofing your child: Mind-body exercises to enhance your child's health.* New York: Bantam Books.

Lieberman, A. (1993). *The emotional life of the toddler.* New York: The Free Press.

Lowenstein, L. (1999). *Interventions for troubled children and youth.* Toronto: Champion Press.

Nerin, W. F. (1986). *Family reconstruction: Long day's journey into light.* New York: W. W. Norton.

Shelby, J. S. (2004). *Developmentally sensitive play therapy for mood disorders.* Presented at the annual meeting of the Georgia Association for Play Therapy, Atlanta, GA.

Taffel, R. (2001). *Getting through to difficult kids and parents.* New York: Guilford.

Webb, N. B. (Ed.). (1991). *Play therapy with children in crisis: A casebook for practitioners.* New York: Guilford.

Intervening with Foster Infants' Foster Parents: Attachment and Biobehavioral Catch-Up

Erin Lewis, Mary Dozier, Michelle Knights, and Mallory Maier

T his chapter recognizes the importance of secure and therapeutic foster care placements and describes how to do family
therapy within the foster home. A case example is provided
involving very young children in foster care.

Infants who enter foster care experience disruptions at a time
when maintaining relationships with primary caregivers is a critical, biologically based task. When they are placed in foster care,
infants lose the partner on whom they are dependent for maintaining regulatory processes, and the attachment figure whom they
need for reassurance and protection. Therefore, it is not surprising
that foster infants have problems developing new trusting relationships with foster parents and developing their regulatory
capabilities. In this chapter, we present evidence for several key
issues faced by infants in foster care, and describe the intervention
program that we have developed to target these issues. We then
present case examples to illustrate the intervention. These examples highlight the importance of tailoring interventions to the
needs of specific clients in order to obtain effective results.

Children in the Foster Care System

As you may know, by the time a child enters foster care, he or she
has often been exposed to a number of early adverse experiences.
It is not surprising that this combination of harmful experiences

and the loss of primary attachment figures often results in increased incidences of emotional, behavioral, and medical problems within the foster child population (Clausen, Landsverk, Ganger, Chadwick, & Litrownik, 1998; Chernoff, Combs-Orme, Risley-Curtiss, & Heisler, 1994; Halfon, Mendonca, & Berkowitz, 1995).

Currently, the number of children in the foster care system is estimated at over 530,000, and 46% of these children are placed in nonrelative foster family homes. Of about 300,000 children who entered foster care during 2002, 14% were less than a year old at placement and another 26% were under the age of five (U.S. Department of Health and Human Services, Administration for Children and Families, 2004). This means that approximately 120,000 children (40% of children in foster care) are particularly vulnerable to poor outcomes because their primary attachment relationships were disrupted at an early age. Our intervention is founded in attachment theory, is the product of over 10 years of work researching foster children (see Dozier, Dozier, & Manni, 2002), and is designed to lessen the detrimental effects of such disruptions.

Empirical Justification of the Attachment and Biobehavioral Catch-Up Intervention

We have discovered some very important things about how infants in foster care and their surrogate parents interact. Since crucial biological, psychological, and social outcomes for those foster children may depend on how these relationships go, we want to share our discoveries with you. Then we will describe how you may optimize things for the families in your care (see Dozier & the Infant–Caregiver Lab, 2002).

Reinterpreting Children's Behavioral Signals: The First Issue Targeted

The first component of our intervention targets infants' tendency to push foster parents away. Our evidence for this came from a study in which diaries were used to assess the developing attachment relationship between foster children and foster parents over the first weeks of the child's placement. Foster mothers recorded their observations of how their foster child responded when distressed over a period of 60 consecutive days (Stovall & Dozier, 2000; Stovall-McClough & Dozier, 2004). Each day, the foster mothers recorded how their child responded to distress on three separate occasions, including when he or she was hurt, frightened, and separated from the foster parent. In addition to their written description of each event, foster mothers also completed a checklist for each instance of distress. The checklist and narrative specified how the child responded to the distressing event, the mother's response to the child, and the child's subsequent response to the mother.

The results of this study indicated that children placed earlier than 10 months of age typically showed secure attachment behaviors when distressed, as long as their foster parents were nurturing. Conversely, children placed after about 10 months of age typically showed avoidant or resistant attachment behaviors when distressed, and these insecure ways of responding continued for the duration of the two-month study. For example, children placed before the age of 10 months responded to nurturing foster parents by seeking physical closeness to the foster parent when distressed and calming down when comforted. Children placed after about 10 months of age responded to distress by either avoiding contact with their foster parents or remaining irritable and uncomforted by them (Stovall & Dozier, 2000; Stovall & Dozier, 2002, Stovall-McClough & Dozier, 2004).

We also found that the type of behavior exhibited by the child elicited a complementary response from the foster mother. In other words, children who responded to distress by actively seeking and obtaining comfort from their foster mothers elicited consistent, nurturing responses from foster mothers. When children responded to distress by avoiding contact with their foster mothers, their mothers acted as if the child did not need any nurture. Lastly, when infants were inconsolable and resistant, their foster mothers behaved in irritable ways. As you can imagine, these complementary responses of foster parents troubled us because they suggested that a self-perpetuating cycle was developing. Instead of participating in this destructive dance, foster parents need to look beyond the avoidant and resistant behaviors often displayed by foster children in times of distress and see the underlying neediness of the child. They need to provide nurture even if the child does not outwardly appear to need it. The first component of the Attachment and Biobehavioral Catch-Up intervention addresses this critical issue.

Providing Nurture When It Does Not Come Naturally: The Second Issue Targeted

Infants form expectations of dyadic relationships based on their history of experiences with their parents. If parents have been responsive and nurturing to their children when the children have been distressed, those children have likely developed expectations that their parents will behave in such a way in the future. These children are said to have a secure attachment because they appear secure about the availability of the foster parent. When parents have been rejecting of children's bids for reassurance, children tend to develop expectations that foster parents will be rejecting. Such infants appear avoidant when distressed and turn away from their foster parents.

Finally, when parents are inconsistent in their availability, their infants tend to be unsure of their parents' availability and they tend to fuss and be difficult to soothe. Although it might appear to be optimal to have a child with a secure attachment, each of these three patterns is organized around the caregiver's availability and is well-suited to maximizing caregiver availability. Problems emerge when children are unable to organize their attachments.

Our research suggests that foster children are at particular risk for failing to develop organized attachments (Dozier, Stovall, Albus, & Bates, 2001). Although biologically intact dyads can develop organized attachments unless their parents behave in frightening ways (Main & Hesse, 1990), foster children seem prone to develop disorganized attachment—especially when foster parents are simply not very nurturing. This is of particular concern because disorganized attachments place children at risk for a host of later problems, including externalizing and internalizing problems (Lyons-Ruth, 1992; Lyons-Ruth, Alpern, & Repacholi, 1993; Lyons-Ruth, 1996), and dissociative symptomatology (Carlson, 1998). Thus, our second intervention target is to help foster parents respond to children in nurturing ways even if it does not come naturally to them.

Helping Children Develop Regulatory Capabilities: The Third Issue Targeted

Work with nonhuman primates (Levine & Wiener, 1988; Levine & Mody, 2003) has suggested that early separations from caregivers are associated with changes in the ability to regulate levels of stress hormones. In humans and other primates, cortisol is the end product of the hypothalamus-pituitary-adrenal (HPA) system. The HPA system is involved in maintaining a daily pattern that helps us function as diurnal creatures. High morning values are followed by a decrease across the day and a low level at night. The HPA system also has the function of mounting a response under conditions of stress. These functions are critical to maintain a biological rhythm and protect the organism from threat.

We followed up the nonhuman primate work by studying the production of cortisol levels across the day among infants in foster care. We found that infants who had been in foster care often showed very anomalous patterns of cortisol production compared with other infants. Some children showed high levels of cortisol across the day and others showed very low levels of cortisol production (Dozier, Manni, et al., 2006). Our interpretation of this finding was that children have difficulty regulating their neuroendocrine system when they have experienced disruptions in caregiving.

In addition to having difficulty regulating their physiology, foster children also have difficulty regulating their emotions and behaviors. Children who entered foster care as infants and toddlers had difficulties identifying how other children would feel in a series of emotion-eliciting situations. Foster children tended to over-report positive emotion compared with children who were raised in their biological families (Manni & Dozier, 2003). Children's deficits in understanding emotion have been linked to social problems (Denham, 1986; Schultz, Izard, Ackerman, & Youngstrom, 2001) and behavior problems (Denham et al., 2002). In addition, foster children have been found to have more difficulties inhibiting behavior than do other children (Lewis, Dozier, Ackerman, & Sepulveda, 2006). Inhibitory control is a self-regulatory skill that is essential for preschoolers' successful adjustment to school. Children with poor inhibitory control abilities are more likely to experience academic, social, and behavioral problems (Blair, 2002).

Supporting children's developing self-regulation has been the target of interventions intended for premature and temperamentally difficult infants (Barnard, 1999; Barnard & Morisset, 1995; van den Boom, 1994, 1995). These interventions suggest that having an interpersonal world characterized by predictability and responsiveness is particularly important for young children who are poorly regulated. This type of social environment is thought to support the development of a child's ability to develop his or her regulatory capability. It is also important for poorly regulated children to feel as if they can have an effect on their interpersonal worlds. Based on this literature, the third component of our intervention helps foster mothers to become responsive interpersonal partners to their children, to follow their children's lead in play, and to hold and touch their children on a regular basis.

Behaving in Nonthreatening Ways with Foster Children: The Fourth Issue Targeted

With few exceptions, foster children have experienced threatening behavior from adults. It could be neglectful behavior, when parents fail to provide a sense of security for their children, or it could be abusive actions, when parents actually become a source of fear and danger to their child. When foster parents directly state or indirectly imply that whether or not the child stays in the family is dependent on how well they behave, they can exacerbate those same fears in foster children. Such threats are overwhelmingly frightening to foster children. In response, a common coping mechanism among foster children is dissociating (in other words, mentally "checking out") from threatening conditions (Perry, 1994; van der Kolk & Fisler, 1994).

The fourth and final component of our intervention involves minimizing foster parents' threatening behavior toward foster children. This component aims to help foster parents understand that certain types of behaviors can frighten children and that threatening behaviors can affect children negatively.

Overview of the Attachment and Biobehavioral Catch-Up Intervention

We have found that children entering the foster care system have several specific needs:

- First, when foster children are distressed, they frequently behave in ways that communicate to new foster parents that they do not need nurture. Therefore, your foster parents must look past the children's rejecting signals and provide nurturing, responsive care regardless of the children's ability to convey their need for such care.

- Second, as a result of their own discomfort with attachment issues, some foster parents are reluctant to provide nurture to children who are distressed. However, foster children need nurturing if they are to develop organized attachments with their new foster parents. Accordingly, foster parents need to learn to respond to distressed children in nurturing ways, even when doing so is uncomfortable for them.

- Third, children in foster care are often dysregulated at neuroendocrine, behavioral, and emotional levels. To modify these atypical patterns of regulation, your foster parents need to provide predictable interpersonal worlds that are responsive to children's needs.

- Fourth, foster children have been exposed to threatening behavior from adults in the past and have limited means of coping with this type of behavior. Your foster parents need to understand that foster children may be particularly sensitive to adults' threatening behaviors, and refrain from engaging in the types of behaviors that are likely to be perceived as threatening by foster children.

These four components are critical for optimal outcomes in foster care. The intervention that we developed to facilitate this is called the Attachment and Biobehavioral Catch-Up Intervention.

We are in the process of evaluating the effectiveness of this intervention in a randomized clinical trial. Foster families who are participating in this study are randomly assigned to either of two interventions: the Attachment and Biobehavioral Catch-Up Intervention and the Developmental Education for Families Intervention. The Developmental Education for Families Intervention focuses on enhancing the development of children's cognitive and language skills by teaching foster parents ways that they can promote intellectual development in their children from an early age. It was borrowed from Sparling, Lewis, Ramey, and Wasik (1991).

The Attachment and Biobehavioral Catch-Up Intervention is composed of ten weekly sessions that last approximately one hour each and are conducted in the homes of the foster parents (Dozier & the Infant–Caregiver Lab, 2002). During these sessions, parent trainers sensitively guide foster parents in their interactions with their foster children. The sessions are videotaped for treatment fidelity purposes, as well as to be used as learning tools for foster parents. By watching the videotapes, the foster parents can observe their interactions with their children and discuss these observations with the parent trainers. Specific content of the ten sessions is described below.

Component 1

The first treatment objective is to help parents reinterpret children's rejecting signals and provide nurture when children are distressed, even if they do not appear to need it. This objective is the focus of the first two sessions.

Session 1: Providing nurture to your child

The trainer introduces herself and the Attachment and Biobehavioral Catch-Up Intervention. Session 1 focuses on the importance of foster parents developing nurturing relationships with their foster children. Foster parents and trainers watch video clips of babies who directly ask for nurture when they are distressed (secure behaviors) and babies who have difficulty doing that (avoidant and resistant behaviors). As a homework assignment, foster parents are asked to keep a diary of times when their children are frightened, hurt, or separated from them and how they respond to their children's distress.

Session 2: Providing nurture—What about the child makes it difficult?

Session 2 focuses on helping foster parents reinterpret their children's behavior and notice their own reactions to their children's distress. The homework from Session 1 is reviewed to help foster parents become more aware of how they respond to their child when he or she is distressed. Foster parents are encouraged to respond to their child's need for love and attention even when the child does not directly ask for such a response. For every day of the following week, foster parents are asked to write down an example of a time when the child was upset and their response to the child.

Component 2

The second treatment objective is to help foster parents understand how their own experiences of being parented affect how they parent their foster children. Because this learning often involves discussion of the foster parents' own potentially painful memories, we postpone it until later in our intervention, namely, we address this topic in Sessions 6 and 7. We precede this work with Sessions 3, 4, and 5 (Component 3, see below) so that the therapeutic alliance has opportunity to grow stronger.

Session 6: Providing nurture—Recognizing shark music

The focus of session 6 shifts from the child to the foster parent. More specifically, session 6 explores how the foster parent's own attachment experiences may affect their ability to parent. To address this sensitive subject matter, the trainer introduces the "shark music" metaphor. The shark music metaphor was developed as a technique for helping parents think about how their own attachment issues could affect their relationship with their children (Marvin, Cooper, Hoffman, & Powell, 2002). First, the foster parents watch a video of a peaceful ocean panorama accompanied by soothing music. Then they are shown the same video but, instead of a soothing melody, it is accompanied by music from the movie "Jaws." Foster parents learn that all parents hear "shark music" at times. In fact, it is important for parents to recognize their own shark music so that when they hear it, they can respond to their children in thoughtful, controlled ways rather than in ways that are reactive and potentially harmful. The trainers help the foster parents identify situations that cause them to experience shark music.

Session 7: Providing nurture even when there's shark music

Foster parents and foster children are videotaped during a brief separation and reunion. Mothers are asked to think about their child's response to the separation relative to their own thoughts and feelings during the separation, and to consider how their own parents would have responded when they were distressed as children. To prevent alienating the parent due to the potentially upsetting nature of session 7, trainers emphasize the parent's individual strengths and approach the parent's feelings very delicately.

Component 3

Five of the sessions (sessions 3, 4, 5, 8, and 10) focus on helping foster parents provide interpersonal environments that are predictable and responsive to children's needs. Foster parents need to allow children to feel that they have some control over their world. By following the session tasks, foster parents help provide a critical link in improving their children's developing regulatory capabilities.

Session 3: Helping the child take charge

The purpose of session 3 is to help foster parents feel more comfortable allowing children to have control over certain aspects of their environment. During the session, parents and children are videotaped as they make pudding together. The pudding activity can be difficult for parents because relinquishing some control in pudding-making could result in an unpleasant end result (for example, a messy kitchen). Trainers and parents then watch the videotape together and the trainer discusses the foster parent's strengths in working with their child. Parents and trainers consider together what was challenging about the task for the parent.

Session 4: Following the child's lead in play

Foster parents are introduced to the concept of following the child's lead in play. Trainers emphasize the importance of allowing the child to have as much control as possible during play because this will give the child a sense that he or she can have an effect on the world. Foster mothers practice following the child's lead during a videotaped interaction of the mother and child reading a book with pull-outs on each page. The foster parent is encouraged to let the child flip the pages, do the pull-outs, and look through the book at his or her own pace. As homework, parents are given several books to look at with their children over the following week. Parents are reminded to try and allow their children to have an increasingly active role in activities as the week progresses.

Session 5: Attending to the child's signals

Session 5 is designed to show foster parents how to interpret children's signals for engaging or disengaging in an activity. Foster parents are shown videotapes of other children reacting to an adult who is trying to play with them with a puppet. In the video clips, one child is curious about the puppet and tries to touch it, but another child is afraid of the puppet and tries to hide from it. Parents are encouraged to consider what the child's behavior in each video clip conveys to the adult with the puppet. The importance of recognizing and being respectful of children's signals is discussed. Videotaped parent–child interactions from past sessions are watched again to help the foster parent identify their own child's cues for engaging and disengaging. At the end of session 5, parents are asked to keep a record over the next week of their child's signals for more or less engagement.

Session 8: The importance of touch

In this session, trainers explain to the foster parents that physical contact is very important if children are to develop good regulatory capabilities. This is especially true when children have experienced disruptions in caregiving. Then, the foster parents are videotaped while playing lap games (for example, "this little piggy went to market," "itsy-bitsy spider") with their children. When reviewing the videotapes, the foster parents' responsiveness to their children's signals, their comfort with the game, their ability to allow the children to take the lead, and the children's enjoyment of the game are discussed.

Session 10: The young child's emotions

The final session focuses on showing the foster parents how to read their children's emotions and how to help their children become comfortable with experiencing and expressing emotions (especially negative emotions). The trainers discuss the value of allowing children to feel and express their emotions, because it helps children organize their negative feelings so they do not become overwhelming.

Component 4

Session 9 targets the fourth component of the Attachment and Biobehavioral Catch-Up Intervention. The foster parents learn about what kinds of behaviors may be frightening to foster children and how frightening behaviors could affect them.

Session 9: Frightening behavior

This session helps foster parents realize that it is important for them to protect their children from frightening conditions, rather than becoming another source of their children's fear. Parents who are frightening or harsh to their children undermine the children's capacity to use parents as a source of support and reassurance. Indeed, frightening behavior destabilizes the relationship between foster parents and their children. In session 9, foster parents are presented with examples of adults' frightening behavior toward children and are asked to generate comparable examples from their own childhood. They are encouraged to think about how these examples would make a child feel and are asked to discuss how they felt as children during such experiences.

Implementation of the Attachment and Biobehavioral Catch-Up Intervention

The Attachment and Biobehavioral Catch-Up Intervention has been made into a workbook so that our treatment is clearly specified and can used by others. However, we expect that sessions will partially depend on who is participating in the program and where it is occurring. Since the treatment itself is presented to foster parents in an interpersonal context, the characteristics of the foster parents and those of the parent trainers will mutually influence both the treatment process and the outcome. As a result of this reciprocal influence, it is essential that the intervention be customized to meet the specific needs of individual clients if it is to be effective.

A number of studies have determined that clients' states of mind regarding their own attachment issues is related to how they perceive treatment and treatment providers (Dozier, 1990; Dozier & Tyrrell, 1997; Korfmacher, Adam, Ogawa, & Egeland, 1997). State of mind refers to the manner in which people process attachment-related thoughts, memories, and feelings. This can make a big difference in the foster parents' ability to nurture their children. Parents with autonomous states of mind have been found to collaborate with treatment providers much more than do parents with nonautonomous states of mind (Dozier, 1990). For example, in our intervention, an autonomous foster mother would be expected to be open to thinking about how her own attachment relationships may affect her level of responsiveness toward her child. This foster mother would believe that her relationship with her foster child would affect the child's development in many ways. Accordingly, she would be willing to work on her own attachment issues and how these might affect that relationship. In most cases, an autonomous foster mother would be eager to work with the parent trainer toward finishing the intervention.

Parents with dismissing states of mind tend to diminish the significance of their own attachment issues. Consequently, when treatment involves reflecting on attachment issues, clients with dismissive states of mind may become resistant to treatment because it makes them feel uncomfortable (Dozier, 1990; Dozier & Kobak, 1990; Korfmacher et al., 1997). A dismissive foster mother might be agreeable to our intervention as long as her own relationship issues were not the topic of discussion. When such an issue arose, a dismissive mother could become defensive and possibly hostile toward the parent trainer. It would be difficult to get this mother to recognize problems with her own relationships and how they could be affecting her foster child.

Parents classified as preoccupied regarding attachment have trouble concentrating on the issue at hand during treatment sessions (Dozier, 1990). Foster mothers with preoccupied attachment states of mind might become caught up in their own relationship issues instead of focusing on session material. These foster mothers would require constant redirection from the parent trainer in order to advance through the sessions in a timely manner.

Mothers with unresolved states of mind regarding attachment frequently experience stressful life events that obstruct their progress in treatment (Korfmacher et al., 1997). An unresolved foster mother might focus on dealing with the numerous crises in her life rather than on parent training. The other emergencies in this mother's life would render our treatment concerns somewhat trivial. An unresolved foster mother would require strong persuasion from the parent trainer that the treatment sessions did provide relevant information.

Foster parents' attachment states of mind are clearly pertinent to consider when implementing our particular intervention. The goal of the Attachment and Biobehavioral Catch-Up Intervention is not to alter foster parents' states of mind regarding attachment, but rather to improve parenting skills so that nonautonomous foster mothers can provide nurture to their children the way that autonomous mothers do. Therefore, it is critical to consider clients' specific needs and beliefs, and to intervene flexibly, modifying treatment content and approach to fit the individual client. The subsequent case studies serve as examples of some of the practical challenges faced by parent trainers as they implement this particular intervention. In addition to intervening with foster parents we have adapted our treatment for use with birth parents who have been reunited with their children after the children have been in the foster care system. This is shown in case study 2.

Case Studies

The following case examples illustrate the tailoring of our treatment to the individual needs of two very different foster parents.

Case Study 1

"Ms. T" is a 65-year-old African American nonrelative foster parent who has been a foster mother for the past five years. Ms. T has a high school education and an income of less than $15,000 a year. Ms. T's mother was a single mother, and she frequently had to leave Ms. T home alone, so she could work. Consequently, Ms. T practically raised her two younger siblings. Ms. T left her mother's home after she graduated from high school and got married at the age of 18. Soon after, she and her husband had two children of their own. Ms. T's husband died five years ago of a heart attack. After her husband's death, Ms. T decided to become a foster parent. In the past five years, she has adopted two foster children and has cared for 12 other foster children.

Darius was 14 months old when he was placed with Ms. T. Darius had been placed in foster care when he was less than a year old because his biological mother could not provide for him. Darius and his mother had been homeless when the Division of Family Services (DFS) took custody of Darius. Darius lived in his first foster home for only 4 months because his first foster mother became too ill to care for him. At 14 months of age, Darius was introduced to his third primary foster parent.

Initially, Ms. T failed to return several phone calls from our parent trainer. When Ms. T and the parent trainer eventually got in touch, Ms. T politely explained that she did not need the Attachment and Biobehavioral Catch-Up Intervention because she had over 50 years of experience raising children as a parent, grandparent, and foster parent. She also expressed that she was too busy to be bothered with the intervention. The Division of Family Services then contacted Ms. T to let her know that participation in the intervention was mandatory for any foster parent who had a foster child less than 20 months old. Ms. T's reluctant agreement to be in the intervention presented a challenge for the parent trainer who would be working with her.

The flexibility of the Attachment and Biobehavioral Catch-Up treatment manual allowed the parent trainer to selectively emphasize content that would be helpful in reducing Ms. T's resistance to training. In approaching a foster parent who was opposed to receiving training, the parent trainer presented herself as a professional colleague rather than as an instructor. She informed Ms. T that the training she had to offer was not unidirectional. Instead her intent was also to learn from Ms. T's extensive experience in caring for foster children. In addition, the parent trainer indicated that what she learned from Ms. T's experience would be used to better understand the effects of disruptions in caregiving on young children.

The combination of respecting Ms. T's opinions and placing emphasis on the importance of her experience dramatically changed Ms. T's attitude toward participating in the intervention. By the end of the first session, instead of feeling reluctant and forced into the training, Ms. T was excited about sharing her own experiences and looked forward to learning new information. As the training progressed, Ms. T participated in every activity, demonstrated her understanding of concepts by expanding on the information presented, and continually made connections between session material and her relationship with Darius. For example, Ms. T was able to reinterpret Darius' behavior toward her when he returned from visitation days with his birth mother. Ms. T had noticed that, following these visits, Darius would look away from her and remain inconsolable when she attempted to soothe him. Placing his behavior in an attachment context, Ms. T realized that his behavior did not mean that he did not need her; rather, he was confused and angry about being separated from her. Ms. T practiced providing nurture to Darius in these situations and could detect a change in his behavior. Ms. T was also able to connect the shark music session to her experience with her own unavailable mother. She realized that when she left Darius alone to cry, she was doing the same thing her mother had done to her when she had been upset as a child.

Ms. T became invested in the Attachment and Biobehavioral Catch-Up training sessions, because her experience as a parent and as a foster mother were validated and respected by the parent trainer. The intervention provided a framework that Ms. T could apply to her own foster child's behavior, and she noticed improvements in their interactions when she employed concepts from the intervention.

Case Study 2

"Jennifer" is a 17-year-old European American birth mother. Emma is her 13-month-old biological daughter. Jennifer has an 8th grade education and is currently working part-time at McDonald's. She herself was placed into foster care when she was three years old because her mother had a substance abuse problem. Jennifer's mother was in and out of jail due to her heroin addiction and Jennifer's father died when she was a toddler. From the age of four until 14, Jennifer grew up in the care of a grandmother who was both physically and verbally abusive. Jennifer was also the victim of sexual abuse perpetrated by one of her distant relatives. Following this incident, Jennifer was again placed into foster care. From about age 13, Jennifer frequently drank alcohol and used marijuana, but she has abstained from drug use over the past year. She is single and currently does not have any other foster or birth children, although she is pregnant with her second child. At the time of the intervention, Jennifer and her daughter were residing in a foster placement because, at the age of 17, Jennifer was still considered a minor.

In contrast to Ms. T, Jennifer did not have experience and knowledge that she could bring to initial training sessions. In fact, Jennifer's immaturity, lack of education, and low self-esteem became quite a challenge for the parent trainer assigned to her case. Early on, it became apparent that Jennifer was very sensitive about her lack of education. Her fear of appearing unintelligent prevented her from speaking up during sessions. To address this issue, the parent trainer was able to use the flexibility of the treatment manual to tailor session material to Jennifer by explaining concepts as simply as possible and by asking for feedback more often than prescribed by the manual. Repetition was also particularly helpful. The parent trainer employed the technique of repeating concepts several times in different ways until Jennifer could say them back to her from memory. In this way, the Attachment and Biobehavioral Catch-Up Intervention became much more conversational than usual, which was more effective in this case.

In addition, the parent trainer modified session content and language to fit with Jennifer's understanding of developmental concepts. For example, Jennifer did not understand that it is important to help children develop autonomy and to give them a sense that they can affect their worlds. However, she did understand that it is a good thing for children to be curious, because children who are curious are also bright. When presented in this way, Jennifer was able to realize that by restricting her child's movement and exploration, she might be hindering Emma's development and consequently, her child's ability to feel a sense of control over her world.

Another factor in this particular case was Jennifer's own tumultuous family history. Jennifer's difficult childhood experiences shaped how the intervention was delivered in a number of ways. For instance, the trainer noticed that Jennifer had difficulty allowing Emma to take the lead during play. Occasionally, Jennifer got so caught up in her own enjoyment of the activities that she would forget to let Emma direct their interaction. To counter this tendency, the parent trainer used many opportunities (including spontaneous mother–child interactions—for example, Jennifer feeding Emma as she listened to the trainer) to remind Jennifer to let Emma partially lead their interactions. The parent trainer also gave Jennifer extensive praise in-the-moment for times when she parented well. The positive feedback about her parenting abilities worked extremely well because Jennifer had rarely received praise growing up.

As the intervention progressed, the trainer realized she would have to risk alienating Jennifer by bringing up Jennifer's difficult childhood experiences in sessions 6 and 7. Connecting session material to her own life would most likely make the sessions more meaningful to Jennifer. However, this course of action would also be very risky because Jennifer had had many painful experiences in her life that she would probably be reluctant to discuss. Jennifer had revealed a lot of information regarding her childhood during the preintervention meetings, so the parent trainer helped her make connections to her own life by gently prompting her with what she knew of Jennifer's past (for example, "I remember that you told me your grandmother yelled at you a lot...").

Luckily, bringing up issues from the past did not alienate Jennifer because she was very committed to her daughter, as a result of all she had missed during her own childhood. For example,

Jennifer desperately wanted Emma to be smart and articulate, get a good education, and to be willing to come to her when she was upset. Jennifer was able to make direct links to her own childhood in both the shark music session (session 6) and the emotions session (session 10). During the shark music session, she realized that sometimes when she responded to Emma, she was responding the way her grandmother had responded to her when she was a child. When Jennifer watched videotapes of her responses to Emma, she could clearly verbalize, "That's my grandmother. That's not me." or "That's me. That's how I want to parent." Being able to identify times when she was treating Emma the way that she had been treated, versus times when she was being a good mother, was a very powerful connection for Jennifer.

Jennifer could also relate the emotions session to her own childhood because she had never learned to express her negative emotions in a nondestructive way. When she was a child, she had always been afraid that her grandmother would yell at her or hurt her if she expressed anger or sadness. Instead of confiding in her grandmother, Jennifer learned to keep all of her anger and sadness to herself. Jennifer recalled feeling overwhelmed by her anger and realized that her inability to express her emotions was probably why she had gotten into so many fights at school. And she recognized that by hitting and yelling at her child she was behaving like a frightening adult. Remembering that her grandmother had frightened her, Jennifer realized that, by acting the same way toward Emma, her daughter would learn not to come to her for reassurance.

Although Jennifer probably would not have the social support system necessary to carry out all she had learned from the Attachment and Biobehavioral Catch-Up Intervention, the parent trainer felt confident that the intervention had made an impact. From week to week, Jennifer remembered things they had discussed and often made references to very early concepts during later sessions. Jennifer also made the effort to always do the homework assignments and she and Emma read all of the pull-out books that the trainer left at the end of session 4. This intervention was effective due to Jennifer's strong commitment to her child, as well as the trainer's ability to simplify intervention concepts, make sessions conversational, provide extra praise for good parenting, sensitively draw on Jennifer's childhood experiences, and emphasize Jennifer's hopes for Emma's future. The outcome of this case would not have been as successful if the Attachment and Biobehavioral Catch-Up Intervention did not provide a flexible framework that allowed for treatment to be tailored to Jennifer's individual needs.

Conclusion

Foster children often experience difficulties in regulating their behavior, emotions, and physiology. They also face difficulties in forming trusting, loving relationships. These problems occur as the result of foster children's early inadequate care, traumatic experiences, and disruptions in attachment relationships. Through our research, we have developed a manualized intervention for foster infants and toddlers that targets four specific, critical needs of these children. Foster children who complete our Attachment and Biobehavioral Catch-Up Intervention are expected to be more likely to develop secure attachments to their surrogate foster parents and exhibit greater regulation of emotional, behavioral, and physiological levels. Our intervention is likely to be most effective when it is delivered in a manner that considers the specific needs of those involved.

References

Barnard, K. E. (1999). *Beginning rhythms: The emerging process of sleep-wake behaviors and self-regulation.* Seattle: Nursing Child Assessment Satellite Training (NCAST), University of Washington.

Barnard, K. E. & Morisset, C. E. (1995). Preventative health and developmental care for children: Relationships as a primary factor in service delivery with at risk populations. In H. E. Fitzgerald, B. M. Lester, & B. Zuckerman (Eds.), *Children of poverty: Research, health, and policy issues* (pp. 167–195). New York: Garland Publishing.

Blair, C. (2002). School readiness: Integrating cognition and emotion in a neurobiological conceptualization of children's functioning at school entry. *American Psychologist, 57,* 111–127.

Carlson, E. A. (1998). A prospective longitudinal study of attachment disorganization/disorientation. *Child Development, 69,* 1107–1128.

Chernoff, R., Combs-Orme, T., Risley-Curtiss, C., & Heisler, A. (1994). Assessing the health status of children entering foster care. *Pediatrics, 93,* 594–601.

Clausen, J. M., Landsverk, J., Ganger, W., Chadwick, D., & Litrownik, A. (1998). Mental health problems of children in foster care. *Journal of Child & Family Studies, 7,* 283–296.

Denham, S. (1986). Social cognition, prosocial behavior, and emotion in preschoolers: Contextual validation. *Child Development, 57,* 194–201.

Denham, S., Caverly, S., Schmidt, M., Blair, K., DeMulder, E., Caal, S., Hamada, H., & Mason, T. (2002). Preschool understanding of emotions: Contributions to classroom anger and aggression. *Journal of Child Psychology and Psychiatry, 43,* 901–916.

Dozier, M. (1990). Attachment organization and treatment use for adults with serious psychological disorders. *Development and Psychopathology, 2,* 47–60.

Dozier, M., Dozier, D., & Manni, M. (2002). Attachment and Biobehavioral Catch-Up: The ABC's of helping foster infants cope with early adversity. *Zero to Three Bulletin, 22,* 7–13.

Dozier, M., & the Infant–Caregiver Lab. (2002). *The Attachment and Biobehavioral Catch-Up Intervention: A training manual for foster parents.* Unpublished manual, University of Delaware, Newark, DE.

Dozier, M., & Kobak, R. R. (1990). Psychophysiology in attachment interviews: Converging evidence for deactivating strategies. *Child Development, 63,* 1473–1480.

Dozier, M., Manni, M., Gordon, M. K. Peloso, E., Gunnar, M. R., Stovall-McClough, K., et al. (2006). Foster children's diurnal production of cortisol: An exploratory study. *Child Maltreatment, 11,* 189–197.

Dozier, M., Stovall, K. C., Albus, K. E., & Bates, B. (2001). Attachments for infants in foster care: The role of foster parent state of mind. *Child Development, 72,* 1467–1477.

Dozier, M., & Tyrrell, C. (1997). The role of attachment in therapeutic relationships. In J. A. Simpson & W. S. Rholes (Eds.), *Attachment theory and close relationships* (pp. 221–248). New York: Guilford Press.

Halfon, N., Mendonca, A., & Berkowitz, G. (1995). Health status of children in foster care: The experience of the center for the vulnerable child. *Archives of Pediatric Adolescent Medicine, 149,* 386–392.

Korfmacher, J., Adam, E., Ogawa, J., & Egeland, B. (1997). Adult attachment: Implications for the therapeutic process in a home visitation intervention. *Applied Developmental Science, 1,* 43–52.

Levine, S., & Mody, T. (2003). The long-term psychobiological consequences of intermittent postnatal separation in the squirrel monkey. *Neuroscience and Biobehavioral Reviews, 27,* 83–89.

Levine, S. & Wiener, S. G. (1988). Psychoendocrine aspects of mother-infant relationships in non-human primates. *Psychoneuroendocrinology, 13,* 143–154.

Lewis, E., Dozier, M., Ackerman, J. P., & Sepulveda, S. (2006). *The effect of caregiving instability on adopted children's inhibitory control abilities and oppositional behavior.* Unpublished manuscript, available from mdozier@udel.edu.

Lyons-Ruth, K. (1992). Maternal depressive symptoms, disorganized infant-mother attachment relationships and hostile-aggressive behavior in the preschool classroom: A prospective longitudinal view from infancy to age five. In D. Cicchetti & S. L. Toth (Eds.), *Developmental perspectives on depression* (pp. 131–171). Rochester, NY: University of Rochester Press.

Lyons-Ruth, K. (1996). Attachment relationships among children with aggressive behavior problems: The role of disorganized early attachment patterns. *Journal of Consulting and Clinical Psychology, 64,* 64–73.

Lyons-Ruth, K., Alpern, L., & Repacholi, B. (1993). Disorganized infant attachment classification and maternal psychosocial problems as predictors of hostile-aggressive behavior in the preschool classroom. *Child Development, 64,* 572–585.

Main, M., & Hesse, E. (1990). Parents' unresolved traumatic experiences are related to infant disorganized attachment status: Is frightened and/or frightening parental behavior the linking mechanism? In M. T. Greenberg, D. Cicchetti, & E. M. Cummings (Eds.), *Attachment in the preschool years: Theory, research, and intervention* (pp. 161–182). Chicago: University of Chicago.

Manni, M., & Dozier, M. (2003). *Emotion understanding in young foster children.* Unpublished master's thesis, University of Delaware, Newark, DE.

Marvin, R., Cooper, G., Hoffman, K., & Powell, B. (2002). The Circle of Security Project: Attachment-based intervention with caregiver–pre-school child dyads. *Attachment and Human Development 1,* 107–124.

Perry, B. D. (1994). Neurobiological sequelae of childhood trauma: Post-traumatic stress disorders in children. In M. Murberg (Ed.), *Catecholamines in post-traumatic stress disorder: Emerging concepts* (pp. 253–276). Washington, DC: American Psychiatric Press.

Schultz, D., Izard, C. E., Ackerman, B., & Youngstrom, E. A. (2001). Emotion knowledge in economically disadvantaged children: Self-regulatory antecedents and relations to social difficulties and withdrawal. *Development and Psychopathology, 13,* 53–67.

Sparling, J., Lewis, I., Ramey, C., & Wasik, B. (1991). Partners: A curriculum to help premature, low birthweight infants get off to a good start. *Topics in Early Childhood Special Education, 11,* 36–55.

Stovall, K. C., & Dozier, M. (2000). The development of attachment in new relationships: Single subject analyses for ten foster infants. *Development and Psychopathology, 12,* 133–156.

Stovall, K. C., & Dozier, M. (2002). *Evolving attachments in new foster care placements.* Unpublished manuscript, University of Delaware, Newark, DE.

Stovall-McClough, K. C., & Dozier, M. (2004). Forming attachments in foster care: Infant attachment behaviors during the first 2 months of placement. *Development and Psychopathology, 14,* 253–271.

U.S. Department of Health and Human Services, Administration for Children and Families (2004). *2002 adoption and foster care analysis and reporting system report.* Retrieved January 21, 2004, from www.acf.hhs.gov/programs/cb.

van den Boom, D. C. (1994). The influence of temperament and mothering on attachment and exploration: An experimental manipulation of sensitive responsiveness among lower-class mothers and irritable infants. *Child Development, 65,* 1457–1477.

van den Boom, D. C. (1995). Do first-year intervention effects endure? Follow up during toddlerhood of a sample of Dutch irritable infants. *Child Development, 66,* 1798–1816.

van der Kolk, B. A., & Fisler, R. E. (1994). Childhood abuse and neglect and loss of self regulation. *Bulletin of the Menninger Clinic, 58,* 145–168.

13

Supporting the Work
of Foster Parents

Paul T. Huber and Jason B. Whiting

U nderstanding the perspective of foster parents in the foster
care system is important for professionals who work with the
children in their care. Foster parents are a vital link in the
chain of caregiving, and they have the potential to be one of your most
important allies. Foster parents undergo many unique experiences in
their work with the agencies and children, and they often feel frustrated or taken for granted. Learning what motivates these parents to
foster, as well as what compels them to quit, is helpful for those of us
who work with foster families.

Foster parents are an indispensable link in the chain of caregiving for children removed from their homes. These parents are the
first line of defense for these children, and they provide most of the
caregiving for children who are in state custody (Rhodes, Orme &
Buehler, 2001). Despite their importance, there are not enough
foster parents available to take the children who are entering the
system in ever-increasing numbers. Between 1987 and the late
1990s, the number of children entering foster care increased 74%,
while the number of foster homes actually declined by a third
(Burry, 1999). Given that foster parents are important allies in protecting and caring for children who have been removed from their
homes, it is important to work well with these parents. They have
unique dynamics, concerns, and stresses we need to understand.
This chapter will review important foster parent dynamics, including why they choose to foster, what they need to be successful, what

their primary stressors are, and how therapists can work with foster parents effectively.

To Be or Not to Be a Foster Parent

The decision to become a foster parent is motivated by many factors. Many foster parents take children for altruistic or spiritual reasons, such as wanting to help children in need or make a difference in society (Baum, Crase, & Crase, 2001; Whiting & Huber, 2007). Some couples choose to become foster parents because they have been unable to have children or because their biological children have grown and left (Gillis-Arnold, Crase, Stockdale, & Shelley, 1998; Sanchirico & Jablonka, 2000). Some are former foster children themselves or individuals who identify with the needs of dispossessed children and choose to pick up the torch. Others are inspired by a family who fosters (Baum et al., 2001; Phelps, 1989). Finally, some simply find rewards in nurturing children and would like more of them in their homes (Hampson & Tavormina, 1980).

Although rewards exist, there also are many disincentives to fostering. In some areas, foster parents have a low social status or are viewed with suspicion. The media often sensationalize the difficulties and dangers inherent in the system (Smith & Gutheil, 1988). Also, there is little support or material assistance for the work, and many couples today are busy with two careers. Some parents fear that taking foster children will result in accusations of abuse, or they worry about the stress on the family or marriage (McFadden, 1996; Pecora & Fraser, 1992). There are also high expectations for foster parents and that can intimidate those considering signing on.

The Characteristics of Good Foster Parents

Good foster homes do not just fall from the sky. Although training will provide some of the skill sets for success in fostering, it is important that foster families have a fundamental capacity to supply a safe haven for the children who come into their care. A good home environment is an excellent indicator of latent foster family functioning (Brown & Calder, 2000; Shlonsky & Berrick, 2001). The active involvement of the male parental unit in the life of the family is also important to successful fostering (James & Meezan, 2002). A stable marriage or long-term partnership is highly beneficial (Brown & Calder, 2000; Wilson, Sinclair, & Gibbs, 2000). Along with emotional stability, it is important that the potential foster family members have a genuine liking for children (Morrissette, 1994).

Agency workers have described high quality foster families as having the following characteristics: The capacity to handle difficult situations with children, the ability to work productively with the biological parents, acceptance of agency workers and procedures, and the ability to provide basic care for the child, including emotional warmth, discipline, positive interaction, and a safe environment (Shlonsky & Berrick, 2001). These parents are also expected to have positive values, good social skills, high energy, resilience, and good judgment (Brown & Calder, 2000; Daly & Dowd, 1992). All of the preceding attributes will be tested by the foster children who enter into their family system, as well as by agency workers.

Foster Parent Stressors

Often the challenges of fostering overwhelm parents—even to the point where they burnout and discontinue. These stressors include problematic interactions with the agency and workers, personal problems, foster children behaviors, strains on the biological children or marriage, and financial problems.

Problems with the agency often include poor communication with caseworkers, a lack of agency support, or feeling devalued (Chamberlain & Moreland, 1992; Rhodes et al., 2001; Whiting & Huber, 2007). A common complaint of experienced foster parents is that their contribution towards permanency planning is ignored, even though they have valuable insight into viable options. Inadequate provisions for respite care, which is intended to provide temporary relief for the foster family from the stresses of foster children, are also problematic (Chamberlain & Moreland, 1992).

An example illustrating the problematic interaction of foster parents and agencies comes from a recent study done in Kentucky (Cabinet for Families and Children, 2002). The state surveyed all family foster homes in 2002. Many parents indicated that they were dissatisfied because of inadequate information from agency workers, not getting calls returned in a timely manner, and too few visits from caseworkers. Responses were broken down among sixteen geographical regions and wide variations in satisfaction appeared. Some areas were doing a much better job in caring for their foster families than others. Fully 55% of the foster parents claimed that receiving limited information about the child interfered with the partnership with the state agency. Changes in caseworkers were cited by 45% of the respondents as a problem. The failure to respond to foster parent needs was a strong reason why less than 50% of foster parents had five or more years of experience.

Many foster parents are not prepared for the intensity of behavior and emotions that foster children exhibit (McFadden, 1996). Often the children are traumatized by their family background, as well as their entrance into care (Barth, 2001; Folman, 1998). Hyperactivity, defiance, and general behavioral problems are common, and many foster parents feel that the discipline techniques they previously learned are inadequate. These behavioral and health problems are difficult for foster parents to handle, especially when they feel disconnected from the professionals who have more expertise in this area.

Other emotional challenges for foster parents include ambiguities about the relationships among the foster family, child or children, agencies, and biological family (Brown & Calder 1999; Hudson & Levasseur, 2002). Also, the loss of a foster child is potentially one of the most difficult times of a family's fostering career. Foster families must learn to deal with the grief of separation when one of the children placed in their care is removed and returned to the biological family (Brown & Calder 1999; Hudson & Levasseur,

2002; Rhodes et al., 2001; Wilson et al., 2000). This can be especially difficult if the foster family does not agree with the decision to reunite and if the caseworker or court system has ignored their opinion. The return of children to homes—homes viewed by foster parents as dysfunctional—is one of most stressful and frequently occurring situations with which they must contend (Jones & Morrissette, 1999). An additional stressor for many foster families is interaction with or the influence of the biological family on the foster children while they are in care, and so indirectly upon the fostering family system (Sanchirico & Jablonka, 2000; Wilson et al., 2000).

Financial problems can also create a great deal of stress for foster families. The cost of raising children is increasing, and reimbursement rates are far below the expenses required to raise a child. This creates a bind for foster parents because their own family's situation is put at risk while they help other children escape the hazards of their biological families (Barth, 2001; Rhodes et al., 2001; Rindfleisch, Bean, & Denby, 1998). Reimbursement rates are uneven across the country. But at least one estimate was that foster families were receiving approximately 60% of what middle-class families expected to spend to raise a child (for example, Barth, 2001).

How Professionals Can Support Foster Parents

Despite the difficulties, many foster parents rise to the challenge and find rewards in helping these children develop physically, emotionally, and spiritually (Whiting & Huber, 2007; Wilson et al., 2000). As one foster parent described, "You live, breathe, and sleep fostering. It actually consumes your life" (Kirton, 2001, p. 200). Foster parents have identified several general areas where they need help if they are to continue to function well (Brown & Calder, 2000). These include increased parenting skills, effective relationships with agency staff, and adequate reimbursement. Support from other foster parents has also been recognized as an advantage (Brown & Calder, 2000; Phelps, 1989; Rhodes et al., 2001).

It is important that professionals who work with foster parents understand how to do this effectively. This section will discuss some of the most crucial areas of support for foster parents. These include support through improved contact, training, and financial assistance (Phelps, 1989).

A relationship built on trust with agency social workers is a necessity (Brown & Calder, 2000; Morrissette, 1994). Frequent high quality contact with agency workers increases the probability that foster parents will remain within the system (Fisher, Gibbs, Sinclair, & Wilson, 2000). And better retention provides the further likelihood that foster children's placement will be with skilled and motivated foster parents (Rhodes et al., 2001).

Another way to improve retention is through better recruitment. State workers involved with recruitment should seek feedback from prospective foster parents about how they came to be interested in fostering, so that effective measures can be continued and ineffective techniques abandoned (Rodwell & Biggerstaff, 1993). The optimum solution to the shortage of foster families is to recruit and train those families with the highest potential for success in fostering, while also providing the requisite incentives that will encourage quality foster families to remain.

Foster parents need to clearly understand agency policy concerning the roles of social workers and foster parents (Rodwell & Biggerstaff, 1993). They also need practical help understanding the procedures for having a child in their home, as well as emotional support and validation. Especially when new to the system, foster parents' anxiety levels can be very high (Morrissette, 1994). New parents often need agency help in getting connected to resources to help with a child's behavioral or emotional problem (Fisher et al., 2000; Hudson & Levasseur, 2002). In addition, as the front line of care, foster parents should have more input into case planning (Rhodes et al., 2001). And if the agency cannot affirm the foster family because they are not performing well enough, then remedial training should be available to increase the skill level of the family. Some states utilize a mentoring program in which experienced foster parents work with new foster parents. These states find that that strategy benefits both parties (Rhodes et al., 2001).

"The quality of training most likely affects the future practical application of the material learned by the participants" (Fees et al., 1998, p. 360). Without adequate training, the chances of success in fostering are severely diminished. There are two essential types of training provided by most states: preservice and inservice (or continuing) education. Before individuals or families are licensed to take in children who are wards of the state, they typically are required to participate in training to prepare them for the needs of foster children. This training is important because the uniqueness of fostering children creates difficulties for even experienced parents (Fees et al., 1998; Hampson & Tavormina, 1980). Training is especially important for those who do not have very much parenting experience (Fees et al., 1998). One way to ensure that potential foster parents understand the challenges they will face is to incorporate experienced foster parents into the teaching team so they can share their own fostering experiences (Morrissette, 1994). Initial foster parent training should discuss in greater detail some of the difficulties that will be encountered with children in out-of-home care (Rhodes et al., 2001). Training is also needed in basic communication, family conflict, and the effects of foster care on the biological children (Brown & Calder, 2000; Chamberlain & Moreland, 1992).

Regardless of how good the preservice training may be, there is a need for continuing knowledge and skill acquisition. To be most effective, there must be a variety of training opportunities that coincide with the skill level of foster parents (Morrissette, 1994). A variety of delivery systems, including on-site and Internet-accessed reading materials, are useful so that diverse additional training needs can be individually achieved. The primary focus of continuing training should be on skill development and coping mechanisms concerning behavioral issues. Of necessity, the skills required will be dependent upon the foster parents and the foster children with whom they are involved (Morrissette, 1994; Pithouse, Hill-Tout, & Lowe, 2002; Rodwell & Biggerstaff, 1993). Quality continuing education is vital for perceived competence and for retention of foster parents.

If reimbursement rates were higher and tied in some way to the rate of inflation or adjusted more often by the respective state legislatures, the financial strain felt by many foster families might be eased (Chamberlain & Moreland, 1992). Respite care provisions could also be attached to reimbursement rates (Barbell & Wright, 1999). That way families could take breaks without concurrent loss of their stipends. Provision for medical insurance coverage for foster families might also bring relief. Such changes are not within the control of those of you who work in the trenches, but your support of legislation could be an indirect aid to the parents.

Case Example—The Karst Family

The Karst family has been involved in foster care for over twelve years. That they have stayed with it for so long attests to their substantial family resiliency. They are unsure of the exact number of children who have passed through their home in those years. Some of the children stayed only a few days, but one girl lived with them for over nine years. Several children were in the family for over two years each. Their experience is typical of foster parents in some instances, and perhaps less so in others.

In 1992, the Karsts became foster parents in response to an emergency in a family they had known for several years. Their nine-year-old daughter told them that they had to take in two girls because there was nowhere else for them to go. The licensing period took longer than they expected, but they appreciated the training and made good connections with the agency worker who led the group. After initial training, the children, Martha, age 15, and Mary, age 10, were placed with the Karsts and the adventure began in earnest.

The first significant contact between a state worker and the Karst family was with Bobbie, who eventually became the trainer who led them through the intricacies of licensing and ongoing training requirements. She also was part of the team who placed children who were new to out of home care with foster families. The relationship with Bobbie was marked by mutual respect and flexibility. In describing Bobbie, Mrs. Karst said that she was affirming, upbeat, unflappable, nurturing, and balanced. Both Karst parents gave her a great deal of credit for helping them stay in the system for the first several years. Somehow, the Karsts went from providing a home for their two children and the two original foster girls, to a home where there was room for one more child whenever it was needed. It was rare to have less than five children, and at one time there were seven in the home. Unfortunately, Bobbie was transferred. Her trainer position was taken by Harriet, who tried hard to maintain the same level of service but was hampered by inexperience and by a larger caseload that affected her ability to interface well with "her" foster parents.

The Karsts' experience with the caseworkers assigned to the children in their care was uneven at best. Many workers did not appear to have the time or the inclination to deal with issues in an expedient manner. Some individuals merely made the minimal contact required by law and were impossible to reach when not carrying out their own agenda. On the other hand, several workers were outstanding, and the Karsts grieved when they were no longer involved with the family.

Ted, the first worker assigned to Martha and Mary, told Mr. and Mrs. Karst that they could not impose household rules on the girls, even if the rules were the same as those for their biological children. He seemed to imply that Martha, as a teenager, could do as she wanted and there wasn't anything the Karsts could do to stop her. After speaking to the parents of Martha and Mary, who attended the same church as the Karsts, an agreement was reached where the family rules were enforced. There were other problematic interactions with Ted, and the Karsts decided they would not take any other children for whom he was the caseworker. They were relieved when he was promoted and transferred. Martha and Mary had several other workers over the years they lived with the Karsts. Some were excellent and some were not. Jackie was one who stood out as particularly difficult. She appeared to have her own agenda concerning the children and would not listen to the Karsts, even though Mary had at this point lived with the family for several years and Martha had aged out of the system. Despite the Karsts' contention that Mary did not need extra services (with an accompanying higher stipend), Jackie put through paperwork that designated her so.

The Karsts were involved with potential adoptions of children in their care on two occasions. In the first case two sibling children, a boy and a girl, were placed and lived with the family for about two and a half years. During that time the biological parents persisted in their problematic lifestyles. The children were administratively moved from regular foster care to the pre-adoptive department. The children did not fully understand the significance of this change, and their new caseworker did not explain to them that they would not be able to live with their mother after her parental rights were terminated.

The Karsts did their best to inform the children about what was going to take place, but the Karsts did not fully understand the process or the potential emotional disruption for the children who were 9 and 11 years old. When the termination of parental rights was granted, the girl disrupted the placement by accusing Mr. Karst of physical abuse. To protect themselves, the Karsts had this girl removed from their home, but kept the boy. The extended family of the children agreed that the boy could be adopted. So did the boy's therapist, because the boy had such a strong attachment to the Karst family. However, the director of the pre-adoptive unit decided that the boy would also be removed so that the siblings could be placed together again. The grief and anger created by what seemed to them to be an insensitive and ill-informed decision caused the Karst family to refuse any new placements for three years. However, they continued to foster the children already in their home. One of the most difficult aspects of the situation for the Karsts was learning that the brother and sister were never placed in the same home during the following two years. The Karsts were allowed to see them each once after that time to try to heal some of the wounds everyone continued to carry.

A second adoption scenario went far more smoothly. Two brothers were placed in the Karst household with their older half-sister. The sister was eventually allowed to move into her biological father's house, and the boys were reunited with the mother after 5 months. Within a few months, the boys were back with the Karst family. After repeated unsuccessful attempts to return them to their mother, the agency decided to change the case goals. The Karsts and the caseworker took a great deal of care to prepare the children for the termination of parental rights and the adoption. It took over a year for the termination of parental rights to be granted. During that time, the children were assured they would be able to have contact with their biological family, as long as the family stayed within the parameters the Karsts set. After the termination of parental rights, the Karsts waited several months before proceeding with the adoption. They wanted the boys to have additional time to internalize the change and be sure they were willing to go on with it. The caseworkers involved allowed the extra time because they were sensitive to the experience of the Karst family. Because the Karsts had many years of experience and their caseworker treated them as valuable members of the child welfare team, the adoption went through with excellent outcomes for everyone involved.

The experiences of the Karsts illustrate some of the points brought out in the research on foster parents. The case study does not illustrate the whole range of issues that occur between caseworkers and foster parents, but it does illustrate some common issues that affect these families. Most notably, when foster parents are included and affirmed by caseworkers, there is a higher likelihood that there will be a positive and collaborative relationship. The case study also shows the incalculable service that occurs when foster parents work well in tandem with the professionals to serve disadvantaged youth. Hopefully, all parties involved are motivated to help the children in the best way possible. Effective partnerships with parents and professionals help the children have a higher chance of living in a stable foster home environment, whether it is a short-term placement, or one that leads to adoption.

References

Barbell, K., & Wright, L. (1999). Family foster care in the next century. *Child Welfare, 78,* 3–14.

Barth, R. C. (2001). Policy implications of foster family characteristics. *Family Relations, 50,* 16–19.

Baum, A. C., Crase, S. J., & Crase, K. L. (2001). Influences on the decision to become or not become a foster parent. *Families in Society: The Journal of Contemporary Human Services, 82,* 202–213.

Brown, J., & Calder, P. (1999). Concept mapping the challenges faced by foster parents. *Children & Youth Services Review, 21,* 481–495.

Brown, J., & Calder, P. (2000). Concept mapping the needs of foster parents. *Child Welfare, 79,* 729–746.

Burry, C. L. (1999). Evaluation of a training program for foster parents of infants with prenatal substance effects. *Child Welfare, 78,* 197–214.

Cabinet for Families and Children. (2002). *Kentucky foster care census: The status of safety and well being among children in out of home care.* Frankfort, KY: Cabinet for Families and Children.

Chamberlain, P., & Moreland, S. (1992). Enhanced services and stipends for foster parents: Effects on retention rates and outcomes for foster parents. *Child Welfare, 71,* 387–401.

Daly, D. L., & Dowd, T. P. (1992). Characteristics of effective, harm-free environments for children in out-of-home care. *Child Welfare, 71,* 487–496.

Fees, B., Stockdale, D. F., Crase, S. J., Riggins-Caspers, K., Yates, A. M., Lekies, K., S., & Gillis-Arnold, R. (1998). Satisfaction with foster parenting: Assessment one year after training. *Children & Youth Services Review, 20,* 347–363.

Fisher, T., Gibbs, I., Sinclair, I., & Wilson, K. (2000). Sharing the care: The qualities sought of social workers by foster carers. *Child & Family Social Work, 5,* 225–233.

Folman, R. (1998). "I was tooken": How children experience removal from their parents preliminary to placement in foster care. *Adoption Quarterly, 2*(2), 7–35.

Gillis-Arnold, R., Crase, S. J., Stockdale, D., & Shelley, M. C. (1998). Parenting attitudes, foster parenting attitudes, and motivations of adoptive and non-adoptive foster parent trainees. *Children & Youth Services Review, 20,* 715–732.

Hampson, R. B., & Tavormina, J. B. (1980). Feedback from the experts: A study of foster mothers. *Social Work, 25,* 108–113.

Hudson, P., & Levasseur, K. (2002). Supporting foster parents: Caring voices. *Child Welfare, 81,* 853–877.

James, S., & Meezan, W. (2002). Refining the evaluation of treatment foster care. *Families in Society: The Journal of Contemporary Human Services, 83,* 233–244.

Jones, G., & Morrissette, P. J. (1999). Foster parent stress. *Canadian Journal of Counseling, 33,* 13–27.

Kirton, D. (2001). Love and money: Payment, motivation and the fostering task. *Child & Family Social Work, 6,* 199–208.

McFadden, E. J. (1996). Family-centered practice with foster-parent families. *Families in Society: The Journal of Contemporary Human Services, 77,* 545–557.

Morrissette, P. J. (1994). Foster parenting: A developmental model. *Child & Adolescent Social Work Journal, 11,* 235–246.

Pecora, P. J., & Fraser, M. W. (1992). Intensive home-based family preservation services: An update from the FIT project. *Child Welfare, 71,* 177–188.

Phelps, D. (1989). Foster home recruitment and retention: A success story. *Children Today, 18,* 7–10.

Pithouse, A., Hill-Tout, J., & Lowe, K. (2002). Training foster carers in challenging behaviours: A case study in disappointment? *Child & Family Social Work, 7,* 203–214.

Rhodes, K. W., Orme, J. G., & Buehler, C. (2001). A comparison of family foster parents who quit, consider quitting, and plan to continue fostering. *Social Service Review, 75,* 84–115.

Rindfleisch, N., Bean, G., & Denby, R. (1998). Why foster parents continue and cease to foster. *Journal of Sociology & Social Welfare, 25,* 5–24.

Rodwell, M. K., & Biggerstaff, M. A. (1993). Strategies for recruitment and retention of foster families. *Children & Youth Services Review, 15,* 403–419.

Sanchirico, A., & Jablonka, K. (2000). Keeping foster children connected to their biological parents: The impact of foster parent training and support. *Child & Adolescent Social Work Review, 17,* 185–203.

Shlonsky, A. R., & Berrick, J. D. (2001). Assessing and promoting quality in kin and nonkin foster care. *Social Service Review, 75,* 60–83.

Smith, E. P., & Gutheil, R. H. (1988). Successful foster parent recruiting: A voluntary agency effort. *Child Welfare, 67,* 137–146.

Whiting, J. B., & Huber, P. T. (2007). *Serious stress and real rewards: The ecological and ambiguous experiences of foster parents.* Manuscript in review.

Wilson, K., Sinclair, I., & Gibbs, I. (2000). The trouble with foster care: The impact of stressful "events" on foster carers. *British Journal of Social Work, 30,* 193–209.

14

"It Isn't Right!" The Need to Redress Experiences of Injustice in Child Abuse and Neglect

Terry D. Hargrave, Robert Brammer, and Laura McDuff

The circumstances leading to foster placement may lead all parties to feel that they have been dealt with unjustly—by life and by society's institutions. Furthermore, those maltreated as children may themselves become maltreating parents. An approach to family therapy is described that addresses the manifold perceptions of injustice on the part of family members and which also is intended to diminish repetition of generational malfeasance.

"This sucks! I don't need to stay here! You all hate me!" was the cry from Elizabeth who had entered the foster care system the day after her fourth birthday. Now age 11, with a history of exits from a biological parent and entries into different foster care situations, Elizabeth displays the very common turmoil manifested by abused children: being needy, isolated, discouraged, and angry. How do you, the therapist, and the other affected parties understand these issues from the past that often resurface in unacceptable or damaging ways? We believe that there is a way of looking at these issues that sheds light on an abused child's behavior and directs effective interventions. This lens is called *contextual therapy*. This is a family therapy that was originally developed by Ivan Boszormenyi-Nagy (Boszormenyi-Nagy & Krasner, 1986). We have adapted this model, applying it and making it more accessible for different therapeutic situations (Hargrave & Pfitser, 2003).

In this chapter, we will look at a family from a contextual therapy perspective in order to give you a framework to understand the history of an abused child. Then we will discuss how to use this framework to assess children and develop goals and strategies for therapeutic work with the child and foster family. The process will be illustrated by the case of Elizabeth, the child who expressed the angry outburst above. We will follow her history of abuse and illustrate how it has resulted in the dysfunctional patterns expressed in her foster home. The case will then describe the interventions used and outcomes experienced by Elizabeth. Finally, we will discuss this case and point out how this theoretical framework gave us insights that were crucial to her ultimate good outcome.

The Contextual Family Therapy Framework

Children growing up in abusive families have experienced severe damage not only to their self-images, but also to their abilities to perceive what is right, fair, and trustworthy in relationships. Family pain and hurt in foster children originate from such a wide variety of sources, it is difficult to decipher where the relational damage has occurred and where first to apply our healing. The theoretical constructs of contextual therapy (see Boszormenyi-Nagy & Krasner, 1986; Boszormenyi-Nagy & Spark, 1984; Boszormenyi-Nagy & Ulrich, 1981) have been particularly helpful for us in conceptualizing how relational damage originates and how it affects the abused child. Contextual therapy is a family therapy approach that integrates several theories of family and psychology (Boszormenyi-Nagy & Spark, 1984). The framework maintains that all relationships exist in four dimensions. Although these four dimensions can be discussed separately, they are inseparable in terms of effect on individuals and relationships (Boszormenyi-Nagy & Krasner, 1986).

1. **Facts.** Facts are anchored in existing environmental, relational, and individual factors that are objectifiable. They include factors such as genetic input, physical health, basic historical facts, and events in a person's life cycle.

2. **Individual Psychology.** The individual's psychology is the subjective internal psychological integration of his or her experiences and motivations. Individual psychology produces subjective influences on relationships as individuals strive for recognition, love, power, and pleasure, and are motivated by aggression, mastery, or ambivalence.

3. **Family or Systemic Transactions.** Family or systemic transactions are the communication or interaction patterns of relationships. These objectifiable transactions produce organization or patterned tendencies, which define power alignments, structure, and belief systems.

4. **Relational Ethics.** Relational ethics deal with the subjective balance of justice, trustworthiness, loyalty, merit, and entitlement between members of a relationship. As members of the relationship interact in an interdependent fashion, relational ethics require them to assume responsibility for consequences and strive for fairness and equity in the process of give-and-take.

Each of these dimensions obviously affects relationships. But we and our predecessors believe that it is the dimension of relational ethics that is the most powerful, because relational ethics are the heart of a family's sense of justice and trust.

In order to understand how relationships and trust function, it is important to look at the philosophical basis of this dimension through Buber (1958). He maintained that individuals are dependent on relationships in order to experience self-understanding and self-delineation. It was Buber who asserted that humans have an innate sense of justice that demands they try to balance what they are entitled to receive and obligated to give in relationships. When relationships are cast into this relational ethics context, the function of human emotions is clear. Emotions are simply gauges that give us a reading on the balance between the give-and-take in relationships. When we do not get what we deserve in relationships, we become hurt and angry. On the other hand, when we over-benefit from relationships to which we have not contributed, most of us feel guilty. Therefore, the dimension of relational ethics encompasses the emotional field of the individual and family relationships (Hargrave, 1994a).

When family members engage in relationships that have a balanced give-and-take between relational entitlements and obligations, this innate sense of justice is satisfied. Balance between give-and-take over a long period of time produces trustworthiness in the relationship.

At the heart of trustworthiness is the security that in each relationship an individual will receive what he or she deserves without having to threaten, manipulate, or retaliate. Trustworthiness also includes the freedom to contribute and give in a relationship without fear or misgiving. This trustworthiness is the key resource that enables family members to give to each other and have relational security and stability (Boszormenyi-Nagy & Krasner, 1980).

When there is consistent or severe imbalance in this family relational give-and-take, individuals feel either cheated or over-benefited from relationships. Instead of a balance that builds trust-worthiness in a relationship, trust is drained and family members feel that their just entitlement is threatened. Instead of providing individuals freedom to give and security to receive, relationships become unstable and members have to fight and struggle to get the love, nurture, and physical requirements they need and deserve (Hargrave, 2001). It is the innate sense of justice that sets individuals in the relationship on this self-justifying claim toward securing compensation for their just entitlement. Boszormenyi-Nagy and Krasner (1986) refer to this violent pursuit of one's entitlement as destructive entitlement. Destructive entitlement can manifest itself in many ways, including paranoid attitudes, hostility, rage, emotional cutoffs, and destructive harm to other individuals. Imbalances in the relational give-and-take and the resulting destructive entitlement may be the result of gradual decline in trust or a single violent and destructive act. Gradual declines between individuals in relationships may result from a number of problems such as emotional barriers, consistent manipulation, emotional distance, and irresponsible behavior. Violent and destructive acts deteriorate relationships rapidly because they insult the balance of give-and-take in a severe fashion (Hargrave, 1994b). Most often, these severe acts are intertwined with behaviors that are associated with gradual declines in trustworthiness. Some examples of violent and destructive acts are retribution or intentional manipulation. These include consistent verbal attacks or threats, physical harm such as abuse and incest, or irresponsible emotional mistreatment that results from neglect or addiction.

In terms of give-and-take, relationships between parents and children are asymmetrical by nature (Hargrave, 2001). For instance, Figure 1 is an example of a relationship ledger between a parent and a very young child. The left side of the ledger shows examples of what we believe a parent is obligated to give to a child such as love, care, nurture, security, protection, and discipline. Notice, however, there is nothing that the child is required to give back to the parent and no entitlement or merit that the parent receives, although the parent most likely would get great emotional satisfaction (Hargrave, 2001). Most would agree that this ledger looks imbalanced. But most would also agree that it is a fair relationship because the parent was once the benefactor of love and trust from his or her parent (Hargrave & Pfitser, 2003).

FIGURE I

Parent and Child Relational Ledger

ENTITLEMENT	OBLIGATION
(Take)	(Give)
(child is entitled to:)	(child is expected to:)
1. Love	No required
2. Care	obligation
3. Nurture	
4. Security	
5. Protection	
6. Discipline	

We believe that "destructive entitlement" is at the root of family pain and hurt. The justice and trust that are necessary for a balanced relational ethic are violated and victims of the destructive behavior learn that people upon whom they depend cannot be trusted. Instead, destructive family members seek to maintain their own well-being at the expense of others in the relationships (Hargrave, 2001). This dimension of family emotion in the relational ethics strongly influences the other three dimensions (Boszormenyi-Nagy & Krasner, 1986).

The most powerful effect of destructive entitlement in the relational ethics is in the dimension of individual psychology (Hargrave & Pfitser, 2003). An individual's psychological development and personality are largely dependent upon how he or she is viewed inside the family—how he or she was loved and whether sacrifices were made for the individual's benefit. In short, how the family loves the individual shapes the individual's self-image. If a person believes he or she is a precious, worthy, and worthwhile human being, it will be because the parents treated the child in such a loving way. When people feel condemned, shameful, and unworthy, it is because their families did not love them in consistent and acceptable ways, and they took it to heart (Hargrave, 2001). This is an intolerable blow to their self-concept and image.

Therefore, internal emotional pain originates in the relational ethics dimension because of a continual imbalance in relational give-and-take. This imbalance drains trustworthiness and individuals feel justified in seeking entitlement through destructive channels. This results in manipulation, dysfunctional patterns, and, in the worst cases, damage to the psyche of others who feel the shame of not being loved (Hargrave & Pfitser, 2003). These violations of love and trust may be large and overt, such as physical abuse, incest, or profound neglect. However, pain and hurt can be just as real from less extreme and less obvious acts of destructive entitlement, for instance, consistent lack of interest, manipulation, and addictions to drugs and alcohol (Hargrave & Williams, 2003). Even though pain and hurt originate from the same source—destructive entitlement—there are varying degrees of pain and hurt. A victim of manipulation from an alcoholic family member and a victim of severe physical abuse will both not trust in relationships. But the victim of the physical abuse may feel more pain because of the violent act taken against him or her. Generally, we believe that the more violent and grievous the violation, the more violent destructive behavior will result in the future (Hargrave & Pfitser, 2003).

Neglected and Abused Children

Sometimes children do not get that to which they are entitled—their parents do not fulfill their obligations. At other times, children are required to fulfill obligations that do not belong to them, such as taking care of their parents physically or psychologically. Both situations are harmful (Hargrave, 2001). As these children grow, they seek to protect themselves from further parental abuse and seek their entitlement in destructive ways (Hargrave & Pfitser, 2003). In order to cope with pain from violations of love and trust we believe that these children—or any individual—will transform the pain into feelings about themselves (primarily violations of love), and beliefs about actions they must take in future relationships (primarily violations of trust). As Figure 2 illustrates, when children are violated in this way, they are likely to feel (1) uncontrolled anger toward victimizing adult or adults, or (2) shame because the parents accused them of being unlovable and not deserving of a trustworthy relationship. Similarly, if children experience painful trust violations, they will likely take actions toward future relationships that are (1) over-controlling because they are trying to minimize their risk of hurt in future relationships or (2) chaotic because they assume that little can be done to form trusting relationships and that they will eventually be hurt no matter what they do to protect themselves (Hargrave, 2001).

FIGURE 2

Model of Violations of Love and Trust

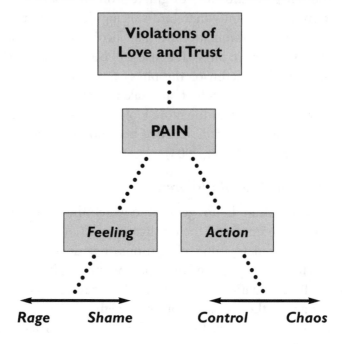

Rage

Some victims of child maltreatment will answer the questions of "Why was I not loved?" and "Why was my family not trustworthy?" with an answer that blames their victimizers with disproportionate vigor. It may start out with confusion about how a father could sexually abuse his own daughter or how a mother could possibly be so unfeeling as to burn her son as a form of punishment. But through re-exposure and re-victimization by family members, the victims begin thinking that the perpetrators must be beyond human reason. Their actions seem so unjustifiable. With this view-point, it is easy for the victims to see perpetrators as dangerous objects, rather than humans, and this becomes generalized to others who may be perceived as a threat. Victims may then experience rage toward persons who may or may not be dangerous to them (Hargrave, 2001).

Shame

Other victims will answer the question of "Why was I not loved?" or "Why was my family not trustworthy?" by blaming themselves. They conclude that the fault for the unreasonable or manipulative actions lies not with their perpetrators, but their own unworthy nature. For a victim to believe that he or she deserved the terrible neglect or abuse that came from an abuser is to be filled with a toxic shame that penetrates every part of the soul and colors every interaction in future relationships. Healthy self-image and relating to others is impossible when this type of shame results from abuse (Hargrave, 2001).

Rage and Shame Cycles

Many victims of abuse will flip-flop in cycles of intense rage and shame. They may feel swept away by unreasoning rage over being abused and feel justified in lashing out at the "monsters" who damaged them—or the current bystanders who remind them of the people that caused the pain. Later, after the victims view the destruction they believe they have caused themselves, they feel a backlash of shame. Victims of abuse will then feel all the remorse and self-condemnation of shameful people and may become distant, depressed, and dependent. After a time, the cycle is likely to repeat itself (Hargrave, 2001).

Control

When individuals feel hurt by relationships on which they have depended, they find ways to avoid hurt in future relationships. At one extreme, this avoidance allows victims to control future interactions in relationships. Simply stated, they protect themselves by dictating the how, what, and when of future relationships. They may do it overtly by threatening emotionally or physically. These individuals are often seen as "little dictators" because they demand certain kinds of behavior from others. They also may show controlling attitudes in relationships through covert methods such as subtle manipulation or withdrawal. In order to deal with the threat of

relationship disappointment, some victims will distance themselves from others or keep all of their thoughts to themselves.
When things go wrong in their relationships, they seldom take any
responsibility for its failure. Instead, they wait until the other
person takes full responsibility for the problem. In this way, the
controllers maintain power over the relationship so it will not hurt
them (Hargrave, 2001).

Chaos

When individuals are violated in areas of trustworthiness, they
may try to escape relationships to avoid future pain or hurt.
Instead of trying to control all the power in their relationships,
they may expend their energies trying to escape the other person's
power and avoid his or her rules. Victims who are driven by chaotic
behavior believe that life and relationships are built to damage
them and that they will be hurt again. They take pleasure in acting
out in ways that provide escape from the gloomy prospect of hurt.
When there is a choice to be made between doing what may be
good for the relationship and narcissistically satisfying themselves,
they choose the latter. These individuals are driven to chaotic
behavior in order to avoid pain, and they appear very irresponsible
toward relationships. However, their behavior is not driven by lack
of maturity or irresponsibility; rather, it is driven by hopelessness.
They believe that they eventually will experience pain in every relationship and they are trying to escape their despair. Often such
individuals become addicted to substances (Hargrave, 2001).
These substances can provide them emotional distraction or relief
without having to engage in social relations.

Control and Chaos Cycles

The control and chaos cycle that occurs in victimized individuals
will remind you of bipolar individuals who vacillate between manic
episodes and periods of depression. However, with the control and
chaos cycle, the individual is trying to deal with emotional pain.
Victims in these types of cycles will overly control relationships and

obsess over their details. Then, when matters become more unruly and out of line with expectations and power, they often will resign themselves from all power and responsibility and instead escape into some type of indulgent behavior designed to calm their anxiety and pain (Hargrave, 2001).

Assessment and Goals from a Contextual Perspective

As you know, there are several categories of maltreatment to which children and adolescents may be exposed. Although each is different, they all inflict a common injury on victimized children. These are the violations of love and trust that cause a poor or confused self-concept and dysfunctional behavior in future relationships. As we discussed earlier, the symptoms of rage, shame, control, or chaos serve a purpose in the human response to abuse. They may lose their function when children are safe in foster care, but they do not go away. These destructive actions are attempts to gain the entitlement of love and trust missed in family relationships. Unhappily, these symptoms serve the opposite effect—they tend to keep the children from building and maintaining healthy relationships in the post-traumatic environment. Moreover, foster parents and other adults who are attempting to love and care for these children often feel frustrated and unloved themselves when interacting with them.

We suggest that you assess foster children with an eye toward these areas of injustice and violations of love and trust. We do not believe that it is important to obtain all of the details of previous maltreatment because this can retraumatize children. You do, however, want to understand how the child in your office uses rage, shame, control, and chaos in response to violations. As you begin to understand these attempts of the child to cope, you can surmise the type of violation the child feels and you can respond with appropriate therapy.

The impact of trauma occurs in three primary dimensions—attachment, self-regulation, and self-perspective—and symptoms can remain dormant for long periods of time only to pop up without warning during stressful periods or events (Levine, 1997). Keeping this in mind, the symptom picture we see displayed in trauma is easily converted into contextual thinking. The symptoms of flashbacks, anxiety, and panic attacks can be understood as chaos reactions. Insomnia, lack of openness, and demanding behavior can be understood best as control reactions. The symptoms of depression, psychosomatic complaints, and lack of openness are most likely a result of shame reactions. Violent, unprovoked rage attacks, repetitive destructive behaviors, and overt acting out are often rage reactions. Looking at the trauma symptomology from a contextual perspective helps us understand the nature of the violation.

The goal of the contextual therapy approach is to redress the issues of violation of love and trust with the child as constructively as possible. We believe that no relationship is as powerful as that of biological parent and child because of the innate sense of justice the child carries and the initial experiences the child has with the parent (Hargrave & Pfitser, 2003). However, we also believe that children can learn that:

- past irresponsible abuse does not have to dictate his or her present behavior,

- professionals, foster parents, and friends can provide the love, trust, and nurture necessary for healing and recovery of normal functioning, and

- children have resources that can be used in constructive ways to rebuild their self-concepts and enable them to function in relationships in a healthy manner.

Contextual therapy is normally thought of as a therapy for adults working on family of origin issues. However, it also is an excellent fit with children who have been maltreated. Working with foster children to address the injustices that existed in their abusive relationships makes sense for all involved relationships. And we also believe that these emotional issues may surface for many years and in many different ways. Therefore, even if maltreated children receive treatment right away, there will be issues to work through during their adolescent and adult years.

Case Study

Elizabeth entered the foster care system the day after her fourth birthday. Evidence of rape and neglect led to quick removal from her family, but she was returned home within a year. Then, at age 6, Elizabeth was placed in a foster home again. Once there, she demonstrated limited skills in most social contexts. She had no friends, remained quiet during most of the school day (except when hitting children or yelling at the teacher), and appeared angry most of the time. As problems escalated, the foster parents intervened by removing teddy bears and video games. They locked up her Barbie dolls and bicycle, but Elizabeth pretended not to care. Then, a day later, she would cry and wail about the loss. She said her foster family hated her and tried to hurt her. The situation grew worse.

In their report, before Elizabeth returned to her family for the final time, the foster family reported in their log, "Elizabeth is a mixture of feelings. She's loving one day and cruel the next. She can comfort our dog, then kick it when it bothers her. She also prefers the company of strangers to those she knows."

Despite problems in the foster family, or possibly because of them, Elizabeth's biological family had won the right for a third try. They kept her for five more years, but then a teacher noted some disturbing behavior: Elizabeth was afraid to use the bathroom, stating, "Bad things happen in there." She also looked excessively tired in the morning, had frequent headaches, became even more isolated, smelled like urine, and had bruises on her arms. When the teacher spent more time with the girl, she saw more troubling signs. Elizabeth performed sexualized dances, stating that her daddy liked "this kind of dancing." She retold stories of watching R-rated movies and had been caught peeping into the boys' bathroom. The police intervened again, and vaginal scarring was found. At age eleven, Elizabeth was removed from her home for the final time and placed with the Peterson family, a foster family with two years of experience.

During their first week together, the Petersons were shocked by the ambivalence of the child. Elizabeth snuggled against them, but erupted into fits of rage when asked to perform menial tasks. Washing dishes resulted in broken china. Requests to take out the trash led to garbage under beds or couches. When confronted about these problems, Elizabeth would explode into a tantrum. She would bite, kick, and hit the Petersons, and scream that she hated them and wanted to return to her family.

Sessions 1–3 (Alone with Elizabeth)

During their intake interview, the therapist spent some time with Elizabeth alone. Elizabeth slumped in her chair and kept her head down. Creases lined her forehead. Given her history, the therapist's goal was to form a relationship in which Elizabeth didn't feel threatened. Gaining information would be helpful, but only within the confines of getting to know each other.

Therapist: Bet you've been to counseling a few times before. Nasty counselors probably made you talk for hours at a time.

Elizabeth: *(squirms in her chair)*

Therapist: Tell you what: Let's play a game. I have a collection of animals. Here's a monkey, a donkey, a gorilla, and most of what else you'd find in a zoo. If I had a magic wand and could turn people into the animals they most act like, who would your foster mom and dad turn into?

Elizabeth: *(grabs a few of the animals and casts a "you've-got-to-be-kidding" look at the therapist)*

Therapist: Pick whatever you want. If it helps, I think my mom would be a cheetah, always running around, and my dad would be the ape. He's big and grumpy but fun to be around.

Elizabeth: The donkey, I guess. My mom is the donkey. My dad— he's like this horse and the giraffe.

Therapist: Hmmm. A two-animal parent?

Elizabeth: Yeah. He's kinda like my mom, but he's always sticking his nose where it doesn't belong.

As Elizabeth becomes more comfortable, she delves into the things she doesn't like about her foster home. "There are too many rules. Pick up this. Put that away. They're always getting on me about something."

Therapist: So, you think they aren't being fair?

Elizabeth: Yeah. I mean, they don't know what it's like to be a kid. I'll have time to work when I'm old like them.

Therapist: When I was growing up, I said something like that to my mom. She agreed. It wasn't fair that I had to put away my clothes. I got all excited until she told me we could switch jobs. She made me fold the laundry, clean the kitchen, vacuum the floors, and clean the refrigerator.

Elizabeth: That sucks.

Therapist: Yeah, but she was right. I just never thought about it. She did that stuff every day.

Elizabeth: Well, I'm still not putting my clothes away.

Therapist: I understand. When you come from a tough place you often don't feel like doing anything more, even if it is reasonable.

Elizabeth: You got that right.

Since the therapist's goal is to establish a trustworthy connection with Elizabeth, he employs multidirected partiality (Boszormenyi-Nagy & Krasner, 1986). This means that the therapist doesn't try to be neutral. Instead, he tries to connect with Elizabeth by appreciating her current circumstances as she experiences them in terms of her relationship ledger. When the therapist tells the story of his own mother and how she taught him about fairness, it is clearly a mistake that feels to Elizabeth that the therapist does not understand her feelings. When the therapist quickly recovers and makes her last statement about understanding, Elizabeth feels the partiality and connects. This connection is essential in building trust that can expand into other relationships. Through the first three sessions, Elizabeth improved slightly. This modest improvement probably occurred because the therapist heard her story and struggle without correcting anything.

Session 4 (With Foster Parents and Elizabeth)

The foster parents began the fourth session with a summary of their week. Elizabeth had one bad day at school and another one at home. Despite the improvement, the foster parents expressed concern. Both the conflicts were intense and more severe than usual. At home, Elizabeth shattered a glass against a wall. Then she locked herself in her bedroom and destroyed clothing and furniture. When the foster parents coaxed her into the living room, she cursed at them and said that she hated them. The conflict ended with Elizabeth marching out the front door. The parents followed, giving her space. Elizabeth stopped a block later, remained quiet, and walked back to the house. None of them addressed the situation until today.

The reports and observed behavior led the therapist to believe that Elizabeth was cycling between spells of rage and shame. Elizabeth often felt desperate and shameful and simply wanted people to respond to her and love her. At these times she would cuddle and come close. However, when Elizabeth felt anger about her past and experienced injustice at being asked to "do her part," it did not matter if the task was large or small. It violated her sense of entitlement and she would respond in an outburst of rage. Additionally, the therapist believed that Elizabeth used this cycle of rage and shame to control her relationship to the foster parents.

Therapist: I want to congratulate you for five days without conflicts. A record. At the end of the session, we'll celebrate by getting a soda. Before we get to that point, it seems we have to address the conflict from home.

Elizabeth: *(keeps her head low but scowls)*

Therapist: Rather than retell what happened, we're going to focus on something different. First, I need everyone to stand in the middle. Not too close, we don't need a group hug or anything. Second, I'm giving each of you a piece of paper. Drop it a few feet behind you. Okay, those papers represent your limit, the level of frustration you can take before you feel like bolting out the door. Every time someone says or does something that bothers you, move a little closer to the paper. When you can't take any more, step on the paper. Who wants to start?

Foster mom: She scared me so much this week. *(tears form)* I don't know how much more I can handle.

Elizabeth: *(jumps all the way back to her paper)*

Therapist: Someone's reached her limit.

Elizabeth: This game sucks. I don't need to stay here. You all hate me!

Therapist: *(kneels to her level)* Scary, isn't it, when people say you hurt them. You're just trying to be the best you can be, and your parents get all stressed out. Was it like this at your birth parents' house?

Elizabeth: No! *(crying and yelling)* They never made me play stupid games. They loved me. Getting a beating was better than coming here.

Therapist: We're almost done. One more step and we're there. *(the therapist stands and returns to the circle)* When someone reaches her limit, we have to draw her back to the circle. Can either of you think of something that might help her feel like returning?

Foster mom: Sweetie, we just want all these problems to go away.

Foster dad: It hurt us when you left.

Elizabeth: *(backs behind the paper, pulling further away)*

Therapist: This whole game ends when we're all part of the circle. Can anyone here help you feel safe enough to return?

Elizabeth:	*(glances to her foster mother then turns away)* No. I want to leave.
Therapist:	You looked to your mother. What can she do to help you end the game?
Elizabeth:	*(lower lip trembles)*
Foster mom:	*(kneels and takes her daughter's hand)* I want one thing from you. Just don't leave home. If you stay, we can work through anything. Okay?
Elizabeth:	I'm sorry. I really am sorry.

The give-and-take component of their relationship is subtle, but the foster mother wanted her daughter's consistent presence. Without this, she became overwhelmed. Elizabeth wanted affection and stability. But she could only receive this by testing the foster parents' rules and reactions. Eventually, the give-and-take would require more, including responsibility, but not yet. Here the therapist was skillful in maintaining partiality to Elizabeth, but also in finding a way for the foster parents to pay attention to love and thus making the rage unnecessary.

Session 8 (With Elizabeth)

Elizabeth went nine days without a violent outburst or problems at school. She still struggled to maintain friendships and appeared sullen most of the time. She locked herself in her room, playing video games, and reading pieces of books. Her foster mother believed the problems stemmed from Elizabeth's refusal to play by the rules. When she lost, she threw raging tantrums trying to make people do something different. When these actions did not work, she felt ashamed and withdrew in the hope that that someone would make her feel better. Viewed through the lens of contextual therapy, Elizabeth's manipulative behaviors stemmed from her history of inadequate and undependable care. The therapist thought that using games in therapy might let Elizabeth momentarily experience a stable world, which she had never experienced.

Therapist:	You said you liked video games, so I brought an old game from my house. It's called Space Duel. Not much graphics, but it takes some planning and skill. Want to try?
Elizabeth:	Sure. Whatever.
	During the game Elizabeth became frustrated. Her spaceship kept running into the sun and she lost points.
Elizabeth:	This game sucks. I'm not playing anymore. *(She slaps the joystick hard; then backs away from the game, forfeiting)*
Therapist:	*(backs away as well—the two ships float alternatively toward the sun, blowing up and then reappearing)* What would you say if I told you I cheated?
Elizabeth:	*(her eyes grow wild)*
Therapist:	I'm not saying I did, but how would you feel if I knew a secret you didn't?
Elizabeth:	That's so unfair.
Therapist:	Wanna know how I won?
Elizabeth:	Yeah!
Therapist:	I suppose this is kind of like cheating. I've been playing this game for twenty years. I've learned how the gravity forces players toward the sun and where ships appear when they reach one side of the screen. In a sense, I have an unfair advantage because I know more.
Elizabeth:	I thought you were going to say something interesting.
Therapist:	It must have felt like cheating to you, because you stopped playing. The problem is, you can't compete with me on this until you've played more. I hoped to teach you how to get better. Can you think of a way to make this feel fair? Want me to run into the sun a few times to give you some points?

Elizabeth: Okay.

Therapist: I don't mind doing it, but I want something from you as well. When you get frustrated, before you walk away from the game, I want you to say, "Arrrrg." Like a pirate. When you do this, I'll try to figure out how to make the game more enjoyable, but it upsets me when we don't get to finish. I want you to have fun, but I want to have fun, too.

Elizabeth responded well to the therapist's request. As she learned that the therapist cared for her and took trustworthy steps to help her, she began to lose the need for control and the rage/shame cycle could be addressed more directly. This technique of balancing give-and-take is an effective response to destructive behavior (Hargrave & Anderson, 1992). However, its effectiveness requires an interpersonal context in which the children have first adequately perceived love and trust from their therapists or foster parents.

Discussion

The healing process for Elizabeth developed because she learned to confront the destructive tendencies in her life. When she was in her birth family, problems with abandonment (violation of love) and tensions in the household led to her removal from her parents, and Elizabeth developed the cycle of rage/shame. Focusing on compliance didn't work for her either, because no matter what she did, the disruptions came (violation of trust). Her only mechanism for survival entailed protecting herself from loss, and pushing people away at the first sign of stress (developing a style of control). When she made a mistake, she reacted by blaming others, threatening them, or leaving.

Therapy helped by providing rules that made the family structure more reliable. It became permissible for Elizabeth to speak her mind, and even rebel at times, as long as she provided her foster parents the respect and commitment that they needed. Stabilizing the family's communication patterns also permitted Elizabeth to take emotional risks. With the foster parents' continued commitment and affection, she learned to trust them—even before she trusted herself. For such children, learning to apologize with feeling is tantamount to a commitment of love. It is risky because they believe the bond between themselves and the other party is tenuous.

Paradoxically, the rules also provided Elizabeth with a sense of autonomy. By obeying the structures at home and school, her effort became an accurate measure of her success. Most foster children struggle with this idea. They see the world as an enemy. It is something that is working against them. They see their own efforts as insignificant, and this inspires them to grasp all they can. By staying within the rules, they achieve a higher level of power. They can have a discernible effect on their grades, families, and friends. The result is profound.

At the end of therapy, Elizabeth went a month without violent behavior or significant problems at school. She continued to make occasional rude statements to foster siblings, but these were similar to the problems that natural siblings encounter. She grasped that the world isn't always fair, but most of the time it is.

Occasionally, Elizabeth continued to make statements about her family of origin, creating a fantasy world in which they did their best to protect her and provided a loving and stable home. Some of the pleasant stories she told of her youth had actually occurred within the foster setting, not her birth family. This confusion was a sign that her present family system approached the ideal she had created in her mind. But it also indicated that there was still much work to be done. Even though Elizabeth was now in a stable environment with enough love, nurturing and dependability to address her destructive behaviors, issues connected to the specifics of her abuse would have to wait until she was old enough to conceptualize other choices. Attempts to make sense of the "why" and "irresponsibility" of her birth parents will likely surface in Elizabeth's early adulthood. But the correct assessment of emotion, multidirected partiality from the therapist, and the rebalancing of give-and-take have provided Elizabeth a foundation from which to approach the future in a more loving and trustworthy fashion.

References

Boszormenyi-Nagy, I., & Krasner, B. (1980). Trust based therapy: A contextual approach. *American Journal of Psychiatry, 137,* 767–775.

Boszormenyi-Nagy, I., & Krasner, B. (1986). *Between give and take: A clinical guide to contextual therapy.* New York: Brunner/Mazel.

Boszormenyi-Nagy, I., & Spark, G. (1984). *Invisible loyalties.* New York: Brunner/Mazel.

Boszormenyi-Nagy, I., & Ulrich, D. N. (1981). Contextual family therapy. In A. S. Gurman & D. P. Kniskern (Eds.), *Handbook of family therapy* (pp. 159–186). New York: Brunner/Mazel.

Buber, M. (1958). *I and thou.* New York: Charles Scribner and Sons.

Hargrave, T. D. (1994a). *Families and forgiveness: Healing wounds in the intergenerational family.* New York: Brunner/Mazel.

Hargrave, T. D. (1994b). Families and forgiveness: A theoretical and therapeutic framework. *The Family Journal, 2,* 339–348.

Hargrave, T. D. (2001). *Forgiving the devil: Coming to terms with damaged relationships.* Phoenix, AZ: Zeig, Tucker & Theisen.

Hargrave, T. D., & Anderson, W. T. (1992). *Finishing well: Aging and reparation in the intergenerational family.* New York: Brunner/Mazel.

Hargrave, T. D., & Pfitser, F. (2003). *The new contextual therapy: Guiding the power of give and take.* New York: Brunner/Routledge.

Hargrave, T. D., & Williams, G. (2003). A contextual therapy model for understanding emotions. *Marriage and Family: A Christian Journal, 6,* 63–71.

Levine, P. A. (1997). *Walking the tiger: Healing trauma.* Berkeley, CA: North Atlantic Books.

Part 3

Important
"Other" Issues

15

"I Want This Child Out of Here Now!" How to Deal with Sexualized Acting Out in the Foster Environment: A "SMART" Approach to Assessment and Treatment

Alice Nadelman and Debra D. Castaldo

A common problem in foster care, often destroying placements, is sexual perpetration from the foster child to other members of the foster household or school. This chapter offers practical advice for the recognition of and intervention with such tendencies. A whole-family approach is outlined.

The care and treatment of sexualized children in foster care can be extremely challenging for even the most highly experienced foster families and professionals. Sexual acting out often results in multiple placements and disruptions (Thompson, Authier, & Ruma, 1994). A major challenge for the child welfare system is the recruitment, training, maintenance, and support of foster and adoptive families who can successfully parent these children.

Two critical keys to the prevention of placement disruption are:

- thorough assessment and preparation of foster families, and

- comprehensive, relational, and team-centered therapeutic approach to care and treatment.

331

Both of these involve incorporating foster parents as integral partners of the professional team. You also need to include extended family members and other important adults and systems in the child's life.

In this chapter, we will discuss a comprehensive, two-pronged approach to effective treatment with sexually reactive children in foster care. These prongs are: the preparation and assessment of foster families, and a treatment model we call the SMART approach. We developed this model over 25 years of practice with foster and adoptive families caring for sexually reactive children. The SMART approach is summarized in Figure 1.

FIGURE I

Working SMART

Foundations of Treatment

S = Solution focused/strength based perspective
M = Multimodal treatment approaches
A = Acceptance and openness
R = Relational approach
T = Team-centered focus

Key Treatment Components

S = Supervision ("eyes on")
M = Mutually defined goals
A = Attitudes and beliefs incorporated
R = Reasonable expectations
T = Trust building

Desired Treatment Outcomes

S = Self-confidence
M = Management of behavior
A = Alternative behaviors
R = Responsibility for self
T = Trust and attachment

The overarching goals of this approach are to provide:

- nurturing, healing, and growth of the child within a family system,
- care of the child in the least restrictive placement setting possible, and
- permanency and prevention of placement disruption.

Foundations of the SMART Approach

The SMART approach includes core beliefs and guidelines that we have found to be integral to successful placement and treatment.

Solution-Focused/Strength Perspective

We firmly believe in the capacity of a child and a family to heal, to use internal strengths and capacities, and to develop solutions to their own problems. Your belief in the healing capacity of the foster family is a critical starting point for treatment. A solution-oriented perspective conveys to children and families that healing is not only possible, but also likely, and that even the most entrenched symptoms and behaviors can be managed and resolved (see deShazer, 1985, 1991). Such an approach recognizes the importance of developing solutions rather than staying saturated in symptoms—a situation that can cause children and families to feel hopeless and helpless (Berg & Dejong, 1996). As you guide your families to focus on the exceptions to problems, rather than the problems themselves, the family members will often develop their own solutions. These solutions will incorporate the families' beliefs, skills, and capabilities in a mutual problem-solving process.

A core component of solution-focused treatment is the use of solution-oriented interventions and tasks (deShazer, 1985, 1991). We have had great success utilizing these tasks with families with sexually reactive children. For example, a common first session task might be: "Pay attention to what is going well that you want to continue." If you are addressing the sexual impulses of the child, a solution-based task might be: Pay attention to what you do when you overcome the urge to masturbate in front of others or play sex games with other kids. A "Do One Thing Different" (O'Hanlon, 1999) task might be: "When you have the urge to act out, do something different, anything different, since there are many routes to solving a problem."

Multimodal Treatment

The treatment needs to be flexible, so the therapist should use a combination of family, couple, individual, and child play therapy as needed. The therapy must address a multiplicity of needs—those of the child, family members, and the family system as a whole. Sometimes foster parents may need bolstering as individuals or as a couple to deal with the stresses of caring for such a challenging child. We encourage a comprehensive family approach that includes foster siblings and extended family. That way you can develop as much family support as possible. Play therapy may provide an opportunity for children to tell their stories, as well as enable them to work through trauma and deal with feelings of shame, guilt, confusion, and grief (see also Chapter 4, "The Perspective of the Consumer: Foster Children Tell Us What They Need," and Chapter 7, "Parent–Child Therapy for Traumatized Young Children in Foster Care").

Acceptance and Openness

A critical challenge for your treatment team is to model acceptance and openness with each other and the child, no matter how trying or unacceptable the child's behavior. That does not mean condoning such behavior, but it does mean letting child and family know that no behavior is too shameful to be dealt with. It may be helpful for all of you, including the foster parents, to use team meetings and case conferencing to openly discuss and brainstorm about the difficult aspects of healing the acting-out child. All team members need to be aware of their own personal beliefs and comfort level with issues of sexuality, child molestation, and sexual acting out.

An environment of acceptance and openness can reassure the child, saying in effect, "we accept you, will help you, and can handle even the most secretive and shameful events or feelings that you need to share with us."

Relational Perspective

The presence of a sexually acting-out child will undoubtedly impact the extended foster family system, including relatives, friends, neighbors, and anyone who lives with, visits, or relates to the child. It is important to view the child as part of a complex, interconnected system of relationships, rather than through the lens of individual pathology (Boscolo, Cecchin, Hoffman, & Penn, 1987). Birth family, foster family, child protective services workers, clinicians, teachers, and medical professionals who interact with the child may be included in the comprehensive team, case conferencing, and even therapy sessions, as needed (see Chapter 2, "An Ecosystemic Approach to Foster Care").

Team-Centered Approach

The creation of the professional team is important when dealing with sexually reactive children. All members of the team can benefit from each other's knowledge and support. This includes foster parents, whom we value as knowledgeable, integral, professional team members who are doing the difficult job of caring for the child on a day-to-day basis. A strong team approach has the benefits of coordination of services, consistency, and sharing knowledge of clinical issues, and often results in reduced acting-out behavior. Ongoing support groups for foster parents and case conferencing that includes all of your team members can provide a great sense of support and value for foster parents. When deemed appropriate by your professional team, inclusion of those birth family members who can be supportive of the child can also be extremely useful in your relational approach.

Preparation and Assessment of Successful Foster Homes

A critical component of successful treatment of sexually acting out is the availability of well-trained foster/adoptive parents who can weather the challenges these children present. Identifying, assessing, training, and supporting these families requires a thorough study process, as well as ongoing support and training once the children are placed (Castaldo, 1996). You should view the home study assessment as a mutual process between the prospective foster parents and social workers— one in which information is gathered that can help both parents and professionals determine if fostering sexually reactive children is appropriate for that family.

It is also an opportunity for professionals to educate prospective families regarding the challenges of this work. As part of a thorough home study process, it is recommended that the assessment include focusing specifically on information in the following categories: education regarding sexually acting-out children, attitudes about sex and sexuality, family structure, parenting skills, beliefs, and values, and capacity to use support systems. Some practice guidelines might be provided for each category. These guidelines are helpful for 1) establishing minimal requirements for the approval of foster parents, 2) determining foster families' potential for successful care of sexually acting-out children, and 3) ruling out foster families with limitations that represent too great a risk for placement disruption.

Education Regarding Sexually Acting-Out Children

It is critically important that clinicians, social workers, and foster families appreciate the impact and effects of sexual abuse on children. Nowhere is the extent of this trauma more evident than in the child welfare system. Many children who are in out-of-home placement for abuse and neglect have also been sexually molested

(Freidrich, 1995). Therefore, it is essential that all of us who work with foster children must learn about what reactions and behaviors might be expected.

The impact of sexual abuse on children has been well documented throughout the literature (Avery, Massat, & Lundy, 2000; Fleming & Belanger, 2000; Freidrich, 1995; James, 1989; Jones, 2004; Mayer, 1985; Ruggiero, McLeer, & Dixon, 2000; Sgroi, 1982; Thompson et al., 1994). Sexual abuse is a betrayal that shatters a child's world of trust and safety and represents a loss of childhood innocence (Fleming & Belanger, 2000; Freyd, 1996). This abuse leaves pervasive scars on children that affect their physical, psychological, and emotional well-being, and often has impact on their behavioral functioning. In our experience, the effects of abuse are most often evident in the areas of physical symptoms, psychological injury (including posttraumatic stress disorder), impaired capacity for attachment, and acting out (see Avery et al., 2000; Deblinger, Steer, & Lippman, 1999; Jones, 2004; Ruggiero et al., 2000). Betrayal at such a core level often results in impaired attachment (James, 1989). This may be exacerbated by multiple moves through the foster care system that continually reinforce the child's feelings of mistrust, unworthiness, and fear of rejection (McFadden, 1992). The original trauma of the abuse experience and subsequent acting-out behaviors can result in a vicious cycle in which the child is repeatedly rejected and abandoned.

Although most sexually abused children do not act out sexually or become sexual abusers themselves, the acting out of sexually reactive children in foster care can test the tolerance of even the most competent caretakers, and jeopardize their ability to continue to provide care. These behaviors are a maladaptive way for children to release feelings of rage, guilt, and sadness regarding the abuse and betrayal they have experienced (Fleming & Belanger, 2000).

Children who have been sexualized and eroticized at young ages may show obsessive/compulsive self-stimulating behaviors.

Attempts to initiate sexual activity with other children and adults may be playful, seductive, aggressive, predatory, and out of control (Thompson et al., 1994). These actions may occur at home with siblings and extended family members, as well as in school and the outside community. They may cause embarrassment, criticism, and rejection by others. It is also not uncommon for foster and adoptive parents to be the focus of abuse investigations due to the sexualized behaviors of their children.

To meet the challenges of caring for sexualized children, we need to help our foster families be open to working with the full range of behavioral and emotional symptoms noted above. Families who welcome support and view themselves as embarking on a therapeutic journey with the child and other professional team members will undoubtedly fare better than those who feel they can "go it alone" and who expect the child's symptoms to simply disappear upon entry into the home.

Attitudes About Sex and Sexuality

It is important to assess the foster family's comfort level in dealing with and discussing sexual issues with adults, as well as with children. It will be difficult for families to parent sexualized children if they feel embarrassment or shame when talking about sexual matters (Duehn, 1990). As child welfare professionals, it is our job to help parents determine their own level of comfort and determine what behaviors they can accept and work with in their home. Placement disruptions occur more frequently when professionals decide what a family can and cannot handle, rather than employing a process of mutual discussion and assessment to assist the family in reaching an understanding of their own capacities. Experience has clearly shown that imposing the placement of a child upon a foster family—when that child's behaviors severely conflict with the family's belief system—is a recipe for disruption.

It is often useful to obtain a general sexual developmental history from each adult separately (Castaldo, 1996). These may be either verbal or in writing. This assists in assessing how beliefs, attitudes, and intergenerational family of origin patterns of communication about sexuality may impact the care of the foster child. Some sample questions that can act as a discussion guide include:

- What were the beliefs and attitudes in your family about sex and sexuality?
- How were sexual behaviors dealt with in your family? Would you handle sexual issues any differently than your parents did? If so how?
- On a scale of 1 to 10, how comfortable would you say you are discussing sexual issues with a child? Explain.
- What would you tell a child about masturbation? Would there be rules in your home about masturbation?
- How would you handle inappropriate sexual behaviors of a child in your home?
- Could you deal with these behaviors as part of raising this type of child?
- Are there any behaviors that you feel you could not cope with?
- How would you handle a child who is sexually provocative with you or other family members?
- How would you handle preparing other family members and friends about dealing with a sexualized child? What would you do if your family and friends do not accept the child?

Family Structure, Boundaries, and Parenting Skills

Since many abused children have experienced chaotic family environments in which boundaries, rules, and roles were unclear and inconsistent (Douglas, 2000), it is important that the child have firm, reassuring, and consistent rules and routines. These provide a framework for managing the child's sexualized behaviors. The foster family must be willing and able to provide a consistent environment.

These foster children are likely to test boundaries. Therefore, in two-parent foster families, it is important that a strong parental subsystem alliance exists (Boscolo et al., 1987). Couple relationships that reflect equal distribution of power and collaborative decisionmaking are more successful in dealing with these children (Goldner, 1992). Couple relationships that are not cohesive enough will allow the child to "triangle" into the parenting relationship and divide the couple. Couple relationships are problematic in which the male is more controlling and less caring. The perceived power differential may render the mother powerless and ineffective in the eyes of the child, and can replicate dysfunctional patterns from the family of origin (Douglas, 2000).

Research has shown that a foster family's ability to be cohesive, adaptable, and supportive increases likelihood of positive treatment outcomes (Cohen & Mannarino, 2000). It is important to assess foster parents' ability to use redirection, close supervision, and positive reinforcement to manage sexualized behaviors. Without the use of these techniques, parents may find themselves entrenched in constant punishments and negative interactions with the child. In effect, these children can provoke abusive cycles that replicate those they have previously experienced. Affection, cuddling, and other forms of physical nurturing encourage attachment and increase the child's motivation to behave appropriately. They also help shape and manage the child's sexualized behavior.

Exploration of parenting styles and skills is a critical part of your assessment process. Questions about intergenerational patterns through use of genogram work and circular questioning can provide information on patterns of parenting. Some sample assessment questions regarding family structure, boundaries, and parenting include:

- What are your strengths as parents and what would you say you do well?

- What would you say you would most like to improve as a parent?

- Who was responsible for child rearing in your childhood? Did your father and mother participate equally?

- What are the basic rules in your family and how are they determined?

- What are the usual routines of the family and how are children involved?

- Who in your extended family would best be able to manage a sexually reactive child? How do you think they would handle acting-out behaviors?

- Who would most help you in parenting a sexually acting-out child?

Beliefs and Values

It is critical that you assess family beliefs and values, including cultural, religious, and spiritual guidelines. These often shape child-rearing practices as well as attitudes about sex and sexuality (Castaldo, 1996). For example, if religious values are rigid regarding abstinence and the unacceptability of masturbation, it will be difficult to parent a child who finds it hard to control self-stimulating behavior. Also, if attitudes about sexuality prevent parents from being open and accepting, but instead include shame, guilt, and secrecy, it will be difficult for the family to be therapeutic and to assist the child in healing (Cohen & Mannarino, 2000; Imber-Black, 1993).

Some guideline questions regarding beliefs and values include:

- What values and beliefs have you been taught about sex and sexuality in formal religious training or from your family?

- What values about sex and sexuality do you believe are important to teach the children in your home?

- On a scale of 1 to 10, how open do you feel you are in your home about issues of sexuality?

- How do you think that community groups in which you are involved would react to a sexually acting-out child?

Openness to Support Systems

A family's openness and ability to incorporate and use support systems are also important in providing successful care. As you know, this capacity may be especially critical for single foster parents. Your practice experience no doubt agrees with the research literature—families who are unwilling to use support from others are often the most overwhelmed and vulnerable, and are most likely to give up on caring for an acting out child (James, 1989; Sgroi, 1982). A rigid attitude of "We can do this alone and we do not need therapy or any other outside assistance" does not bode well for successful placement of the sexualized child. Conversely, families who view themselves as part of the therapeutic team and welcome assistance from other professionals are often able to weather crises and continue providing therapeutic care for the child. Networking with other foster families can also be a tremendous source of support for foster parents.

Some questions to assess parents' willingness to use support include:

- Who among your family, friends, and relatives would be most able to help you with problems you may have with the child?
- How do you feel about being a part of the child's therapy?
- Are you willing to commit to consistent therapy for the child?
- What other resources and connections do you have in the community that would be helpful to you in parenting sexually abused children?
- Who would help you if you reached a crisis point and needed a break from the child?

Figure 2 condenses the critical components in the assessment of prospective foster families (Castaldo, 1996). The desirable characteristics represent qualities that contribute to successful placement. The warning indicators represent issues that need further exploration and may prevent families from providing therapeutic care.

FIGURE 2

Assessment of Foster Families' Capacity to Provide Therapeutic Environments for Sexually Acting-Out Children

Desirable Characteristics	Warning Indicators
• Family is accepting and open to dealing with sexualized behavior through use of supervision, structure, and attachment behaviors.	• Family expects sexualized behaviors to disappear and child to quickly conform to family's own values.
• Family understands normal childhood sexual behaviors and can openly deal with them as any other behavior.	• Family is unable to comfortably deal openly with sexualized behaviors.
• Communication about sexuality and other emotionally charged issues is open, honest, and age-appropriate.	• Sexuality is a taboo subject. Difficult topics are not communicated openly. Family struggles with embarrassment.
• Family has clear, firm boundaries and structure. Parents are clearly in charge of protection and supervision of children.	• Family is too loosely organized and chaotic, with inappropriate lack of boundaries.
• Family uses a repertoire of behavior management techniques and is willing to try alternative methods.	• Behavior management techniques are limited and primarily negative.
• Family is receptive to professional help and values and supports use of therapy.	• Family denies the need for therapy and resists or refuses participation.
• Family has a supportive network and openly uses resources in the community.	• Family is isolated and withdrawn.
• Parents display a strong parenting coalition.	• Parenting is unbalanced, with one spouse assuming the majority of responsibilities.

The desirable characteristics listed in Figure 2 should be on your wish list for foster/adoptive families caring for your sexually acting-out children. Families are human, and no family or person should be expected to possess all of these traits and abilities. However, we have found that families who possess the above desirable traits are best able to weather the challenges these children present. Families will remain committed to care of the foster children to the extent that they are willing to accept a child as he or she is, flexibly adapt to that child's needs, and appreciate small successes.

Case Illustration

Adam was 6 years old when his new foster parents, Mr. and Mrs. S, with whom he had lived for 2 months, brought him in for family therapy. Adam had been removed from his elderly foster mother, Mrs. N, who had raised him since birth. Mrs. N, whom Adam called "Momma," also fostered three teenage boys. Mrs. N infantilized Adam. She had him sleep in her room, fed and dressed him, and gave him several bottles daily. Adam had not attended any pre-school programs and he did not play with other children his age. He spent much of his time watching television with his Momma or going with her while she did errands, visited friends, and attended church.

Mrs. N resisted changing her parenting of Adam and was unwilling to accept supportive services, including preschool. A decision was made by the agency to move Adam to a therapeutic foster home to help him separate from Mrs. N and to develop more age-appropriate self-care, social, and academic skills before placing him with an adoptive family. Mrs. N was very upset about Adam leaving her home. She refused to participate in the good-bye process or to continue contact with Adam after he left.

Initial Treatment

The therapist first met with Mr. and Mrs. S without Adam present to develop a foundation for working together. The SMART approach to therapy was shared with them, with its emphasis on solution-focused, strength-based interventions. They responded positively to the idea of working with the team to help Adam build on his strengths and expand his repertoire of coping and mastery skills. They were open to seeing themselves as the primary healers for their foster son and using their skills and experience as parents. The role of the therapist would be to help them expand their parenting resources and assess and facilitate Adam's healthy development.

In answering: "What is Adam good at and what does he do well?" Mr. and Mrs. S described him as bright, inquisitive, cooperative, timid, curious, and fearful of new people and activities. They observed that he was easily frustrated and prone to crying when things did not go his way. Adam often said he was sad and missed Momma. He asked for his bottle at these times and rubbed his genitals while drinking it. Adam did not seem eager to play with children except the Ss' grandson, Danny, who was three years old and spent much time with the family. Adam's favorite activity was dancing and he "danced up a storm" whenever he heard music. Mrs. S described Adam's dancing bumps, grinds, and grunts, and said he danced like a "macho man."

Mr. and Mrs. S's goals for Adam were to help him adjust to living with their family and to develop age-appropriate self-care and social skills. Initially, they were inclined to avoid mentioning Mrs. N since it seemed to upset Adam. However, as therapy progressed, they accepted his need to mourn this loss.

Mr. and Mrs. S identified their primary strength as having a strong marriage of over twenty years, during which they successfully dealt with many challenges, especially raising five children together. They felt they knew how to provide structure, consistency, supervision, and encouragement for kids. Their primary motivation in becoming foster parents was to give back, in appreciation of their many blessings.

A crucial family belief was revealed in response to a question about what kind of child might be most challenging to them. Mr. S immediately responded, "No bullies and no sex fiends!" He explained that he had little tolerance for abusers, whether verbal, physical, or sexual, and believed he would do better with children who had been victimized rather than those who had hurt others. This opened a discussion about how victims can become victimizers, and how children who feel threatened sometimes attack first in order to feel safe. Normal, age-appropriate sexual curiosity and exploration, as well as inappropriate sexual activities were also discussed. An educational approach was used to inform this prospective foster family how sexualized children might introduce sexuality into nonsexual situations.

Mr. and Mrs. S were surprised to learn that a very high percentage of foster children have been exposed to sexual stimuli, including sex acts on television and videos, real life sex, and being seduced and/or forced into sexual activity with older children or adults. They were told that this information often is not known when a child enters foster care and only emerges once the child is living in a foster home. Mr. and Mrs. S continued to feel it would be difficult for them to parent a sexualized child, but they seemed less overwhelmed by the prospect. Discussion of their experiences dealing with other inappropriate childhood behaviors such as cursing, pilfering, and fibbing enabled them to realize that they had developed the resources to cope with a multitude of parenting challenges.

Therapeutic work with Adam began with a welcoming statement from Mr. and Mrs. S, telling him how glad they were to have him as their foster son, while recognizing that it had been very hard for him to leave Momma and her family. Mrs. S held Adam on her lap when he began to cry about Momma. She told him it was okay to feel sad or have any other feelings and that he could let them know when he was thinking about Momma. Adam immediately said, "I miss her every minute!" This was a powerful indication of how much pain this little boy was internalizing. Mr. S praised Adam and encouraged him to share more feelings and ideas. He told Adam that he was proud of him for being willing to become part of their family even though he still wanted to be with Momma. This grief work done with the new foster family was important for Adam's healing and beginning attachment to them.

During the next weeks, the foster parents did a number of family rituals as "claiming" activities (Imber-Black, Roberts, & Whiting, 1988), such as putting Adam's picture on the mantle, posting his artwork on the refrigerator, and introducing him to extended family and friends. Adam and Danny declared themselves "blood brothers" and, with help from Mrs. S, created matching hats and capes. At the same time, Mrs. S worked with Adam to create a Life Book, which told the story of his life and contained his pictures of Momma and his previous foster family. Adam decided to write to Momma with the help of his foster mother. Even though he received no response to his letter, Adam seemed to gain some closure. Adam also included Momma in his prayers and said he felt good that God and the stars in the sky were watching over both of them.

During their therapy sessions, the family played games that fostered communication, expression, and acceptance of feelings. The focus was on Adam's strengths. These included his "million dollar smile," what Adam had done well that week, and what had happened that was considered "good stuff" (Berg & Dejong, 1996). With encouragement from his foster parents, Adam became less timid and more willing to interact with new people and try new activities. As he developed six-year-old self-care skills, such as feeding and dressing himself and brushing his own teeth, Adam began to take pride in learning to do things by himself. He entered a morning kindergarten program and seemed eager to learn. In the therapy sessions, the foster parents and the therapist celebrated each new milestone Adam achieved.

Mrs. S helped Adam expand his Life Book with pictures and mementos of his current life, while honoring his past by continuing to share memories about Momma. Adam continued to express sadness about losing her, and this was validated by the family. As Adam became more comfortable with the family, discussions of adoption as his ultimate plan were begun. After four months of treatment, Adam was doing well at home and school and was able to make a list of his accomplishments. Since the family spent extended time in their summer home, the therapist and the foster family planned a summer break from therapy. Everyone agreed to meet again when Adam returned to school in the fall.

The Crisis

In mid-summer, Mr. S called the therapist and frantically reported that Danny's mother (his daughter-in-law) was hysterical in his living room. She was insisting that Adam had sexually abused Danny. She said she had just discovered Danny mutually rubbing genitals with the three-year-old girl next door. Danny had told her that Adam taught him this special game, but that it was a secret so the little girl shouldn't tell anyone. Mr. S said that he and his wife confronted Adam. Adam at first denied everything, and then insisted that Danny had made him touch his penis, even though Danny is half Adam's size. Mr. S reported that Danny's parents decided to keep him away from his grandparents until they got rid of Adam. Mr. and Mrs. S were very worried and upset, and did not know what to do.

A session was held immediately to help assess the foster parents' ability to keep Adam and to develop solutions to the current crisis. They were assured that the therapist would be fully available to them to deal with this problem as a team. The therapist empathized with their predicament of being caught between competing commitments to Adam as well as to their son, daughter-in-law, and grandson. Prior discussions about the frequency of sexualized behavior among foster children and the need for foster parents to respond to it were reviewed. Mr. S repeated his belief that he couldn't deal with "sex fiends." Mrs. S immediately said they'd known Adam for over six months and he certainly wasn't a sex fiend, but that he might have more problems than they originally had anticipated. Mr. S was adamant that they could only keep Adam if they could be sure he would never again molest another child. The therapist reminded them there were no guarantees with any child.

Discussion began around how to clarify what had actually happened between Adam and Danny. Then the therapist and the family considered approaches to working with Adam that would help and protect him as well as other children. After two hours of soul-searching discussion, Mr. and Mrs. S decided to honor their commitment to Adam, even if it meant not seeing their grandson for some period of time. They discussed how to apologize to their son and daughter-in-law and how to reassure them they would deal with this issue with Adam. They decided to provide "eyes-on" supervision whenever Adam was with other children. They also would ask to see Danny outside their home, without Adam.

SMART Components of Treatment

A treatment approach was developed with the foster parents that implemented both the SMART foundation of treatment and SMART components of treatment (Figure 1). This clinical model enabled the foster parents to create a family environment to help heal their sexually reactive child. Adam was an active participant in all aspects of treatment, beginning with a family session in which the foster parents assured Adam of their ongoing commitment to take care of him and help him. They promised that neither he nor Danny was in trouble and he became willing to discuss his touching games with Danny. We made a plan to teach Adam more about his body and how to take care of it, as well as how to respect other's people's bodies. Adam was initially reluctant to talk about touching games and secrets other than to say we should talk to one of his previous foster brothers. Over the next few weeks, in individual, play, and family sessions, Adam disclosed observing and participating in extensive sex play with his previous foster brothers. These activities included watching each other masturbate, mutual fondling, and oral sex. In addition, Adam had sometimes been present while the older boys were "making out" with their girl-friends. This information was disclosed through discussion as well as drawing, puppet play, and storytelling with Adam. And it was verified by at least one of Adam's previous foster brothers.

Supervision

Supervision is a key to the healing process since it is an essential method of parental protection. By remaining physically close to the child, able to see exactly what the child is doing at all times, the parent prevents the child from behaving in unacceptable ways. Rather than isolating the child via punishment, the parent provides external control, cues, and positive reinforcement to strengthen the child's own controls. This protects the child from getting into trouble, getting hurt, or having negative experiences. It also builds closeness and fosters attachment between parent and child, rather than separation. In contrast to isolation techniques such as time out or being sent to one's room, supervision enables the parents to prove that they can and will protect the child, even from him/herself.

Mr. and Mrs. S decided that the best way to be sure that Adam would not engage in sex play with other children was to provide eyes-on supervision at all times. They immediately realized that given Adam's age and previous sexual exposure, he did not have the self-control to restrain his own impulses and sexual curiosity when no adult was present. They were able to develop a plan in which one of them or their regular sitter would maintain eyes-on supervision when Adam played with other children. They explained to Adam that their supervision was designed to help him play with other kids in better ways, and to remind him that kids needed their personal space and should not be touching each other's bodies. Adam said his favorite place to play was the toy room. However, Mr. and Mrs. S realized they often needed to work in the kitchen while Adam played. We devised a plan under which they would do certain household tasks in the playroom so Adam and friends could play there. We also planned kitchen play activities so the adult could do kitchen work while the children played. Telephones were in both rooms so calls could be taken without interrupting supervision. Adam liked this plan, especially the part about the grownups playing with the children some of the time.

Mutually defined goals

Mutually defined goals increase the chances for success and everyone's investment in the therapeutic process. It demonstrates that foster parents and you, the therapist, are truly working as a team. It conveys to the child that he/she is valued and respected and that his or her active participation is essential to progress. Mutual goal selection is also an important part of solution-focused treatment. Goals are generated from the ideas and input of the family and child, with your guidance. It is presumed that the foster families know which solutions are most feasible and have the best chance of success.

The therapist and the foster family developed the following goals to discuss with Adam:

- Explore and understand the origin and meaning of Adam's sexualized behaviors.
- Teach Adam about his body: how to take care of, enjoy, and protect it.
- Teach boundaries and how to respect them, and explain why private parts need to be private.
- Teach other ways Adam could explore his body and satisfy his curiosity, including private touching.
- Encourage fun and nontouching ways to play with other children, so parents would want their children to play with Adam.

Adam was initially reluctant to talk about how he learned the secret games he taught Danny. However, he became willing when he was assured that no one would get in trouble and that his foster parents wanted to learn more about him to help him be happy in the family. Adam wanted to have play dates with other children and to be able to play with Danny again. He also wanted his foster parents to teach him some games they had played when their birth children were little and they agreed to do so.

The therapist helped Adam and his foster parents talk together about specific rules about touching and sexual behavior. Family sessions were supplemented with individual play therapy time with Adam, during which the rules and boundaries were reinforced through play. Adam was proud to recite the rules to his parents, stating, "no kissing fresh, only short kisses on the cheek, nose, or forehead, no touching butt or private parts." He could identify and point to private parts of his body. He also was able to state who was allowed to touch him or another child: "Only mommy, daddy, or grandma when they are bathing me and the doctor at my check-ups." Work also focused on helping Adam protect himself should anyone try to touch him in a sexualized way. He stated: "I would tell them to leave me alone or I would kick them in the butt if they tried to do that! Then I would tell mommy, daddy, or my teacher." These rules were also reinforced in drawings, games, and puppet shows that Adam would create.

Over time, Mr. and Mrs. S were able to persuade their son and daughter-in-law to join the family therapy sessions to discuss what had occurred between Adam and Danny, and how to insure the children's safety while also repairing their relationship. Everyone decided that Danny and his parents should be included in some future family sessions. The purpose of these sessions would be to nonjudgmentally process what had occurred, teach the boys about their bodies, and give them guidelines for appropriate play in the future.

Attitudes and beliefs

Attitudes and beliefs powerfully influence families' actions (Boscolo et al., 1987). Mutual trust and respect will be facilitated when you and your foster parents share relevant attitudes and beliefs. Such sharing leads to plans which tend to be more realistic and comfortable for all parties. It also decreases the passive resistance that often accompanies hidden agendas. As a SMART family therapist, you need to respect the power of these family beliefs and develop treatment goals that support and use those beliefs, rather than opposing them.

In discussing attitudes and beliefs, the therapist and foster family returned to Mr. S's concerns about "bullies and sex fiends." They discussed what he meant by the phrase "sex fiend." Mr. S described someone who forced others to engage in sexual activity against their will. His belief system included a hatred of bullies. This was related to his own childhood experience of feeling powerless against them. As he grew older and stronger, Mr. S had gone out of his way to defend smaller children and to help them band together for self-protection. Mrs. S asked her husband if he viewed Adam as a bully or sex fiend. Mr. S replied that he did not, but that he feared that Adam had intimidated Danny into their mutual masturbation. Mrs. S said she doubted that anyone had to make little boys touch themselves, and that most boys learned that it felt good. Mr. S admitted that he was never comfortable when seeing little boys walking around with their hands inside their pants. He reminded his wife how he had persuaded her to sew up the pockets on their sons' sweatpants when they were in preschool, so it wouldn't be so easy for them to fondle themselves. He said he knew that wasn't the modern way to deal with this, but that he was "an old-fashioned guy with old-fashioned beliefs."

This facilitated a discussion of his beliefs about his role as father, and how guilty he felt about having let down both Adam and Danny by not preventing them from engaging in sex play. Mr. S concluded that his initial anger at Adam was really at himself. His wife admitted she also felt guilty and had worried that Mr. S blamed her for not adequately supervising the boys. These moving and honest exchanges seemed to break down barriers and enabled everyone speak more openly and nondefensively in developing goals, expectations, and strategies.

Reasonable expectations

If you have reasonable expectations, the chances of successful goal attainment are increased and the probability of frustration and disappointment is decreased. The process of mutually developing reasonable expectations is an important step in creating a therapeutic team. This involves sharing knowledge, attitudes, and experiences, and melding them to produce expectations that can be achieved. In a solution-focused approach, it is useful to help clients consider what is the most feasible of all the possible expectations they can devise. It is important that you help the family take the lead in setting expectations that fit within their specific family culture and belief system.

An important part of Adam's treatment program was the use of periodic team case conferences, which included the therapist, supervisor, foster parents, extended family members, foster care worker, teachers, and babysitters. The purpose of these conferences was to refine the treatment plan and assure that everyone agreed on expectations and interventions. Team conferences also provided consultation and support for all of Adam's caregivers. Adam's foster parents and teacher often said they felt less isolated and stressed after these meetings.

In order to formulate reasonable expectations, there needed to be an understanding of age-appropriate, normal sexual behavior, as well as the consequences of early childhood sexualization. Adam's natural curiosity and desire to explore his body had been distorted by being sexually stimulated by his older foster brothers, whom he admired and sometimes feared. Adam had experienced sexual arousal and gratification at a very young age and had been indoctrinated into a secret and exciting brotherhood. His desire to recreate these experiences was understandably strong and he had little understanding of why it was wrong. Mr. and Mrs. S realized that Adam would remain a sexualized child, easily stimulated and drawn to sexual activity, but they could help him channel this into acceptable behavior. They also understood that change would be gradual and come in small steps, with each step needing to be recognized and reinforced. Setbacks would be likely and shouldn't be treated as catastrophes. Rather, their efforts should be directed toward helping Adam achieve realistic goals, one step at a time. They made a deal with Adam: He would try to tell them when he felt "that sexy feeling" and they would reward him and suggest nonsexual activities that he enjoyed, such as jumping and dancing. Individual sessions were also used to help Adam recognize what triggered sexual feelings and help him develop strategies to deal with them.

Trust building

Trust building is crucial for foster children because they have usually experienced loss, betrayal, and trauma. They need to learn that they can trust their foster parents—to meet their needs, provide good care, and protect them from harm. Foster parents earn this trust through their actions toward the child. Similarly, you, the therapist, must earn the child's trust. You will do this through deeds rather than words. Mutual trust must also be developed between you and the foster parents if you are to function as an effective team. Trust is based on honesty, respect, and open discussions that include differences and disagreements.

The seeds of trust between foster parents, Adam, and the therapist had been sown during the early months of therapy, when they worked together to help Adam settle in and become part of the foster family. Trust was further nurtured by the therapist's availability to the family, coupled with honest sharing and mutual problem solving, during the crisis of discovering Adam's sexual involvement. Adam showed trust toward his foster parents and the therapist by his willingness to reveal past and present experiences and feelings. Everyone else showed their trust of Adam by believing his words as well as his agreement to work with them to change his behavior. The therapy process required each party to take risks and expose vulnerabilities. This strengthened their interdependence and mutual trust.

SMART Outcomes of Treatment

Self-confidence

Self-confidence is a key outcome of SMART treatment. The child learns that he or she is capable of achieving goals and making the foster family proud. Such children begin to believe in themselves and their abilities. Similarly, foster parents develop confidence in their parenting skills and view themselves as effective in dealing with highly challenging children.

After four months of SMART treatment, using a combination of individual and family sessions, Mr. and Mrs. S, the therapist, and Adam felt that he was ready for some unsupervised time with other children. This was tried for short time periods and was successful. They developed a "confidence scale" in which Adam rated how confident he was that he could control his sexual impulses in a variety of situations, using a range of 1 to 5. For a rating of 4 to 5, Adam required no direct supervision and only periodic check-ins from his foster parents. For 3 ratings, the foster parents provided "eyes-on" supervision. For 1-2 ratings, where Adam still felt highly stimulated and uncertain of his own controls, further therapeutic work was needed before Adam could be placed in those situations, with or without supervision.

Adam's teacher reported that he seemed more confident and assertive in school and was making major academic progress. Adam proudly reported that he was in charge of his own body, other people were in charge of theirs, and that friends didn't touch each other's private parts. Mr. and Mrs. S developed greater confidence in their ability to parent Adam, despite his being a sexualized child. They became confident that they could nurture, guide, and protect him, and help him to believe in himself.

Management of behavior

Management of behavior occurs when the foster parents have developed their own process for creating effective behavior management strategies, to be used whenever needed. This involves assessing the problem, separating behavioral patterns into their component parts, and developing a repertoire of behavior management skills.

Mr. and Mrs. S were able to identify the process they had used to help Adam control and redirect his inappropriate sexual behavior, and to envision how they might use these skills in a range of situations. These included focusing on specific targets of behavioral change, listing preferred behaviors, rehearsing and practicing desired behaviors, and giving positive reinforcement of incremental change. Their list of behavior management skills included supervision, redirection, positive reframes, and praise and other rewards.

Alternative behaviors

Alternative behaviors are the basis of successful solutions. Therapists, foster parents, and children develop new behaviors that can replace inappropriate ones. A positive cycle is created once children learn that they can choose and implement behaviors that satisfy themselves and others.

A useful solution-focused question of "What can you do to overcome the urge to do something sexual?" helped Adam think of alternative behaviors. Adam and the family were also instructed to observe what was happening when Adam overcame inappropriate urges and what behaviors he was using instead.

Adam had learned a number of alternatives to engaging in sex play with other children and was able to discuss and use them spontaneously in sessions and at home. He became able to tell his foster parents when he "felt sexy" so they could all brainstorm what to do about it. Sometimes he decided to push the feelings away and absorb himself in an activity. Sometimes he would sing or dance so he could "get the sexies out of me," ask for private time in his room, or talk about how he was feeling until his sexual arousal diminished. Adam and his foster parents used his "confidence scale" to determine how he felt about certain activities and playmates. This enabled them to plan together how Adam would deal with various situations and what help he needed to handle them.

Responsibility

Responsibility occurs when each participant in the therapeutic process accepts his or her own part of that process and carries out agreed-upon actions. All parties agree that no one can do the work of another, but can provide help and support while doing his or her own job. A solution-focused question that can facilitate responsibility is: "What are you willing to do or can you do to make this situation better?"

Mr. and Mrs. S developed a greater understanding of their role as primary healers. They no longer expected the therapist to fix Adam or take away his negative behaviors. They accepted responsibility for supervising, teaching, and helping Adam, while looking to the therapist for information, ideas, and support. The therapist was responsible for sharing knowledge and strategies with the family, while modeling the support and encouragement the foster parents were expected to provide for the child. Adam became responsible for his own choices and actions—to the extent that a six-year-old can be. He learned that his foster parents were there to help and protect him, but he also learned that they could best help him when he allowed them to do so by helping himself.

Trust

Trust is the ultimate outcome of successful SMART treatment. This includes trust of others and trust of oneself. Trust must be earned through positive experience. The children learn to trust that foster parents will provide care and protection. Then the children learn to trust parental rules, structures, and control. The children also learn to trust other adults of whom the foster parents approve. The children begin to accept care and control from teachers, relatives, family friends, and therapists. Finally, the children learn to trust themselves to do what is best, with the help of adults. The children learn that they are not alone. The foster parents and therapists learn to trust each other as therapeutic teammates. As they demonstrate honesty, reliability, and respect, they learn to count on each other. Gradually, they learn to trust that the children will accept their help, care, and control.

During the course of treatment, Adam came to know that he could count on his therapist and foster parents to be there for him, even during difficult times. He discovered that they kept their word, tried to meet his needs and do what was best for him. He learned that things usually worked out for him when he accepted their care and control. This provided the foundation of trust that Adam needed to begin to heal. He expressed this with 6-year-old eloquence one morning after he told his foster mother he should only play with his next-door neighbor if his foster mother stayed in the room because he "had the sexies." When she praised him for being honest and keeping his part of their deal, Adam smiled and said "I keep my word, just like you and Dad. Remember, we're a family!"

Conclusion

In this chapter, we have presented a two-pronged model for effective treatment of sexually reactive and acting-out children in foster care. These prongs are equally important for successful outcomes. Only through comprehensive assessment and thorough preparation can foster families—the primary healers of the child—be ready and able to do this difficult job.

We recognize that there is no magic bullet or quick fix for children who have been betrayed by trusted adults, had their innocence stolen, and whose survival mechanisms include sexual acting out. Many parents and families are not able to deal with these issues emotionally, let alone care for these children in their own homes. As professionals, we must give the utmost respect to parents and families who are willing to care for these children—children who are too frequently shunned by much of society. It is in this giving of respect and imparting of hope that we can team with foster parents as therapeutic partners and enable the family to become the primary healers for the child. Families like the family of Mr. and Mrs. S are most likely to be able to weather the predictable crises of caring for these children. They are courageous and open enough to accept and work with sexual acting-out behaviors, have flexible attitudes and beliefs, provide consistent and reassuring structure and boundaries for children, and accept support from others.

Despite the shortcomings of the child welfare system, we maintain a strong belief in the resilience of children and the healing capacity of foster families. After years of clinical practice, we remain committed to the work of restoring children's trust and helping them build competence and self-control. Witnessing the return of a child's capacity to give and receive love within the context of a protective, healthy, and nurturing family environment is surely motivation for all of us to continue this important work.

References

Avery, L., Massat, C. R., & Lundy, M. (2000). Posttraumatic stress and mental health functioning of sexually abused children. *Child and Adolescent Social Work Journal, 17,* 19–34.

Berg, I. K., & DeJong, P. (1996). Solution building conversations: Co-constructing a sense of competence with clients. *Families in Society, 76,* 376–391.

Boscolo, L., Cecchin, G., Hoffman, L., & Penn, P. (1987). *Milan systemic family therapy: Conversations in theory and practice.* New York: Basic Books.

Castaldo, D. (1996). *Assessing foster and adoptive families for placement of sexually abused children.* Milwaukee: Families International, Inc.

Cohen, J. A., & Mannarino, A. P. (2000). Predictors of treatment outcome in sexually abused children. *Child Abuse and Neglect, 24,* 983–994.

Deblinger, E., Steer, R. A., & Lippman, J. (1999). Two-year follow-up study of cognitive behavioral therapy for sexually abused children suffering post traumatic stress symptoms. *Child Abuse and Neglect, 23,* 1371–1378.

deShazer, S. (1985). *Keys to solution.* New York: W.W. Norton.

deShazer, S. (1991). *Putting difference to work.* New York: W.W. Norton.

Douglas, A. R. (2000). Reported anxieties concerning intimate parenting in women sexually abused as children. *Child Abuse and Neglect, 24,* 425–434.

Duehn, W. D. (1990). *Beyond sexual: The healing power of adoptive families, a guide for adoptive parents.* Pittsburgh: Three Rivers Adoption Council.

Fleming, S. J., & Belanger, S. K. (2000). Trauma, grief, and surviving childhood sexual abuse. In R. B. Neimeyer (Ed.), *Meaning reconstruction and the experience of loss* (pp. 311–330). Washington, DC: American Psychological Association.

Friedrich, W. N. (1995). *Psychotherapy with sexually abused boys: An integrated approach.* Thousand Oaks, CA: Sage Publications.

Freyd, J. J. (1996). *Betrayal trauma: the logic of forgetting childhood abuse.* Cambridge, MA: Harvard University Press.

Goldner, V. (1992). Making room for both/and. *Family Therapy Networker, 16*(2), 55–61.

Imber-Black, E. (Ed.) (1993). *Secrets in families and family therapy.* New York: Norton.

Imber-Black, E., Roberts, J., & Whiting, R. (Eds.) (1988). *Rituals in families and family therapy.* New York, Norton.

James, B. (1989). *Treating traumatized children.* Lanham, MD: Lexington Books.

Jones, D. A. (2004). Intelligence and achievement of children referred following sexual abuse. *Journal of Paediatrics & Child Health, 40,* 455–460.

Mayer, A. (1985). *Sexual abuse: Causes, consequences, and treatment of incestuous and pedophilic acts.* Holmes Beach, FL: Learning Publications.

McFadden, E. J. (1992). The inner world of children and youth in care. *Community Alternatives: International Journal of Family Care, 4*(1), 1–17.

O'Hanlon, W. (1999). *Do one thing different.* New York: William Morrow and Co.

Ruggiero, K. J., McLeer, S. V., & Dixon, J. F. (2000). Sexual abuse characteristics associated with survivor psychopathology. *Child Abuse and Neglect, 24,* 951–964.

Sgroi, S. (1982). *Handbook of clinical intervention in child sexual abuse.* Lanham, MD: Lexington Books.

Thompson, R. W., Authier, K., & Ruma, P. (1994). Behavior problems of sexually abused children in foster care. *Journal of Child Sexual Abuse, 3*(4), 79–91.

16

Combating a Family Culture of Violence

John Seita

J ust as with sexual abuse, foster children may bring aggressive
   behavior into their foster homes and school settings. Besides mas-
   tering their own experiences of having been abused, many foster
children are socialized to see physical violence as an appropriate
response to frustration or anxiety. This chapter describes how family
therapy in both the birth and foster families can contain this behavior and provide a different orientation.

Violence is often a way of life for children who have been abused
and neglected in their families of origin. And many children enter
foster care angry. These are children who are injured, are in deep
emotional pain, and may have learned a set of coping strategies that
include lying and other mechanisms intended to outwit adults.
The use of violence by angry and relationship-wary young people
is a particularly powerful way to accomplish their goals.

Predisposition to Everyday Violence

Foster children's predisposition toward aggressive and sometimes
violent behavior is typically a product of two things, namely, abuse
inflicted upon them or which they have witnessed, and their current psychosocial state.

Past Abuse

Some children in foster care report witnessing abuse among their
first memories:

I was only five years old when I watched my father inexorably and brutally beat my mother's head against the kitchen wall. Their argument at dinner had been brief, ending quickly when, burning with rage, he jumped over the garage sale Formica table and pulled her out of her chair by the hair. A clump of her hair drifted soundlessly to the floor. He grabbed her by the hair and banged her head repeatedly against the kitchen wall, with a *crack, crack, crack* sound that I could hear for years. Blood began to spurt from her skull, splattering the wall.

My mother screamed first. Then she pleaded with him. I crumpled in the corner watching with horror, fear, and fright. "You may as well go ahead and kill me," she screamed toward his contorted, vein-swollen face. Her own face was a bit different—a bluish gray and it reminded me of a cartoon I once saw where the bad guy was beating up the good guy.

The beating ended abruptly. Maybe the blood-speckled kitchen wall let him know she was nearly dead, maybe her crying awoke him to his brutality. Maybe she was simply lucky that he was out of energy. Anyhow, he dragged my mom toward his old blue rust-pocked Pontiac. As she sat in the front seat, he almost gently intoned "Are you OK, I didn't mean to hurt you, are you OK? Please be OK, I won't ever do that again, honey, I promise." My mom did not reply, she simply sat slumped near the passenger door sobbing very quietly, as if trying to muffle her pain and anguish. She seemed almost embarrassed in her pain. I sat in the back. It was as if I wasn't there at all. I liked it that way, pretending that I was invisible. I curled up deep in the back seat, wondering, "Am I next?" "Why did he beat her, anyway?" (Seita, unpublished manuscript)

The above description is not unusual among the experiences that are reported by children who enter foster care. The consequences may be dulled or heightened social sensibilities, anomie, and the notion that violence is an accepted method of goal attainment.

Decades of research are clear in their findings that children who experience abuse instead of love fail to develop adequate conscience and empathy for others. There are many theories for why these former victims may go on to repeat the horrible acts inflicted on them. These theories include managing the anxiety and self-images associated with victimization, identification with those who had such power, or exoneration of the perpetrating parents ("I'm no better than them"). An early review of the domestic violence literature (Nichols, 1986) is helpful. A child's inclination to act in violent ways in the home requires two things. First, the child must feel absolutely powerless in a situation perceived as important. Second, the child has learned from other family members that violence is an acceptable response to such feelings of impotence. This combination of circumstances is likely to characterize children who are in foster care, especially those who have been placed because of the violence in their former households.

State of Mind

Foster children often are torn by confusion and doubt. They may feel abandoned by their parents, the primary caretakers whom they loved, trusted, and depended upon. They may feel betrayed, alone, scared, emotionally hurt, confused, sad, and unsure about what might happen next (see Chapter 4, "The Perspective of the Consumer: Foster Children Tell Us What They Need"). They may wonder about their new foster parents, their new home, and how long they will be there. They may also wonder if or how they might fit in with their new family. In fact, many do not want to fit in and, in spite of abuse in their home of origin, many children fantasize about when they will return home (Seita, 2004; Seita, Mitchell, & Tobin, 1996). A common response to such uncertainty is irritability and temper.

Because they have been abused and neglected, almost without exception, children who enter foster care are traumatized and have attachment disorders, behavior disorders, and emotional problems (Seita & Brendtro, 2005). They often do not trust adults, even those who are trying to help. After all, in their own private logic, adults created the misery that is their lives.

In short, many children have not entered foster care voluntarily and may not be happy to be there. It is not a positive adventure for them, such as going away to camp. Many are in a state of denial about what has happened and what will happen to them. Moreover, they are entering into a strange home. Most likely, even if it is a placement with kin, the home is not like their home. There are different people, with different ways. They are probably unlike their parents and unlike their siblings.

Violence as Problem-Solving

Angry aggressive acts normally are not children's preferred strategy for coping. Some aggression is driven by unconscious motives. Sometimes aggression toward adults and others is an extreme approach that is used when children are left without appropriate ways of goal satisfaction and meeting needs. Instead of pathologizing this rebellious, antisocial behavior, you may find it helpful to view it as an adaptive attempt by children to improve their lives—albeit employing dysfunctional approaches. In his book *Lost Boys,* James Garbarino (1999) writes: "Some of these boys appear so tough on the outside. But when I get a glimpse of their inner life, I am deeply touched by their vulnerability and their pain, and I come to see their toughness as a survival strategy, as something that helps them get through another day" (page 83).

Aggression is an instinctual, protective survival mechanism. Research on aggression shows pathways by which a young child may become, to use a term coined by Athens (1989), "violentized." Below is a synthesis of such studies:

- Children who have been brutalized, rejected, subjugated, or terrorized experience extreme negative emotions of anger, fear, shame, and depression.

- When a crisis persists, children typically brood over the problem. Some become depressed and blame themselves. Others become belligerent and begin to fantasize ways of getting revenge at attackers. Violent ideation is intensified by what the children may have experienced to date. Violent action also may have been coached. "Don't be a sissy! Stand up and be a man."

- Many children who have been hurt fantasize about hurting back. But most don't follow through. They may exercise self-restraint because of nonviolent values, fear, or a lack of opportunity. However, if they are big and strong, and there is continuing provocation, some youth experiment with aggressive coping strategies. Deciding they won't take any more abuse, they choose a situation and a method to fight back. Antisocial youth tend to follow one of three pathways: overt violence, covert delinquency, or authority conflict. The typical course of things is for aggression to progress over time from minor to more serious behaviors. Their aggression may be directed against an abuser or displaced on a more ready target, such as a peer or less threatening adult. If the violent behavior succeeds, it is likely to continue. If aggression doesn't work, the youth may develop another solution or endure victimization.

- When aggression works, it can become entrenched as a stable lifestyle. Children become comfortable with aggressive behavior because it brings many benefits. They have surmounted the initial crisis, extricated themselves from the victim role, and now feel comfortable, vindicated, and less distraught. The power of the bully brings new status, at least within their private logic. Any possible discomfort of guilt about hurting others is managed by thought distortions that justify violence. Violence becomes fashionable as these children cut ties with prosocial peers and gravitate to associates who applaud this behavior and to victims who tolerate abuse.

In summary, children who experience violence are impacted in a variety of ways. Some internalize it and turn it against themselves.

Others externalize it and use violence as a strategy to solve frustration and to cope with the daily problems of life. However, their preoccupation with violence may become a barrier to appropriate developmental opportunities. Children who have lived in violent family systems often experience difficulty in school, in peer and adult relationships, and may join in with negative peer culture.

Family Therapy with the Goal of Management

There are two treatment goals when dealing with potentially violent foster children: behavior management and addressing of root causes. These must always be dealt with sequentially, with the first goal being management of the behavior. You are probably quite familiar with the urgent calls of case managers—driven by the acute concerns of foster parents—to do something immediately to make a child stop acting up. Even though we believe in the emergency, we also believe that the problematic behavior is a symptom of something else. We would prefer to delve a little deeper and deal with the root cause. But we can't. We must deal quickly with the perceived emergency, or the placement is likely to be disrupted and a difficult case will become much worse. We need to settle things down now to afford everyone the opportunity for more profound individual and contextual remedies.

Much of what we need to know has already been covered in Chapter 15, "'I Want This Child Out of Here Now!' How to Deal with Sexualized Acting Out in the Foster Environment: A 'SMART' Approach to Assessment and Treatment." The principles and remedies are largely the same whether the child is active sexually or aggressively. Foster families fear for the security of those already in the home, and may be alienated by behavior that is far from their own family ways. This means that aggressive children need to be placed in foster families who are prepared for them. In advance of making their decision to accept the child, these brave families must be fully informed about the child's potential violent behavior, including what triggers it, its range, and management techniques with a good probability of success.

As in the SMART approach to managing sexual behavior in the foster home, we need the security of a team-centered approach with mutually-defined and reasonable expectations. Those aspects of the team members that would inhibit effective work—attitudes, values, anxieties, and limited knowledge—need to be addressed and resolved before the child enters the home. We need to agree on our short-term outcome, namely, managing the violent behavior, and our longer-term goals. The latter include the foster child accepting responsibility for self-control, replacing the violent behavior with prosocial behavior, and cultivating self-confidence and a realistic trust in others. The foster parents must recognize and accept the need for constant "eyes-on" supervision.

Typically, there are two kinds of violent behaviors that may be exhibited by foster children: one is bullying; the other is an emotional spell. Bullying is managed by eyes-on supervision, clarification of what is occurring, limit-setting, and modeling of prosocial behavior. In contrast, when children are emotionally and aggressively volatile, no reasonable approach will work until they calm down. In the meantime, all one can do is keep them in a safe place until the emotional spell subsides. Typically, such children cannot be touched or moved, so foster parents need to remove objects that might hurt the children or which the children might use to hurt others.

There is a very good behavioral control technique that involves the alert use of anticipatory time-outs. With experience, we can ascertain what signals that a specific child is about to lose control. Perhaps the child's voice will take on a certain volume or pitch. Perhaps the child's movements will become more driven, fists will clench, toys will be roughly handled, or there will be a look on the child's face. In our experience with a child, these signs are consistently followed by an escalation of mood and behavior. Once we have identified these signs, we use eyes-on supervision and implement a time-out for as long as it takes for the mood to diminish. When calm, the child can return to whatever he or she was doing— until the signs once again appear and there is another time-out. The idea is to intervene before things get out of control and thereby keep the child relatively tranquil and his or her behavior in a tolerable range. Since these emotional children lack the capacity to self-regulate, our immediate task is to do it for them. With increasing age, the children can be collaborators in this and, eventually, be responsible for their own self control.

Family Therapy with the Goal of Resilience

Family therapy can be used to teach both the family of origin and the foster family new skills to address the child's acts of violence. Family therapy can also teach the child more socially acceptable and prosocial ways to express his/her frustration when goals or needs are denied. However, your therapy will be complicated by the fact that there are two families in the consultation room. Even if one of the families is not physically there, they will be a presence nonetheless. Every family system has its own priorities and standards and its ways of enforcing those norms.

Before attempting to engage in any type of family therapy, all stakeholders must address a stark reality that might seem obvious: The culture and practices in the family of origin are likely to be dramatically different than the culture and the practices within the foster family or within any healthy and functioning family. Therefore, values, beliefs, and coping mechanisms for the child are more than likely not going to be like those of the foster home. Presumably, the foster family is where the violent child is expected to learn prosocial behavior and appropriate conflict resolution skills. The birth family is where the child has learned that violence and anger are an appropriate mechanism for conflict resolution or for goal attainment.

When children enter into foster families they are entering into a new culture. Therefore, our interventions should recognize two things.

- Different values, mores, and worldviews are in competition inside and outside of our consulting room.
- The ways of the birth family have influenced the private logic of the children and the choices of the adaptive coping mechanisms that they use.

Private Logic

All individuals construct their own private logic. This is their way of making sense of the world based upon their life experiences. This private logic forms the basis for personal coping strategies, including whether or not to approach others with trust or distrust. Individuals reared in appropriately nurturing families typically see others as a source of protection and support and will seek them out in time of need for help and companionship. In contrast, individuals with a private logic colored by violence view others with fear and anger and cope by avoiding interdependent relationships.

Clearly the value of understanding private logic and decoding the thinking errors of children in foster care is a valuable tool in working with these children. Yet there are limitations. For example, family therapy may not change the personal space or the environment that prompted the development of the aggressive orientation of the child.

The Importance of Family Therapy

Family therapy provides a forum for the members of both the birth and the foster families to discover and understand the individual and family circumstances that elicit and maintain aggressive behavior in their children. A relational therapy orientation is very important in this regard. Often families describe a child as aggressive—this view sees the problem as a personality trait and the emphasis is then on how the child is to be changed or controlled. We find it more helpful to ask all of the disparate family members to think of exceptional situations, that is, circumstances in which the child was angry but was not demonstrating violent behavior. In so doing, we remind all the parties that the child does not act violently all the time, with all people, and in every setting. We then can ask what is different about those settings in which the child is not acting violently? What are the other people doing and what is the child doing?

We also can explore each family's legacy with regard to physical aggression. If they are inclined to or appalled by such behavior, from whom and how did they learn that lesson and why is it so compelling? Typically, these are multigenerational matters. For example, the adults are emulating or reacting against the attitudes and behaviors of their own parents. We then can ask, "How did your parent come to be like that?" If it is a negative trait, we can add, "How do you think your parent might have liked to be different?" The point to be made is that uncovering and understanding these family legacies can allow family members to be more comfortable with themselves and with each other, and less automatic and more purposeful in their actions (see, for example, Chapter 14, "'It Isn't Right!' The Need to Redress Experiences of Injustice in Child Abuse and Neglect").

Many of the techniques of individual cognitive psychotherapy also work well in family therapy. Interventions common to rational–emotive and cognitive–behavioral psychotherapies will allow everyone to identify and explore thinking errors and the private logic being used by the respective parties.

Individual and Relational Resiliency

Not all children "crash and burn" as a result of their maltreatment. Many not only survive psychosocially, they even thrive (for example, see Rutter, 1985; Werner & Smith, 1992). There is a growing interest in exploring this resiliency in at-risk youth. Resilient youth are able to withstand stress and even rebound from adversity with greater strength to meet future challenges. We now know that even serious disruptions in a child's life can offer unexpected opportunities for growth and that children exposed to severe trauma can turn their lives around to the extent that they possess intelligence, imagination, a likable personality, the ability to set goals, a sense of purpose, the ability to form close positive personal relationships, and a sense of spirituality (Brown, 1983; Everson, 1994; Garmezy, 1985; Rhodes & Hoey, 1994; Vorrath & Brendtro, 1985).

Resiliency is not only a personality trait. It also can be a characteristic of relationships (Walsh, 1996). Social systems may help family members withstand, rebound, and even grow from stress—to the extent to which they are cohesive, flexible with regard to responsibilities under changing circumstances, practice open communication, have good problem-solving skills, and have affirming belief systems.

Young people who emerge victorious and grow from traumatic and other unfortunate circumstances are the result of both internal and external factors. They can experience success and positive growth, if they connect with teachers, coaches, clergy, neighbors, or other adults. The role of these caring external others is to provide support, set positive expectations, and encourage the child as he or she seeks a purpose in life.

The message to all of us from the resiliency literature is clear: We do not need to be pessimistic about the life trajectories of youth and families in foster care. These can be altered by external influences. Life crises can become opportunities for growth to the extent that we help our clients acquire the individual and corporate traits that support resiliency.

When we are assessing our foster children and planning for them, we want to remember that resilience is nurtured by (Brown, 1983; Fisher, 2001; Seita, 2004):

- a safe environment,
- a structured environment in at least one system of their lives,
- at least one adult who is tenaciously and consistently caring and who holds high expectations of them,
- a school that holds high expectations for them and believes in them,
- caregivers who acknowledge their accomplishments, and
- positive peers.

To the extent that any of these factors are absent, we need to find a solution or amplify the other factors so as to minimize the influence of that which is missing.

Practical Approaches for Foster Care Practitioners

Sometimes there is confusion among many practitioners and scholars about the needs of those in foster care and how to meet those needs. Those who work with young people who are in foster care, their families, and foster families should have a set of tools, standards, and expected outcomes.

Fundamentally, the needs of young people in foster care are no different than the needs of young people who are raised with family privilege (Seita & Brendtro, 2005). What is different about young people in foster care is that those who are responsible for their care might need to be more consciously intentional about what they are doing and how it might be experienced. Moreover, because placement in foster care is a blending of two family systems, the participants may have special needs for family therapy.

Another way that foster parents, case managers, and birth parents may address the primary developmental needs of their children is to use the Connectedness, Continuity, Dignity, and Opportunity model (CCDO; Seita et al., 1996). CCDO provides a common language and a common understanding of what foster children need for healthy growth. Then it provides common actions. This straightforward, strength-based, and ecological approach can be used in both the foster and birth homes. It can stand alone or it can be a useful supplement to family therapy. We believe that young people whose needs are met by CCDO are less likely to strike out in anger.

- *Connectedness* meets the young person's need to belong, for strong attachments, and intimate and prosocial adult relationships. Foster parents, birth parents, and others can work with their children to (1) create a network of friends, (2) actively involve themselves in a community where they are respected, (3) encourage extended family members, siblings, and other adults to provide counsel, safety, and support in the event that primary family are absent or inattentive, and (4) participate in school and community programs. Community connections should also be explored to find appropriate supports such as Boys and Girls Clubs, churches, developmentally appropriate educational opportunities, and family counseling, if necessary.

- *Continuity* is a sense of continuous belonging to a group and a general feeling of permanence. It also includes an appreciation for one's place in the world, a sense of one's legacy, and a sense of spiritual eternity.
- *Dignity* includes respect, courtesy, safe environments, access to health care and food, boundaries, and limits.
- *Opportunity* is the chance to explore, learn to see new ways of living, capitalize on one's strengths, build new strengths, and have one's talents recognized and strengthened.

The basic needs of all children, if they are to be resilient, are affiliation, competence, autonomy, and purpose (Benard, 1993). Strengths develop naturally to the extent that we create the circumstances in which the children are able to meet these growth needs.

Summary

Working effectively with children who enter foster care is to be mindful of the various challenges that they bring into that setting. Anger and aggression are frequently used to meet needs. Family therapy that is informed by what is known about cultivating resiliency in individuals and social systems is a useful approach for both birth and foster families.

References

Athens, L. (1989). *Creation of dangerous violent criminals.* New York: Routledge.

Benard, B. (1993). Fostering resiliency in kids. *Educational Leadership, 51*(3), 44–48.

Brown, W. K. (1983). *The other side of delinquency.* New Brunswick, NJ: Rutgers University Press.

Everson, T. (1994). Resiliency and skill-building: A spiritual perspective. *Journal of Emotional and Behavioral Problems, 3*(2), 25–29.

Fisher, A. (2001) *Finding fish: A memoir.* New York. William Morrow.

Garbarino, J. (1999). *Lost boys: Why our sons turn violent and how we can save them.* New York: The Free Press.

Garmezy, N. (1985). Stress-resistant children: The search for protective factors. In J. E. Stevenson (Ed.), *Recent research in developmental psychopathology* (pp. 213–233). Oxford, UK: Pergamon Press.

Nichols, W. C. (1986). Understanding family violence: An orientation for family therapists. *Contemporary Family Therapy, 8,* 188–207.

Rhodes, W. A., & Hoey, K. (1994). *Overcoming childhood misfortune: Children who beat the odds.* Westport, CT: Praeger.

Rutter, M. (1985). Resilience in the face of adversity: Protective factors and resistance to psychiatric disorder. *British Journal of Psychiatry, 147,* 598–611.

Seita, J. R. (2004). Strength based approaches expand into leadership. *Reclaiming Children and Youth: The Journal of Strength Based Interventions. 13*(1), 22–25.

Seita, J., & Brendtro, L. (2005). *Children who outwit adults.* Bloomington, IN: National Educational Service.

Seita, J., Mitchell, M., & Tobin, C. (1996). *In whose best interest? One child's odyssey, a nation's responsibility.* Elizabethtown, PA: Continental Press.

Vorrath, H. H., & Brendtro, L. K. (1985). *Positive peer culture* (2nd ed.). New York: Aldine.

Walsh, F. (1996). The concept of family resilience: Crisis and challenge. *Family Process, 35,* 261–281.

Werner, E., & Smith, R. S. (1992). *Overcoming the odds: High-risk children from birth to adulthood.* Ithaca, NY: Cornell University Press.

17

"We're in It Together" Family Therapy Where Substance Abuse Is a Problem

John K. Mooradian

S ubstance abuse by birth parents is a factor that often contributes to the placement of children in foster care. In cases where the parent takes steps toward recovery, reunification may occur, but ongoing treatment is indicated as a means of preventing placement recidivism and improving family relationships. In this chapter, we view substance abuse as a family issue, clarify the effects of parental substance abuse on family functioning, discuss assessment processes, and consider concrete methods for strengthening the family system.

Case Example

It was a warm summer evening. Robby (age 9) and Jim (age 12) were out in the yard throwing frogs against the trunk of the apple tree behind the house. Robby started swearing at Jim because he wanted to smash the amphibian that Jim had just snatched from him. The yelling got louder after Jim pushed Robby, and they started to fight. Their mother, Betty, had just come home from her job as an administrative assistant at the local university, and was in the kitchen when she heard them fighting. She dashed to the freezer and clutched her bottle of vodka. As the frigid liquid splashed on the back of her throat, she felt a familiar rush of relief spread through her body. She savored the sensation for a moment and gathered her resolve before screaming out the window for the boys to stop. They only fought harder. Betty raced outside and pulled them apart, telling them not to kill each other, or else she would.

It really came as no surprise when Robby and Jim were later removed from the home by Child Protective Services. There were multiple reports of neglect filed by teachers, neighbors, and the school social worker. When Robby and Jim were placed in foster care, Betty drank every day. She felt even guiltier, but it seemed like she couldn't stop. The foster care worker came to her house one Wednesday around 3:30 P.M. for a routine visit, and found Betty inebriated. The worker reminded her that she could not have her children back until she got sober.

Overview

We all recognize that parental substance abuse has a profound influence on families. Families experience great stress and progressive dysfunction as they attempt to integrate or eliminate substance abuse (Jackson, 1954; Lemert, 1960; Steinglass, Bennett, Wolin, & Reiss, 1987). Parental substance abuse is associated with marital instability, including fighting, physical violence, prolonged separations, and divorce. It also is associated with parenting problems, including lack of structure, inconsistency, emotional neglect, and inability or unwillingness to perform responsibilities. Often weak parent–child boundaries may be manifest in role reversal and parentification of a child, or in physical or sexual abuse. Families in which the parents abuse substances often are characterized by isolation of the family from its external environment and between members of the family. Also, in such families the members often are confused by each other's incongruent communications, lack of trust, and concerns about family secrets (Lawson & Lawson, 1998).

In addition to these effects on overall family functioning, there are also effects on the children. Compared to other children, the children of substance abusers are more likely to experience many problems, such as depression and repressed emotions; antisocial behavior; difficulties with attachment and social relations; lack of self-confidence and life-direction; fear of abandonment and the future; cognitive problems and low school achievement; and eventual substance abuse themselves (Elkins, McGue, & Malone, 2004; Lawson & Lawson, 1998; Logue, 1991; McNichol & Tash, 2001; Seilhamer, 1991). The substance-abusing parent often has mood changes, blackouts, aggressiveness, withdrawal cycles, and self-centeredness. These create an unstable home environment that requires children to develop chameleon-like behavior in response. It has been noted that such a family context negatively affects organization, cohesiveness, predictability, discipline, emotional support, and training in basic life skills (Seilhamer & Jacob, 1990).

Given all of these pervasive and destructive effects, it is not surprising that parental substance abuse is often a major contributor to the decision to place children in foster care (Gregoire, 1994; Peterson, Gable, & Saldana, 1996; Semidei, Radel, & Nolan, 2001; Terling, 1999; Tracy & Farkas, 1994; Wolock & Magura, 1996). As a result, those of us who perform clinical work within the child welfare system need specialized knowledge of substance abuse and family dynamics in order to be effective.

This chapter offers you useful ways to think about substance abuse in the family context, clarifies its effects on family functioning, and provides concrete suggestions for strengthening the family system. We will focus on family therapy in those situations where the substance-abusing adult has become involved in a recovery process and family reunification is possible. We will be concerned with the interconnected relationships within the family, and the steps that can be taken to support recovery for the family as a whole.

Conceptual Framework

In the field and in the literature, there often is a split between professionals who favor an individual treatment approach, usually based on the disease model, and those who prefer a systems model. In brief, the disease model views substance abuse as a progressive medical problem with biological, psychological, and spiritual characteristics (Jellinek, 1960). Addiction represents a loss of control over the substance, the addict is never cured, and sobriety is a life-long challenge that is accomplished one day at a time (Alcoholics Anonymous World Services, 1972). It is often seen as a primary problem that overshadows all other life tasks, because of its far-reaching effects on judgment, thinking patterns, emotions, and behaviors. Intervention requires total abstinence as the overall goal (Lawson & Lawson, 1998).

Traditionally, systems-oriented therapists have been reluctant to embrace the disease model because it centralizes an individual instead of the family system, and describes the problem as a deficit rather than a need for different forms of interaction (Substance Abuse and Mental Health Services Administration, 2004). This critique recognizes the role of family interaction in maintaining substance abuse and attends to the needs of family members as well as those of the substance abuser.

One way to bridge this gap and explain the processes of inter-action within families of chemically-dependent people is the concept of codependency. From this perspective, substance abuse is viewed as a family disease, from which whole families must recover (Beattie, 1992; Koffinke, 1991; Wegscheider-Cruse, 1989; Wegscheider-Cruse & Cruse, 1990). Although researchers have not established empirical validity for codependency, clinicians often use it to explain interaction patterns (Gotham & Sher, 1996). Characteristics of codependency include the following:

- thinking and feeling responsible for other people in regard to their thoughts, feelings, actions, well-being, and ultimate destiny;
- feeling compelled to help other people solve their problems through unsolicited advice, rapid-fire suggestions, or sidestep-ping signs of interpersonal discord;
- feeling angry when the help that is offered isn't effective;
- doing things for people that they are capable of doing for themselves;
- saying yes instead of no, and doing more than a fair share of the work;

- being attracted to needy people;
- anticipating conditions, problems, and outcomes, and trying to control them to maintain a sense of safety;
- denying a fear of loss of control; and
- engaging in sex when angry or hurt, as a way to placate unpleasant feelings and avoid conflict.

We recommend integrating both traditional individual treatment with family therapy. This approach is encouraged by several investigators and clinicians (Brown & Lewis, 2002; Dulfano, 1992; Liddle & Hogue, 2000), and endorsed by the United States Department of Health and Human Services (Substance Abuse and Mental Health Services Administration, 2004). Such an approach recognizes that substance abuse afflicts the individual in body, mind, and spirit, and is often progressively destructive. It also acknowledges the development of family interaction patterns that are heavily influenced by—and affect the progression of—substance abuse. This approach puts into action a combination of 12-step and family systems interventions in order to bring powerful resources to bear on this complex problem.

Processes for Intervening with the Family

Useful processes for intervening with the families of substance abusers are presented below, followed by more of the case example. The general course of treatment is approximately six to nine months, with weekly sessions for the first four months, and biweekly sessions for the remainder. These processes represent the product of clinical experience that draws from structural family therapy (Minuchin, 1974; Minuchin & Fishman, 1981), strategic family therapy (Haley, 1987, Madanes, 1984), solution-focused therapy (De Jong & Berg, 2002; Walter & Peller, 1992), and cognitive therapy (Beck, 1976; Ellis & Dryden, 1997). Interventions were also selected on the basis of empirical investigations that substantiated the need to combine psychological treatments and 12-step models to effectively treat substance abuse (Roth & Fonagy, 2005).

Although the processes identified below follow a general sequence, the reader is cautioned not to think of them as separate stages that must be accomplished in sequence. Matching individual recovery efforts with changes in family interactions is required.

Identify Relapse Prevention Plan

Responsible intervention with substance abusers recognizes the high likelihood of relapse, especially during transition and early recovery phases, and helps the individual make plans to prevent it (Brown & Lewis, 2002). Assuming that the individual substance abuser is engaged in a treatment program, a relapse prevention plan should be identified by the time the therapist begins to work with the family. If not, it should be addressed first. There are two important elements.

- *Family education* that includes understanding the relapse process; identifying and developing strategies to handle high-risk situations, cravings for the drug, and social pressures; managing anger; using leisure time appropriately; building a long-term sobriety plan; knowing what to do if a relapse occurs; and monitoring efforts with a daily relapse prevention inventory (Daley & Raskin, 1991).

- *Identification of psychological issues* such as shame, guilt, and anger, their triggers, such as family conflict, and the situations in which they are likely to arise (Freeman, 2001). Concurrently families should develop methods, tools, and strategies to use when these psychological issues arise. Moreover, knowing to whom to turn for support during a crisis, as well as knowing what significant others are most likely to block the plan, can increase the likelihood of success (Rotunda, Scherer, & Imm, 1995).

In Betty's case, the worker obtained written permission to discuss her situation with the substance abuse counselor who had treated her. This communication indicated that a careful and realistic relapse prevention plan was identified and implemented.

Use Environmental Controls

Although it is not possible to guarantee sobriety by simply limiting access to the drug of choice, it is helpful to build barriers to obtaining it. Removal of the drug from the home can help the recovering person deal with the cravings and impulses to use. Limiting access, especially during transition and early recovery stages, can also serve to protect the recovering person against the triggers that exist in the family environment.

With the help of her substance abuse counselor, Betty decided to make a firm rule that her household would be alcohol-free. That meant that she would not purchase her customary stock of vodka, and she would not allow anyone else to bring alcohol into her home.

Establish Accountability and Support

You and the foster care worker can make an invaluable contribution to the health of the family by creating accountability structures for the substance-abusing parent (Smith, 2003). When children are initially placed out of the home, it is important to set firm limits about substance use. The worker should be clear that children will not be returned until the parent demonstrates a genuine willingness to accept the reality of addiction. Research indicates that substance-abusing mothers often believe that their use does not interfere with parenting, so you and the worker are strongly encouraged to directly address this risk (Baker & Carson, 1999). It is possible that the substance-abusing parent may pull herself together in an effort to reunite with the children, but the rest of you should insist that she or he actively participate in a treatment program or intervention effort (Hohman & Butt, 2001). Even at this early stage, it is important to instill a realistic level of hope that children can be returned whenever possible. In many cases, this limit and accompanying hope serve to motivate adults to seek sobriety. In later stages of preparation for reunification, and once it has been achieved, the limit can shift to center on compliance with the individual intervention program. It is crucial that individual support mechanisms, such as 12-step programs, be activated as soon as the parent seeks sobriety. Generally the threat of court action alone is not enough to make sure that substance abusers remain in recovery. As a result, it is also valuable to build in external accountability during the early stages of recovery. Many substance-abusing parents will relapse quickly without it (Gregoire & Schultz, 2001). As recovery progresses, you should find ways to encourage the adults to build self-accountability. You do this by reinforcing efforts to change, pointing out the positive results of a sober lifestyle, and establishing a clear structure for self-monitoring of impulses and behavior.

Those involved in Betty's case helped her family by insisting on active involvement in alcohol counseling. In addition, Betty was told that she could have her children back only when these and other conditions were met. The therapist and caseworker also encouraged Betty's participation in Alcoholics Anonymous.

Assessment

It is useful to apply an ecological approach to assessing families that takes into account the family's interaction with its environment, as well as its internal structure. Useful tools for ecological assessment include the genogram (McGoldrick, Gerson, & Shellenberger, 1999), the eco-map (Hartman & Laird, 1983), and the Clinical Rating Scale of the Family Adaptability and Cohesion Evaluation Scales (Thomas & Olson, 1993).

Relationship patterns

Along with universal assessment processes that identify strengths, needs, and risks (especially violence) at the individual and family levels, the worker should also consider the general pattern of relationships across generations of the family.

The genogram has particular utility for work with substance abusers (McGoldrick et al., 1999). It is an intergenerational family map (or family tree diagram) that can range from simple to comprehensive. It may be used to display patterns of relationships, functioning, and substance abuse across three or more generations. Family members cooperate in obtaining information about family history and current relationships. The genogram can increase information and focus attention on transmission of substance abuse patterns from one generation to the next. Often, attention to generational patterns is helpful in increasing family members' motivation to work together as they experience a collective challenge and build support for the individual who is engaged in the recovery process. An additional benefit of the genogram is that it counteracts the patterns of isolation and secrecy that characterize families of substance abusers.

Betty's family genogram indicated patterns of disruption in relationships, alcohol use, and stress. Betty's father was an alcoholic who was verbally and physically abusive to her mother. Betty remembers her father yelling at all of the children and often using corporal punishment. "He would hit us with his belt, or a cord, or whatever was handy." Her two older brothers were the most frequent targets of his wrath. Her younger sister was considered the cute one who escaped most often. Betty's mother stayed married to her father until his death in a car accident after Betty turned nineteen. Her mother still lives alone in another state, and Betty talks with her on the phone once a week. Betty suspects that her maternal grandfather was also an alcoholic, but her mother never talked about him much.

Betty's ex-husband Lincoln is Robby and Jim's father. Married shortly before Jim was born, Betty and Lincoln "went through a rocky period ... that lasted ten years" and eventually divorced. Betty says he seemed like a nice guy at first, but he turned out to be an alcoholic. After a while, Betty recognized his behavior as similar to that of her father, and decided to get out of the marriage and take the kids. She divorced him. Betty drank very little until she met Lincoln. From that time on, she began to party with him. As Lincoln's alcohol use increased, Betty began to drink more, and more often. Lincoln stopped drinking after a few arrests for DUI and after he started to lose his sight, but at the time of this assessment, he was very moody and critical of Betty. He had contact with the children sporadically.

Social connections

The eco-map is a diagram that can be used to identify and display the interactions of the family with its environment (Hartman & Laird, 1983). The family is represented by a circle in the center of the diagram and the subsystems of the family's environment are represented by more circles arranged around the family. Examples of subsystems might be church, Alcoholics Anonymous, employment, extended family, peers (both substance-using and nonusing), and the legal system (Kaufman, 1999). Various lines are drawn from the family to each of the relevant social subsystems to depict the strength, quality, and the amount of energy expended relative to what is received. Substance abusers' families generally are socially isolated because of shame. Identifying potential social involvements can be very useful in linking family members to outside resources as they struggle to reorganize their internal interactions.

Betty's family eco-map exhibited social isolation. Her friends from the bar were identified as social contacts that provided her with comfort, but Betty was able to recognize them as threats to her sobriety. Betty's mother, who lived several states away, was depicted as intrusive and critical. The only positive social connections shown on the eco-map were weak links to the children's school, Betty's employment at the university, occasional church attendance, and recent involvement with Alcoholics Anonymous. Conspicuously absent were other subsystems that could promote connection, growth, and health. In conversation with her caseworker, Betty identified the need for additional supportive friends, spiritual development, and time for hobbies and fun. Robby and Jim were excited by the idea that the family could find ways to have fun, such as sledding at the park, and going to church together more often.

Function of substance abuse

Identifying the function of substance abuse within the family is a crucial aspect of family assessment. Understanding what substance abuse accomplishes for the individual and the family will make it easier to intervene effectively (Barnard, 1990). In many cases, substance abuse is an attempted solution to a problem. It is important for the worker to identify the sequence of interactions that maintains the substance abuse, rather than trying to locate its historical causes.

In Betty's case, it was important to recognize that her drinking initially served to connect her with Lincoln. It was a shared activity that put her on the same (inebriated) plane with him. This does not excuse her addiction, but helps explain it.

It was also important for the worker to recognize that Betty used alcohol to cope with stress and reduce her anxiety, such as when she calmed herself with the vodka and tried to get her sons to stop fighting. This is evidence of an attempted solution to a problem that went wrong. Even when her children were removed from the home, Betty continued to use alcohol to reduce her anxiety and maintain control. Although no responsible professional would condone this use of alcohol, it is important to recognize that her drug use represents an attempt to fulfill personal and parental needs. Understanding the function of the substance abuse aided her therapist in helping the family develop suitable replacement behaviors. In Betty's case, it was necessary to support her efforts to reduce anxiety with healthy cognitions and behaviors, as well as to teach Betty more appropriate methods of child rearing.

Cohesion and adaptability

When you focus on family change, it is valuable to identify the interactions that characterize levels of cohesion and adaptability in the family structure. These concepts were first described by Minuchin and his colleagues in their work with families of delinquent youth (Minuchin, Montalvo, Guerney, Rosman, & Schumer, 1967). Substance abusers' families tend to fall in the extreme ranges of both cohesion and adaptability. The family's placement on either dimension is, in part, determined by the progression of the individual disease and the drug of choice. It is important to uncover family patterns and individual preferences for particular substances. Families of active alcoholics, for example, most often present as enmeshed and rigid (Brown & Lewis, 2005).

Enmeshment means that family members are extremely close and emotionally reactive to one another. Disengagement is the opposite extreme, wherein family members have very little emotional connection, or are fragmented and distanced from one another. As noted above, families of substance abusers are often isolated, with limited opportunities to share in mutual understanding. At the same time, they may be stuck in codependent patterns and denial. We may be tempted to view these families as disengaged, but it is probably more useful to focus attention on the family's shared compulsion to think, feel, and act the same way—in codependent interaction with one member's addiction. In a sense, family members collectively share the common experience of isolation. They are compelled to sacrifice their own well-being for the good of the family. Consequently, they embrace the family myth that everything is fine, put on a brave face to the external world, and sink deeply into self-negation.

Adaptability refers to the range of flexibility the family uses in responding to problems or challenges. These families may appear to be essentially chaotic. They exhibit wildly variant control processes along with abortive and ever-changing attempts to solve problems. However, they also may be very rigid. Regardless of their ineffectiveness in actually solving problems, they may exhibit overly powerful controls and use repetitious attempted solutions. In these cases, familiar processes are selected and comfort is drawn from the familiarity. As the therapist, you may find it most useful to focus on the rigid approach to problem solving that limits creative and effective solutions to problems and challenges. A rigid parenting style may show up as repeated threats to hurt children even after these threats fail to control children's behaviors.

To clarify levels of family cohesion and adaptability, you may apply the clinical rating scale developed for the Family Adaptability and Cohesion Evaluation Scales (Thomas & Olson, 1993). This tool is a rating scale that you complete after interviewing and observing the family. It provides clear descriptors of family behaviors for levels of cohesion and adaptability, and can be used to guide your clinical decisions. Determining the family's operations on these two dimensions will help you formulate goals for changing relationships and functioning within the family. For example, in enmeshed families, it will be useful to help individuals find ways to obtain more personal space for their own interests, thoughts, and emotions. In rigid families, it will be helpful to expand the strategies used to provide control for family members and solve life problems.

Betty's family was enmeshed and rigid. Her approach to parenting was highly emotional and reactive. Whenever the boys did anything wrong (like smash frogs, burn toys, or break windows), Betty felt like it was her fault and that she was a bad mother. When this happened, she decided that she had to control them immediately and tried to do so with threats ("I'll kill you") that were generally ineffective. It was clear that Betty's frustration increased as the boys got older and became even less susceptible to her control efforts. Unfortunately, she did not learn new methods of providing effective controls. The patterns of enmeshment and rigid parenting were seen as contributing to the perpetuation of Betty's substance abuse, and the placement of the children in foster care.

Define a Workable Treatment Unit

Family therapy requires that we make some decisions about who to involve in primary therapy, who to engage occasionally, and who to view as outside the process. This is a matter of setting a practical boundary that allows work to progress and to build a sense of accomplishment within the family. Assessment data can help us specify membership in the family and define a workable treatment unit. It is also useful to consider all members of a household as candidates for family therapy, and to consult with family members about who they consider capable of helping to bring about the desired changes.

The primary treatment unit in our example was defined as Betty, Jim, and Robby. Lincoln's membership in the family was recognized, but he was not routinely involved in sessions because he did not reside in the household or have regular contact with any of the primary members. Despite the fact that he exerted notable emotional impact on Betty and the children, his consistent presence in sessions was judged not to be conducive to goal accomplishment. We acknowledged his relationship with Betty and the children in an early session and agreed that he could be included in sessions where his presence would be especially helpful.

Compose a Cognitive Map

Family change is accelerated when you and the family share a clear picture, or cognitive map, of the territory you will cover together. This means that the family develops a useful understanding of the goals and the process of change. The concept of codependency can be used as a powerful conceptual tool to increase understanding of what happens inside the families of substance abusers and to shape efforts toward family recovery. It can be used to help family members make sense of their personal experience, counteract isolation by recognizing that other families have faced similar dynamics, and instill hope that the future can be more satisfying than the past. It is not helpful, however to attribute codependent behaviors to family members. It is more productive to take an exploratory approach, ask family members to describe their experience, and listen for evidence that supports or dispels codependent patterns. If the family describes patterns that are consistent with the codependency concept, then it is appropriate to apply the idea as a means of drawing them together to resolve the challenges they face in reorganizing their relationships (Wegscheider-Cruse, 1989). In doing so, it is important that you provide encouragement to acknowledge and address the relational patterns that the family describes, rather than casting these patterns as unchangeable and universal across all families with chemically dependent members, and beyond the family's capability to change (Levin, 1998). Working from a positive perspective toward change, it is possible help the family to quickly recognize the scope of the problem and the potential solution (Minuchin & Fishman, 1981).

In Betty's situation, it became clear that she and her children were locked into a codependent relationship, and the family was clearly organized around her alcohol use. In the session where codependency was explored, she said, "I see ... we're in it together." The children expressed concern about their mother's frequent headaches and wanted her to be happy. Jim had the role of a parentified child. He watched Robby after school until his mother got home, attempted to keep Robby occupied, and often scolded him for being too loud or doing wrong things. Of course, Jim was not prepared developmentally for this role and, despite his best effort, bungled the job by getting into physical fights with his brother. Robby, according to Jim, acted goofy and would often flop around on the floor in a pretty drastic way to get attention. Robby saw Jim as bossy and, sometimes, mean.

Set Clear Goals

Any application of family therapy requires explicit goals (Haley, 1987). Family work with substance abusers' families in the foster care system, especially, requires clear, realistic, specific, and positive goal statements. Goals should address individual sobriety and family functioning. The following express typical goals:

- The substance abuser will maintain sobriety.
- Family members will use social supports.
- Parent(s) will provide flexible leadership for the family.
- Family members will state intentions and desires directly, but considerately.
- Family members will express a full range of emotions without harming another person.
- Family members will accurately identify challenges, supports, and consequences.
- Family members will use positive coping strategies to manage stress.

- Family members will heal resentments and emotional hurts.

For work with Betty's family, these goal statements were personalized and used to shape therapy. People's names were listed directly in the goal statements (for example, "Betty will maintain sobriety"). Betty and the boys were directly involved in listing the goals, actively engaged in specifying them, and encouraged to view them as realistic.

Encourage Change

During the process of change, family members should be encouraged, connected with resources, and guided to find their own best solutions to the problems they face. Change will advance as the worker respects clients, collaborates with them, and helps them build their own social competence. This process should focus on the following components.

Employ natural community supports

Natural community supports should be in place early for the substance-abusing member as indicated above. These should also be expanded so they are available for other family members. It may be particularly useful for spouses or children to participate in their own 12-step programs, such as Al-Anon or Alateen. It is important to counteract the family's social isolation and to connect members to outside relationships. Spiritual support through organized religion, meditation, or group experiences may also prove to be useful in this regard. Community involvement can also take the form of healthy leisure-time activities. When it is safe for parents and children to interact with each other, it is advisable to encourage fun family activities to engage them with each other in the community.

Betty continued attending Alcoholics Anonymous meetings. She also started to attend church services more regularly, and started to talk with her pastor, who encouraged her to get involved in church activities. The boys enjoyed going to the local Al-Anon Club because of the ping-pong and pool tables. They also liked the cookies that were always there. As Betty's church involvement increased, the boys got involved in separate Sunday school classes and met other children.

Change thinking patterns

Often, thoughts lead to feelings, and feelings direct behavior (Ellis & Dryden, 1997). In situations where people experience unpleasant emotions in repeated patterns, such as the anxiety and shame that are common in substance abuse, it is useful to distinguish the event, the thought, the feeling, and the behavior. New behaviors often emerge when people understand and exercise control over their thoughts. It is important to replace negative self and family cognitions with hopeful, positive, and accurate thinking in a substance abuser's family.

To accomplish this, the worker may use a "three-column technique" (Freeman, Pretzer, Fleming, & Simon, 2004). On a sheet of paper, three columns are headed, "Events," "Thoughts," and "Feelings," and the client is asked to work across the page to describe one sequence at a time. The resultant behavior is also identified. A therapist asks the client the following questions: "When 'X' happens, and you think 'Y', do you feel better or worse? When you feel that way, what do you do? What thought could you have instead that would help you feel better? If you feel that way, what will you do?"

Work with Betty focused on her self-statements and the effect they had on her feelings. For example, misbehavior by the children would trigger the belief that Betty was a bad mother, and then she would feel shame and anxiety. These emotions negatively impacted her parenting. Betty was encouraged to replace the negative thought with one that focused on her ability to be an effective parent. She learned to say "I can do this." As she gained experience with the use of logical consequences, her confidence increased and she felt calmer.

Work with Jim centered on his belief that he needed to be a parent to his mother. He was encouraged to try to trust his mother's efforts. He was cautioned that she might make mistakes, but it was her job to take care of both boys.

Work with Robby centered on his use of immature behavior to distract from the tension in the family. Robby was encouraged to say out loud that he was scared instead of acting too young. Betty was encouraged to respond with recognition of his fear, and reassurance that he would be all right.

Expand and clarify communication

Communication is the process through which people express and experience closeness and distance. Therapy should create conditions that model and support clear, direct, and compassionate communication. Such communication creates opportunities for family members to safely express anger, fear, guilt, shame, and pain, as well as commitment, support, and connection.

In families where emotions are constricted, there may be no existing language for expression of feelings. In such cases, it is helpful for you as a professional to provide the words. Various "feelings charts" are available for this purpose. Such tools list words with different shades of meaning on a page, and arrange them in groups of pleasant and unpleasant feelings. You can orient family members to these charts and refer to them as members search for the right words to express their experience. For young children, it is helpful to use posters of various facial expressions to teach them how to label their feelings.

In order to develop the family's capacity to understand personal and interpersonal meanings, it is useful to practice a communication process in your family therapy sessions. This process involves one member stating a message briefly and clearly. It is helpful to structure the message as a self-statement using the format, "I feel ____, when you ___, because ____." This structure offers a personal statement of a feeling that arises when another family member takes a particular action, and helps minimize defensiveness in the hearer. Another family member then restates the message in his or her own words, and the process continues until the first person is satisfied that he or she is understood. It is generally a good idea to start with the adults if two are available, and include children in the process after appropriate modeling has occurred. You must be active in this process and intervene if the communication becomes hurtful or is misunderstood. It may be easiest for the family to practice with less intense events and feelings at the outset, and move toward conversations about more deeply felt events and more difficult emotions after the process is learned.

With Betty's family, the therapist explained the importance of using words that describe feelings, showed the feelings charts, and set ground rules for talking that included listening to each other and listening to understand. The use of "I-messages"—declarative sentences that start with "I feel ..."—was also taught. Betty, Jim, and Robby practiced using these techniques in family sessions and were given homework to use them between sessions. The content of these conversations focused first on current feelings about current events, such as Betty's experience of stress in her job, Jim's confusion about his role as the oldest brother, and Robby's problems in school. As the process of communication became more comfortable, the therapist encouraged family members to tackle more difficult areas such as Betty's experience in substance abuse treatment and the boys' experiences in foster care.

Address adaptability

In the recovery process, it is important to help families develop the flexibility to change behaviors that were supporting the substance abuse. In early family sessions, codependent dynamics were explored, identified, and used to encourage change. Betty and the boys understood that they would have to play expanded roles in order to improve family functioning and stay together. Betty would have to learn new parenting methods, and these would be enhanced as she better identified what needs her children were expressing through their misbehavior. For example, Robby's disruptive flopping around came to be understood as a need for security, so Betty could provide structure in a loving manner. These new ways of relating were explained as getting free of the old ways and making good things happen together.

In the mid-phase of treatment Betty learned to use behavioral contracts with the boys to specify acceptable behaviors and to encourage them. Responses to their behaviors employed safe, natural, and logical consequences that emphasized a rational and caring parental stance. She was encouraged to remain calm by using her cognitive procedures and to respond deliberately to the children's needs for control, rather than to react out of her own anxious need to take action.

Jim's role as the parentified child was also addressed. He was asked to talk with his mother about his belief that he needed to take care of her and to supervise Robby. Betty was coached to thank Jim for his concern and explain that she was working to become a more effective parent by taking care of herself, staying sober, and learning new ways to be a good mother. As Betty's confidence became stronger, her words became more convincing to Jim.

Address cohesion

Cohesion is addressed by helping family members balance closeness and distance. This can be accomplished by creating a safe environment. A safe environment is one that promotes emotional stability and predictability, calms anticipatory anxiety (the fear that arises when family members sense that the codependent patterns are about to activate), and provides opportunities for expressing feelings while providing space for individual differences. This work includes helping family members set functional boundaries. Such boundaries encourage members to describe their thoughts, feelings, and behaviors. Sharing personal experiences connects family members at the same time that they clarify individual differences between them.

In work with Betty's family, early efforts to address cohesion centered on reducing the level of enmeshment that characterized family interactions. The family therapist recognized that work to help codependent family members become more independent must be balanced with their need to belong. Therefore, the views of the children were encouraged in talks about family business, but

Betty's position as the parent was emphasized and her functioning as an adult was supported. For example, talks between the adults were used to suggest a distinct boundary between Betty and her children. Moreover, even when Betty described her efforts to maintain sobriety, the details of her meetings and her activities were not shared with the boys. Also, discussions of emotions were used to explicitly distinguish the feelings of each family member and to highlight the differences between the various parties.

Later sessions emphasized the emerging strength of the family as a unit that could protect, nurture, and grow independent people who would always have a place to belong. Betty told the children that she would always love them and be available to them. She also shared her dreams that they would be healthy, happy, have good educations, and be successful in whatever areas of life they chose.

Consolidate emotional healing

Although emotional healing is addressed throughout the processes already outlined, it is important to focus directly on it after treatment has progressed to the point that recovery is firm and functioning is orderly. It is useful to hold at least one session that compares each family member's feelings at the beginning of family therapy with those present toward the end of it. By this time, family members generally don't need to use feelings charts and have incorporated words that describe feelings into their vocabulary. Family members can draw two columns on a sheet of paper and list their feelings at the beginning of treatment and at the end. For some family members, it may help to anchor the beginning to some outstanding event so they have an experience in mind, rather than an abstraction. You can then highlight changes and note similarities. Positive changes are identified and amplified. Decisions are then made about the areas that remain.

Another way of centering on emotional healing is to use a forgiveness session. If possible, time the forgiveness session to match the recovering person's steps. Healing in this manner may be most important in cases where there is a substance-abusing partner and a nonusing partner who have elected to stay together. Forgiveness sessions can help family members accept the pain of the past, integrate the pain with a positive present experience, and move beyond it (Enright, 2001; Enright & Fitzgibbons, 2000). If forgiveness sessions are used, it is important to explain that forgiveness is not forgetting, but a way to let go of the pain that another person inflicted. The session is for the person who has been injured by the behavior, not for the benefit of the offender. General steps in forgiving include recognizing the hurt that has been inflicted and the intent that motivated it, expressing regret and apologizing, asking for forgiveness, and granting forgiveness. If you are interested in using this approach it is important to learn the model thoroughly before trying it with a family.

A forgiveness session was not used with Betty's family, because their emotional experience was significantly improved by the end of treatment. Had there been concerns about the children holding grudges about their mother's problem and the problems it caused (such as their removal), a session would have been orchestrated to help them release the impact.

Betty was able to contrast her initial anxiety over parental responsibilities with a new sense of her ability to do the right things most of the time. She described her current state as "pretty peaceful" most of the time, and felt encouraged by her movement. She was proud of her new ability to think positive thoughts and to turn around the shame by recognizing that she had done the best she could and now was doing better.

Jim said that he felt OK about his mother's changes, and this was interpreted to mean that he trusted her ability to be in charge. His fear about again being placed into foster care was subsiding. Robby still communicated his feelings through his behavior more than words. A notable reduction in his flopping around was interpreted to mean that he sensed less tension in the home. He was able to say that he liked being with his mom more now than before.

Check-up sessions

You will find it useful to arrange a series of follow-up sessions after your primary therapy with a family is complete. At a minimum, check-ups at thirty and ninety days are a good idea. Try to conduct face-to-face follow-ups so the actual interaction among family members is evident and each family member's voice is heard.

At the thirty day follow-up, Betty remained sober and reported attending Alcoholics Anonymous meetings once a week. She said that she continued to work her steps and felt like she was developing new sober friendships. Her anxiety level would still rise occasionally, but she was usually successful in calming herself with positive ideas, reflections on her daily performance, and reliance on social support.

Jim occasionally lapsed into his parent role, but would respond well to his mother's gentle reminders that she was in control and that he could be her child. Jim learned to release his belief that he had to control his brother's behavior, and let Robby answer directly to Betty. Robby remained most sensitive to tension levels in the family. However, he rarely engaged in his flopping around, and was responsive to his mother's calm tone of voice and reassurance that she could manage her tasks.

By the time of the ninety day follow-up, Betty remained sober and recognized that she had to work at it each day. The family was going to church every Sunday, and enjoyed their contacts with other families. The boys were getting along like brothers do. There were occasional fights, but no violence. Everyone reported a calm confidence in facing the future.

Summary

It is possible to successfully help families recover from the effects of substance abuse, even in cases where the children have been placed in foster care. As long as the substance-abusing parent seeks recovery, practical changes in daily operations, family organization, and relationships can be realized. Emotional healing is also possible and the children will not need serial placements.

This is challenging therapeutic work. It requires viewing individuals as members of families, and families as members of communities. It also works best when we use an integrated set of interventions, rather than relying on one approach, or hoping that recovery alone will heal the family. This work is also extremely rewarding, because individuals, families, and relationships can be strengthened, and subsequent generations can be protected.

References

Alcoholics Anonymous World Services. (1972). *A brief guide to Alcoholics Anonymous.* New York: AA Grapevine.

Baker, P. L., & Carson, A. (1999). "I take care of my kids": Mothering practices of substance-abusing women. *Gender and Society, 13,* 347–363.

Barnard, C. P. (1990). *Families with an alcoholic member: The invisible patient.* New York: Human Sciences Press.

Beattie, M. (1992). *Codependency no more: How to stop controlling others and start caring for yourself.* St. Paul, MN: Hazelden.

Beck, A. T. (1976). *Cognitive therapy and the emotional disorders.* New York: International Universities Press.

Brown, S., & Lewis, V. (2002). *The alcoholic family in recovery: A developmental model.* New York: Guilford.

Daley, D. C., & Raskin, M. S. (1991). Relapse prevention and treatment effectiveness. In D. C. Daley & M. S. Raskin (Eds.), *Treating the chemically dependent and their families* (pp. 128–171). Newbury Park, CA: Sage Publications.

De Jong, P., & Berg, I. K. (2002). *Interviewing for solutions* (2nd ed.). Pacific Grove, CA: Brooks/Cole.

Dulfano, C. (1992). *Families, alcoholism, and recovery.* San Francisco, CA: Jossey-Bass.

Elkins, I. J., McGue, M., & Malone, S. (2004). The effect of parental alcohol and drug disorders on adolescent personality. *The American Journal of Psychiatry, 161,* 670–676.

Ellis, A., & Dryden, W. (1997). *The practice of rational–emotive therapy* (Rev. ed.). New York: Springer.

Enright, R. D. (2001). *Forgiveness is a choice: A step-by-step process for resolving anger and restoring hope.* Washington, DC: American Psychological Association.

Enright, R. D., & Fitzgibbons, R. P. (2000). *Helping clients forgive: An empirical guide for resolving anger and restoring hope.* Washington, DC: American Psychological Association.

Freeman, E. M. (2001). *Substance abuse intervention, prevention, rehabilitation, and systems change strategies: Helping individuals, families, and groups to empower themselves.* New York: Columbia University Press.

Freeman, A., Pretzer, J., Fleming, B., & Simon, K. M. (2004). *Clinical applications of cognitive therapy.* New York: Plenum.

Gotham, H. J., & Sher, K. J. (1996). Do co-dependent traits involve more than basic dimensions of personality and psychopathology? *Journal of Studies on Alcohol, 57,* 34-39.

Gregoire, T. K. (1994). Assessing the benefits and increasing the utility of addiction training for public child welfare workers: A pilot study. *Child Welfare, 73,* 69–81.

Gregoire, K. A., & Schultz, D. J. (2001). Substance-abusing child welfare parents: treatment and child placement outcomes. *Child Welfare, 80,* 433–452.

Haley, J. (1987). *Problem-solving therapy.* San Francisco, CA: Jossey-Bass.

Hartman, A., & Laird, J. (1983). *Family centered social work practice.* New York: Free Press.

Hohman, M. M., & Butt, R. L. (2001). How soon is too soon? Addiction recovery and family reunification. *Child Welfare, 80,* 53–67.

Jackson, J. (1954). The adjustment of the family to the crisis of alcoholism. *Quarterly Journal of Studies on Alcohol, 15,* 562–586.

Jellinek, E. M. (1960). *The disease concept of alcoholism.* New Haven, CT: United Printing Service.

Kaufman, E. (1999). Family therapy: Other drugs. In M. Galanter & H. Kleber, (Eds.), *Textbook of substance abuse treatment* (2nd ed., pp. 389–400). Washington, DC: American Psychiatric Press.

Koffinke, C. (1991). Family recovery issues and treatment resources. In D. C. Daley & M. S. Raskin (Eds.), *Treating the chemically dependent and their families* (pp. 195–216). Newbury Park, CA: Sage Publications.

Lawson, A., & Lawson, G. (1998). *Alcoholism and the family: A guide to treatment and prevention* (2nd ed.). Austin, TX: Pro-Ed.

Lemert, E. (1960). The occurrence and sequence of events in the adjustment of families to alcoholism. *Quarterly Journal of Studies on Alcoholism, 21,* 679–697.

Levin, J. D. (1998). *Couple and family therapy of addiction.* Northvale, NJ: Jason Aronson.

Liddle, H. A., & Hogue, A. (2000). A multidimensional family therapy for adolescent substance abuse. In E. F. Wagner & H. B. Waldron (Eds.). *Innovations in adolescent substance abuse interventions* (pp. 229–261). New York: Pergamon.

Logue, M. E. (1991). Young children of substance-abusing parents: A developmental view of risk and resiliency. In T. M. Rivinus (Ed.), *Children of chemically dependent parents: Multiperspectives from the cutting edge* (pp. 55–73). Philadelphia: Taylor and Francis.

Madanes, C. (1984). *Behind the one-way mirror: Advances in the practice of strategic therapy.* San Francisco: Jossey-Bass.

McGoldrick, M., Gerson, R., & Shellenberger, S. (1999). *Genograms: Assessment and intervention* (2nd ed.). New York: Norton.

McNichol, T., & Tash, C. (2001). Parental substance abuse and the development of children in family foster care. *Child Welfare, 80,* 239–256.

Minuchin, S. (1974). *Families and family therapy.* Cambridge, MA: Harvard University Press.

Minuchin, S., & Fishman, H. C. (1981). *Family therapy techniques.* Cambridge, MA: Harvard University Press.

Minuchin, S., Montalvo, B., Guerney, B., Rosman, B., & Schumer, F. (1967). *Families of the slums: An exploration of their structure and treatment.* New York: Basic Books.

Peterson, L., Gable, S., & Saldana, L. (1996). Treatment of maternal addiction to prevent child abuse and neglect. *Addictive Behaviors, 21,* 789–801.

Roth, A., & Fonagy, P. (2005). *What works for whom? A critical review of psychotherapy research* (2nd ed.). New York: Guilford.

Rotunda, R. J., Scherer, D. G., & Imm, P. S. (1995). Family systems and alcohol misuse: Research on the effects of alcoholism on family functioning and effective family interventions. *Professional Psychology: Research and Practice, 26,* 95–104.

Seilhamer, R. A. (1991). Effects of alcoholism on the family. In D. C. Daley & M. S. Raskin (Eds.), *Treating the chemically dependent and their families* (pp. 172–194). Newbury Park, CA: Sage Publications.

Seilhamer, R. A., & Jacob, T. (1990). Family factors and adjustment of children of alcoholics. In M. Windle & J. S. Searles (Eds.). *Children of alcoholics: Critical perspectives* (pp. 168–186). New York: Guilford.

Semidei, J., Radel, L. F., & Nolan, C. (2001). Substance abuse and child welfare: clear linkages and promising responses. *Child Welfare, 80,* 109–128.

Smith, B. D. (2003). How parental drug use and drug treatment compliance relate to family reunification. *Child Welfare, 82,* 335–365.

Steinglass, P., Bennett, L., Wolin, S., & Reiss, D. (1987). *The alcoholic family.* New York: Basic Books.

Substance Abuse and Mental Health Services Administration. (2004). *Treatment improvement protocol 39: Substance abuse and family therapy.* Washington, DC: United States Department of Health and Human Services.

Terling, T. (1999). The efficacy of family reunification practices: Reentry rates and correlates of reentry for abused and neglected children reunited with their families. *Child Abuse & Neglect, 23,* 1359–1370.

Thomas, V., & Olson, D. H. (1993). Problem families and the circumplex model: Observational assessment using the clinical rating scale. *Journal of Marital and Family Therapy, 19,* 159–175.

Tracy, E. M., & Farkas, K. J. (1994). Preparing practitioners for child welfare practice with substance-abusing families. *Child Welfare, 73,* 57–68.

Walter, J. L., & Peller, J. E. (1992). *Becoming solution-focused in brief therapy.* New York: Brunner/Mazel.

Wegscheider-Cruse, S. (1989). *Another chance: Hope and health for the alcoholic family* (2nd ed.). Palo Alto, CA: Science and Behavior Books.

Wegscheider-Cruse, S., & Cruse, J. (1990). *Understanding codependency.* Pompano Beach, FL: Health Communication Press.

Wolock, I., & Magura, S. (1996). Parental substance abuse as a predictor of child maltreatment re-reports. *Child Abuse and Neglect, 20,* 1183–1193.

18

Teaching Developmentally Appropriate Parenting

Ann M. Stacks

*S*upervised visitation and extended visits—as opposed to didactic classes—are the ideal opportunities to provide child development and parenting skills for birth parents. You want the parents to develop realistic expectations of their children and the capacity to recognize and respond to their children's cues in an appropriate and timely manner. This chapter describes a four-stage model of developmental guidance to help birth parents accomplish these goals.

We all recognize that optimal development occurs in environments that are stable and nurturing (Herrenkohl, Herrenkohl, & Egolf, 2003). Placement in foster care occurs because households lack these critical traits. Partially because of this lack, foster children demonstrate developmental delay at the following rates (Reams, 1999): personal and social functioning, 14%; adaptive functioning, 17%; receptive language, 8%; expressive language, 15%; cognitive functioning, 23%; and sensory–integration dysfunction, 23%. Many foster children have difficulty regulating their emotions (Klee, Krondstadt, & Zlotnick, 1997; Osofsky, 1995) and distrust others (Osofsky & Fenichel, 1994; Toth, Cicchetti, Macfie, & Emde, 1997). As many as 25% of children in foster care demonstrate clinically significant levels of internalizing behavior and 34% have clinically significant levels of externalizing behavior.

A critical factor in any child's biological, psychological, and social development is the extent to which his or her needs have been accurately perceived and met, in a timely, appropriate, and complete manner. In households where children have been maltreated, their needs presumably are not being met reliably. Maltreating parents have been found to process child-related information differently than do nonabusive individuals (Dopke, Lundahl, Dunsterville, & Lovejoy, 2003). Maltreating parents score lower on test that measure perception and empathy, especially with regard to warmth and compassion for others (Belsky, Rovine, & Taylor, 1984; Frodi & Lamb, 1980; LeTourneau, 1981). They also report more feelings of anxiety and discomfort in response to observing another's negative experience (Albeniz & de Paul, 2003; Milner, Halsey, & Fultz, 1995; Perez-Albeniz & de Paul, 2004; Wiehe, 2003). These parents have a limited ability to perceive their children's needs and feelings (Kropp & Haynes, 1987; Wiehe, 1997, 2003). For example, maltreating parents are more likely to perceive crying as spoiled and manipulative (Zeifman, 2003). They also may respond aggressively or punitively when there is conflict (Azar & Rohrbeck, 1986; Bavolek, 1989).

Foster parents must provide the nurturing climate that may have been lacking in the child's birth home. They must recognize their foster children's needs and requests for nurture and respond appropriately. However, placement in foster care means a change in homes, caregivers, childcare routine, and neighborhood (Herrenkohl et al., 2003). As we have all discovered, these changes can elicit acute emotional and behavioral episodes in foster children, and may also exacerbate any developmental problems (see Chapter 8, "Providing Developmentally Appropriate Family Therapy"). Infants and toddlers in foster care are a particularly vulnerable population. They experience extreme stress prior to placement, which may result in emotional dysregulation, trouble with transitions, regressive behavior, and developmental problems (Fish & Chapman, 2004; Heller, Smyke, & Boris, 2002). Young children in foster care exhibit multiple problems that most foster parents do not anticipate (Heller et al., 2002). For example, some might have odd eating behaviors, such as refusing to eat, hoarding food, or overeating. They may have difficulty staying asleep or sleeping alone. They may have night terrors. Even toddlers may exhibit extreme externalizing behavior such as self-endangerment, indiscriminate sociability, aggression, and sexualized behavior.

Many foster parents do not expect these things and may even have negative reactions and be unable to manage their foster children's symptoms. The children's symptomatic behavior, in turn, may be exacerbated by the foster parents' developmentally inappropriate attempts to set things right (see Chapter 12, "Intervening with Foster Infants' Foster Parents: Attachment and Biobehavioral Catch-Up").

Based on their life experiences with caregivers, children in foster care have learned to expect less-than-positive responses from adults or to behave in ways that elicit such responses (Gauthier, Fortin, & Jeliu, 2004; Stovall & Dozier, 2000). Our challenge as family therapists is clear: Foster care can be a protective and healing experience for young children, but only if the children and their parents—foster and biological—are sensitive to each other's needs and respond to cues for nurture in timely, appropriate, and complete ways. This is a reciprocal process. If they distrust their caregivers, children won't engage in actions with a high probability of obtaining appropriate nurture. In turn, caregivers are likely to respond negatively to children who are avoidant, anxious, or hostile. Foster children need the corrective emotional experience of the present being different from their past experiences. Our job is to educate and coach their birth and surrogate parents to provide this corrective emotional experience. Not all children who have experienced maltreatment and subsequent foster care have poor prognoses, but those who do best have had a stable attachment to a nurturing caregiver (Perry, Pollard, Blakley, Baker, & Vigilante, 1995; Stovall & Dozier, 2000).

Treatment Considerations

A primary goal of intervention for families involved in the foster care system is to decrease family risks and improve the parents' abilities to cultivate opportunities for optimal child development (Schellenbach, 1998). Therefore, almost all birth parents are required to attend parenting classes. However, as you know, these classes have shortcomings. What works best for at-risk families are educational programs that include the parents and children together, focusing on parent–child interaction (Thomlison, 2003). These use modeling, practice, and feedback to improve parenting skills (Geeraert, Van den Noortgate, Grietens, & Onghena, 2004; Kolko, 1996; Liaw & Brooks-Gunn, 1994; MacLeod & Nelson, 2000; Schellenbach, 1998; Thomlison, 2003). In contrast, when parents involved with the foster care system are referred for parent education classes, the courts often rely on community-based classes that are didactic in nature, and have no empirical support for their effectiveness (Huebner, 2002). These programs often rely on cognitive–behavioral or behavioral approaches and take place in a classroom setting. In general, these programs may not be effective because they happen away from the parents' interactions with their children (see Chapter 6, "The Case for Relational Therapy with Young Children in Foster Care"), probably do not address abusive parents' perceptions, interpretations, and evaluations of their children (Milner, 2003; Wiehe, 2003), do not focus on empathy (Wiehe, 1997), and may not be specific to the needs of the unique family (Lee & Lynch, 1998). In fact, what was learned in these classes may have been forgotten by the time the parents and children are reunited (Lee & Lynch, 1998). In addition, most of the services are offered only to parents, despite the evidence that it is the children in foster care who are likely to have devastating developmental issues. It is extremely rare for foster children to receive the developmental assessment and regular screenings that allow appropriate treatment recommendations (Malik, Crowson, Lederman, & Osofsky, 2002).

We need to recognize that families with infants need specialized services. There are many developmental and biological constraints associated with this period of life. If optimal foster infant and toddler development is to be realized, then we need predictable environments with nurturing caregivers who have learned to reinterpret abused infants' behaviors so that they can respond in developmentally appropriate ways (Dozier, Higley,

Albus, & Nutter, 2002; see also Chapter 12, "Intervening with Foster Infants' Foster Parents: Attachment and Biobehavioral Catch-Up"). Research indicates that programs intending to aid abused infants and toddlers should focus on educating parents in the following areas: knowledge of child development, parenting skills, and discipline; mental health treatment; child physical health; parental social support; and community support (Schellenbach, 1998). A secure parent/caregiver–child attachment may be established by addressing all of these interacting parts.

We also recognize the reality of the foster care system. Although parents are referred for educational and other services, many do not follow through with their treatment plans and others fail to make progress. Research has shown that the most noncompliant parents tend to be those who frequently change residence, have serious substance abuse problems, suffer from relationship violence, are involved in criminal behavior, or sexually or physically abuse their children (Butler, Radia, & Magnatta, 1994; Famularo, Kinscherff, Bunshaft, Spivak, & Fenton, 1989). These parents may need interventions that work to stabilize their lifestyles before working on parenting issues (Butler et al., 1994; also see Chapter 2, "An Ecosystemic Approach to Foster Care"). Moreover, families who persistently deny that the abuse or neglect occurred, refuse to accept help, have severe personality or psychiatric disorders, lack empathy, and are severely abusive are the least likely to show improvements as a result of treatment (Jones, 1987). Psychological evaluation of all parents along with consideration of their case histories may help the courts consider treatment plans that are more effective for these families.

Development Guidance

Interventions with the highest probability of success involve improvement in at least four parent–child spheres (Milner, 1993, 2003). They promote increased:

- awareness of children's emotional states;
- accuracy of the perceptions, interpretations, and evaluations of the children's emotional displays and behavior;

- reality-based expectations with regard to children's thoughts, feelings, and behavior;
- knowledge of a range of parenting techniques; and
- capacity to monitor, inhibit, and change one's responses to the children.

Because foster children expect maltreatment, they require nurturing caretakers who have learned to reinterpret abused infants' behaviors so that they can respond in developmentally appropriate ways (Dozier, et al., 2002). Parents need to know about child development and how to nurture those children who are emotionally injured and developmentally delayed. They need to possess a reservoir of good parenting and disciplinary skills, and need to know about and use support services in their community (see Schellenbach, 1998).

Developmental guidance is one approach to meeting these parents' complex educational needs (see Fraiberg, Shapiro, & Cherniss, 1980). It can be an initial step in parent–infant psychotherapy or it may be used in cases when parental psychotherapy is not indicated or is unlikely to be successful. For example, developmental guidance may be used when parents have good parenting skills, but the child's history and developmental status are straining the parents' abilities. Developmental guidance is also recommended when children have developmental problems, or their parents are emotionally or intellectually impaired. When babies exhibit developmental delays and disorders of attachment, and their parents have psychological problems that are distorting their relationship with their baby, parent–infant therapy—which often includes developmental guidance—is indicated (Fraiberg et al., 1980; see also Chapter 6, "The Case for Relational Therapy with Young Children in Foster Care"; Chapter 8, "Providing Developmentally Appropriate Family Therapy"; and Chapter 11, "Creative Ways to Strengthen Family Bonds").

A variety of professionals can engage families in developmental guidance, including therapists, early intervention specialists, nurses, foster care workers, and case supervisors. It is important that the professionals who intervene are trained in observation of child development, especially language and social–emotional development. Service providers who offer developmental guidance must understand how infants and toddlers respond to trauma and be able to recognize mental health issues in biological and foster parents (Azar & Bober, 1999).

Since developmental guidance can only take place where the children and parents are mutually present, it will either take place in your office or during supervised visitation at an agency. Supervised visitation is the way in which the foster care system supports the parent–child bond, and is often a good fit for developmental guidance (Fish & Chapman, 2004). Developmental guidance also may facilitate a less defensive relationship between parents and agencies. Moreover, it also may be a time when court workers observe the parent and child in order to make recommendations to the court. Therefore, doing developmental guidance in the presence of these evaluators may provide education and support a more valid recommendation to the court regarding permanency placement.

Wherever the developmental guidance takes place, your job is to educate the caregivers about the physical and emotional needs of their children. This includes teaching the age-appropriate reactions of children who have been separated from them and who may have established an attachment with an alternate caregiver. Teaching the parents about meeting children's needs includes giving information about nutrition and child development, as well as helping parents secure employment, transportation, and housing. The child's needs are central to the unique education that takes place with each family. The interactions that occur naturally between parents and children prompt the conversations that take place. These conversations are between the parents and you, on behalf of the children. They are intended to highlight a child's experience, increase the parents' empathy, and make the parents aware of their own psychological obstacles to appropriate responsiveness to the child (Lyons-Ruth & Zeanah, 1993).

The following program of developmental guidance involves four stages (Fraiberg et al., 1980; Lyons-Ruth & Zeanah, 1993; Milner, 1993; Stovall & Dozier, 2000).

Referral

In the first stage, referral, the caseworker presents you with several things: The family's history with child protective services and foster care; demographic information for parents, foster parents, and children; and any medical history that is available. It is important that families are referred to the program as soon as possible, so that a proper assessment and recommendations regarding scheduling of parent–child visitations can be made.

Between the first and second meeting, you observe the children in the foster home and in their childcare settings, if available. You pay special attention to each child's attachment behaviors, withdrawal, and developmental progress relative to normative benchmarks. You also ask the foster parents about these areas. The biological parents will be observed with their children during their next supervised visitation session.

Introduction and Assessment

In this stage, you contact the parents to explain the program and set up a time to meet at your office. It is important that this initial meeting take place outside of the foster care agency to assure confidentiality and allow the parents to see you as a helping person who is separate from the foster care system. During the first meeting, the parents are given the opportunity to share their perspectives regarding the removal of their children and provide a detailed medical history and a description of their own childhoods. The parents also provide information about the children's personalities, likes, dislikes, and schedules. They are asked to share their personal hopes and dreams, and those they have for their children. The respect we show them at this stage serves as the foundation for building a good working relationship. In this meeting, you also can get an initial sense of the parents' ability to accurately perceive the circumstances surrounding the removal and to reflect on their own history. Finally, you can obtain information regarding the parents' values that can be used during play-based interventions.

Developmental Assessment

The third stage may take place during supervised visitation at the child welfare agency or at your office. The parents are asked to arrive 45 minutes early to complete questionnaires regarding their level of stress, psychiatric symptoms, empathy, parenting beliefs, and medical history. When their children arrive, the parents help you administer a developmental assessment that measures each child's progress in each domain of development. We like to use the *Ages and Stages Questionnaire* (Bricker & Squires, 2006). The results of the developmental assessment, parent self-report measures, and similar surveys completed by the foster parents are used to make a treatment plan. This information also is used in making a recommendation to the court regarding developmentally appropriate services for the child, including recommendations concerning frequency and duration of developmental guidance sessions.

Parent–Child Developmental Guidance

This stage lasts for approximately six months. In weekly one-hour sessions, the parents and children interact in a room that resembles a family-type setting equipped with developmentally appropriate toys. You, the parents, and the children generally all sit on the floor. But very little interaction takes place between you and the children unless it is initiated by them. With the parents' permission, the visitation may be video-recorded to facilitate discussions surrounding successful visits.

We have found it helpful to begin each session talking about one domain of development and providing parents with a colorful handout describing what they can expect from each of their children at that particular stage of development. There are two very good sources for these handouts: *Partners for a Healthy Baby Home*

Visiting Curriculum (www.cpeip.fsu.edu/books/cfm?assetID=74) and *Healthy Families, San Angelo* (www.hfsatx.com/curriculum).

This portion of the session lasts approximately 10 minutes. After this, you watch the parents interact with their children and you comment on the children's attachment behaviors and developmental accomplishments. Questions regarding a child's intentions, thoughts, or feelings, and behaviors are posed to the parents and occasionally you offer suggestions regarding what the child might want. In doing that you sometimes might speak for the baby (for example, "Mom, I get really frustrated when you won't let me knock down your tower. I like to knock it down because it helps me to understand that my actions cause something to happen."). You also pay close attention to the child's reaction to the parents' emotions and gestures. Then you can draw the parents' attention to the child's positive and negative responses. You always interpret a child's behavior within a developmental framework and take into consideration the child's history with the parents. Parents are also advised about what kinds of behavior and feelings are typical for children who have experienced separation from their parents, and counseled about ways in which they may comfort their children.

Following each parent–child session, you and the parents meet to discuss their feelings about the session, their perspectives about the children's progress, and any issues surrounding relationships with family or significant others, or employment, or the court treatment plan—anything in the parents' emotional environment that may be impacting their ability to relate to their children during the parent–child interaction sessions.

After six months of developmental guidance, the third stage, developmental assessment, is repeated and the parents and foster parents complete the same surveys. You also observe the children with their parents, with their foster parents, and in their childcare settings. That way you can make notes regarding the children's developmental progress and their attachment behaviors with all of their important adults. On the basis of these observations, you make recommendations to the foster care worker regarding continued treatment and permanency planning.

Throughout treatment you collaborate with the other community agencies that are working with the children, biological parents, and foster parents. No doubt, many of your parents have also been referred to individual therapy and substance abuse treatment. They probably also are required to maintain suitable housing and employment. It is especially important that you maintain regular contact with those professionals who provide services to the foster families, for example, speech and language therapists, occupational therapists, public health nurses, and physicians. Maintaining these connections increases the probability that the children will consistently receive nurturing care in high quality, stable environments.

Case Example

Stage 1—Referral

Seven-month-old Sarah was removed from her biological mother, Bette, at birth. Bette's parental rights had been terminated three times previously and it was assumed by all parties at the child welfare agency that her parental rights with Sarah would be terminated shortly after birth. Sarah was placed at birth with the Alden family, who had fostered her older sister (now 3 years old) from her birth until age two. The Alden family was led to believe that it would be impossible for Bette to gain custody of Sarah and that foster care would just be a formality. However, at the six-month hearing, the judge agreed to allow Bette to have visitation based on her lawyer's argument that she was progressing in therapy at a community-based domestic violence shelter.

At the time of the referral, the foster care worker explained that Bette's two oldest sons were removed seven years ago, when they were 5 and 7. According to the case file, the boys had been exposed to domestic violence between their mother and father (who is the father of all four of Bette's children). The boys had also been picked up by the police on several occasions. Each time they were wandering outside, inappropriately dressed, near a busy city street in the winter. The boys were finally placed in foster care when neighbors reported to the police that the children were seen hanging out of an attic window. When the police arrived, the children were found locked in an attic that was covered in human waste. They had not been fed or bathed. At the time of their removal, Bette explained that she had to leave town. She allegedly left the boys locked in the attic so that they would not run in the street and get hurt. At the time of Sarah's referral, both boys were living in specialized foster homes and had severe emotional and behavioral disorders.

Bette's third child, Bailey, was born four years later and visitations were progressing well. Bette had decided to leave her abusive husband, Mark. Just before the court was to recommend unsupervised visits, Bette began seeing Mark again and then she began living with him. During her one of her last visits, she attempted to hand Bailey out the window to Mark.

The foster care worker knew that we only accepted families who had recently been referred to foster care. But she was certain that the judge was going to give custody of Sarah back to Bette and she wanted Bette to have the skills to care for Sarah.

Stage 2—Introduction/Assessment

At Bette's first meeting, she reported that the foster agency was out to get her because they didn't like Mark. She said that she really liked her lawyer and the judge who were helping her with Sarah's case. They believed in her and could see that she had changed as a result of her involvement in counseling at the local domestic violence shelter. Bette explained that, after she lost custody of Bailey, she left Mark for good. She recognized that she had given Mark too many chances.

When the therapist asked Bette about the circumstances under which her sons were removed, she reported that her sons were wild like their dad and would take off their winter clothes when they were playing outside. "They loved to play outside with the neighborhood kids," she explained. "Sometimes I would notice that it had gotten dark and they had not come in the house." Bette reported that they were so wild when they were in the house that she was happy to have them play outside. She said that they usually played outside between four and six hours a day. Bette reported that she missed her older boys, but she had heard that they were doing well in school and had a lot of friends. She expected that they would come to live with her again once they turned 18.

When asked to describe her relationship with Sarah, Bette reported that Sarah was the smartest of her four children. She liked to dress Sarah in the new outfits that she bought her, but was upset that Sarah cried at the visits. She surmised that the foster mother was undermining the visits because she could not have children of her own.

Stage 3—Developmental Assessment

Prior to the developmental assessment the therapist observed Sarah at her foster home and during her supervised visit with her mother. When the therapist arrived at the Alden home, Mrs. Alden informed her that she had invited a family member to play with the children so that she could share some information with the therapist that she did not share with the children. She reported that Sarah's development was progressing well and that she was an active and affectionate baby. Her only concern was that Sarah would be returned to her biological mother.

Mrs. Alden explained that she would not have fostered Sarah if she knew that there was a possibility of her returning to Bette. In fact, her experience working with Bette, when Bailey was in foster care, had been very difficult. Mrs. Alden was aware of Bette's parenting history, and she and her husband had considered adopting Bette's two boys when they adopted Bailey so that the siblings could stay together. However, they soon changed their minds. "When we visited those boys we knew that having them in our home would put Bailey and our animals in danger." The boys had each been kicked out of several foster placements and their current foster parents had to keep their kitchen locked at night so that the boys wouldn't steal food or take the knives. Mrs. Alden's eyes filled with tears as she tried to explain what the boys had gone through when they were young. "How could a judge let that woman have access to children? What will happen to my sweet little Sarah if she lives with that woman? How will I explain to Bailey why her sister doesn't live here and why she can't see her?" The therapist reflected Mrs. Alden's feelings and agreed that these feelings and questions needed to be addressed. She suggested that another member of the program work with Mrs. Alden, Sarah, and Bailey on a bi-weekly or monthly basis and that this person would be part of a "team" to understand how Sarah develops best.

After their private conversation, Mrs. Alden and the therapist went downstairs to the playroom. Sarah was sitting next to her aunt who was showing her a picture book. When Mrs. Alden walked through the doorway, Sarah pointed at her and smiled. Sarah turned to the therapist and stared blankly at her. Mrs. Alden introduced Sarah and Bailey to the therapist and explained that she was there to watch their family play. Throughout the play session, it became clear that Sarah was thriving in the foster home and was developing a secure attachment to Mrs. Alden. She explored the room in Mrs. Alden's presence, went to her when she pinched her finger, and was able to be comforted. Sarah also used vocal signals to gain assistance and let Mrs. Alden know that she wanted her to join in her favorite game of peek-a-boo.

A very different picture emerged when the therapist observed Sarah and her mother, Bette, during a supervised visitation. Sarah was sleeping when the caseworker brought her into the visitation room. Bette picked Sarah up out of her car seat, kissed her fore-head, and shook her gently. "Wake up and see your mommy, Sarah," Bette said in a gentle tone. When Sarah did not respond, Bette continued to talk to her softly and began undressing her, changing her diaper, and putting her in a new dress that she had brought. When Bette removed her diaper, Sarah woke up and began to cry. Bette tried her best to console Sarah, but Sarah's cries became more fierce. After Sarah had cried for several minutes, Bette put her back in her car seat. Sarah cried herself to sleep. As soon as Sarah was asleep, Bette picked her up, and shook her gently to wake her. Sarah began to cry. Bette tried to hold her in several positions and she walked her around the room. Eventually she sat in a rocking chair with Sarah, who was screaming, cradled in her arms. Bette seemed to "check-out" at this point. She stared into space as if she couldn't hear Sarah screaming. After several minutes the caseworker who had been supervising the visit went into the room to help. She took Sarah from Bette's arms and held her close. Sarah calmed down almost immediately.

Two days later Bette arrived at the clinic, filled out the required surveys and then helped administer the developmental assessment. Sarah did not score in the "of concern" range on most domains of development. However, after seeing her in the foster home, it was clear that she did not perform to her potential. Sarah did not vocalize during the assessment, which is a minimum language requirement for a child between 4 and 7 months of age. She did not go to Bette when she was upset, initiate social contact, or become upset when a toy was taken from her. These are considered to be minimum requirements for coping behavior.

Bette and the therapist met after Sarah had gone home. The therapist asked Bette if she thought that Sarah's performance was an accurate reflection of her abilities. Bette insisted that it was. Bette reported that the visits at the clinic seemed to go better than they did at the child welfare agency. She cried as she described the visit that had taken place at the agency two days before and admitted that visit was pretty typical of her visits with Sarah at the agency. "Every time they bring her to me she is asleep. How am I supposed to show them that I can be a good parent when she is sleeping? I want to play with her and dress her up, but she is always sleeping." She accused Mrs. Alden of giving Sarah cold medicine to make her sleepy and manipulating the visits so that Sarah would cry. The therapist agreed that this must be very frustrating for Bette. It did not give her an appropriate chance to form a relationship with Sara and it was disruptive to Sarah to have a visit during a time period that was designated for a nap.

Stage 4—Parent–Child Developmental Guidance

Developmental guidance sessions were scheduled two times a week for 90 minutes. The first 60 minutes were scheduled playtime and the last 30 minutes were spent processing the play session. Prior to the first session, Mrs. Alden asked if she could come early to play with Sarah at the clinic so that she could ease Sarah into the new schedule. Sarah played comfortably with Mrs. Alden for 40 minutes and cried for her when she left the playroom. The therapist was able to comfort Sarah before Bette arrived. When Bette entered the playroom she was very excited to see Sara rocking on all fours and babbling. She picked up Sarah and kissed her, which made Sarah cry. The therapist asked Bette why she thought Sarah was crying and Bette explained that Mrs. Alden had trained Sarah to cry whenever she saw Bette. The therapist told Bette that she could certainly understand how she might feel this way, but that there were other reasons why Sarah might be crying. They could talk about these after Sarah became used to her new environment and calmed down. The therapist then helped Bette try different calming strategies. Eventually they discovered that Sarah could be calmed when she was held facing away from Bette and distracted by a puppet on Bette's hand. Bette seemed pleased that she was holding Sarah and was able to use the puppet to engage her.

After the play session the therapist and Bette talked about how good it felt to have positive interactions with Sarah and how difficult it can be to learn how to comfort a baby. The therapist praised Bette for trying many things and eventually being successful. She also normalized Bette's suspicions about Mrs. Alden and then took the opportunity to share some information about the cognitive and emotional development of a 7-month-old infant. "Sarah's experiences with you have only been once a week when her body needs to sleep. She also does not have a very good memory and could be scared when she wakes up in an unfamiliar place with someone who to her might seem like a stranger. It is very unfortunate that your relationship has started this way and we are going to work hard to help Sarah have enjoyable times with you more frequently. Our first step was changing the time of her visit with you and allowing you to see her more than one time each week. It is common for infants in foster care to react to their parents this way and it is very common for parents to feel very upset." Bette and the therapist discussed strategies that she might use to lessen Sarah's fear during the next visit.

Three months after her referral to the program, Bette and Sarah's interactions had improved. Bette entered the playroom and greeted Sarah from a distance. She then drew nearer to Sarah, watched her play, and waited patiently for Sarah to approach and share her toy. Although Sarah seemed to tolerate the session and began to interact with Bette, it was with much reservation. She expressed very few emotions even when she was proud of accomplishments such as releasing a cube into a cup or standing on her own. Bette brought a healthy snack for Sarah, as she did every week, and then changed her diaper. The therapist noticed that when Bette changed Sarah's diaper, Sarah laid on the floor appearing to be frozen, with wide eyes. She did not look at her mother or vocalize during the diaper change. The therapist recognized that this was a possible indication of fear. Although Bette had made some improvements in her parenting, she still could not accurately perceive Sarah's emotional states.

In the last three months of treatment the 30-minute periods following the play sessions were devoted to reflection on how Bette's past had influenced her. The therapist began to ask Bette to reflect on how she had grown as a parent since her sons had been removed. Bette reported that her parenting had not changed, and that it did not need to be changed. She also reported that her parents were very supportive of her efforts to regain custody of Sarah, and that they were her primary source of support. Bette said that her parents would provide childcare when Sarah was returned to her.

At her initial meeting with the therapist Bette had reported that she wanted Sarah to feel loved and that she was an important part of her family. She said that this was something that her own family had done especially well. In the fifth month of treatment the therapist reminded Bette of her wish for Sarah and asked her some of the ways in which she had been made to feel special as a child.

Bette remembered a neighborhood family who played board games together. They sat and watched Bette play with their children, and asked her questions about herself. As Bette began talking about her family she revealed that her parents actually never paid that much attention to her. They sometimes made her feel special when they bought her pets—she received a new pet every year. But every year, Bette's father would get angry with her for something, which resulted in Bette, her pet, and her father taking a ride in the car. Bette's father would drive until they reached an empty field or a patch of forest. He would then put Bette's pet outside of the car and drive away. "It must have been so hard to lose so many pets that you loved," the therapist reflected. Bette admitted that it had made her very sad, and that to make up for it, she had been taking care of stray animals since she moved out of her parents' home. Bette's description of her parents seemed incongruent with the examples she gave of her parenting style.

Stage 5—
Recommendation to the Court and Case Discussion

After six months of developmental guidance, Bette was able to play with Sarah in an appropriate manner. She reflected Sarah's actions, brought her age-appropriate toys and snacks, and applauded Sarah's developmental accomplishments. She reported that she felt much closer to Sarah and that their relationship had improved. While it was true that the climate of their visits had improved, there was a clear distinction between Sarah's behavior with her foster family and with Bette. Sarah's behavior during developmental guidance was indicative of her continued fear of her mother. She did not show her affection, did not approach her for help, and did not display positive or negative emotions in the session. Bette would not consider the possibility that Sarah was distressed by these visits and that she could adjust her parenting to help Sarah cope. And Bette's defensiveness and inability to reflect on the consequences of her behavior were not limited to Sarah. Bette also was not able to openly reflect upon the mistakes that she had made with her three older children, how her relationship with Mark had affected her and the children, or how her family history might have influenced her and her parenting. Bette's individual therapist reported that their conversations had remained superficial for 18 months and that Bette continued to describe her relationships with her family of origin, with Mark, and with the children in a glorified manner. Because we did not have evidence that Bette could reflect upon her situation, or that she could be empathic in regard to Sarah's needs, we ultimately recommended that Bette's parental rights be terminated.

Although, on the surface this does not seem like a success story, ultimately it is. Sarah remained with her sister and the family with whom she had formed a secure attachment and was developing appropriately. Bette was given the opportunity to build a relationship with a child whom she would never raise and now has positive memories of the time that they spent together. Some of the greatest tragedies in foster care occur when children must be returned to foster care because the birth parents have not been given an appropriate chance to form a relationship with their children, or when the children are separated from an attachment figure and returned to a home that is unsafe. One of the most difficult parts of working in child welfare is knowing that whatever you recommend, your decisions will hurt someone—a parent, foster parent, or child. Without our program, the judge and the child welfare agency would not have had the evidence they needed to make the best decision for Sarah. To date, Bette is the only parent who has completed our program and has not had her child returned to her. We are confident that we made a very difficult, but appropriate recommendation.

References

Albeniz, A. P., & de Paul, J. (2003). Dispositional empathy in high and low risk parents for physical child abuse. *Child Abuse and Neglect 27*, 769–780.

Azar, S. T., & Bober, S. L. (1999). Children of abusive parents. In W. K. Silverman & T. H. Ollendick (Eds.), *Developmental issues in the clinical treatment of children* (pp. 371–392). Needham Heights, MA: Allyn and Bacon.

Azar, S. J., & Rohrbeck, C. A. (1986). Child abuse and unrealistic expectations: Further validation of the Parent Opinion Questionnaire. *Journal of Consulting and Clinical Psychology, 54,* 867–868.

Bavolek, S. J. (1989). Assessing and treating high-risk parenting attitudes. *Early Child Development and Care, 42,* 99–112.

Belsky, J., Rovine, M., & Taylor, D. G. (1984). The Pennsylvania Infant and Family Development Project: III. The origins of individual differences in infant–mother attachment: Maternal and infant contributions. *Child Development, 55,* 718–728.

Bricker, D., & Squires, J. (2006). *Ages and Stages Questionnaire (ASQ): A parent-completed, child monitoring system* (2nd ed.). Retrieved December 18, 2006, from http://www.brookespublishing.com/store/books/bricker-asq/.

Butler, S. M., Radia, N., & Magnatta, M. (1994). Maternal compliance to court-ordered assessment in cases of child maltreatment. *Child Abuse and Neglect 18,* 203–211.

Dopke, C. A., Lundahl, B. W., Dunsterville, E., & Lovejoy, M. C. (2003). Interpretations of child compliance in individuals at high- and low-risk for physical child abuse. *Child Abuse and Neglect 27,* 285–302.

Dozier, M., Higley, E., Albus, K. E., & Nutter, A. (2002). Intervening with foster infants' caregivers: Targeting 3 critical needs. *Infant Mental Health Journal 23,* 541–554.

Famularo, R., Kinscherff, R., Bunshaft, D., Spivak, G., & Fenton, T. (1989). Parental compliance to court-ordered treatment interventions in cases of child maltreatment. *Child Abuse and Neglect 13,* 507–514.

Fish, B., & Chapman, B. (2004). Mental health risks to infant and toddlers in foster care. *Clinical Social Work Journal 32* (2), 121–140.

Fraiberg, S., Shapiro, V., & Cherniss, D. S. (1980). Treatment modalities. In S. H. Fraiberg & L. Fraiberg (Eds.), *Clinical studies in infant mental health: The first year of life* (pp. 49–77). New York: Basic Books.

Frodi, A., & Lamb, M. (1980). Child abusers' responses to infant smiles. *Child Development, 51,* 238–241.

Gauthier, Y., Fortin, G., & Jeliu, G. (2004). Clinical application of attachment theory in permanency planning for children in foster care: The importance of continuity of care. *Infant Mental Health Journal 25,* 379–396.

Geeraert, L., Van den Noortgate, W., Grietens, H., & Onghena, P. (2004). The effects of early prevention programs for families with young children at risk for physical child abuse and neglect. *Child Maltreatment 9,* 277–291.

Heller, S. S., Smyke, A. T., & Boris, N. W. (2002). Very young foster children and foster families: Clinical challenges and interventions. *Infant Mental Health Journal 23,* 555–575.

Herrenkohl, E. C., Herrenkohl, R. C., & Egolf, B. P. (2003). The psychosocial consequences of living environment instability on maltreated children. *American Journal of Orthopsychiatry 73*, 367–380.

Huebner, C. E. (2002). Evaluation of a clinic-based parent education program to reduce the risk of infant and toddler maltreatment. *Public Health Nursing 19*, 377–389.

Jones, D. P. H. (1987). The untreatable family. *Child Abuse and Neglect, 11*, 409–420.

Klee, L., Kronstadt, D., & Zlotnick, C. (1997). Foster care's youngest: A preliminary report. *American Journal of Orthopsychiatry, 67*, 290–299.

Kolko, D. L. (1996). Individual cognitive behavioral treatment and family therapy for physically abused children and their offending parents: A comparison of clinical outcomes. *Child Maltreatment, 1*, 322–342.

Kropp, J. P., & Haynes, O. M. (1987). Abusive and nonabusive mothers' ability to identify general and specific emotion signals of infants. *Child Development, 58*, 187–190.

Lee, R. E., & Lynch, M. T. (1998). Combating foster care drift: An ecosystemic treatment model for neglect cases. *Contemporary Family Therapy, 20*, 351–370.

LeTourneau, C. (1981). Empathy and stress: How they affect parental aggression. *Social Work, 26*, 383–389.

Liaw, F., & Brooks-Gunn, J. (1994). Cumulative familial risks and low-birthweight children's cognitive and behavioral development. *Journal of Clinical Child Psychiatry, 23*, 360–372.

Lyons-Ruth, K., & Zeanah, C. H. (1993). The family context of infant mental health I: Affective development in the primary caregiving relationship. In C. Zeanah (Ed.), *Handbook of infant mental health* (pp. 14–37). New York: Guilford Press.

MacLeod, J., & Nelson, G. (2000). Programs for the promotion of family wellness and the prevention of child maltreatment: A meta-analytic review. *Child Abuse and Neglect, 24*, 1127–1149.

Malik, M., Crowson, M. M., Lederman, C. S., & Osofsky, J. D. (2002). Evaluating maltreated infants, toddlers, and preschoolers in dependency court. *Infant Mental Health Journal, 23*, 576–592.

Milner, J. (1993). Social information processing and physical child abuse. *Clinical Psychology Review, 13*, 275–294.

Milner, J. S. (2003). Social information processing in high-risk and physically abusive parents. *Child Abuse and Neglect 27*, 7–20.

Milner, J., Halsey, L., & Fultz, J. (1995). Empathic responsiveness and affective reactivity to infant stimuli in high- and low-risk for physical child abuse mothers. *Child Abuse and Neglect, 19*, 767–780.

Osofsky, J. D. (1995). The effects of exposure to violence on young children. *American Psychologist 50,* 782–788.

Osofsky, J. D., & Fenichel, E. (Eds.). (1994). *Caring for infants and toddlers in violent environments: Hurt, healing, and hope.* Arlington, VA: Zero to Three National Center for Clinical Infant Programs.

Perez-Albeniz, A., & de Paul, J. (2004). Gender differences in empathy in parents at high- and low-risk of physical abuse. *Child Abuse and Neglect, 28,* 289–300.

Perry, B. P., Pollard, R. A., Blakley, T. I., Baker, W. L., & Vigilante, D. (1995). Childhood trauma, the neurobiology of adaptation, and "use dependent" development of the brain: How "states" become "traits." *Infant Mental Health Journal 16,* 271–291.

Reams, R. (1999). Children birth to three entering the state's custody. *Infant Mental Health Journal 20,* 166–174.

Schellenbach, C. J. (1998). Child maltreatment: A critical review of research on treatment for physically abusive parents. In P.K. Trickett & C.J. Schellenbach (Eds.), *Violence against children in the family and community* (Chap. 10). Washington, DC: American Psychological Association.

Stovall, K. C., & Dozier, M. (2000). The development of attachment in new relationships: Single subject analysis for 10 foster infants. *Development and Psychopathology, 12,* 133–156.

Thomlison, B. (2003). Characteristics of evidence-based child maltreatment interventions. *Child Welfare, 83,* 541–569.

Toth, S. L., Cicchetti, D., Macfie, J., & Emde, R. N. (1997). Representations of self and other in the narratives of neglected, physically abused, and sexually abused preschoolers. *Development and Psychopathology, 9,* 781–796.

Wiehe, V. (1997). Approaching child abuse treatment from the perspective of empathy. *Child Abuse and Neglect 21,* 1191–1204.

Wiehe, V. R. (2003). Empathy and narcissism in a sample of child abuse perpetrators and a comparison sample of foster parents. *Child Abuse and Neglect, 27,* 541–555.

Zeifman, D. M. (2003). Predicting adult responses to infant distress: Adult characteristics associated with perceptions, emotional reaction, and timing of intervention. *Infant Mental Health Journal, 24,* 597–612.

19

"Ready or Not, Here I Come!" Equipping Families for Transitions

J. Matthew Orr and Rachel Brown

Current policy no longer allows children to linger in foster care. *This chapter discusses what therapists can do to equip families for the transition of children from the foster family to the birth or adoptive family. We first identify the central issues that must be resolved and provide a framework for conceptualizing the phases of this transition. We then provide a case example that illustrates how therapy can help the various systems involved resolve the identified transition tasks.*

Eventually the foster children with whom you are working will be sent back to their birth parents or placed for adoption. Granted, some middle adolescents may be considered for supervised independent living, but we are assuming that most of your foster cases are children younger than middle teenagers. We who work with children in foster care are faced with many complex issues that are not easily explained by specific theories or traditional interventions. This is one of them.

Current policy requires a search for and transition to a permanent placement. The challenge is to provide for the welfare of the children in foster home placements—which are likely to be temporary—while also helping the children's birth families to eventually be able to adequately care for them. As a result, when a judge orders that the child be returned to the birth home or placed for adoption, what are we supposed to do?

In this chapter, we talk about how to equip children's caregiving systems for the transitions involved with moving children from the foster family to the birth family or to an adoptive family. We first address the nuts and bolts of what needs to be done with each of these family systems to enable them to successfully manage the transition effectively and, above all, to create an environment that promotes safety, stability, and security in the children. We then provide a case example to illustrate how this conceptual framework is applied, and discuss its indications and limitations.

In order to be useful, this chapter must be understood in the context in which we wrote it. First, we assume that you have a basic understanding of attachment theory and its implications on development. If not, we recommend the book by Levy and Orlans (1998), which offers a thorough introduction to attachment and the issues related to disrupted attachment processes (see also Chapter 6, "The Case for Relational Therapy with Young Children in Foster Care"; Chapter 8, "Providing Developmentally Appropriate Family Therapy"; and Chapter 12, "Intervening with Foster Infants' Foster Parents: Attachment and Biobehavioral Catch-Up"; all are chapters in this book). Second, this chapter will focus on what the foster and birth/adoptive families need to do to meet the demands of the transition from foster care to home. We will consider what these families must do to meet the socioemotional needs of these children in general. We assume that any existing mental or physical health needs of an individual child and family will be receiving ongoing clinical attention. These needs should be considered in the context of the framework provided here. Third, given the complexity and intensity of the issues related to working with multiple systems and relationship dynamics, we believe that family therapists play a critical role in foster care. However, we also recognize and appreciate that professionals on the front lines of foster care represent a wide array of agency roles and may be interested in learning about this therapeutic process. All of you comprise our audience.

Conceptual Framework

We first discuss concepts and issues that should be considered when assessing the assets and needs of families. This discussion

includes two concepts—expectations and buffers—that play important roles in the foster, birth, and adoptive families' processes during
this period. We also identify and discuss particular concepts that
relate specifically to each family system. Second, we outline three
phases that frame the transition from foster home to permanent
placement—anticipation, preparation, and adjustment.

Assessment

Expectations

At the outset of the transitional process it is imperative that we assess
what the various families expect from each other, the child, and the
participating social service agencies. Knowing what the individual
members expect from the rest of the system will help us understand
their actions and their decisions. For example, foster parents and
birth parents each have ideas about how children should be raised.
Their ideas often do not match and this can create a chaotic emotional atmosphere for children (see Chapter 9, "An Integrative
Approach Involving the Biological and Foster Family Systems").

You may wonder why it matters what the foster parents expect
regarding parenting, if children are going back to their birth parents. It matters because it is a critical element of the intervention
process. As will be discussed below, it is essential to the stability
and security of children that they experience as much consistency
in their routine as possible. It is our experience that expectations
often translate into standards for living, which encompass not only
the daily routine but also the types and levels of financial and
social resources provided to the child. Therefore, we need to determine what kinds of expectations and standards the foster family
has of themselves and their children. We want to know if these
standards are reasonable, whether the type and level of the standards are within the means of the birth family, and if the birth
family will be able to maintain them. Some birth or adoptive families might even perceive that foster family expectations were set
too low and that the children have been underachieving.
Conflicting expectations must be addressed from the outset.

Buffers

In a perfect world, children could be inoculated against the potential stressors and chaos that occur in an unhealthy psychosocial environment. Because the world is not perfect, we have the foster care system that attempts to isolate children from the potential harm these environments can cause. However, the reality is that children cannot be isolated from the relationships and the emotional contracts (in other words, attachments) formed with their birth families. Current policies no longer allow children to linger in foster care. Agencies are pressured to return children home as quickly as possible. This can promote more contact with biological caregivers and other family members through visitation, but it does not prevent children's exposure to the patterns of behavior and relationships that led to their foster placement in the first place. In these cases, the foster home becomes a mere respite—a shelter from the storm—which acts as a buffer against the unhealthy functioning in their birth home.

When you are working with families during this final transitional period of foster care, it is vital that you identify and promote any properties, characteristics, or relationships in the children's psychosocial milieu that can act as buffers against potential harm. This involves identifying protective factors not only for the child, but also for the parents. The idea is to assess the whole family system to identify not only what properties or characteristics may serve a protective function, but also those factors that represent potential liabilities to healthy family functioning. One common example of this is when you identify and institute active buffers against undue stress and relapse for a parent who is recovering from a substance abuse problem. This concept is discussed further below.

Identifying buffers or protective factors is often easier than promoting them. For instance, children may make great strides in their social–emotional development in foster care, especially if they have been with the same family for a substantial period of time. We must be able to identify the environmental factors that have been helpful in the child's development, and then seek to integrate them, as appropriate, in the next home environment. We must also assess everyone's level of comfort with contact between foster and birth or adoptive family. This can range from a situation where the various adults have never been introduced, to one where the adults have regular contact in each other's homes. Furthermore, at times we may identify some of the same birth parent problems that were concerns to the social service agency or the foster parents. This may cause the birth family to perceive you as judgmental and make addressing those issues all the more difficult.

Routines

One of the more challenging issues of the transitional period is the need to surround the children with as much consistency and certainty as possible. Daily routines established in the foster homes are difficult to transport intact to the birth home. Instead, we must assess the routines to determine which of their qualities and characteristics seem most helpful for the children. We can then help the birth or adoptive families create helpful routines that fit within their capacities.

Routines are more than scheduled events. They involve important issues such as parenting style, family rituals, and maintaining established relationships with foster families and with the friends made during foster care. Many times children form strong attachments to the family and friends gained during their stay in foster care. In order to foster security and stability during the transitional period and beyond, we believe that these relationships should be maintained as much as possible. Birth families who allow these relationships often find that this conveys the kind of security and adaptability children need to promote their own security and sense of self. Of course, the intensity and focus of these relationships may not be the same as during foster care. But we need to help parents give their children permission to maintain these relationships without feeling as though they are betraying their parents. We can help families gauge the amount and duration of this contact depending on the individual needs of each child. The needs of the identified child must be primary. However, ongoing contact between child and foster family is likely to be beneficial to the foster family in supporting their ability to continue to provide loving, but temporary, care to children under extraordinary stress.

Your emphasis should be on the permanence of relationships and not the permanence of placement. Foster care workers seek to identify placements that will allow children to have as permanent a residence as possible. What gets lost in this effort is the tremendous need for all children to be exposed to permanent relationships. We must continually remind other professionals of the importance of maintaining established relationships for children, no matter how difficult they may be to negotiate with all of the people involved (see Chapter 5, "Ambiguous Loss: A Key Component of Foster Care").

Another important relationship is the one between the children and their schools. Among all of the changes that children experience during foster care, one that agency workers are often able to keep constant is the school children attend. This is important, given the amount of time that children spend in school and the opportunities it gives them to engage in age-appropriate activity. The predictable nature of daily school routines provides a sense of certainty for foster children. Consequently, teachers can contribute a great deal to the intervention milieu through their constant interaction with these children. We can help families promote an open line of communication with teachers and staff and help the parents develop a sense of competence and confidence in dealing with academic and social school issues.

Family rituals comprise activities and traditions that are symbolic, and from which family members derive meaning regarding personal and family identity. Traditions include birthdays and holiday celebrations. But weekly activities such as movie night, pizza night, and church dinners, also can play a major role in providing children with a sense of connection and belonging in the family. This can help children overcome feelings of rejection or disloyalty. We can assess families for the existence of these rituals and educate them about their potential usefulness.

Triggers and Warning Signals

Clinical issues that must be assessed and addressed include the circumstances within the birth family system that led to the removal of the child. This issue is complex because it involves not only getting rid of those circumstances, but also preventing their return. For example, there is a strong association between child maltreatment and parental alcoholism and drug problems (Jung, 2001; Miller-Perrin & Perrin, 1999). It is imperative that agency professionals work together both to identify the systemic antecedents to such problems and find ways to intervene in them effectively (see Chapter 17, "'We're in It Together'—Family Therapy Where Substance Abuse Is a Problem"). Veterans in this field know that is not enough to simply require that parents complete drug and alcohol education classes or complete drug counseling. To truly provide a protective buffer within the family and between the family system and the outside world, it will take the involvement of a systems-savvy therapist. It is our task to help the family negotiate its way through its psychosocial milieu, including the social service agencies.

Birth families must feel safe to ask for help with problems without fear that their children will be removed. This is true no matter what the problematic issues are. This is why a family therapist should be involved as a point person during the transition from foster home to permanent placement. The families are not as likely to view us as part of the child welfare agency, although they must understand that we work in collaboration with them. Birth families often experience crises during the transitional period but are afraid to ask for help because they fear that they will be punished for having problems and their children will be taken away again. If we provide a safe context for the family in which the limits of confidentiality are clear, we can help these families learn the triggers that precipitate maladaptive behavior and the warning signals that the behavior may be happening again. This helps families gain a sense of control over their situation, increased responsibility in managing crises, and the ability to effectively communicate when they need help.

Concerns Specific to the Three Types of Families

The foster family

We must be sensitive to the needs of foster families regarding the potential feelings of loss associated with foster children being moved back home (see Chapter 5, "Ambiguous Loss: A Key Component of Foster Care"; Chapter 9, "An Integrative Approach Involving the Biological and Foster Family Systems"; and Chapter 12, "Intervening with Foster Infants' Foster Parents: Attachment and Biobehavioral Catch-Up"). It is not uncommon for foster parents and foster children to develop secure attachment relationships to each other. This can make the process of "letting go" difficult, or even traumatic. If such an attachment exists it is likely that the child will experience grief and will need support. At the same time the foster parents, while supporting and celebrating a positive outcome to their task, may be grieving the departure of a loved child (who may be going to a risky setting), while they still must support the siblings left behind.

The birth family

Child development is the most elementary concept in this framework (see Chapter 8, "Providing Developmentally Appropriate Family Therapy"). It informs all the other aspects because it points directly to the needs of the child. We include this concept because it is our experience that issues related to basic child development are often overlooked as children are transitioned out of foster care. That is not to suggest that the issue is neglected. It is just that we become very focused on the logistic and pragmatic issues related to moving children from one placement to another. As a result, little time is spent assessing what the families who are receiving the children actually understand about children's basic needs relative to their developmental stage. For example, many of us have focused on behavior management strategies as the primary target in birth families. Although this focus may have been very appropriate, it may mean that an important educational component was omitted—one that might have taught the parents about antecedents to child behavior or how parents' responses could help promote security in their parent–child relationship.

Many agency professionals are inadequately trained in the area of child development. If we see that this is the case, we need to be sure that developmental issues are being considered. There are too many issues to name and discuss here, but it is essential that children's development, in general, be made a primary focus from the outset. One important concept for foster children is that of the transitional object (Winnicott, 1987). We are all familiar with the tendencies of infants and toddlers to suck their thumbs, carry around blankets or teddy bears, or perhaps demand to wear a certain article of clothing to bed. If it appears that children become obsessed with these items, then these items may have become the objects that children use to soothe themselves in times of stress or discomfort. Older children often use cards, games, puzzles, videos, action figures, or drawing tablets to provide a sense of security in their anxious worlds. Essentially, the transitional object of the child is a relationship over which the child has control and can determine its permanence. We must allow for these types of objects, because children use them to manage their anxiety and adjust to the chaos around them.

Parenting styles encompass not only the strategies and techniques parents use to discipline their children, but also the extent to which they can comfort and soothe their children in an age-appropriate manner. It is not our intention in this chapter to advocate a particular model or method of parenting. We believe that there is a range of appropriate and effective parenting approaches. The key is to work with parents to help them to be able to nurture and teach (that is, discipline) their children in a manner that promotes more positive parent–child interactions than negative ones.

The adoptive family

The practical issues we have discussed above in regard to birth families—routines, relationships with schools, rituals, and parenting styles—are also relevant for adoptive families. Many people assume that, with adoptive families, many of the more clinical issues have been assessed and addressed in order for them to qualify for adoption. However, it is still necessary to assess adoptive families for their preparedness for the transitional period, a matter that involves collaboration with the multiple systems discussed earlier. Most of the issues that are more specific to adoptive families relate to the concept of leaving room—this refers to the delicate process of creating boundaries within and around the family, so that the children can:

- maintain relationships with people with whom they have strong ties;
- grieve the loss of their birth and foster families; and
- develop an appropriate attachment to their adoptive parents

Some adoptive families seem to have a difficult time with the idea that they may need to involve a family therapist during the transitional period and beyond. One foster mother admitted, "I guess it's just that I know how he was treated by his biological parents, and I didn't expect to have to be the one that had to go to therapy because of it." We can pave the way for a more smooth transition by helping adoptive parents and siblings understand the intensity of the feelings and cognitive perceptions that adopted children have. This is especially true of older children who are more likely to remember their experiences prior to adoption.

We recommend that adoptive parents become involved in an adoptive parent support group, preferably before the child comes home. These groups can help ease the transition by providing opportunities for parents to engage in catharsis, receive troubleshooting tips, and develop an overall sense of community and contact with others who can relate to this unique parenting experience. From a clinical standpoint, it is often useful to assign movies or books (fiction or nonfiction) that families, especially those with older adopted children, can discuss together. This provides a forum for important topics that may otherwise be left untouched because of emotional insecurity, fear of hurting another family member's feelings, or reticence to be disloyal to someone. We do not recommend one book over another. Rather, we believe that you should make your selections according to the topic about which you are trying to stimulate discussion. This is as much about your personality and style as any other aspect of intervention. The point is to be creative!

Goals and Strategies

The general goal during the final transitional stage of foster care is to successfully resolve the issues and complete the tasks discussed earlier. The strategies used to achieve that goal will vary depending on your approach and the unique circumstances of each situation. However, there are typically three phases—anticipation, preparation, and adjustment—that comprise this transitional period and form the context in which these issues must be addressed.

Three Phases of Transition

Anticipation

The anticipation phase is that time when members of the various families begin to start thinking (more than just sporadically) about the child going home. Theoretically, this phase can begin during the beginning of the foster care placement and continue throughout. This phase is marked by stress and the anxiety of not knowing what will happen next. Even with the help of a treatment plan and goals that outline what needs to happen for the child to return home, there are likely to be difficulties.

At this point, you may not be involved unless there are adjustment problems or mental health issues that have been previously identified. However, as the conversation among the parents and professionals begins to turn toward completing the treatment plan and moving the child out of foster care, you will probably be needed to help promote the stability and permanence of relationships no matter with whom the child may be placed.

There are three goals of the anticipation phase:

- Join with the members of the various families.
- Identify stable parent–child relationships and/or develop them.

- Get to know the children and their environments, especially watching for temperament, attachments, transitional objects, and routines.

It is tremendously helpful if we observe the children in their natural environments, such as at home and at school. If this is not possible, then we can watch them play in our office while the parents also observe. This way we and the parents can identify and share information about the meaning of behavior patterns as they happen in front of us (see Chapter 18, "Teaching Developmentally Appropriate Parenting"). Our goal is to educate the parents about the basic developmental needs of their children and the appropriateness of their children's and their own behavior.

As we work with these families we must get to know them without aligning with one family over another. It often takes time for each family to trust that we have their best interests in mind. This is understandable given that foster families are often skeptical of the birth families' ability to care for the children, and the birth families are often quite guarded about talking to us if they know we are also involved with the foster family. Joining appropriately involves helping the families realize that our primary focus is on the welfare of the children.

Preparation

The preparation phase typically begins when a specific plan for a child is made by the agency or by the court, when the treatment plan is nearing completion, or when the court intends to place the child for adoption. There is a marked increase in the intensity of planning toward that specific end and, accordingly, in everyone's emotion. This defined focus allows us to offer more of an organized therapeutic effort. The previous phase had been marked by a general flavor of joining and trust building. Now our essential task is to prepare the foster and birth/adoptive families for the transition. We want these families to be seen by the child as operating collaboratively in a stable fashion.

One major strategy for accomplishing this is to institute family rituals designed to mark the passage from the foster family to the birth/adoptive family. We recommend that you help the foster families create a memory box, photo album, or scrapbook together with the foster child. The value in doing such an activity lies in the process of putting the product together, with the essential ingredient being the child and foster parents discussing the meaning of the items. The child will be able to take this memory box with him or her and pull it out as desired. This will give the child a sense of control and an outlet during distress during the transition. Furthermore, the foster parents should also make their own memory box together with the child. This will help to continue the permanence of the relationship (assuming it is positive). The child will see that he or she is important enough to the foster parents that they want to remember and, perhaps, continue the relationship.

For the birth and adoptive families, this phase must involve the establishment of routines that allow for them to identify with and occupy a specific position in the family. These include daily routines, but, more importantly, they should also include meaningful rituals. For example, these families may institute a pizza and movie night every Friday. That will give the children something to anticipate and it promotes a sense of belonging and family identity. The simplest routines quickly become meaningful rituals on which the children learn to depend as buffers to stress and anxiety. In the case of adoption, you should help your foster families, and later the adoptive families, assist the children in resolving the loss of (and often feelings of rejection by) their birth families. This may come in the form of creating a scrapbook, writing letters, drawing pictures, or any other creative activity preferred by the children.

The key is to equip the families to be able to help the children externalize their thoughts in a manageable way. They must understand that there will be times when children will want to talk about what they think and feel, and times when they will want to just go outside and play. Parents must learn the art of giving children room to ask questions and express themselves, no matter how choppy or unclear, without pressuring them for more information or offering advice. Children often want to release just a little bit at a time. When parents allow children to spout off about "whatever," it goes a long way toward helping the child feel safe and secure and makes it more likely they will continue to express themselves.

Adjustment

The adjustment phase encompasses all of the action and emotion that follows the bang of the judge's gavel. This phase is the dance between you and all of the different systems involved: The birth family, foster family, child, school, agency, and adoptive family. It can last indefinitely, because it involves every level of functioning in every system involved. You must help the birth and adoptive families establish clear boundaries, not only to develop an organized structure and identity that includes the "new" children but also to leave room for appropriate relationships with the foster family and friends. You may find this challenging because the newly formed family often wants to hunker down and be rid of all of the outside influences.

During this phase it is essential that you help the birth families come up with a system for communicating their needs to you, especially about the triggers and warning signals they discovered in the preparation phase. Birth families often do not want to ask for help because they are tired of having to deal with "all of those people." However, you must help them understand that it is better to deal with any problems through therapeutic means, before harm occurs and removal of the children is threatened. If you are dealing with an adoptive family, your focus is also on establishing communication between them and you.

Whichever family receives the child, you want them to accept the reality that they are not expected to know how to handle every situation. You can help these parents understand that asking for help is not a sign of incompetence. You can also help these families maintain the healthy relationships that the children have with people outside of their family, such as with the foster family. This is a major challenge because—although the families may have been willing to discuss and imagine the maintenance of these ties before—when the child actually comes home the idea can lose its luster and the hunkering-down effect tends to take hold. You can take some responsibility for keeping these relationships active where they are appropriate.

Case Examples

We will give you two illustrative case vignettes. The first is very detailed and describes a complex case wherein a child is being returned to his biological family. The second, briefer, vignette highlights some differences when a child is placed for adoption.

Return to Biological Parents

Tommy (three years old) was home when his mother, Carrie, stabbed his stepfather, John, in the hand with a steak knife during an argument. John received a deep cut and needed stitches to sew it up. The neighbors called the police when they heard the fight, and when the officers arrived, they believed that Tommy was in imminent threat of harm and they placed him in protective custody. He was placed with foster parents, Sara and David, who had sons ages eleven and eight. The following discussion outlines the process of preparing these families for the transition of Tommy out of foster care.

Anticipation phase

The family therapist became involved three months into the placement when it was time to set up visitation with Carrie and John. They had attended the anger management and parenting classes ordered by the court, and it became clear to the caseworker that the parents were set on completing the treatment plan and regaining custody of Tommy. Thus, the anticipation phase was in full swing and the agency wanted a family therapist to work with the families in order to facilitate a smooth transition to home. Further, the staff were concerned that Carrie and John needed more than the parenting classes to be able to care for Tommy effectively and appropriately.

The family therapist began by assessing both the foster family and the birth family for their strengths and needs according to the framework discussed above. He met with the foster family and Tommy to observe, interact with, and ask questions about him in the relational context in which he was living. It appeared to the therapist that Tommy had grown accustomed to the foster family's routines and had developed a meaningful connection to his foster brothers. Sara and David also appeared to allow Tommy to talk about his mother and stepfather. They encouraged him to so without offering judgments.

Then the therapist conducted a separate interview with Tommy together with his birth parents, Carrie and John, to get to know them as a family. He paid special attention to the parent–child interaction. By this time, Tommy was four years old, and his parents had just informed him that they were pregnant and that he was going to have a little brother. He seemed excited about this. Moreover, the therapist observed that Tommy was appropriately engaged with his parents and that they attended to him in an age-appropriate manner. One other session was completed with Carrie and John. It focused on identifying the triggers and warning signals for the explosive disagreements to which they were prone. Carrie indicated that much of their difficulty had been about money. Things improved when she started working. Their income increased and she perceived herself to be more structured and organized.

However, soon Carrie and John began to miss appointments. The therapist later explored this issue with the caseworker and it appeared that Carrie and John had become complacent because they had been allowed to coordinate their visits with Tommy directly with the foster parents. Since these visits were one to two days long, Carrie and John thought this arrangement meant that they no longer needed a therapist.

Preparation phase

The beginning of the preparation phase for both families was signaled when the agency let the foster and birth families coordinate their visitation schedule. It also marked the end of their cooperation with the therapist and with each other. After that, neither family attended the therapy sessions on a regular basis and the caseworker began receiving complaints from each family regarding the uncooperativeness of the other. She directed them to the therapist to work through the matter. In the next session, Carrie and John expressed their extreme displeasure with the process and declared that they did not need help. They felt that, when the agency gave them responsibility for arranging visitation, it was a vote of absolute confidence in their abilities. They further proclaimed that they were suspicious of the therapist, since the therapist talked about the same issues regarding parenting and child development that Sara—the foster mother— would try to discuss with them during their conversations. Simply put, Carrie and John felt ganged up on.

Sara admitted to the therapist that she was being deliberately uncooperative because she was having what she termed an "intense moral conflict" with the custody arrangement. She revealed that her cousin, a mother, had recently died after a long struggle with cancer. This had caused her to question the justice in her cousin's children losing their "great loving and caring" mother while "Carrie treats her son the way she does." When asked to further elaborate, she made known her suspicion that Carrie was using marijuana and beer during her visits with Tommy at their house (by Tommy's report). The therapist spent a couple of sessions working with Sara and her husband around this issue. Their discussion included recognition that their expectation that Tommy would be going home at some point in the near future was activating feelings of loss and grief in them. They agreed to work on a memory box and elicited the help of their sons and Tommy. They reported that it was quite a positive experience and that both Tommy and the family had a box.

The therapist reported concern about Carrie's possible drug use to the caseworker and the caseworker pursued it. In fact, Carrie admitted to using marijuana on a regular basis but denied using it around Tommy. At about the same time, the caseworker informed the therapist that Tommy's biological father, Mike, had been located and was living about two hours away. By now, Tommy had been in the care of the foster family for almost a year, and had little contact with his father prior to that. According to the history given by the caseworker, Mike and Carrie had never been married and Carrie made it difficult for him to participate in Tommy's life during the first year. Once each of them got married, Mike was afraid that Carrie would sabotage his marriage and he decided to keep his distance for a while. He was only able to negotiate a few weekends with Tommy over the next two years. During the period when Tommy was in foster care, Carrie never informed Mike about what was going on for fear that he would try to intervene.

In fact, this is exactly what happened when Mike made a call to social services to complain about Carrie withholding Tommy from him. Mike wanted custody of Tommy and he took legal steps to petition the court. Therefore, in the spirit of the framework presented here, it was imperative that the caseworker involve Mike in the therapeutic process.

It was clear to the therapist that Mike was in preparation mode. He had complete faith that the court would obtain evidence of Carrie's erratic and impulsive pattern of behavior and award him custody. This was despite his own past complacency regarding his lack of visits with Tommy. Still, the therapist spent time joining with Mike, his wife, and his mother who was a source of support for the couple. The therapist made it clear that he was not involved as a custody evaluator and that, as the family therapist, his sole role was to help Tommy and his family construct an adaptive environment and make the transition out of foster care as smooth as possible. This resonated with Mike. He described how he had changed his own life over the last couple of years and became more responsible and family-minded.

Several sessions followed with Mike, Tommy, and Beth, Mike's new wife (and Tommy's potential stepmother). In these sessions, the therapist observed Tommy playing and eliciting the participation of his parents in much the same way that he did with the other sets of parents. The therapist's focus was on affirming the adults' awareness of Tommy's needs in general, and the meaning of his behavior, specifically. Time was spent discussing plans for establishing routines and maintaining established relationships. For example, this family had established a ritual of going to a particular pizza restaurant on the weekends they had Tommy with them. Tommy was still with the foster parents Sara and David during the week, and the family maintained contact with the therapist. Sara reported that Mike was cooperative and checked in on Tommy frequently. Tommy's visits with his father increased to four days a week. During this time, Carrie began attending outpatient drug and alcohol treatment on a consistent basis and her visitation sessions were reinstated at every other weekend. The therapist became involved in helping Carrie and Mike and the stepparents communicate effectively about Tommy. He emphasized that it was crucial that Carrie and Mike set aside any personal differences to focus on Tommy's need to be surrounded by secure and stable relationships.

The family seemed to accomplish this for the most part, so the therapist was needed less. He received updates from the caseworker who reported that Sara maintained her concerns about Carrie as a mother. While Mike appeared to be putting forth his best effort, he also became complacent and was less cooperative in communication with Carrie and Sara. However, Carrie and Sara believed Mike to be providing a secure home environment for Tommy. The situation was made more clear when Mike's petition was heard before the court and he was awarded sole physical custody, with Carrie getting regular visitation. This was a decision that no one expected. It moved the process into the adjustment phase.

Adjustment phase

The therapist began working with the family system again to address several adjustment issues: The grief of the foster family in losing Tommy; Mike and Beth getting used to full-time parenthood; Carrie's frustration and disappointment about losing full custody of Tommy; and the need for Mike and Carrie to develop an effective co-parenting relationship. First, the therapist helped Mike and Beth understand the importance for Tommy to maintain contact with his foster family. This was especially important given the close connection that he had formed with his foster brothers, who offered positive models for him. He visited them once or twice a month.

Next, the therapist worked with Carrie about her disappointment and anger that Tommy had been taken from her. Little headway was made, and Carrie was reactive and uncooperative. In fact, most of the parenting in their home came from John because Carrie worked most weekends when Tommy was there. However, the situation improved when Carrie learned that she was pregnant. According to the caseworker, Carrie then seemed to become more satisfied with the visitation schedule and her interactions with Tommy were more pleasant and adaptive.

Mike and Beth continued to bring Tommy in for "booster" sessions once a month for six months following the transition home. The therapist addressed their consistent concerns about Tommy's preoccupation with a superhero shirt that he had to sleep in every night, as well as his insistence that they eat pizza every Saturday. This opened the door for discussing transitional objects and rituals and their importance in helping Tommy soothe himself in an age-appropriate manner. This gave Mike and Beth insight into some of Tommy's other behaviors, such as rough play and sassy talk, when he returned from visits to the foster parents' home or his mother's home. Mike and Beth began to understand that Tommy used these to discharge tension. The therapist helped them develop a system in which Tommy was required to do 10 minutes of release time after his visits. He was told that he could do nothing else until he did something to release his tension, such as draw, yell, run around outside, or sit quietly. This eventually lost its novelty and Tommy was able to adjust after his visits fairly quickly without disrupting others.

Outcome

The six months following the placement with the father proved to be productive. The foster family was able to maintain a connection due to Mike's belief that it was good for Tommy. Tommy began kindergarten, which gave him other positive routines in which to engage. The busy schedule this created for him, Mike, and Beth—who were also expecting another child—provided additional buffering from the chaos that seemed to engulf Tommy in his mother's home. Carrie and John maintained a tenuous relationship and neither parented much in their home. Carrie's mother stepped in often to take care of their infant son as well as Tommy during his visits.

For a time, Tommy had bouts of tantrums and defiance when he returned from visits with his mother. It appeared that her interactions with him were limited to times when he misbehaved and needed to be disciplined. Tommy conveyed a sense of giving up on his mother, and complained about visiting her. There was little Mike could do at that point except petition the court for full custody. However, he believed that if he did so, Carrie would be much less flexible with the visitation schedule and would even pull further away from Tommy. The therapist sought help from the caseworker to get Carrie involved again in therapy; if not with him, with another therapist. But there was little anyone could do to encourage her participation.

Consequently, the therapist addressed this issue by working with Mike and Beth to institute buffers against the maladaptive mother–child relationship. They followed through on the release time ritual and started a new ritual in which they allowed Tommy to pick out a game, movie, or other activity that the family could do together to foster a sense of light-heartedness and low pressure following each visit. This seemed to help Tommy adjust. Mike and Beth also got Carrie's mother to visit Carrie when Tommy was scheduled to be there. She became the primary caregiver to Tommy when he was at his mother's house. Tommy also continued his monthly visits with the foster family. These became less frequent over time as each family became more engrained in their regular routines. The last time the therapist spoke with family members about Tommy, he was in second grade and doing average to above-average work. He was playing T-ball and soccer, and his parents believed that he adjusted well to most situations.

Adoption

In the case of adoption, there is additional work to which therapists must attend. It is plausible to assume that if Tommy's father had not stepped into the picture and his mother continued to deviate from the treatment plan (essentially disobeying the court order), Tommy would have been placed for adoption. But then he would have to deal with the reality that he would not be going home and the associated feelings of loss, rejection, and/or abandonment.

For example, Juan, a 9-year-old boy, was placed in foster care after his mother and her boyfriend were arrested for narcotics trafficking. After a couple of months, he learned that she was going to be released from detention because she agreed to testify against the boyfriend. Juan realized that she would have to complete a series of requirements ordered by the court before she could regain custody of him. However, this never happened. The mother never completed any of the requirements on the treatment plan and moved to another state. Other family members were contacted but none felt they could care for Juan. After several more months, the mother signed a Termination of Parental Rights agreement and Juan was placed for adoption. One focus of treatment with him was to nurture the relationships that had been established within the foster family, who might adopt him. However, the greatest work centered on Juan's feelings of rejection by his mother. He was keenly aware that, if she had tried, she could have regained custody of him.

Although the therapist talked with Juan one-on-one and assigned him activities such as storywriting and drawing to promote self-expression, the most important work was reinforcing the foster parents as a buffer. That is, the foster parents facilitated Juan's grieving process by helping him create a memory box. They did this only when he asked, and this helped to promote a sense of control on his part. They further fostered a sense of security in him by allowing him to continue life as usual—going to school, playing sports, playing with friends—without pressuring him to either remember or forget his mother. The family developed a system whereby no one was to bother Juan for 30 minutes if he was exploring his memory box. If he needed more time he would ask for it. If his homework was finished, Juan could spend as much time as he wanted with the box. If it was not finished, then he was limited to one hour with the box until the homework was done. After one month, Juan was visiting the box as a way to diffuse stress. He eventually replaced this with other solitary activities such as drawing, juggling a soccer ball, or playing video games. This type of approach is critical to fostering security in children who are placed for adoption upon being abandoned by their parents. They are desperate for a sense of control in response to something so devastating over which they have felt powerless. If they are given prosocial and adaptive outlets they will be less likely to develop maladaptive patterns of behavior. The central unit for accomplishing this task is the family.

Discussion

This chapter has described a framework for helping families constructively manage the transition when children move from foster care to a permanent placement. It is a highly complex undertaking because you must work with several different family systems to create an environment that fosters adaptive growth and development. We did not try to offer a cookbook recipe approach. That would presuppose an unrealistic amount of uniformity among all of the family systems with whom you will work. Instead, we provided an outline of the essential tasks that must be completed and the general issues that must be resolved, when working in the final stage of foster care—the transition to a permanent home.

The framework described here does not address many of the mental health problems often associated with children in foster care. However, it does provide many of the basic building blocks necessary to working with all children in foster care and the families involved in the final transition. Still, you must be aware of the potential challenges that diagnosable disorders—such as oppositional–defiant disorder, attention deficit hyperactivity disorder, major depressive disorder, and posttraumatic stress disorder—place on the milieu, and you must be prepared to address them either through treatment or referral. This includes parents with disorders as well as children.

This framework also does not explain in detail about how to collaborate with schools, physicians, or other larger systems. However, you and the other child welfare professionals must consider them as part of the child's interpersonal world. Therefore, you must develop the knowledge and skills necessary to collaborate effectively with these systems, because they potentially offer vital support in the intervention approach. They may also obstruct progress if concerns related to them are not addressed (see Chapter 2, "An Ecosystemic Approach to Foster Care").

The most important thing we can do for the children is to promote safe and stable environments that are based on permanent secure relationships. These relationships promote adaptive behavior and healthy child development. However, the transition out of foster care can be one of the most difficult times to maintain or establish these relationships. This conceptual framework can help you facilitate this important process.

References

Jung, J. (2001). *Psychology of alcohol and other drugs.* Newbury Park, CA: Sage.

Levy, T. M., & Orlans, M. (1998). *Attachment, trauma, and healing: Understanding and treating attachment disorder in children and families.* Washington, DC: Child Welfare League of America.

Miller-Perrin, C. L., & Perrin, R. D. (1999). *Child maltreatment: An introduction.* Newbury Park, CA: Sage.

Winnicott, D. W. (1987). *Through paediatrics to psycho-analysis.* London: The Hogarth Press.

20

"But I Don't Trust You" Recognizing and Dealing with Parents' History of Trauma: The Story of Amy

Kathleen Burns Jager

The personal traumas experienced by the birth parents involved in foster care often keep them from adequately using services meant to be supportive. These individuals have been disappointed by family members, other significant members of their social network, and their communities. There is an ongoing breech of trust and connection. This chapter gives examples of this and describes approaches to removing these barriers.

Many birth families involved in the foster care system have a multigenerational legacy of trauma, oppression, and loss. As you have discovered, parents accused of maltreating their children may themselves have been maltreated in past or current relationships. Consequently, they have learned to distrust other people, including those who society has designated to protect and help them. Their negative views no doubt have been magnified by their current experiences with the authorities associated with having their children removed (see Chapter 14, "'It Isn't Right!' The Need to Redress Experiences of Injustice in Child Abuse and Neglect"). Once their children are in foster care, you are expected to offer these parents and children supportive therapy, namely: resources, hope, and healing. You probably have discovered that your efforts are been thwarted by obstacles such as distrust, crises, and other daunting problems. In fact, your fellow therapists may expect that these families will change very little over time (Boyd-Franklin & Hafer Bry, 2000). If you are not going to accept such a poor prognosis for the families referred to you, you need to discover how you can begin to facilitate trust, connection, and empowerment in spite of these challenges.

Much of what you need to consider is incorporated in the family-based services movement. This movement also is known as family preservation services, community-based services, or home-based services. In seeking to provide a viable alternative to out of home placement for children, family-based services therapists have learned about how to engage alienated families in order to develop family strengths (Pecora, Fraser, Nelson, McCroskey, & Meezan, 1995). They gain acceptance by focusing on the families' own choices for change and by helping them discover, appreciate, and expand their adaptive resources. This collaborative and strengths-oriented orientation makes it possible for distrusting families to address those factors that place their children at risk for removal (Koren, DeChillo, & Friesen, 1992).

Best practice advises us to find solutions that work in one setting, and then see if they apply in a closely related one. In this arena, the idea would be to take what works with defensive families—who are at risk for losing their children—and to apply it to families one step removed—those whose children are already in foster care.

The Central Role of Trust

"Empowerment," in the sense of improved individual and family functioning, can be an appealing goal for parents who themselves have experienced traumatic abuse and who perhaps are parenting children with special needs. These victimized individuals must appreciate and accept the role of the community if they are to gain the power needed to influence their environment. Therefore, it is essential that we explore how parents' experiences of trauma have affected their experiences of getting help for their families and children through family-based services. They need knowledge of what external support is available, trust that they will not be disappointed or harmed, skill in forming working alliances, and a sense that they can bring about positive change in their lives. These traits comprise the foundation of individual and family resiliency (Walsh, 1996).

Unfortunately, traumatic abuse experienced by birth parents can lead to situations requiring child removal in two ways. First, the parents' traumatic memories of their own maltreatment as children can make them operate in a continual crisis mode. This distracts them from their pain and channels and discharges anxiety (Boyd-Franklin & Hafer Bry, 2000). Second, having themselves been victimized, any sustaining bonds between these adults and their communities are destroyed (Herman, 1997). As a result they often have a poignant personal sense of disconnection, loss, and disempowerment. These attitudes may become associated with their current significant others, potential significant others (including you), and the social systems in which you both are embedded (for example, the child welfare system). Moreover, caught up in a multigenerational abuse cycle, parents may abuse their children, collude with others who abuse their children, fail to protect their children from abuse, or simply be too depleted to care for their children (Walker, 1999). However, we therapists should not view trauma experience as simply a deficit. In the in-depth study of 16 abused mothers now involved in a family-based services program described below (Jager, 2002), I came to appreciate how individuals', couples', and families' capacity to survive trauma can bolster their realistic self-esteem and highlight individual and group strengths.

Working through the hurts and losses that parent–survivors have felt and continue to feel may help parents be more empathic towards their children (see Chapter 6, "The Case for Relational Therapy with Young Children in Foster Care"). However, in my study, I came to recognize that, for many survivors of abuse, empowerment also requires working against beliefs and behaviors that are supported by or embedded in current social structures (Koren, DeChillo, & Friesen, 1992). These include unequal distribution of power and resources, exacerbated by sexism (Heflinger & Bickman, 1996; Jager, 2002; Vanderslice, 1984). It is important to address gaps in services that do not acknowledge these particular obstacles to empowerment that survivors of traumatic abuse may face.

Assessment of the Family Empowerment Process

I explored the family empowerment process for mothers who have survived traumatic abuse and who were participating in family-based services with their children (Jager, 2002). I interviewed 16 women about their personal experiences with trauma survival and discovered how this experience led them to be cautious in dealing with others and influenced their participation in agency services.

Their stories showed that the women's strengths exceeded the obstacles that they have faced and that they continue to face. Their stories demonstrated their will to survive, and their courage, creativity, strength, and hope. Many lived through the atrocities of abuse, and yet continued to move forward, love their children, and work towards a better life. Some had fallen prey to anger, isolation, and desperation; had begun abusing their own children, or acting out against others. All experienced oppression, isolation, and obstacles to their development. All had made attempts to overcome some of their hardships by participating in family-based services and asking for help. What they taught me can be profitably applied to your foster care clients. As their therapists, you need to coach:

- more benign perception and expectations of relationships,
- changes in perception of the self, and
- positive involvement in self- and family-empowerment services

These qualities are illustrated and discussed in the following case study.

Case Study

Amy is a 29-year-old, single, white female with three children: Brittany (15), Jacob (14), and Emily (11). Amy was court-ordered to participate in family-based services when her children were returned to her custody. Their return followed Amy's escape from her family of origin, in which she was abused and wherein the children's father's refusal to let Amy have contact with her children. The children's father, who was also Amy's uncle, lived with Amy's family of origin and had been raping Amy since she was 10 years old. Amy reported that her abusive uncle was violent and physically abusive to her and their children in the family home. Amy's immediate family, who were aware that the uncle was the children's father, blamed Amy for the sexual misconduct of her uncle. Although others outside of the family attempted to get Amy out of that situation, they were generally unsuccessful. Amy had spent some time as a preschooler living with her grandmother, only to be returned to her home through the court system. As she grew older, Amy's uncle closely monitored her behavior and only allowed her out of the family home to go to school or to work. Amy's mother colluded with this abusive behavior. At the age of 28, Amy reached her breaking point. She began to suspect that her uncle was sexually assaulting their oldest daughter. Amy, who feared for her life, decided that she would escape first and send the police back for her children.

It took four months for her children to be returned to her custody. Although placed in Amy's new home away from their father, the children remained wards of the court until Amy proved she was able to maintain minimum parenting standards in the home. Family-based services were accessed and child protective services remained involved. The therapists began implementing the family-based services model and accessed mentors, psychiatric services, and community funding for supports for Amy and the children. The goal of the therapy was to increase both family functioning and resources of natural support. Amy maintained a full-time job, but she earned little more than minimum wage. She continually had difficulty making ends meet, but received food stamps and qualified for assistance with car repairs and bills through various programs in the community. Juvenile court later became part of the treatment team when her son Jacob was charged with stealing and operating a neighbor's car. At one point it was estimated that Amy's family was participating in an average of about 10 hours of services a week.

Perceptions and Expectations of Relationships

Throughout her past life, during the time that she was living through the rapes, physical, and sexual abuse, Amy reported that no one was there for her. No one in her family helped her, "even my own mother really." She explained, "That's why it took me so long to actually get to actually trust somebody, even in a clinical type of manner. I had a problem trusting people."

At the time of the interview, Amy had been participating in family-based services with her children for about nine months. I asked her how her trauma experiences impacted her relationships. She reported that she questioned a lot of things, like people's reasons for helping or for being there for her at times. She stated that her abuse had affected her relationships, including how she participated in therapy and in other supportive community services: "You know, you get a little bit leery of what is going to happen when you do tell somebody something, especially when you have been abused as long as I have." Amy stated that it took her a little while to feel safe talking with her family-based services therapists, and said that at first the therapist seemed a little bit "stand-offish." When asked what helped her to feel safe talking to her therapists, she stated: "Mainly, I think it was getting to know you guys to where I could have some type of rapport to where I knew that you guys were on my side, you know, that you know what had gone on and you weren't going to feel that I was a bad person because of it."

Amy went on to discuss the impact of her own family not being supportive of her during the years that she was being abused by her uncle in the family home. "It still hurts me to actually think about it because it's like—what type of family could just sit there and just let it happen and know about it and not do anything? When it was going on, I didn't feel like I had anybody to turn to, really ... I was too scared to say anything. I was afraid of what he [uncle] might do, if he found out that I did say something to somebody."

In contrast to that awful time in her life, Amy now feels that the community response to her needs has been and will be different. In fact, when she listed people to whom she could turn if needed, Amy listed the police, her family-based services therapists, friends from work, and some extended family members. This was an important shift in Amy's beliefs, feelings, and attendant behaviors. She now can expect, locate, and use outside help. In contrast, in the past, Amy experienced both her abuse and the lack of protection as a natural part of her environment. She coped with this otherwise intolerable state of affairs by acting like it didn't happen. Many of the women I interviewed did the same thing. Amy began to recognize that this was her way of coping when she observed her children, particularly her oldest daughter, beginning to act just like her. This prompted Amy to escape the family home.

Amy teaches us to be respectful, strengths-oriented, and empathic when working with adults who have been abused. She needs the corrective emotional experience of seeing herself in positive ways and seeing others as helpful to her. However, we need more than empathy to correct the multigenerational abuse system in which families develop. For this to happen, the family needs to discover and nurture its own natural support mechanisms. If this can be done effectively through family therapy, there is potential for healing the emotional wounds and restoring healthy individual and family functioning. However, this should not be done naively. Well-meaning attempts to include perpetrators and colluders to abuse in a family's natural support system could set up the family members for revictimization (Jager, 2002).

Having expressed this cautionary note, it is important to point out that consumer choice is central to how many of us look at things. We believe that people cannot feel empowered if they are not the ones to interpret family context, needs, and resources available, and to choose the course of action they think is best for them (MacMillan & Turnbull, 1983; Nash, Rounds, & Bowen, 1992).

There is no simple answer to the quandary raised by the pairing of choice with an abusive family system. We therapists often have clear ideas about what our clients and their families need at this particular time. However, when we don't begin with our clients' choices, our system itself may act in arrogance and become abusive in its own right. Should perpetrators of violent abuse have choice in the treatment processes of their families and children? One might be quick to respond, "No." In some cases of multigenerational abuse, it is quite clear who are the perpetrators and who are their victims. In other families, empowerment can be difficult to negotiate when victims become abusers and vice versa. Indeed, some of the abuse-surviving mothers I interviewed reported abusing their own children, and some of these children had already victimized others. However, like Amy, the other mothers were actively seeking help for themselves and their children. Impinging upon their choice would only serve as one more barrier that increased the isolation of these women and their children, and increased the risks and threats to the development of both.

If the participants are to realistically feel safe and empowered, and we are to break the repetitive cycle of multigenerational abuse, they may need new, nonabusive contacts and informal support systems. Also, we probably need additional protective agencies involved in the family empowerment process. Amy and the other mothers agreed that the police, child protective services, and the courts played various roles in protection and prevention in partnership with mental health services.

Perception of the Self

When we think about what additional protective and supportive agencies are needed, we must consider our clients' skills and their willingness to use them effectively (Heflinger and Bickman, 1996). For example, trust in others is usually a precursor to looking for and accepting help. In order to feel safe, connected, and respected in her relationship with her family-based services therapist, Amy reported that she needed "… the ability to actually tell the therapist something that's personal, and know it's not going to get out to somebody that I don't want it to get out to. That's a big thing … you know, it builds trust."

Self-efficacy is another important attitude in this regard. Self-efficacy in this context is the parents' belief that their involvement in their children's mental health treatment will make a difference (Heflinger & Bickman, 1996). Amy discussed her strengths and expectations for her life. "I am very strong willed, I think if I wasn't, that I would have caved a long time ago… . I've gone through a lot of stuff throughout my very short life … I've gone through more stuff than a lot of people could handle …. And, I think my biggest thing is my strength, my ability to just pick up and keep going, you know. And a lot of things lately have been piling up on me and I just kind of just pick up and just keep going, you know. You can't change it, and you're just going to have to live with it. My expectations sometimes, I wonder if I have accomplished them. Um, just to make sure that my kids are safe, make sure that they have what they need to prosper, you know, they need their education, they need food and a house over their head."

In fact, many of the mothers I interviewed indicated that they now believed that they could make a difference in their children's lives and treatment. For example, many of them reflected that their own survival skills helped them appreciate what their children were going through. Moreover, they believed that experiencing the effects of trauma on their own lives made them want to do things differently, so their children would be protected from harm.

When asked how she accomplishes her expectations, Amy stated, "Work everyday, no matter what." Amy reported that when it comes to recovery from her experiences of trauma and loss "I'm doing better, but I still know that I've got some ways to go. I think that the healing process—I believe that you go through the rest of your life, because, I mean, you can go through any type of counseling, you can go through any type of program—it's not going to make all that's gone wrong, go right. You know, it's still gonna be there. So I guess you know, your whole life is going to be a recovery program, because you're just slowly knowing that it's better now, you don't have to worry about that [abuse]. You don't have to wake up in the morning and wish you didn't wake up … I think a lot of it that I've got to deal with is the fact that I let people make me feel guilty—like my family. I let people make me feel that I was the bad person—that I was the person that, you know, at 10 years old, obviously made everything happen in my life. And I guess I need to forgive myself for actually letting it go on as long as it did because you know yes, it was very hard to get out ... when I did get out it was like this thing had been taken off my chest—that I couldn't breathe for so many years ... . I was my own person for once in my whole life ... and that was very, very lifting, you know, because I could actually say I'm finally free, and then I had to get to the part where I had to free my children ... So, I guess my biggest thing was when I walked out and didn't turn back, because if I did, I would have never gotten out of there ... and the kids would've never been safe."

Amy also appreciated how, in helping her, our therapeutic program made it possible for her to help her children. "I think that it will help a lot, because once I can actually heal myself, I can help them by better knowing how I went about doing so. Not to mention maybe even them seeing me how I'm healing and getting ... that might help them, to where they can get through it a lot easier."

Positive Participation in Family-Based Services

We can expect that previously traumatized individuals will become constructively involved in the remedial course they believe to be appropriate, to the extent that they:

- are able to feel a sense of safety in some relationships,
- have appropriate expectations of help, and
- believe in their own capacity to bring positive change in their lives (studies summarized in Walsh, 1996).

Recovery from trauma is based upon the empowerment of a survivor. This empowerment includes the creation of new connections within the contexts of relationships (Herman, 1997; van der Kolk & McFarlane, 1996). Our therapy made this true for Amy. From her new perspective of trust and self-efficacy, she saw the therapy program as a collection of valuable resources for her and her children. "I think this program is doing a good job, because I think a lot of the things that the kids need is somebody there to actually bring out what had happened in one sense or another. Even if you kind of hit on something accidentally, it's helping them bring it out, it's helping them deal with it. If I've got a problem, you know I will talk to you guys the next day. Like I had that problem with what my aunt was saying. [The therapist] could see that I was visually upset about it, and if I get upset, I know that you guys are there … I'm not by myself, I'm not alone—that's the biggest thing."

It is interesting to observe that Amy's trust is not all-inclusive. The staff of our therapy program have been designated trustworthy. But the world is still seen as dangerous. "Because that's what predators feed on—people like myself—that's because they know if you can get them alone to where nobody wants to be around them, nobody wants to segregate them from everybody else. It's just like a zebra, out in the wild and you got these animals that want to eat, to attack 'em and kill 'em, and that's the type—they're on the prowl for people that are weak, and for people that are away from the pack. And that's what these people do, is they segregate you from your family, from everybody else. They don't allow you to be with anybody that's going to give you the help that you need, to make sure that they can do what they want, get away with it, and you're too terrified to say anything because you don't know who to go to." Many of the women I interviewed talked about their trust in us, but continued to describe how their communities had let them down. They were, after all, abused and unprotected, and many perpetrators and colluders were not punished.

Amy was given information about family empowerment as the goal for the services in which she was participating. She was then asked to comment on what she needed from her family-based services therapists to help her to increase family empowerment: "I think I just need to mainly get control of what's going on, and that's the hard part with the kids because that's what they're fighting against … they don't want me to have that control. … My biggest thing is that I don't know what to do when they get out of hand … my house is demolished because of it. I guess I need to know what actions to take that are gonna work with these kids and let them know that they are going to have to conform to the rules and they're going to have to realize that there are rules."

Amy was also asked to comment on how she has worked with the family-based services therapists to help her family. Her answer reflected both the choice and collaboration present in the family empowerment process. "I guess, mainly, I just work with you therapists, when we just sit there and work it out with each other … keeping each other posted … knowing everything that's happening, right down to how the kids are acting."

It is interesting to observe that Amy's sense of trust in and cohesion with her program staff mirrored what she was experiencing in her household. There was more cohesion among them than in the past. All of them, mother and children, were working together as a family more than they used to. Her children were taking better care of themselves and they were helping around the house.

Amy's growing trust in her family-based care providers and the community also was spreading to her children. They could see their mother "telling people what was going on," in contrast to what had happened in their original home with the perpetrating uncle present. "[The children] know if I'm going to trust these people, they're going to think … my mom's trusting … they're not bad people and I can tell them what I think and what I feel. … They're trying to help me get through this …" Amy's children were acquiring some of traits important to their own resiliency.

Recovery of Trust Is a Lifelong Process

My interviews found that the majority of these mothers viewed their recovery from trauma as a lifelong process. They had suffered abuse of varying severity at different times in their lives. They also differed in where they were in the recovery process. Many of them felt that they had specific trauma-related healing left to do. Some believed that family interventions could help them best, if they helped with their children rather than themselves. Many others felt that their own healing and recovery would help their children. In either case, these mothers believed that the family-based services they received actively helped them to help their children. Either the services directly aided the children, or they aided the parents' relationships with their children.

A number of women reported working through trust issues with therapists and making supportive connections with both formal and informal supports in their communities. It may not have been only their participation in family-based services that helped these women reconnect and restore trust in their communities. However, a primary goal of the empowerment services they received was to support the development of basic safety for the family and the self-respect needed to reestablish a sense of personal worth and autonomy (Jager, 2002).

The women's communities also played a role in the restoration of trust. Many of the women reported that their communities had let them down when it came to dealing with their abuse. However, the women gradually became involved in wraparound services coordinated by the initial helpers. In this way their circle of trust expanded to include the various agencies and persons who were working with them. Two good things were happening here. First, based on the autonomy and self-confidence the women had developed, they were able to seek and obtain help on their own. This meant that they developed even more security and confidence because of their successful outreach to the community. Second, the women understood that the abuses they had suffered were finally being acknowledged by the community, because they were being given family-based services. This affirmation enabled them to move beyond the previous neglect and instead to focus on the restoration that was occurring now. And our efforts through the program to provide order and justice in their current lives gave these women the hope of a better life for their children.

It might be best to think of these women as being in recovery. I found that these mothers experienced the effects of traumatic abuse survival everyday in their lives. Throughout their recovery process, the experience of abuse continued to affect their perceptions of self, family, social, and community relationships. Accordingly, these parents also continued to behave in ways designed to protect themselves and families. Sometimes their preservation instincts and skills came out in ways that were beneficial for themselves and their children—for example, they engaged in support services, and noticed and addressed stresses that their children were experiencing. However, at other times, these skills resulted in shame and isolation for the mothers and their children. Sometimes, small children were locked in their rooms because their parents were afraid of abusing them. Or the parents isolated themselves from other people, because they were not able to identify whom they could trust.

Implications for Practice

I had first given this section the heading of "Implications for Treatment." However, what we are discussing is an orientation that needs to be shared by every member of your families' treatment teams and not just characterize you, the therapist. The parents' circle of security will expand only if their entire team systemically incorporates behaviors that cultivate realistic trust and self-efficacy. These behaviors include:

- *Acknowledgement of women's experiences of abuse survival.* It may be your responsibility as their therapist to initiate therapeutic conversations with these women, concerning how their traumatic abuse experiences affected and continues to affect their connections or disconnections with themselves and with others, including institutionalized authorities and agencies. However, it is the obligation of the entire service provision team to facilitate individual and family empowerment by reestablishing basic safety in contextual relationships and supporting survivors in the development of their personal worth (Herman, 1997).

- *Facilitate a level of resolution for traumas.* You, the therapist, are both a representative of the community and a witness to a survivor's stories of abuse and survival. Therefore, you can facilitate survivors telling their stories, change the dominant themes from victimization to survival and resiliency and, on a personal level, provide and make explicit trustworthy relationships. You may be the first step for these parents in forming working alliances with the service provision team. The service provision team, in turn, provides a corrective emotional experience. In contrast to the survivors' toxic memories of shame, blame, and isolation, the service provision team behaves in ways that empower their clientele.

- *Combat your own and the team's tendency to collective denial.* Collective denial is when helping professionals, family members, and/or friends minimize or deny the occurrence of incest, don't accept the harm that was done, or fail to respect the survivor's healing process (Dinsmore, 1991). Collective denial impedes the recovery process. Behaviors of helping professionals that minimize or deny incest survivors' experiences include missing cues, denying the truth of incest stories, or acknowledging the fact that the incest occurred, yet failing to address it.

- *Acknowledge the continuing risk to basic safety and empowerment posed by perpetrators who are still active in the natural and community contexts of the survivor and her children.* The survivors of abuse in your offices exist in a larger system that includes not just the service provision team, but officers of the court, various agencies, therapists, counselors, and foster families who see their obligation as "planning for the best interests of the children" (see Chapter 2, "An Ecosystemic Approach to Foster Care"). All of you should find a way to be in agreement about the facts of the case and, eventually, its disposition.

- *Facilitate the creation of new, nonabusive contacts and informal supports.* This is necessary to break the repetitive cycle of multigenerational abuse. Although the families' past experiences may not have been positive, police, child protective services, and the courts have diverse and important roles in protection and prevention in partnership with mental health professionals. If the woman so chooses, protective agencies can be invited to participate as a support in the family empowerment process.

• *"Choice" remains a crucial component of an empowering parent-professional collaborative relationship* (Heflinger & Bickman, 1996). Family empowerment at the level of the social service system means that it is up to each family member to interpret the family context, needs, and resources available, and to choose the best course of action for a given family member at a given time (MacMillan & Turnbull, 1983; Nash, Rounds, & Bowen, 1992).

Finally, some fundamental principles were suggested long ago for clinical work with women, families, and larger systems (Imber-Black, 1989). They remain relevant for your empowerment work with families involved in the foster care system. For example, all of us need to continually examine the implicit sexist, classist, and racist assumptions that are communicated from our referring systems and from the larger system in which all of us are situated. Then we need to accept referrals in ways that begin to alter those assumptions. We do this by viewing problems from a systemic point of origin, as opposed to blaming the parent or family. We also need to consistently examine the larger context—of which our practice is a part—for patterns of escalating complementarity and triangulation that serve to disempower women. To counteract that, we need to develop interventions that introduce symmetry among the team of participants, support women's effectiveness, and detriangulate women out of childlike positions (for example, positions that imply that a woman should defer to those "who know what's best for her"). Throughout, all of us need to examine things that we believe, feel, say, and do, and root out that which engenders doubt in women regarding their own decisions and actions.

References

Boyd-Franklin, N., & Hafer Bry, B. (2000). *Reaching out in family therapy: Home-based, school, and community interventions.* New York: Guilford.

Dinsmore, C. (1991). *From surviving to thriving: Incest, feminism, and recovery.* Albany, NY: State University of New York Press.

Heflinger, C. A., & Bickman, L. (1996). Family empowerment: A conceptual model for promoting parent–professional partnership. In C. A. Heflinger & C. T. Nixon (Eds.), *Families and the mental health system for children and adolescents: Policy, services and research. Vol. 2. Children's mental health services* (pp. 96–116). Thousand Oaks, CA: Sage.

Herman, J. L. (1997). *Trauma and recovery: The aftermath of violence—from domestic abuse to political terror* (Rev. ed.). New York: Basic Books.

Imber-Black, E. (1989). Women's relationships with larger systems. In M. McGoldrick, C. Anderson, & F. Walsh (Eds.), *Women in families: A framework for family therapy* (pp. 335–356). New York: W. W. Norton.

Jager, K. B. (2002). *Connecting trauma survival and family empowerment: A qualitative inquiry of the implications for family-based services.* East Lansing, MI: Michigan State University. UMI Dissertation Abstract 3075022.

Koren, P. E., DeChillo, N., & Friesen, B. J. (1992). Measuring empowerment in families whose children have emotional disabilities: A brief questionnaire. *Rehabilitation Psychology, 37,* 305–321.

MacMillan, D. L., & Turnbull, A. P. (1983). Parent involvement with special education: Respecting individual preferences. *Educating and Training of the Mentally Retarded, 18,* 5–9.

Nash, J., Rounds, K., & Bowen, G. L. (1992). Level of involvement on early childhood intervention teams. *Families in Society, 73*(2), 93–99.

Pecora, P. J., Fraser, M. W., Nelson, K. E., McCroskey, J., & Meezan, W. (1995). *Evaluating family-based services.* New York: Walter de Gruyter.

van der Kolk, B. A., & McFarlane, A. C. (1996). The black hole of trauma. In B. A. van der Kolk, A. C. McFarlane, & L. Weisaeth (Eds.), *Traumatic stress: The effects of overwhelming experience on mind, body, and society* (pp. 3–23). New York: Guilford.

Vanderslice, V. (1984). Empowerment, a definition in process. *Human Ecology Forum, 14*(1), 2–3.

Walker, M. (1999). The intergenerational transmission of trauma: The effects of abuse on the survivor relationship with their children and on the children themselves. *European Journal of Psychotherapy, Counseling & Health, 2,* 281–296.

Walsh, F. (1996). The concept of family resilience: Crisis and challenge. *Family Process, 35,* 261–281.

21

When the Helper Becomes Traumatized: Taking Care of You

Tracy Woodard-Meyers

It was once thought that foster care workers and therapists, because of their training, were immune to traumatic stress reactions. We now know that people who work directly with trauma victims are also likely to experience traumatic stress symptoms and disorders. They can suffer stress simply by learning about traumatic events. This chapter discusses the phenomenon of secondary traumatic stress (STS) and its effects on helpers. Prevention and intervention strategies are presented.

At the end of the nineteenth century, special laws were passed and public authorities were hired to protect children from abusive caretakers. Since that time, social service agencies throughout the country have reported difficulties in recruiting and retaining foster care workers. Although attrition is common among many human service professionals, the losses are particularly heavy and the costs more substantial in the foster care field. In this group, high turnover results in higher costs for hiring and training of workers, lower quality services, and a decrease in the agencies' ability to protect children (Balfour & Neff, 1993).

Although the consequences of this high turnover rate are understood, the reasons for it are less apparent. Other professions such as law enforcement, disaster relief, and therapists have acknowledged the effects of working with trauma victims.

However, the effects of regular daily exposure to maltreated children have not received adequate attention. A common assumption of researchers, theorists, and administrators is that foster care workers are forsaking their commitment to protect children because they are suffering from burnout (Balfour & Neff, 1993; Daley, 1979a, 1979b; Jayaratne & Chess, 1986; LeCroy & Rank, 1986; Lee, 1979; Savicki & Cooley, 1994; Walden, Gettelman, & Murrin, 1993). Burnout is a feeling of emotional exhaustion (Maslach, 1982)—possibly caused by organizational stressors, including ever-increasing caseloads, lack of resources, unrealistic policies, and the possibility of being criminally charged for errors. But, surprisingly, these organizational stressors and burnout do not appear to contribute significantly to foster care worker turnover rates (Balfour & Neff, 1993; Fryer, Miyoshi, & Thomas, 1989; LeCroy & Rank, 1986). New discoveries in the field of traumatic stress suggest alternative explanations why foster care professionals abandon their vocation.

Professionals who work with traumatized children sometimes become traumatized themselves and, as a result, suffer from symptoms that affect their ability to function. These professionals are often directly exposed to traumatic material on a daily basis. It was once thought that, because of their training, these workers were immune to traumatic stress reactions. However, according to Figley's (1995; 1999; 2002a) secondary traumatic stress (STS) theory, people who work directly with or have direct exposure to trauma victims are just as likely as the primary victims to experience traumatic stress symptoms and disorders. "People can be traumatized without actually being physically harmed or threatened with harm. They can be traumatized simply by learning about the traumatic event" (1995, p. 4).

Traumatization of Foster Children

As you know, most children in foster care have endured some type of abuse and/or neglect. This maltreatment may have included sexual abuse, abandonment, and physical abuse. When children undergo traumatic experiences, their coping abilities are overwhelmed and they suffer from traumatic stress (Figley, 1995; van der Kolk & McFarlane, 1996). Traumatic stress includes the behaviors and emotions that result from being exposed to an event that terrifies, horrifies, or renders one helpless (Figley, 1999). It is a normal response to an abnormal situation and is characterized by a unique set of symptoms.

After foster children encounter traumatic events it is not unusual for them to experience what are called the three symptoms of traumatic stress: intrusion, avoidance, and arousal (see also Chapter 7, "Parent–Child Therapy for Traumatized Young Children in Foster Care"). Such symptoms may appear as nightmares, feelings of detachment, and irritability. In addition to traumatic stress symptoms, general psychological distress and somatic complaints have been noted in traumatized children; feelings of fear, anxiety, guilt, depression, and shame, as well as somatic problems such as headaches, stomachaches, and back pain are also common (Bremner, Southwick, & Charney, 1999). Symptoms tend to vary across individuals and situations, and are influenced by a number of factors. Coping resources, available support, and the nature of the traumatic event all have an impact on the severity and longevity of symptoms (Litz, Gray, Bryant, & Adler, 2002). Most children displaying traumatic stress and psychological symptoms adapt effectively within three months. However, others continue to suffer and are at risk for developing posttraumatic stress disorder (PTSD).

The likelihood of developing posttraumatic stress disorder is difficult to predict. Recent studies suggest that childhood abuse may be the most common predictor of PTSD in children and adult women (Dubner & Motta, 1999; Kessler, Sonnega, Bromet, Hughes, & Nelson, 1995; McCauley, Kern, Kolodner,

Dill, Schroeder, DeChant, Ryden, Derogatis, & Bass, 1997; McLeer, Deblinger, Henry, & Orvaschel, 1992). According to the *Diagnostic and Statistical Manual (DSM–IV,* American Psychiatric Association, 1994), several criteria must be met before a diagnosis of PTSD can be made. The individual must be exposed to a traumatic event to which he or she responds with intense fear, helplessness, or horror. If they are very young, children may instead exhibit disorganized or agitated behavior. Finally, the individual suffers persistent *reexperiencing* of the traumatic event, *avoidance of stimuli* associated with the traumatic event, and *increased arousal.* Reexperiencing the event may be seen in the form of nightmares, repetitive play of the trauma themes, and flashbacks (sudden thoughts, images, and perceptions of the event). When a child enters a state of avoidance, symptoms appear, such as isolation, detachment, withdrawal, inability to recall, diminished interest in activities, and avoidance of thoughts and activities. It is during this period of numbing, that the mind is protecting itself against the onslaught of unbearable emotional pain. Symptoms of increased arousal appear as irritability, outbursts of anger, difficulty concentrating, difficulty falling or staying asleep, and an exaggerated startle response. A child must display at least one reexperiencing, three avoidance, and two increased arousal symptoms to be diagnosed with PTSD. These symptoms must coexist, occurring together for more than one month and they must cause significant distress or impairment in the child's social, occupational, or other important areas of functioning.

Traumatization of Foster Care Workers

The *DSM–IV* criteria present an example of the common assumption that only those who come in direct contact with a traumatic event can experience traumatic stress reactions. However, new scholarship suggests that *helping* a traumatized person can similarly cause trauma symptoms (Figley, 1995;

1999; 2002a). This phenomenon, experiencing traumatic stress through helping trauma victims, is referred to as secondary traumatic stress (STS). STS is defined as "the natural, consequent behaviors and emotions resulting from knowledge about a traumatizing event experienced by a significant other. It is the stress resulting from helping or wanting to help traumatized or suffering persons" (Figley, 1999, p. 10). The negative effects and symptoms of STS are identical to those who are directly exposed to traumatic events and it is "becoming viewed as an occupational hazard of providing direct services to traumatized populations" (Bride, Robinson, Yegidis, & Figley, 2004, p. 28).

Foster care workers are faced with children's traumatic events on a daily basis. Through disclosure or reading a case file, workers learn about grievous acts inflicted upon innocent children. They thereby become indirect victims of trauma. It is not surprising that foster care workers report experiencing symptoms that mimic those found in the children of their caseloads (Cornille & Meyers, 1999; Meyers, 1996; Meyers & Cornille, 2002; Nelson-Gardell & Harris, 2003). Table 1 provides examples of trauma-specific symptoms and psychological distress endured by foster care workers. Although the severity and longevity of the symptoms vary among individuals, when these symptoms linger too long (more than one month) or have a delayed onset, they are considered pathological. The pathological response of being exposed to another's trauma is called secondary traumatic stress disorder (STSD).

Although not a diagnostic category in the *DSM–IV*, secondary traumatic stress disorder is conceptualized as "a syndrome of symptoms nearly identical to posttraumatic stress disorder, except that exposure to knowledge about a traumatizing event is associated with the set of symptoms" (Figley, 1995, p. 8). The symptoms arise quickly and without warning and are accompanied by feelings of confusion, isolation, and helplessness. These symptoms often cannot be connected to their real cause.

TABLE I

Secondary Traumatic Stress Symptoms
and General Psychological Distress
in Foster Care Workers

Somatic	Cognitive	Emotional	Behavioral
Faintness	Trouble remembering things	Lonely	Temper outbursts
Dizziness	Trouble concentrating	Blue	Poor appetite
Pain in heart or chest	Difficulty making decisions	Hopeless	Trouble falling asleep
Nausea	Mind going blank	Worthlessness	Double checking what to do
Trouble catching breath	Thoughts of death or dying	Depression	Getting into frequent arguments
Hot or cold spells	Thoughts of ending your life	Anger	Restless (can't sit still)
Numbness or tingling	Having urges to break things	Guilt	Spells of terror or panic
Feeling weak	Having urges to harm someone	Fear	Avoid thoughts/ feelings
Aches	Thoughts that others are to blame for your troubles	Anxiety	Avoid activities/ situations
Rapid heartbeat	Thoughts that most people can't be trusted	Withdrawn	Exaggerated startle response
Nervousness/ shakiness	Flashbacks	Numb	Nightmares
Tense/keyed up	Recurrent recollections of trauma		

Some workers who help traumatized children never develop severe STS symptoms or STSD. Although scholarship is preliminary on the causes and factors associated with STSD, there are several factors that seem to be associated with worker vulnerability to STS and STSD. Age, gender, exposure levels, personal trauma history, and coping mechanisms are factors most often associated with the severity of STS symptoms. Younger counselors have reported experiencing more severe levels of secondary trauma symptoms than their older colleagues (Arvay & Uhlemann, 1996; Ghahramanlou & Brodbeck, 2000). Compared to their male counterparts, female child protective service workers reported more symptoms such as anger, irritability, jumpiness, exaggerated startle response, trouble concentrating, hypervigilance, nightmares, intrusive thoughts and images, and numbing of responses (Meyers, 1996). Women also reported experiencing more cardiovascular problems, gastrointestinal problems, respiratory problems, and muscular pain and discomfort. Increased symptom severity has also been found to be positively related to the length of professional experience (Birck, 2001; Meyers, 1996; Wee & Myers, 2002) and working overtime. Child protective service workers who worked more than 40 hours a week experienced more anger, irritability, jumpiness, exaggerated startle response, trouble concentrating, hypervigilance, nightmares, and intrusive thoughts and images than those who worked fewer hours per week (Meyers, 1996). Several studies found intense STS symptoms in workers with a personal history of trauma (Ghahramanlou & Brodbeck, 2000; Kassam-Adams, 1999; Meyers, 1996; Nelson-Gardell & Harris, 2003; Pearlman & Mac Ian, 1995). Negative coping strategies seem to be associated with more trauma symptoms (Follette, Polusny, & Milbeck, 1994).

Taking Care of You

In this next section we want to talk about how STSD can be prevented and what can be done about it once it occurs.

Recognition and Normalization of STS and STSD

Educating new or prospective employees about what to expect is a key component in preventing STSD. As a professional in the foster care system you need to know that you are going to be exposed to traumatized children. As a result you are probably going to experience traumatic stress symptoms. Therefore, you need to be able to recognize and anticipate STS symptoms (Table 1), and be prepared to cope with them. These symptoms are an unfortunate occupational hazard of working with traumatized children and their families. The good news is that these symptoms usually do not last long; often less than a month. Symptoms can range from mild to severe, but awareness of them and the connection between your job and what you are experiencing helps decrease their intensity. If symptoms persist for longer than one month and disrupt your functioning, you might be suffering from STSD. If so, you should remember that this too is a normal reaction to an abnormal situation. Your mind and body are asking for help to cope with an overwhelming situation.

Establishing Positive Coping Strategies

It is helpful to recognize your own tendencies in coping with stressful situations. Some use positive coping skills and others rely on negative skills, including using alcohol, drugs, spending money, or withdrawing from others. Particularly in this line of work, you will want to develop the best stress management skills possible. You might consider the following stress management suggestions:

- *Eat regularly and properly.* Eat frequent small meals, and stay away from excessive sugar, fats, and caffeine. Drink plenty of fluids.

- *Get adequate sleep.* Most people are sleep deprived, and this makes them more physically and psychologically vulnerable to stress. Learn relaxation techniques that can help you fall and stay asleep.

- *Exercise.* Incorporate physical activity into your daily routine. Walking, yoga, biking, and other such activities help reduce the tension in muscles and have positive emotional effects, including reducing depression, anxiety, and sleep disturbances.

- *Use positive self-talk.* In the stressful situations that are inevitable in the foster care system, it is easy to become discouraged or beat ourselves up mentally. Talk about yourself in a positive manner. "Given the many challenges that are around, I am doing the best that I can do."

- *Give yourself permission to take care of you.* As caregivers we think it is our job to put everyone else first. You may have heard the old joke: Don't forget that the "MSW" degree stands for "must save the world." As helpers we want to do everything we can to alleviate suffering, but we must be realistic lest we overextend ourselves. In order to have the energy and resources to care for others you have to care for yourself first. By doing so, you will be more helpful to the vulnerable people you are working for.

- *Have fun.* Make time to do something that you enjoy. Fun and laughter replenish your emotions and energy, and creative expression is especially refreshing.

- *Relax and get a massage.* Learning to relax is a key component in handling difficult stressors. There are numerous techniques that teach you to relax muscles in your body and calm your mind. Take a five minute "breathing break" to quiet your racing mind. Stretch your muscles for 10 minutes on the floor of your office. Walk around the building on a nice day. Massage therapy is especially helpful in removing the tension that builds up in your mind and body.

- *Keep a journal.* Writing about a distressing situation can help you put the event in perspective and move past it. Keep a personal diary in which you note especially disturbing situations and how you felt. Writing has a cathartic effect.

- *Give yourself a break.* Make sure that you take time away from work to refresh your thoughts and energy. Vacation time with friends and family is a great way to accomplish this goal. Even if you do not leave town, you should take time off from work.

Establishing Support Systems to Talk It Out

People who work with traumatized populations sometimes believe that if they get upset or experience symptoms, they are weak and in the wrong field. This belief can lead to shame and a reluctance to talk about personal struggles. Figley (2002b) refers to this as "the conspiracy of silence." Talking about particularly disturbing events is effective in keeping STS symptoms to a minimum. When people can express their feelings, they do better work and have more energy. Foster care supervisors could minimize the traumatic symptoms of their caseworkers and therapists by providing supportive environments and debriefing those who work in the trenches. Creating a safe place to express emotions and talk about traumatic events could help.

If supervisors do not provide a supportive environment, you can develop your own peer support groups. Ask coworkers with whom you feel comfortable to be part of your group. Make an agreement with your group members to listen to each other's feelings and give each other encouragement. You may also want to monitor each other's functioning levels and STS symptoms. Be sure you tell your group members how to know when you are reaching your breaking point. "If I start to do X ..."

Seeking Professional Help

Most of the STS symptoms you encounter from your job will go away on their own in a timely manner. When symptoms persist (more than one month) or are so severe that they affect your ability to function, you may want to seek an outside source for help. There are a number of therapists who are specially trained and certified to deal with secondary traumatization. Keeping yourself whole and happy is a critical component in your helping others to do the same.

Case Study

Martha has been a foster care worker for the past three years. During that time she has been exposed to children who have been hit, burned, neglected, and sexually abused by their caregivers. She has written and read reports that include overwhelming details about these experiences, and she has taken and viewed photographs that document the maltreatment. Martha's caseload has continued to grow, and as she becomes more experienced, new workers talk to her about their cases because they value her opinion and advice. Although Martha does not mind helping her coworkers, it has become difficult to do so lately, because she has been extremely tired.

For the past two months, Martha has been waking up at 3:00 A.M. unable to breathe. She gets out of bed and goes into the living room so she can lie on the couch with the ceiling fan on high. She is hot and sweaty, her heart is racing, and her arms are hurting. She cries because she thinks she is having a heart attack and is afraid she is going to die. When she does not die and the symptoms subside, she assumes she is crazy. Finally she falls back to sleep at 5:30 A.M. only to have to get up at 6:00 A.M. for work.

Although she gets up at 6:00 A.M. to be at work by 8:00 A.M., Martha has been late for work for the last three weeks. While at work, Martha has been having problems staying focused and accomplishing her duties. Two weeks ago, she was on her way to a home visit, when halfway there she turned her car around and went back to the office. Although Martha needed to see the foster family, she just didn't have the energy. Martha called the family, made up an excuse for not keeping the appointment, and rescheduled for a later date. She sat in her office and cried. However, she could not understand what she was crying about. Martha then was angry at herself for being weak.

After her last sleepless night, Martha promised herself that if she lived until morning she would go and see her family physician. At the physician's office, Martha disclosed that she had been having a number of symptoms and she was afraid she was dying. Martha told the physician about waking up each night, and confessed that she had also been having severe pains in her legs, and at times it was difficult to walk. She explained that it had been difficult to keep food down and she had lost 15 pounds in the last four weeks. After the examination, the physician questioned Martha further about her symptoms. Martha admitted that she "cries all the time," and was having problems concentrating and remembering things. She stated that at times she found herself very angry, but most the time she just felt numb. She also stated that, when she tried to go to sleep at night, her mind races about all the things she has to do at work.

After a full battery of medical tests, the physician was unable to find any physical cause for Martha's symptoms. Although relieved she was not dying, Martha was upset when the physician suggested she take an antidepressant to help with the symptoms. Since that visit, Martha has not told anyone about the symptoms she is still experiencing, or the doctor's suggestion to take an antidepressant. Martha does not know what could be making her depressed. Since none of the other foster care workers talk about these kinds of experiences, she assumes that she is the only one who is having such difficulties.

As part of in-service training, Martha attended a secondary traumatic stress workshop. It was during this workshop that she learned that what she was experiencing was normal for a person exposed to the job-related trauma she has seen on a daily basis. Martha also learned that other workers were experiencing similar symptoms, but no one thought they should talk about them. They feared that they would be perceived as weak and not cut out for their jobs.

Once Martha understood that her symptoms were associated with her job, she was extremely relieved. She learned in the workshop that she needed to discuss job stress with others. So she talked to colleagues about forming an informal support group. Martha decided to work on making some lifestyle changes to include positive coping strategies, for example, eating properly, exercising, and taking time to have fun. She opted to stay on the antidepressant to help eliminate some of the depression and anxiety symptoms. But she no longer feared being crazy.

References

American Psychiatric Association. (1994). *Diagnostic and statistical manual of mental disorders* (4th ed.). Washington, DC: Author.

Arvay, M., & Uhlemann, M. (1996). Counselor stress in the field of trauma: A preliminary study. *Canadian Journal of Counselling, 30*(3), 193–210.

Balfour, D., & Neff, D. (1993). Predicting and managing turnover in human service agencies: A case study of an organization in crisis. *Public Personnel Management, 22*(3), 473–486.

Birck, A. (2001). Secondary traumatization and burnout in professionals working with torture survivors. *Traumatology, 7*(2), Article 2. Retrieved December 15, 2006, from http://www.fsu.edu/%7Etrauma/v7/Working withTortureSurvivors.pdf.

Bremner, D., Southwick, S., & Charney, S. (1999). The neurobiology of posttraumatic stress disorder: An integration of animal and human research. In P. A. Saigh & J. D. Bremner (Eds.), *Posttraumatic stress disorder: A comprehensive text* (pp. 103–143). Boston: Allyn & Bacon.

Bride, E., Robinson, M. Yegidis, B., & Figley, C. (2004). Development and validation of the secondary traumatic stress scale. *Research on Social Work Practice, 14*, 27–35.

Cornille, T., & Meyers, T. (1999). Secondary traumatic stress among child protective service workers: Prevalence, severity, and predictive factors. *Traumatology, 5*(1) Article 2. Retrieved February 10, 2005, from http://www.fsu.edu/~trauma/art2v5il.htm.

Daley, M. (1979a). Preventing worker burnout in child welfare. *Child Welfare, 58*, 443–450.

Daley, M. (1979b). Burnout: Smoldering problems in protective services. *Social Work, 9*, 375–379.

Dubner, A., & Motta, R. (1999). Sexually and physically abused foster care children and posttraumatic stress disorder. *Journal of Consulting and Clinical Psychology, 67*(3), 367–373.

Figley, C. (1995). Compassion fatigue as secondary traumatic stress disorder: An overview. In C. Figley (Ed.), *Compassion fatigue: Coping with secondary traumatic stress disorder in those who treat the traumatized* (pp. 1–20). New York: Brunner/Mazel.

Figley, C. (1999). Compassion fatigue: Toward a new understanding of the costs of caring. In B. H. Stamm (Ed.), *Secondary traumatic stress: Self-care issues for clinicians, researchers, and educators* (2nd ed., pp. 3–28). Lutherville, MD: Sidran Press.

Figley, C. (2002a). *Treating compassion fatigue.* New York: Brunner-Routledge.

Figley, C. (2002b). Compassion fatigue: Psychotherapists' chronic lack of self care. *Psychotherapy in Practice, 58,* 1433–1441.

Follette, V., Polusny, M., & Milbeck, K. (1994). Mental health and law enforcement professionals: Trauma history, psychological symptoms, and impact of providing service to child sexual abuse survivors. *Professional Psychology: Research and Practice, 25,* 275–282.

Fryer, G. E., Miyoshi, T. J., & Thomas, P. J. (1989). The relationship of child protection worker attitudes to attrition from the field. *Child Abuse and Neglect, 13,* 345–350.

Ghahramanlou, M., & Brodbeck, C. (2000). Predictors of secondary trauma in sexual assault trauma counselors. *International Journal of Emergency Mental Health, 2,* 229–240.

Jayaratne, S., & Chess, W. (1986). Job stress, job deficit, emotional support, and competence: Their relationship to burnout. *Journal of Applied Social Sciences, 10,* 135–155.

Kassam-Adams, N. (1999). The risks of treating sexual trauma: Stress and secondary trauma in psychotherapists. In B. H. Stamm (Ed.), *Secondary traumatic stress: Self-care issues for clinicians, researchers, and educators* (2nd ed., pp. 37–50). Lutherville, MD: Sidran Press.

Kessler, R., Sonnega, A., Bromet, E., Hughes, M., & Nelson, C. (1995). Posttraumatic stress disorder in the national comorbidity survey. *Archives of General Psychiatry, 52,* 1048–1060.

LeCroy, C., & Rank, M. (1986). Factors associated with burnout in the social services: An exploratory study. *Journal of Social Service Research, 10,* 95–105.

Lee, D. (1979). Staying alive in child protective services: Survival skills for worker and supervisor—preliminary examination of worker trauma. *Arete, 5*(4), 195–208.

Litz, B., Gray, M., Bryant, R. & Adler, A. (2002). Early intervention for trauma: Current status and future directions. *Clinical Psychology: Science and Practice, 9*(2), 112–234.

Maslach, C. (1982). *Burnout: The cost of caring.* Englewood Cliffs, NJ: Prentice Hall.

McCauley, J., Kern, D., Kolodner, K., Dill, L., Schroeder, A., DeChant, H., Ryden, J., Derogatis, L., & Bass, E. (1997). Clinical characteristics of women with a history of childhood abuse: Unhealed wounds. *Journal of the American Medical Association, 277,* 1362–1368.

McLeer, S., Deblinger, E., Henry, D., & Orvaschel, H. (1992). Sexually abused children at high risk for post-traumatic stress disorder. *Journal of American Academy of Child and Adolescent Psychiatry, 31,* 875–879.

Meyers, T. (1996). *The relationship between family of origin functioning, trauma history, exposure to children's traumatic traumata and secondary traumatic stress symptoms in child protective service workers.* Unpublished doctoral dissertation, Florida State University, Tallahassee, FL.

Meyers, T., & Cornille, T. (2002). The trauma of working with traumatized children. In C. R. Figley (Ed.), *Treating compassion fatigue* (pp. 39–56). New York: Brunner-Routledge.

Nelson-Gardell, D., & Harris, D. (2003). Childhood abuse history, secondary traumatic stress, and child welfare workers. *Child Welfare, 82,* 5–26.

Pearlman, L., & Mac Ian, P. (1995). Vicarious traumatization: An empirical study of the effects of trauma work on trauma therapists. *Professional Psychology: Research and Practice, 26,* 558–565.

Savicki, V., & Cooley, E. (1994). Burnout in child protective service workers: A longitudinal study. *Journal of Organizational Behavior, 15,* 655–666.

van der Kolk, B. & McFarlane, A. (1996). The black hole of trauma. In B. van der Kolk, A. McFarlane, & L. Weisaeth (Eds.), *Traumatic stress: The effects of overwhelming experience on mind, body, and society* (pp. 3–23). New York: Guilford Press.

Walden, N., Gettelman, T., & Murrin, M. (1993). Understanding occupational stress in child welfare supervisors. *Journal of Applied Social Psychology, 23,* 2043–2054.

Wee, D., & Myers, D. (2002). Stress responses of mental health workers following disaster: The Oklahoma City bombing. In C. R. Figley (Ed.), *Treating compassion fatigue* (pp. 57–84). New York: Brunner-Routledge.

Index

12-step programs, 197, 381, 384, 392. *See also* Alcoholics
  Anonymous, substance abuse

A

abandonment, 112, 422, 449, 471
ABC intervention project, 108
abstract thought, development of, 159, 161, 171
abuse, denial of, 90, 94
abuse, spousal, 364–365, 415–416
acting out. *See also* behavior management
  as anger reaction, 318
  as avoidance behavior, 137
  in foster home, 5, 32, 275
  lack of, in securely attached children, 155
  by repeating traumatic events, 144
  sexually, 331, 334–335
  during visitation, 204
active listening, 98
adaptability, 387–388, 395–396
adaptive development, 246
adaptive skills, 33, 66
addiction. *See* substance abuse
addiction treatment programs, 197, 381, 384, 392
adjustment to stressful events, 83

H

I

S

safety
    after sexual abuse, 174
    immediate, of children, 28, 228
    by promoting mastery of trauma, 139
    talking to therapist, 456
Satir, Virginia, 255
scapegoating, 169
schizophrenia, 22
school, 33, 130, 432, 438. *See also* delinquency
school-age children, and powerlessness, 236
screening, developmental, 109
sculpting, 264
secondary traumatic stress disorder (STSD), 473
secondary traumatic stress (STS), 470–471, 473–474, 476,
    478–480
self-accountability, 384
self-assessment, 222
self-awareness, 201
self-care, 345, 347
self-concept, 157–159, 318
self-confidence, 355
self-efficacy, 459
self-esteem, 7, 93, 97, 183–184
self-identity, 230
self-perspective, 317
self-reflection, 109, 239
self-regulation, 266, 274, 317, 370
self-reliance, 128, 233
self-soothing, 446
self-statements, 394
self-sufficiency, 163, 164
self-talk, 477

and interventions, 41–42

for sexual abuse, 333

teaching foster parents to find strengths in birth parents, 206–207

using birth parents' input, 191–192, 196

stress hormones, 273

stress, post-traumatic, 129, 148, 471–472

stressors on foster parents, 295–297

STS. *See* secondary traumatic stress (STS)

STSD. *See* secondary traumatic stress disorder (STSD)

substance abuse

and 12-step programs, 381, 384, 392

in adolescents, 162, 237

by birth parents, 197

in birth parents' parents, 286

case example of, 377–378

case goals for, 391

and chaotic behavior, 316

cohesion and adaptability of families with, 387

and destructive entitlements, 313

disease model of, 370–379

due to foster care drift, 37

early in therapy, 31

and extended family, 386

genogram, 384–385

and guilt feelings, 382

and isolation, 385, 388, 390, 464

and kinship care, 243

and neglect, 378

and noncompliance with treatment, 409

with one nonusing partner, 398

parental accountability for, 383–384

and parentification of children, 378, 391, 393

and physical abuse, 378–379